Theatre: A Way of Seeing

THEATRE

A Way of Seeing

Fourth Edition

Milly S. Barranger
The University of North Carolina
Chapel Hill

 Wadsworth Publishing Company
An International Thomson Publishing Company

Belmont • Albany • Bonn • Boston • Cincinnati • Detroit •
London • Madrid • Melbourne • Mexico City • New York • Paris •
San Francisco • Singapore • Tokyo • Toronto • Washington

Theatre Editor: Todd Robert Armstrong
Editorial Assistant: Joshua King
Production Editor: Carol Carreon Lombardi
Interior and Cover Designer: Andrew H. Ogus
Print Buyer: Diana Spence
Permissions Editor: Robert M. Kauser
Copy Editor: Barbara Kimmel

Page Dummier: Barry Age/Beach City Graphics
Photo Researcher: Christine Pullo
Technical Illustrator: Carol Lawson
Cover Photograph: *Les Atrides,*
   Michele Laurent/Gamma Liaison
Compositor: Thompson Type
Printer: R. R. Donnelly & Sons/Crawfordsville

*Printed on
acid-free
recycled paper.*

For more information, contact Wadsworth Publishing Company:

Wadsworth Publishing Company
10 Davis Drive
Belmont, California 94002, USA

International Thomson Publishing Europe
Berkshire House 168-173
High Holborn
London, WC1V 7AA, England

Thomas Nelson Australia
102 Dodds Street
South Melbourne 3205
Victoria, Australia

Nelson Canada
1120 Birchmount Road
Scarborough, Ontario
Canada M1K 5G4

International Thomson Publishing GmbH
Königswinterer Strasse 418
53227 Bonn, Germany

International Thomson Editores
Campos Eliseos 385, Piso 7
Col. Polanco
11560 México D.F., México

International Thomson Publishing Asia
221 Henderson Road
#05-10 Henderson Building
Singapore 0315

International Thomson Publishing Japan
Hirakawacho Kyowa Building, 3F
2-2-1 Hirakawacho
Chiyoda-ku, Tokyo 102, Japan

1 2 3 4 5 6 7 8 9 10—01 00 99 98 97 96 95

Library of Congress Cataloging-in-Publication Data

Barranger, Milly S.
    Theatre: a way of seeing/Milly S. Barranger.—4th ed.
      p.   cm.
    Includes bibliographical references and index.
    ISBN 0-534-24024-0
    1. Theater. I. Title.
PN2037.B32 1995
792—dc20   94-14860

To Heather

CONTENTS

6 STRUCTURES OF SEEING 134

7 DRAMA'S CONVENTIONS 166

8 THEATRE LANGUAGE 192

9 THE IMAGE MAKERS: THE ACTOR 220

PREFACE

Theatre *as a way of seeing* is the subject of this book. We will talk about the experience of *theatre*—who sees, what is seen, and where and how it is seen—largely from our own viewpoint as audiences engaged in the direct experience of a complex, living art. We will also try to place ourselves in the creative process of those artists engaged in creating the theatre event. Many persons—writers, actors, directors, designers, technicians, craftspeople, managers, producers—contribute to what is truly a collective, all-encompassing art.

Theatre is where people make art out of themselves for others to watch, experience, think, feel, and understand. Chiefly through the actor, theatre is humanness, aliveness, and presence. Nor does theatre exist in any book. A book, like this one, can only *describe* the passion, wisdom, and excitement that comes with experiencing theatre—in its motion, color, and sound.

This edition of *Theatre: A Way of Seeing* has been revised to discuss theatre as an experience of art, life, and human imagination: people, spaces, plays, designs, staging, forms, language, and productions. For this purpose, the book is divided into fourteen chapters. Ten of the fourteen deal with the complex answer to the question: What is theatre, and who are the "makers" of this collaborative art? There are discussions of theatre aesthetics, theatrical spaces, artists and the artistic process, and dramatic forms and conventions. Five chapters discuss playreading and theatre language. The final chapters examine theatre's response to cultural diversity and the influence of theatre criticism on our theatregoing. In addition, there are diagrams, definitions, quotations, sections of texts of plays, and photo essays illustrating theatre's variety, color, tools, and styles. If instructors want to change the order of the chapters, they will find that they can readily do so. None of these discussions, of course, takes the place of sitting with others in a darkened theatre and experiencing the actors, text, scenery, costumes, changing lights, music, and sound effects in a carefully crafted event demonstrating the human imagination in its many forms.

Written for the basic course, this book *introduces* students to theatre as a way of seeing women and men in action: what they do and why they do it. After all, Shakespeare said that "All the world's a stage,/And all the men and women merely players. . ." (*As You Like It*). Because many students are probably discovering theatre for the first time and perhaps even attending their first performances, I have limited the number of "model" plays used as examples of trends, styles, and forms in theatrical production. Ranging from the Greeks to the moderns, these representative plays are: *Oedipus the King, The Trojan Women, Hamlet, Tartuffe, Ghosts, The Cherry Orchard, The Little Foxes, The Caucasian Chalk Circle, A Streetcar Named Desire, The Bald Soprano, Waiting for Godot, Marat/Sade, Buried Child, Rockaby, The Grapes of Wrath, Fences, Glengarry Glen Ross,* and *Angels in America: A Gay Fantasia on National Themes.* Each of these plays has a special place in the ongoing history of theatrical writing and performance. They also represent, in combination, the extraordinary range and magnitude of human expression and theatrical achievement.

In addition, the complete text of Samuel Beckett's *Rockaby,* along with extensive excerpts from *Hamlet, The Trojan Women, The Three Sisters, The Bald Soprano, Marat/Sade, Buried Child,* and *Glengarry Glen Ross* are included in an effort to keep this book self-contained for classroom use.

In this new edition, the reader will also find sections discussing such current stage directors as Peter Brook, Ariane Mnouchkine, Robert Wilson, Julie Taymor, JoAnne Akalaitis, and Martha Clarke; women playwrights and solo performers; current stage technology, especially sound and computers; and photo essays on contemporary stages, theatrical design, and great actors.

I have also provided tools to help students with questions of history, biography, definition, and example. Included are synopses of the model plays and short biographies of playwrights, actors, directors, designers, producers, and critics along with an expanded Glossary of theatre terms. Wherever possible, terms are briefly defined within the text itself, but the Glossary provides more extensive explanations. Other elements that should be useful for instructors and students include study questions; suggested plays and readings; and a guide to related films and videocassettes that provide "recorded" performances of the model plays and feature such distinguished actors as Laurence Olivier, Jessica Tandy,

James Earl Jones, Derek Jacobi, Irene Worth, Marlon Brando, Vivien Leigh, Billie Whitelaw, Spalding Gray, Vanessa Redgrave, Joan Plowright, Sidney Poitier, John Malkovich, Anna Deavere Smith, Kevin Kline, and Kenneth Branagh. These films represent work by such renowned stage directors as Peter Brook, Elia Kazan, Jerzy Grotowski, Laurence Olivier, Tyrone Guthrie, Alan Schneider, Ariane Mnouchkine, and Robert Wilson.

Finally, this book is in no way a definitive treatment of theatre practice, history, or literature but an attempt to put students in touch with theatre as a performing art and humanistic event. Most important, it introduces students to theatre as an *immediate* experience, engaging actors and audiences for a brief time in a special place. The Greeks called that special place where audiences sat to watch performances a *theatron*, or "seeing place." Let us, as informed spectators, make theatre as a way of seeing our guide to understanding and enjoying theatrical writing and performance.

My thanks are due to colleagues for their encouragement and assistance in the preparation of the several revisions of this book. Those who advised on this fourth edition are: Gayle Austin, Georgia State University; Kurt Daw, Kennesaw State College; Marilyn Hoffs, Glendale Community College; Charles Harbour, University of Montevallo; Christopher Jones, Northern Illinois University; and Jared Saltzman, Bergen Community College.

Milly S. Barranger
The University of North Carolina
Chapel Hill

I can take any empty space and call it a
bare stage. A man walks across this empty
space whilst someone else is watching him,
and this is all that is needed for an act of
theatre to be engaged.

PETER BROOK
The Empty Space[1]

While we are watching, men and women
make theatre happen before us. In the
theatre we see human beings in action—
what they do and why they do it—and we
discover things about ourselves and our
world by seeing them through others' eyes.

1

DISCOVERING THEATRE

The Immediate Art

Theatre is a performance art that places human experience before a group of people—an audience—in the present moment. For theatre to happen, two groups of people, actors and audience, must come together at a certain time and in a certain place. There, on a stage or in a special place, actors present themselves to an audience in a story usually involving some aspect of being human. The audience shares in the story and the occasion. We listen, gather information, feel emotions, and *actively* interact with the actors and their events that define in some way what it means to be a human being in certain circumstances—both familiar and unfamiliar.

Theatre is a way of seeing men and women in action, of observing what they do and why they do it. Because human beings are both theatre's subject and its means of expression, theatre is one of the most immediate ways of experiencing another's concept of life—of what it means to be human.

In this first chapter, we want to ask: What is theatre? How is theatre *a way of seeing*? What makes theatre different from other arts, particularly the mass media? How do we, as audiences, respond to and experience theatre?

Let us define theatre and describe our experience of theatre. Let us consider theatre's special qualities that set it apart as a form of art: its immediacy, aliveness, doubleness, fictions, spaces, and audiences. Theatre's *immediacy* is our first concern.

Theatre's Immediacy

Theatre always involves two groups of people, actors and audiences, in the present moment. Unlike video, television, and film, theatre is not a "canned" product to be mailed about the country and broadcast to millions of people. It is a limited art, requiring that artists and audiences come together in a designated place for the few hours of the performance. That performance may, of course, be taped for television, but the theatre's special immediacy and aliveness is lost when transposed to another medium.

Theatre is most often *contrasted* with the mass media and technical arts: film, television, radio, and music videos. Certainly, there are shared influences among these arts, and artists participate in them in varying degrees. Here the comparison ends, for the mass *media* is the sum of its current technology, which produces, transmits, and receives an artistic product. In addition, the electronic media is forever expanding its number of spectators in various corners of the world, recording images of human experience from Sarajevo, Moscow, and Beijing to beam into our living rooms in Chicago and Los Angeles. Theatre, on the other hand, is limited in all respects: number of spectators, technology, reproducibility, and outreach.

For theatre to happen, there must be a direct exchange between actor and spectator in the present time of the performance. Whereas we respond to the theatre event from moment to moment over a period of an hour or two, radio, film and television require no immediate feedback from viewers. Unless we are watching television with friends, we are essentially alone with the medium.

It is undeniable that media arts have a large and significant place in our daily lives. Radio is often background music to such activities as driving a car or studying for an exam. The television set is part of our household furniture, and the video recorder lets us show films of our own choosing in our own homes. Our favorite movie houses are numerous and widely located. In contrast, theatre is found in limited places, takes place at unique hours (we say that the "curtain is at eight," meaning that the performance begins at eight o'clock), and engages us in an *active* construction of meaning in regard to human experience: Shakespeare's *Hamlet* engages us in untimely revenge and its deadly consequences; David Mamet's *Oleanna* presents us with the use and abuse of power in the classroom; María Irene Fornés confronts us with the family as mirror of totalitarian societies; and so on.

One vital difference between theatre and media arts is *high technology*. Madonna's music videos, for example, produce effects of a theatrical event, but technologies for reproducing sound, images, and permanent records on tape for worldwide dissemination are not part of the theatre experience. For one thing, the theatre's technology has not changed remarkably over 2,500 years. For another, theatre, unlike music video, is ephemeral. Once the theatrical performance concludes, it is gone forever. What is unique (and even disheartening) about the theatrical event is that, even as it is taking place, it is lost forever. We can read about the first performance of Shakespeare's plays, but we can never fully know what it was to experience *Hamlet* on stage in the Elizabethan period. We can have our own first experience of Shakespeare's play, but we cannot make permanent our experience except in memory, photographs, or film. What is it, then, that makes this ancient art so elusive? It is the centrality of human beings—actors and spectators.

As director Peter Brook says about making theatre happen, "A man walks across this empty space whilst someone else is watching him, and this is all that is needed for an act of theatre to be engaged." It is theatre's *immediacy* that makes it different from other arts. Theatre presents human beings playing fictional characters who move, speak, and "live" *before* us, creating recognizable events and places. For a short time we share an experience with actors that is imitative, provocative, entertaining, and magical. Theatre's living quality sets it apart.

Theatre's Aliveness

In many ways, theatre parallels life. On stage, actors represent our humanness (our bodies, voices, minds, and souls) in an imitation of certain human truths and realities. In *Tartuffe*, for example, Molière presents the perils of a phony religious person's greed; in *The Caucasian Chalk Circle*, Bertolt Brecht demonstrates the selfless act of a young woman saving a child in time of war. As we sit in the audience, we constitute a human community—a collective presence as we laugh, cry, enjoy, and applaud.

FIGURE 1.1

This still from the 1951 movie version of Tennessee Williams' play A Streetcar Named Desire *captures for all time a moment between Vivien Leigh (as Blanche DuBois) and Marlon Brando (as Stanley Kowalski). Each time we see the movie (and it may be many times), we can experience again this interaction between these two particular actors. A similar moment in the theatre is lost to us even as it takes place before us on the stage.*

Theatre is thus "alive" in its immediate communion with its audience. Film is a means of recording and preserving that "aliveness" for all time. The television program "Live from Lincoln Center" is one highly successful effort to record on videotape a stage performance with its audience. From our homes we can watch opera stars Luciano Pavarotti and Jessye Norman and hear the audience's enthusiastic response, but we are removed from the original event. We know that both theatre and film/video are equally convincing in their story-telling powers, but their modes of presentation are vastly different.

For example, the great performances of Marlon Brando and Vivien Leigh as Stanley Kowalski and Blanche DuBois in *A Streetcar Named Desire* are captured in the 1951 film (see Figure 1.1). But the wonderful theatrical performances of Laurette Taylor, Jessica Tandy, Vanessa Redgrave, Natasha Richardson, and others in plays by Tennessee Williams are lost to us as the performance ends (see Figure 1.2). Theatre is an evanescent art, lasting only those two or three hours it takes to see the play. The experience can be repeated night after night as long as the show is running, but once the play is closed and the cast is dispersed, that performance is lost.

Although admittedly frustrating, this intriguing quality of theatre, which critic Brooks Atkinson calls the "bright enigma," is the source of its vitality and our pleasure.

FIGURE 1.2
Actress Jessica Tandy as Blanche DuBois with Marlon Brando as Stanley Kowalski in the original New York production of A Streetcar Named Desire *(1947), directed by Elia Kazan.*

Theatre, then, is a *living* art form, continually before us in present time until that final moment when Shakespeare's Hamlet is lifted from the stage to Fortinbras' command: "Take up the bodies," or when Samuel Beckett's tramps do not move from the appointed place for their meeting with "Godot," who never comes. Theatre also bears a unique relationship to the aliveness (and humanity) it mirrors. What are these parallels between theatre and life? There are four essential ones:

       actors ↔ humanity
    simulation ↔ reality
     rehearsal ↔ spontaneity
    audiences ↔ society

At all times in the theatre we are aware of a double quality about life and art. The actors are human beings playing at being other people; the stage is a platform that pretends to be another world. Shakespeare said it best in *As You Like It:* "All the world's a stage/And all the men and women merely players." Theatre's doubleness is another special quality.

TYPES OF CONTEMPORARY THEATRES

Today's theatres are found in large cities as well as in small towns. Just as their locations are diverse, so theatre buildings and stages differ in size and shape.

London's National Theatre, located on the south bank of the Thames River, was completed in 1976. The huge complex contains three theatres (the Lyttelton, the Cottesloe, and the Olivier, shown here), rehearsal rooms, workshops, offices, restaurants, and foyers. Named for English actor Laurence Olivier, the Olivier Theatre has an open stage and 1,150 seats. The audience encircles the stage.

Interior of the 400-seat Cottesloe black box theatre. Modeled on an Elizabethan courtyard with balcony above and flexible seating below, it has been used largely for experimental work, staged readings, and seminars.

The Guthrie Theater, Minneapolis, built in 1963, houses a large auditorium (1,441 seats) encircling the unique seven-sided thrust stage. No seat is more than fifty-two feet from the center of the stage. The photo shows the audience's relationship to the actors and stage.

The Oregon Shakespearean Festival Theatre in Ashland (founded in 1935) is an open-air theatre. The audience sits in front of a platform stage. A multilevel building serves as a permanent background for plays by Shakespeare and other playwrights. Compare this photo with the picture of Shakespeare's Globe on page 36.

In Arena Stage, built in 1960 in Washington, D.C., the audience completely surrounds the stage action. Lighting instruments are visible above the stage, and scenery and furniture are minimal. Actors enter and exit through the alleyways, called voms, for the Roman vomitorium or entrance-ways into the seats in the early amphitheatres.

The Eisenhower Theatre in Washington, D.C.: a modern proscenium theatre, showing the characteristic picture-frame stage. The curtain is closed, awaiting the arrival of the audience—who will "discover" the play's world only when the curtain rises.

Chapter One

Theatre's Doubleness

It has been said by Shakespeare and others that there is a doubleness about the theatrical experience that provides a sense of life reflected on stage. For instance, the audience experiences the actor both as actor—the living presence of another human being—and as fictional character. We experience Kevin Kline as Hamlet, and James Earl Jones as Othello. Likewise, the performing space is a stage and at the same time an imaginary world created by the playwright, designer, director, and actor. Sometimes this world is as familiar to us as a New Orleans tenement or a Midwestern farmhouse. The stage might resemble a modern living room or a hotel room or a front yard. Sometimes it is unfamiliar, like Hamlet's blighted castle at Elsinore, Oedipus' plague-ridden city of Thebes, or Othello's storm-tossed island of Cyprus.

The Elizabethans thought the theatre mirrored life. Shakespeare had Hamlet describe the purpose of acting, or "playing," in this way:

> . . . the purpose of playing, whose end, both at the first and now, was and is to hold as 'twere the mirror up to Nature, to show Virtue her own feature, scorn her own image, and the very age and body of the time his form and pressure. (3, ii)

Hamlet speaks here of the Elizabethan idea that the stage, like a mirror, shows audiences both their good and bad qualities along with an accurate reflection of the times.

The Elizabethan idea of the stage as a mirror, related as it is to the act of seeing, can help us understand the dynamics of theatre and its aesthetics. Looking into a mirror is, in a sense, like going to the theatre. When we look into a mirror we see our double—an image of ourselves—and possibly a background and anyone standing around the reflection. The image can be made to move; we make certain judgments about it; it communicates to us certain attitudes and concerns about our humanness. Our humanity as reflected in the mirror has shape, color, texture, form, attitude, and emotion; it is even capable of limited movement within the mirror's frame. Onstage the actor's living presence as a fictional character—as Oedipus, Othello, Hamlet, or Blanche DuBois—creates the doubleness that is theatre's special quality. It is both a stage world and an illusion of a real world.

Jaques' speech from Shakespeare's *As You Like It* provides us with one of the most famous discussions on the similarities between theatre and life:

All the world's a stage,
And all the men and women merely players.
They have their exits and their entrances,
And one man in his time plays many parts,
His acts being seven ages. At first the infant,
Mewling and puking in the nurse's arms.
And then the whining school-boy, with
   his satchel
And shining morning face, creeping like snail
Unwillingly to school. And then the lover,
Sighing like furnace, with a woeful ballad
Made to his mistress' eyebrow. Then
   a soldier,
Full of stange oaths, and bearded like
   the pard,
Jealous in honor, sudden and quick
   in quarrel,
Seeking the bubble reputation
Even in the cannon's mouth. And then
   the justice,
In fair round belly with good capon lined,
With eyes severe and beard of formal cut,
Full of wise saws and modern instances,
And so he plays his part. The sixth age shifts
Into the lean and slippered Pantaloon,
With spectacles on nose and pouch on side,
His youthful hose, well saved, a world
   too wide
For his shrunk shank, and his big
   manly voice,
Turning again toward childish treble, pipes
And whistles in his sound. Last scene of all,
That ends this strange eventful history,
Is second childishness and mere oblivion,
Sans teeth, sans eyes, sans taste, sans
   everything.
(2, vii)

Theatre is life's double, but it is also something more than a reflection of life. It is a form of art—*a selected reflection*. It is life's reflection *organized meaningfully* into stories and fictions about events and people.

Theatre's Fictions

Theatre presents itself as a fiction—the performance of stories about events and people. We are emotionally and intellectually pulled into the lives and feelings of the characters before us. We would like Blanche DuBois to find that handsome mythical gentle-man who will make life tolerable and kind for her, but we know her destructive tendencies and cringe before the inevitable ending to her life.

In contrast, radio and television programming make extraordinary efforts to separate fact from fiction. Anchorpeople, like Connie Chung, announce programs; journalists, like Dan Rather, assure us that we are being told the facts of the day's news; program credits tell us that we are watching a fiction of Roseanne Arnold's make-believe family.

In the case of such films as *Henry V* and *Much Ado About Nothing*, Kenneth Branagh did not first stage Shakespeare's plays prior to capturing the stories on film. The cutting, editing, framing, and camera movements rearranged Shakespeare's text while retaining the language pertinent to telling the film version of the story. The theatrical dimension is concentrated in certain scenes of *Henry V*, for example, when the comic rogue Falstaff exhorts his friend in the tavern, or when King Henry proposes marriage to Katherine of France. These are concentrated scenes like those found in a play, but in the film as a whole the rapid editing from place to place, the contrasts of faces and images, the realistic scenes of horses falling in battle, and the rearranging of the old text into useful fragments create the medium of film.

In film, we are transported by images into new worlds of discovery. Theatre uses other means to persuade us that we are sharing in new experiences. As the proverbial curtain goes up, we enter into a form of artistic illusion that is now 2,500 years old.

Theatrical Illusion

Theatre creates the *illusion*, as we watch, that we are sharing an experience with others for the first time. As members of the audience we tacitly agree with the actors that, for the time of the performance, the play is a living reality. We know that theatre is not life, but we suspend this knowledge for the few hours we watch the play. We share with the actors the illusion that life is being lived on stage as we observe their actions, which can be repeated night after night. As we watch and listen, we share their experiences—both spontaneous and rehearsed. Moreover, actors contribute further to the illusion, for they are both actors and characters. We are simultaneously aware that Oedipus, the central figure in *Oedipus the King*, is Sophocles' central character and that he is being played by an actor named John Gielgud. Theatre's grand fiction is twofold: that the actors are other than who they are in the present moment, and that life is taking shape before us *for the first time.*

In the theatre we both believe in what is happening before us ("suspend our disbelief," as the poet Coleridge said) and disbelieve in the pretense. We give way to theatre's magic and fiction as our minds and emotions are involved, yet we exist apart.

Theatre's Spaces

At the heart of the theatre experience, as Peter Brook suggests, is the act of seeing and being seen. That requires a special place. We are told that the word *theatre* comes from the Greek word *theatron*, meaning "seeing place." At one time or another during the history of Western culture, this place for seeing has been a primitive dancing circle, an **amphitheatre**, a church, an Elizabethan platform stage, a marketplace, a garage, a street, or a **proscenium** theatre (see Glossary). Today, it may be a Broadway theatre, a university playhouse, or a renovated warehouse. But neither the stage's shape nor the building's architecture makes a theatre. Rather the use of space to imitate human experience for an audience to see makes that space special—a seeing place. And this seeing place, *theatron*, or theatre is where we learn about ourselves and others. It is the place where we perceive the how, the what, and the why of our humanness in the company of others.

The three basic components of theatre are, as we shall discover, the actor, the space, and the audience. The history of theatre has been, in one sense, the record of the changing physical relationships of actor and audience. The audience has moved from the hillside of the Greek theatre to a place before the Christian altar, to standing room around the Elizabethan theatre's platform stage, to seats in a darkened hall before a curtained proscenium stage, to the floor of a modern environmental production.

In the same historical sequence, the actor has moved from the dancing circle of the Greek theatre to the church, to the open stage of the Elizabethan theatre, to the recessed stage of the proscenium theatre, to the environmental space of some contemporary productions. The effect of historical trends and social institutions on theatre is important but not crucial to this discussion of theatre as a way of seeing. What is crucial is an understanding of the common denominators, unchanged since

SHAKESPEARE INTO FILM

In the 1990 film of Hamlet, *starring Mel Gibson as the Prince of Denmark, Glenn Close (Gertrude), Alan Bates (Claudius), and Ian Holm (Polonius) stare in disbelief at Hamlet's antics. Directed by Franco Zeffirelli.*

An intimate moment between Gertrude and Claudius in the 1990 film.

Gertrude (Eileen Herlie) and Claudius (Basil Sydney) try to persuade Hamlet (Laurence Olivier) to join in their festivities in the 1948 film of Hamlet, also directed by Olivier.

Kenneth Branagh (who also directed) as King Henry V comforts an English soldier (above) and exhorts his troops (right) on the battlefield of Agincourt in the 1989 film of Shakespeare's Henry V.

Actor/director Laurence Olivier in the title role of Richard III rides to his defeat during the battle of Bosworth Field in a scene from the 1954 film of Shakespeare's chronicle history play.

Kenneth Branagh as the English king woos Emma Thompson as Princess Katharine of France in the 1989 film of Shakespeare's Henry V, *also directed by Kenneth Branagh.*

Marlon Brando, as Mark Antony in the 1953 film of Shakespeare's Julius Caesar, *addresses the Roman mob in the famous speech that begins "Friends, Romans, countrymen, lend me your ears . . ."*

The wedding scene with Kenneth Branagh and Emma Thompson in the 1993 film of Shakespeare's Much Ado About Nothing, *also directed by Kenneth Branagh. Note the cameramen to the left and top.*

John Gielgud as Prospero (with Isabelle Pasco) in director Peter Greenaway's loose interpretation of Shakespeare's The Tempest *in the 1991 film titled* Prospero's Books.

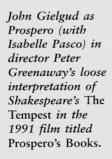

the time the legendary Thespis, credited with being the first actor, stepped apart from the Greek chorus and created dialogue for the listener. It is no accident that the Greek word for actor is *hypokrites*, meaning "answerer." That first actor literally answered the chorus' questions.

Whether the physical space becomes more elaborate or less so, whether the performance occurs indoors or out, the actor–audience relationship is theatre's vital ingredient. In one sense, the formula for theatre is simple: *A man or woman stands in front of an audience in a special (or prepared) place and performs an action, usually interacting with another performer.*

Theatre's Audiences

A modern audience enters a theatre lobby with an air of excitement and a sense of anticipation. There is usually a last-minute crush at the box office to pick up tickets, then to get programs and find seats. An audience is not an unruly crowd but a very special group assembling for a special occasion; it is the final, essential participant in the theatre event. The audience is the assembled group for which all has been written, designed, rehearsed, and produced.

What, then, are our expectations as we wait for the house lights to dim and the curtain to rise? Our expectations are essentially the same whether we are in the Shubert Theatre on Broadway or the Guthrie Theater in Minneapolis.

1. *As audiences, we expect plays to be related to life experiences.* (It goes without saying that audiences expect plays and performances to hold their attention and to be entertaining.) This does not mean that audiences actually expect to have experienced the events taking place on stage. None of us would willingly exchange places with Oedipus or Blanche DuBois. Instead, we expect the play's events (and also the actor's performances) to be *authentic* in feelings and experiences. We are moved by *A Streetcar Named Desire* because it rings true in terms of what we know about ourselves and others. It confirms what we have studied, read, and heard about human behavior. Williams' characters and situation may not be literally a part of our lives; yet we all recognize the need for fantasies, self-delusion, and refuge from life's harsh realities. In short, we go to the theatre expecting the performance to be an

authentic representation of some aspect of life as we know it or can imagine it.

2. *Most of us go to the theatre expecting the familiar*. These expectations are based largely on plays we have already seen or on our experiences with movies and television. Audiences enjoy the familiar in plots, characters, and situations. For this reason, daily television soap operas, like "The Young and the Restless" and "As the World Turns," are popular with all ages. Also, audiences frequently have difficulty understanding and enjoying plays from the older classical repertory or from the contemporary avant-garde. We are not as comfortable with the concerns of Oedipus or Estragon as we are with the domestic affairs of Roseanne Arnold or Jerry Seinfeld.

All audiences come to the theatre with certain expectations that have been shaped by their previous theatregoing experiences. If those experiences have been limited to musicals, summer stock, or local community theatre, then they may find the first experience of a play by Anton Chekhov or Samuel Beckett a jarring, puzzling, or even boring experience. But masterpieces somehow ring true! In them we find authentic life experiences, even if the language is difficult, the situations strange, or the production techniques unfamiliar.

The response to the first American production of *Waiting for Godot* is a good example of audiences being confronted with the unfamiliar and having their expectations disappointed on their first experience with the play. Audiences in Miami and New York were baffled by it. But in 1957, Jules Irving and Herbert Blau's San Francisco Actor's Workshop presented *Waiting for Godot* to the inmates of San Quentin Prison. Because no live play had been performed at San Quentin since Sarah Bernhardt had appeared there in 1913, the director and actors were apprehensive.

Of the 1,400 convicts assembled to see the play, possibly not one had ever been to the theatre. Moreover, they were gathered in the prison dining room to see a highly experimental play that had bewildered sophisticated audiences in Paris, Miami, and New York. What would be the response? It was simply overwhelming. The prisoners understood the hopelessness and frustration of waiting for something or for someone that never arrives. They recognized the meaninglessness of waiting and were aware that if Godot finally came, he would probably be a disappointment.[2]

A radical adaptation of Shakespeare's A Midsummer Night's Dream *directed by Peter Brook in 1970 for Britain's Royal Shakespeare Company. Oberon (Alan Howard) and Puck (John Kane) speak Shakespeare's lines while perched like acrobats on trapezes.*

By now, *Waiting for Godot* is no longer considered experimental, and most audiences are no longer baffled by it. It has become a classic of the modern theatre, exemplifying how initial audience expectations can change over a period of years in response to an unusual, profound play.

Even though audiences desire to see the familiar—this is probably the reason there are so many revivals of *Arsenic and Old Lace* and *Charley's Aunt*—they also appreciate and look forward to novel experiences in the theatre. Imagine the surprise of audiences in 1970 when director Peter Brook reinterpreted Shakespeare's *A Midsummer Night's Dream*, exploring the complications of young love in a white boxlike setting with actors in modern clothing on trapezes (Figure 1.3). Most audiences around the world were delighted with the new concept for staging a very old play, although a few were dissatisfied by not having their expectations fulfilled.

Like all great art forms, the theatre gives us a heightened sense of life and self-awareness. Great theatre also provides a sense of *new* possibilities. We go to plays (whether consciously aware of our reasons) to realize a fuller, deeper understanding of our lives, our society, and our

The 1956 Broadway premiere of Waiting for Godot *(directed by Herbert Berghof) with Kurt Kasznar as Pozzo, E. G. Marshall as Vladimir, Bert Lahr as Estragon, and Alvin Epstein as Lucky.*

Waiting for Godot, by the Irish playwright Samuel Beckett, was first produced at the Théâtre de Babylone, Paris, in 1953. On a country road in a deserted landscape marked by a single leafless tree, Estragon and Vladimir are waiting for someone named Godot. To pass the time, they play games, quarrel, make up, fall asleep. In comes Pozzo, leading Lucky by a rope tied around his neck. Pozzo demonstrates that Lucky is his obedient servant, and Lucky entertains them with a monologue that is a jumble of politics and theology. They disappear into the darkness, and Godot's messenger (a boy) announces that Mr. Godot will not come today.

In Act II, a leaf has sprouted on the tree, suggesting that time has passed, but the two tramps are occupied in the same way. They play master-and-slave games, trade hats, argue about everything. Pozzo and Lucky return, but they are not the same: The master is blind and the slave is mute. Godot again sends word that he will not come today, but perhaps tomorrow. As the play ends, Vladimir and Estragon continue waiting, alone but together. In this play Beckett demonstrates how each of us waits for a Godot—for whatever it is that we hope for—and how, so occupied, we wait out a lifetime.

universe. When we are satisfied, we no longer cling to our need for the familiar.

3. *Another facet of audience expectations is more difficult to pin down—the collective response.* We experience a performance as a group—as a collective thinking and feeling presence. Psychologists tell us that being in an audience satisfies a deeply felt human need: the need to participate in a collective response, whether with laughter, tears, appreciative silence, or thundering applause. As part of an audience, we become very much aware of group dynamics at the conclusion of a powerful and moving play. Sometimes when audiences are deeply moved, there are moments of silence before the beginning of applause. At other times applause is instantaneous, with audiences leaping to their feet clapping and shouting "bravo." The response to a great performance, as it was to Kenneth Branagh's Hamlet, is immediate and unrestrained.

Even though applause is a theatregoing convention, it is also a genuine expression of our appreciation and approval of a performance. One major element of our experience of live theatre is this sharing of feelings with others around us. Sometimes this even happens in movie houses, especially in horror films, but rarely does it happen when we sit before the television set at home—because we are often watching alone, or we are distracted by movements around us. An audience by definition is a sharing with others—of laughter and tears, expectations and delight.

Summary

Theatre takes place as we watch actors present themselves to us in stories usually about human beings. The heart of the theatrical experience is the act of seeing and being seen; hence, we have subtitled this book "A Way of Seeing."

Theatre, like life, happens within the present moment. Theatre has an immediacy that most other art forms do not have or require. For theatre to happen, two groups of people—actors and audience—must come together in a certain space. There the actors present themselves to the audience. The space, the actor, and the audience are the three essential ingredients of the theatre event. Most effectively of all the arts, theatre captures the experience of what it means to be human because human beings are both its medium and its subject: The actor (the medium) on the stage is also Hamlet (the subject) at Elsinore Castle.

Contrasting theatre with film and other forms of entertainment helps clarify the special qualities of the theatre. Theatre's *immediacy* and *aliveness*—living actors presenting themselves before a live audience—are the most notable differences between theatre and film.

Theatre is also an act of discovery. When the curtain goes up, we discover a world that is both familiar and unfamiliar to us. We discover new ways of learning about ourselves, our society, and our world. Great plays always raise questions about what it means to be a human being. Great performances communicate this knowledge to us in fresh, entertaining, and challenging ways.

Because we, as audiences, first experience the theatrical space as we enter a theatre and since that space influences the way in which we see theatre, we begin the next discussion with the types of theatrical spaces found through the ages.

Questions for Study

1. How does theatre differ from other art forms, such as film, television, music, dance, and painting?

2. What did the ancient Greeks mean when they called their theatre a "seeing place" or *theatron*?

3. What types of theatres are we likely to find today on our campuses and in our cities?

4. What is special about theatrical space?

5. Why are the actor, the space, and the audience the theatre's three unchanging components?

6. What do we mean when we say that each night in the theatre there is an "illusion of the first time"?

7. How does Shakespeare define the "purpose of playing"?

8. What do we mean when we say that theatre is an *immediate* art?

9. How are human beings both theatre's subject and its means of expression?

10. What did Shakespeare mean by writing in *Hamlet* that a performance is like a mirror held up to nature?

11. What kinds of *audience response* are we likely to experience in the theatre?

12. Why does Brooks Atkinson call theatre a "bright enigma"? What does it mean?

13. *Plays to Read*: Sophocles' *Oedipus the King*, Shakespeare's *Hamlet*, Williams' *A Streetcar Named Desire*, Beckett's *Waiting for Godot*.

14. *Suggested Reading: The Empty Space* by Peter Brook (New York: Atheneum, 1968).

There are, for example, privileged places, qualitatively different from all others—a man's birthplace, or the scenes of his first love . . . as if it were in such spots that he had received the revelation of a reality other than that in which he participates through his ordinary daily life.

MIRCEA ELIADE
The Sacred and the Profane:
The Nature of Religion[1]

Since its beginnings, theatre has been a place for seeing—for viewing, presenting, perceiving, understanding. Places for theatre to happen are found in all societies, ancient and modern. Throughout history the theatre space has been arranged so that audiences can see and performers can be seen.

2

THE SEEING PLACE

Let us begin the discovery of theatre with the places, stages, and auditoriums where it all happens. All cultures, no matter how primitive or sophisticated, have theatrical performances and places for *seeing* these events. The earliest theatrical spaces were areas for performance of rituals dealing with life and death.

Ritual and Theatre

First Performance Spaces

When we examine the origins of ritual and theatre, we discover that the earliest actor always performs in a special or privileged place. The priest, the guru, the dancer, or the actor performs in a threshing circle, or in a hut, a building, or an enclosure that is shared with the onlooker or audience. In some ritual spaces, a circular area is surrounded by spectators in much the same way that the semicircular Greek theatre is configured. In others, special buildings are constructed for the occasion and often destroyed at the end of the rite in the same sense that a modern production is "struck," or removed at the end of the play's run. Some groups moved from place to place in early societies, like today's touring companies.

Since the publication of Sir James Frazer's *The Golden Bough* in 1890, theatre historians have connected the origins of theatre with agrarian and fertility rites and with *special places* for enactment of these rites. Primitive people staged mock battles between death and life in which the king of the old year, representing death, perished in a duel with the champion of the new year. In these rituals we can see the beginnings of theatrical modes of today: *enactment, imitation,* and *seasonal performances*—all held in special or privileged spaces so designated by the community.

Dramatic overtones were added to ceremonies designed to win favor from supernatural powers. The rain dance ceremonies of the Native Americans of the Southwest were meant to ensure that the tribal gods would send rain to make crops grow. Early societies acted out seasonal changes—patterns of life, death, and rebirth—until their ceremonies became formalized dramatic rituals. Harvest rituals, for example, celebrated abundant food supplies. Imitation, costume, makeup, masks, gesture, and pantomime were theatrical elements in these early rituals. (See Figure 2.1.)

Whereas primitive ritual was concerned with the protection of the tribe, theatre's most common objective is to please and entertain rather than to pacify, protect, or heal. And its audiences are not secondary to what's going on onstage, as they may very well be in the practice of ritual magic. Theatre's audiences, as we have seen, are central and indispensable to the theatrical experience.

Theatre, on the other hand, deals with the mystery, history, and ambiguity of human events. Plays speak to us of individuals, as well as of groups. They hold the mirror up to our joys and our sorrows, to our questions and our tentative answers about life. Theatre aims to provoke thought while entertaining us, rather than to provide concrete answers. We spoke in the previous chapter about the playwright's concern for the human condition. Shakespeare demonstrates the sensitivity of a supreme dramatic artist in this speech by Hamlet:

> What a piece of work is a man, how noble in reason, how
> infinite in faculties; in form and moving how express and
> admirable, in action how like an angel, in apprehension how
> like a god: the beauty of the world, the paragon of animals! And
> yet to me what is this quintessence of dust? (2, ii)

Hamlet speaks about himself, but he also speaks in universal terms about all of us. He raises questions about human nature; insights are there for those who want them. But even so, the play's essential function is to entertain. For without diversion, all else in the theatre must inevitably fail and audiences become bored, restless, "turned off." Although ritual performances are often entertaining, their objective is

FIGURE 2.1
The shaman *of early hunting cultures was both a healer and an artist. As well as healing the sick, the shaman brings psychic calm and confidence to the tribe by revitalizing and intensifying its notions of the world. The annual hunting rites carried out by the shaman are a good example. The photo shows a Siberian shaman's coat and mask. (From* Shamanism: The Beginnings of Art.*)*

largely practical: Crops will grow, the hunt will succeed, warring tribes will be placated or defeated. In ritual, entertainment is a bonus for the onlooker: in theatre we share in a complex experience that is simultaneously entertaining, imitative, provocative, subversive, and even magical.

Although theatre evolved from early ritual and those special places reserved for enactment of communal rites, theatre differs from ritual in several essential ways. Unlike participants in a ritual, actors create fictional characters. Actors also present themselves on a stage, or in a special place, using the playwright's words to create a sense of place and life. That the actor appears *on a stage* is important not only for an actor, and for the other artists and technicians involved, but also for the audience.

What is certain in these early beginnings is that theatre, as we know it now, is a kind of ritual act performed not in a hut or other temporary structure that will be dismantled after the ceremony, but in a permanent building that will be used again and again. Theatrical space as we know it in modern terms has two components: the *stage* and the *auditorium*. And the first such permanent theatre building we know of in Western culture stands in the curve of a hillside in Greece.

The Greek Theatre
Orchestra and *Skene*

The most celebrated theatre of fifth-century Athens, called the Theatre of Dionysus in honor of the fertility god, was an open-air structure located on the slope of the hill below the Acropolis.

In time, there were two performance areas cradled within the curve of the hillside: the dancing circle (or *orchestra*), and the area backed by the scene building (or *skene*). The chorus, usually portraying ordinary human society, performed in the dancing area. One speaking actor (later three) portrayed mythical and historical characters, first in an "empty space" and later in front of the rectangular scene building, which formed a neutral background easily representing many places—a palace, temple, house, cave, or whatever was needed. A late addition to the theatre was the wooden scene building erected on a stone foundation. The actors may also have performed in the *orchestra*, although no one knows for sure. The chorus, actors, and audience all entered the theatre through passageways called *parodoi*, and the audience stood, or were seated on the ground and later on wooden or stone benches, on the hillside "auditorium."

In the ancient Greek theatre there were no barriers between the performing area and the auditorium. The audience on the hillside had an unbroken view of actor and chorus as they do in the photo of the Theatre at Delphi (see Figure 2.2). The spectators in the lower tiers near the orchestra, in fact, were so near the chorus that they were practically an extension of it.

The Chorus as Spectator

The Greek chorus, which was eventually reduced from fifty people to fifteen or twelve by the time Aeschylus, Sophocles, and Euripides were

FIGURE 2.2

The Theatre at Delphi, an ancient Greek theatre, is built on a hillside with seats on three sides surrounding the dancing circle, or orchestra. *The temple of Apollo is in the background. Eventually, scene buildings were built behind the playing area. Audiences could look past the stage to the mountains and the sea in the distance. The photo shows the stone benches placed on the hillside for the audience, the flat dancing circle for the chorus (and possibly actors) at the foot of the hill, and the remains of the stone foundation of the scene building.*

writing for the festivals, shared the audience's reactions to events and characters, and sometimes interacted with the actors. Functioning as the play's community or society, the chorus gave advice, expressed opinions, asked questions, and generally set the ethical framework by which events were judged. They frequently served as the "ideal spectator," reacting to characters and events as the playwrights hoped audiences would. Their costumes and masks added spectacle—movement, song,

AESCHYLUS AND THE ATHENIAN FESTIVALS

Aeschylus (525/4–456 B.C.), Sophocles, Euripides, and Aristophanes are four Greek playwrights whose work has survived. Aeschylus began at an early age to write tragedies for the annual festivals in the Theatre of Dionysus, Athens, winning thirteen first prizes during his lifetime.

Sometime before or during Aeschylus' career, the features of Greek tragedy became fixed: At an Athenian festival, three groups of players, each consisting of a chorus and two (later three) actors, competed in acting four sets of plays. Each set contained three tragedies and a satyr play, a burlesque of Greek myth, for comic relief. The plays were based on Greek legend, epic poems, or history. Costumes were formal, masks elaborate, physical action restrained; violent scenes occurred offstage. The playwright expanded and interpreted the characters and stories of legend or history.

Although Aeschylus wrote over seventy plays, we have inherited scripts for only seven: *The Suppliants, The Persians, The Seven Against Thebes, Prometheus Bound, Agamemnon, The Libation Bearers,* and *The Eumenides.* These last three make up the *Oresteia* (458 B.C.), the only surviving Greek trilogy, or sequence of three tragedies. Its satyr play is missing.

We know little about Aeschylus as a person except that he fought at Marathon (490 B.C.) and probably at Salamis (480 B.C.) during the Persian Wars. His epitaph, which he wrote himself, shows that he was most proud of his military record:

Under this monument lies Aeschylus the Athenian, Euphorion's son, who died in the wheatlands of Gela. The grove of Marathon with its glories can speak of his valor in battle. The long-haired Persian remembers and can speak of it too.

dance, and visual interest—to the occasion, and their moods heightened the story's dramatic effectiveness.

Unlike the chorus, the actor, representing a heroic figure like Oedipus or Orestes, stood apart in the performance space, just as he stood apart from ordinary mortals in life. Thus, the dancing circle and the

FIGURE 2.3
From the audience's perspective in the Epidaurus Festival Theatre, Greece. The modern audience looks down upon the ancient orchestra, or dancing circle. The raised platforms for the stage and the scenic background are modern reconstructions.

chorus formed a kind of bridge between actor and audience, serving as both commentator about and spectator for the deeds it witnessed (see Figure 2.3).

The arrangement of spaces in the Greek theatre indicates how the Greeks saw their world: Classes separated physically by space and social status found themselves on common ground when faced with spectacles of terror and misfortune. They found mutual comfort in being part of a cosmos dominated by gods and heroes. Sophocles' *Oedipus the King* speaks to master and slave when the chorus concludes: "Count no man happy until he has passed the final limit of his life secure from pain."

From the classical to the Hellenistic period (c. 990–30 B.C.), the Greek theatre underwent changes: Wooden seats were replaced by stone; the addition of the scene building made the actors' area more complex, providing a scenic background and dressing area; a raised stage was probably added sometime after the fifth century for the actors to perform on. (See Figure 2.3.) But the theatres remained in the open air, with well-defined places for the audience to sit and for the actors and chorus to perform. As we shall discover in a later chapter, the division of space and other conventions such as the formal entrances, choral odes, and two to three speaking actors dictated the structure of the plays performed there. The plays of Aeschylus, Sophocles, Euripides, and Aristophanes were shaped by the theatre's conventions.

TROPES

The *trope*, made up of chanted dialogue, was the beginning of medieval church drama and the first step toward creating plays after the Dark Ages. The tenth-century *Quem Quaeritis*, from a Benedictine abbey in Switzerland, consisted of questions and answers sung by the two halves of the choir during an Easter Mass. The Angels and the Marys were not actually impersonated, but the seeds of character and dialogue were there. Ultimately, the trope expanded into a little play or opera. It is significant that a question and answer, so familiar to us in theatrical dialogue today, was used so long ago to introduce the Easter Mass.

Question (*by the* ANGELS): Whom do ye seek in the sepulcher, O followers of Christ?

Answer (*by the* MARYS): Jesus of Nazareth, who was crucified, just as he foretold.

ANGELS: He is not here: He is risen, just as he foretold. Go, announce that he is risen from the sepulcher.

Medieval Theatre

The medieval theatre (c. 950–1500) began in churches with Latin playlets performed by priests. (An early example is the *Quem Quaeritis* trope; see above.) Gradually, performances moved out of the churches into the marketplaces. Lay performers replaced priests, and scripts grew longer and more complex, mixing the serious with the boisterous and farcical.

Like the Greek and Roman amphitheatres, the medieval European theatre was an open-air festival theatre. There were few permanent structures. The plays, grouped in *cycles*, dealt with Biblical events and ranged from the creation to the destruction of the world. One cycle contained as many as forty-two plays. They were performed in spring and summer months on religious holidays such as Corpus Christi, Easter, and Whitsuntide. Productions were sponsored by town councils, often with the help of local priests. Religious confraternities or secular trade guilds usually produced them; they hired a director or stage manager and recruited actors from the local population, who turned out en masse to be part of the event.

FIGURE 2.4

The fixed stage used for the Valenciennes Passion Play in 1547. The mansions or huts represent specific locations (from left to right): Paradise, Nazareth, the temple, Jerusalem, the palace, the golden door, the sea, and Hell's Mouth.

Types of Medieval Staging

Precursors of the medieval *fixed stage* are to be found in the permanent Greek and Roman theatres and in the Christian churches with their aisles, naves, and raised altars. The *movable stage* had its beginnings in the medieval processions that celebrated religious and state occasions. We can see the influence of the medieval theatre on our own fixed and movable stages, open-air theatre buildings, amphitheatres, street theatre, festival theatres, and holiday parades.

The Fixed Stage One of the best-known fixed stages was constructed in 1547 for the Valenciennes Passion Play, in northern France (see Figure 2.4). Other important medieval fixed stages include the Roman amphitheatres, the "rounds" in Cornwall, England (see Figure 2.5), and the stages, like the Valenciennes stage, set up in public squares in France.

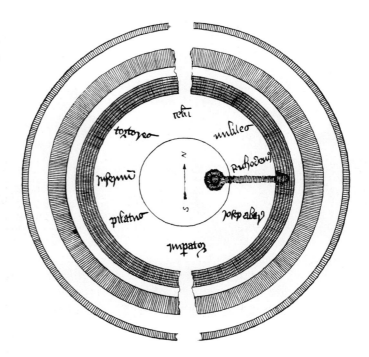

FIGURE 2.5
A Cornish circular amphitheatre (fixed stage). A typical permanent open-air theatre in Cornwall (also called a round) was made out of earth with circular turf benches surrounding a level area 130 feet in diameter. Openings on two sides of the earthen mound provided entrances and exits. This diagram (of the fourteenth-century theatre at Perranzabulo) shows the staging for a Biblical cycle called The Resurrection of Our Lord Jesus Christ. *There are eight scaffolds located in the round's center. Action requiring a specific locale took place on the scaffolds, progressing from one scaffold to another around the circle. The audience, seated on the earthen tiers of seats, could follow the scenes with ease.*

The fixed stage at Valenciennes was a rectangular platform with two chief areas. One contained the "mansions," or huts, which depicted specific locales; the other was the *platea*, an extended playing space. There were no scene changes as we know them in our theatre. The actor merely went from hut to hut to indicate change in locale. Heaven and hell were usually represented on each end of the stage, with earthly scenes of humor, travail, and so on occurring between them. The fixed stage made it possible to present numerous scenes and actors, along with the necessary costumes, **properties**, and special effects.

In the Roman and Cornish amphitheatres, the audience probably viewed the action from two or more sides. When the stage was the platform type, viewers might be grouped around three sides of the playing areas, or they might gather at the front only. Whichever way, the stage was always in the open air; there was a definite performing space for the actors and a definite audience area. The actor was close to the audience, and performances sometimes continued from dawn to dusk.

The Pageant Wagon Although fixed stages were common in many parts of Europe, theatrical space sometimes took on entirely different forms.

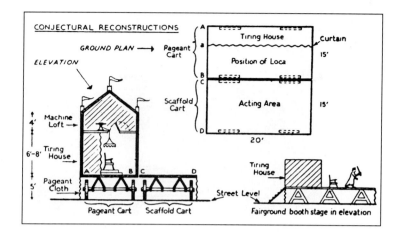

FIGURE 2.6
Glynne Wickham's drawing is a conjectural reconstruction of an English pageant wagon and ground plan of the overall playing arrangement. The drawing shows the essential features of what was to be the Elizabethan playhouse: a platform acting area, a tiring-house with a recessed area (the loca) for interior scenes and costume changes, and an area above the cart for machinery.

In Spain and England, for example, the pageant wagon and processional, or portable, staging were used. The pageant wagon (in Spain called a *carros*) was a platform on wheels, something like our modern parade float (see Figure 2.6). It was a portable playing area with a hut, or **tiring-house**, on top for the actors, which could also serve as a scenic background or acting area. No one is certain of the wagons' dimensions, but they had to move through the narrow streets of medieval towns. The wagons stopped for performances at a number of places and may have been used individually or in groups.

The audience stood around the wagons to watch, so the actors were very close to the audience, just as they were on the fixed stage. The flexible playing space encouraged vigorous action (especially by the Devil, who was booed and hissed energetically by audiences); episodic, loose-knit plot structure; and some sort of scenic element to fix locale. *The Crucifixion Play*, one of thirty-two surviving plays of the English Wakefield cycle (c. 1375), is based on Biblical scenes of Christ's torture at the hands of soldiers, followed by his death on the cross. The cycle requires continuous action from the scourging of Christ to his raising on the cross to his death.

The Elizabethan Theatre

By the late sixteenth century, permanent structures were being built in England and on the continent to house a new kind of theatrical entertainment, one that was losing its ceremonial and festive qualities and focusing more on plays with commercial appeal and acting companies.

FIGURE 2.7
An enlargement of a theatre labeled "The Globe" from the engraving by J. C. Visscher, c. 1616.

In 1576, James Burbage built London's first theatre, naming it simply "The Theatre." It was an open-air structure that adopted features from various places of entertainment: innyards, pageant wagons, banquet halls, fixed platforms, and portable booth-stages.

Shakespeare's Globe

In 1599, Richard Burbage, James' son and leading actor for The Lord Chamberlain's Men (Shakespeare's company), and associates built the Globe Theatre, which became a showcase for Shakespeare's talents as actor and playwright. The most famous of all Elizabethan theatres, the Globe was an open-air building with a platform stage in the middle surrounded on three sides by open standing room (see Figure 2.7). This space was surrounded in turn by a large enclosed balcony topped by one or two smaller roofed galleries. The stage was backed by a multi-level facade as part of the superstructure, called the tiring-house. On the stage level were places for hiding and discovering people and objects,

WILLIAM SHAKESPEARE

William Shakespeare (1564–1616) was an Elizabethan playwright of unsurpassed achievement. Born in Stratford-on-Avon, he received a grammar-school education and married a twenty-six-year-old woman when he was eighteen. He became the father of three children, Susanna and twins Judith and Hamnet.

Few other facts about Shakespeare's life have been established. By 1587–1588 he had moved to London, where he remained until 1611, except for occasional visits to his Stratford home. He appears to have found work almost at once in the London theatre as an actor and a writer. By 1592 he was regarded as a promising playwright; by 1594 he had won the patronage of the Earl of Southampton for two poems, *Venus and Adonis* and *The Rape of Lucrece*.

In 1594–1595 he joined James Burbage's theatrical company, The Lord Chamberlain's Men, as an actor and a playwright; later he became a company shareholder and part owner of the Globe and Blackfriars theatres. He wrote some thirty-seven plays for this company, suiting them to the talents of the great tragic actor Richard Burbage and other members of the troupe. Near the end of his life he retired to Stratford as a well-to-do country gentleman. Shakespeare wrote sonnets, tragedies, comedies, history plays, and tragicomedies, including some of the greatest plays written in English: *Hamlet, King Lear, The Tempest, Macbeth,* and *Othello.*

highly influenced by the variety of medieval stages with their many huts or mansions. A roof jutting out above the stage platform was supported by two columns; the underside of the roof, called "the heavens," was painted with moons, stars, and planets. After paying an admission fee, the audience stood around the stage or—for an additional charge—sat in the galleries or private boxes. Like the medieval audience, they were never far from the performers.

With little scenery and few properties, the Elizabethan theatre encouraged both playwright and actor to create unlimited illusions, transporting the audience from Juliet's tomb in one play to a raging storm at sea in another.

ELIZABETHAN THEATRES
AND RECONSTRUCTIONS

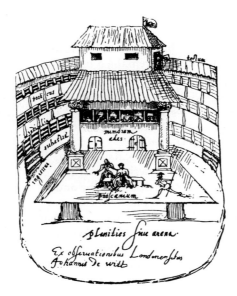

The De Witt drawing of the Swan Theatre in London dates from about 1596; it is the first sketch we have of the interior of an Elizabethan theatre. In The Globe Restored (1968), C. Walter Hodges describes the Elizabethan theatre as self-contained, adjustable, and independent of any surroundings other than its audience.

Hodges' detailed reconstruction of the Globe Playhouse (1599–1613) shows the building's superstructure, with galleries, yard, and railed stage. Notice the trapdoor in the stage, stage doors, curtained inner and upper stages, tiring-house (as backstage area with workrooms and storage areas), hut with machines, "the heavens," and playhouse flag.

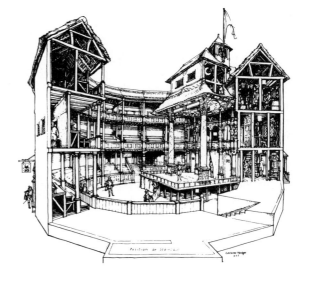

It is generally agreed that the tiring-house (*the area around and within the house wall at the back of the stage as shown in Hodges' drawing*) *was divided from the stage by hangings of some sort, usually curtains opening in the middle.*

The inner stage or discovery space *is thought to be a small, recessed area with curtains in the tiring-house wall. Hodges shows a discovery area surrounded by curtains. The permanent upper level or upper stage is a characteristic feature of the Elizabethan stage; it was used for scenes such as the balcony scene in Romeo and Juliet. Hodges' reconstruction of the inner and upper stages brings them forward into the main acting area.*

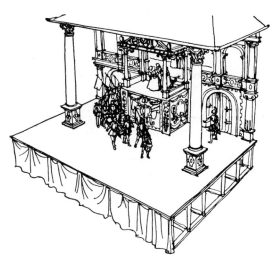

FIGURE 2.8

The Oregon Shakespearean Festival Theatre is a modern reconstruction similar to The Fortune Theatre of Shakespeare's London, which was built in 1599. Although the seating and lighting facilities are modern, the stage and tiring-house are patterned after the earlier theatre.

Theatrical Influences

The Elizabethan theatre, like that of Greece and medieval Europe, was a festive theatre depicting cosmic drama that touched all people: peasant, artist, and noble. Its architecture, as we shall see, affected the structure of the plays written for it. Yet it all happened so long ago. Why do we study these ancient modes of theatre, whose traditions are often so hard to trace? Do they really tell us anything about our own theatre buildings and stages? Are they related to the buildings and performance spaces that we think of as being so modern?

The answer is yes, and you will agree next time you see a Mardi Gras or mummers' float or an open-air theatre designed for summer productions of Shakespeare (see Figure 2.8). In large parks, plays with historical themes are performed outdoors for audiences looking for family entertainment; touring groups travel widely to college campuses with portable stages, costumes, and properties to present plays about current themes. And street theatre performers—aided by puppets, mimes, musicians, loudspeakers, and colorful displays—trumpet political and social messages with the spectacle and passion of a medieval pageant.

FIGURE 2.9
The Farnese Theatre in Parma, Italy, was one of the earliest to have a permanent proscenium arch. Our modern proscenium theatre with perspective scenery had its origins in Italy. Between 1500 and 1650, a typical theatre eventually developed with an auditorium, painted scenery, proscenium, curtain, and musicians' pit. Spectacle, illusion, and entertainment were its primary purpose.

The Proscenium Theatre

The proscenium theatre dates from the Italian Renaissance of the early seventeenth century. The Farnese Theatre built in 1618 at Parma was one of the early proscenium theatres (see Figure 2.9). An ornamental facade framed the stage and separated the audience from the actors and scene.

The development of the proscenium arch, framing the stage and masking its inner workings, brought innovative scenery techniques. Renaissance architects painted perspective scenery on large canvas pieces placed on a *raked*, or slanted, stage. In the seventeenth century, an architect named Giambattista Aleotti created a new system for changing scenery with movable, two-dimensional wings painted in perspective.

FIGURE 2.10
The principles of perspective painting were introduced to theatrical scene design in the sixteenth century. Perspective scenery was painted to create the illusion of large streets or town squares, with houses, churches, roofs, doorways, arches, and balconies, all designed to appear exactly as they would seem to a person at a single point. This kind of painted background was intended to give a sense of depth to the scene. In his book Architettura, *Sebastiano Serlio (1475–1554) explained the construction and painting of scenery for* comedy, *including the houses, tavern, and church shown in the drawing.*

This method, now called a wing-in-groove system (because grooves were placed in the stage floor to hold the scenery), replaced the raked stage.

Most of the theatres built in the Western world over the last 350 years are proscenium theatres. The concern of scenic designers working within this *picture-frame stage* was to use perspective scenery (see Figure 2.10) and mobile scenic pieces to achieve the effect of life being lived within the picture frame. The result was literally to frame the actors so that an audience, sitting in an enclosed, darkened space, could observe the actors in their setting. Playgoers were confined to the tiered galleries and to the orchestra or pit, as the ground-level seats were called.

The Picture-Frame Stage

As audiences grew larger and playhouses became more profitable in the eighteenth century, the auditoriums of public theatres increased steadily in size. And as the auditoriums expanded, theatre architects added boxes for the affluent and cheap seats in the galleries for the less well-off. In the nineteenth century the proscenium opening was enlarged to exploit the pictorial possibilities of the stage space. The auditorium was made shallower so that the audience was drawn closer to the stage, where spectators could see the actors' expressions and the details of their environment.

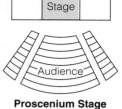

Proscenium Stage

FIGURE 2.11

A box set. The setting for the 1904 Moscow Art Theatre production of The Cherry Orchard *includes box set (with ceiling), details of a recognizable room (notice the dog), and morning light coming through the windows as essential details.*

Today our proscenium theatres (many built in the late 1800s) contain a framed *stage* with scenery, machines, and lighting equipment; an *auditorium* (possibly with balconies) seating 500 to 600 or more; and *auxiliary rooms*, including foyers, workrooms, dressing rooms, and storage space.

The function of the proscenium theatre is to create illusion. In this complex, technicians, designers, directors, playwrights, and actors collaborate to create make-believe worlds. For instance, the **box set** of Anton Chekhov's *The Cherry Orchard* (1904) contains the world of the play—Madame Ranevskaya's drawing room on her bankrupt estate in rural Russia at the turn of the century (see Figure 2.11).

In the proscenium theatre, the stage is usually hidden by a curtain until it is time for the play's world to be "discovered" by the audience (see Figure 2.12). Staging, scenery, lighting, and production style all work together to suggest that inside the proscenium arch is a self-contained world. The room may look like a typical living room. The street, garden, factory, or railway station may resemble places audiences know. But in the proscenium theatre, audiences are intentionally kept at a distance. They are primarily onlookers or witnesses to an event.

FIGURE 2.12
The Eisenhower Theatre, a proscenium theatre, at the John F. Kennedy Center for the Performing Arts in Washington, D.C. The audience is seated before the closed curtain.

The Thrust, or Open, Stage

Variations of the proscenium theatre often display features from Elizabethan inn-theatres and open stages. Today's thrust, or open, stage is an example (see Figure 2.13). Thrust stages were largely designed to minimize the separation of actor and audience created by the proscenium arch and the recessed stage. The actor literally performs on a platform that thrusts into the audience, and audiences have a keen sense of the actor's presence in direct communication with them, sharing the spoken word and the world of the play.

Non-Western Theatre

Until this century, the theatrical traditions of Eastern cultures have been curiously removed from the West by geography, politics, and culture. The music-drama of China flourished in the thirteenth century during the Yüan Dynasty, with the Beijing (formerly Peking) Opera becoming the dominant theatrical form by the mid-nineteenth century. The Japanese Noh theatre, developed in the late fourteenth century and unchanged

FIGURE 2.13

The thrust stage at the Stratford (Ontario) Festival Theatre has a permanent facade or background resembling Shakespeare's theatre (see page 38). In contrast, the Guthrie Theater in Minneapolis is a proscenium-thrust stage utilizing changeable, perspective scenery (see page 10).

since the seventeenth century, has only recently influenced Western directors and actors. The same is true of Kabuki performances, despite their popularity in Japan since 1600.

China's Beijing Opera

The Classical Theatre China enjoyed one of the theatre's golden ages during the Yüan Dynasty (1280–1368). Yüan dramatists created the classical drama of China with stories from history, legend, epics, and contemporary events that advocated the virtues of loyalty to family and friends, honesty, and devotion to work and duty. The staging traditions in this period required a bare stage, with one door on either side at the rear for exits and entrances, and an embroidered, decorative tapestry hanging between the two doors. Performers (both men and women) wore makeup, colorful clothes of the period with long wide sleeves, and beards for the men.

Each play consisted of four acts with ten to twenty songs or arias, all sung by the main character. If all the dramatic action could not be represented in four acts, a wedge (*chieh tze*), one or two short arias,

FIGURE 2.14

A performance of a drama during the Yüan period (1280–1368). The five men in the foreground are the actors. Behind them are the musicians. The bearded musician on the left is playing a drum; behind him, to his left, a musician is playing a ti-tzu; *the second musician from the right is playing a clapper. Behind the stage there is a curtain. From a wall painting in a temple in Shansi province, 1324.*

provided a prologue or interlude. Simple, unadorned musical accompaniment using a seven-tone scale was played onstage by an orchestra consisting of gong, drums, clapper, and *p'ip'a* (a plucked instrument similar to a lute). (See Figure 2.14.)

During the Ming Dynasty (1368–1644), a new drama emerged in the southern province of Hangchow, where T'ang Hsien-tsu (1550–1616) perfected a new drama with five or more acts accompanied by five-tone scale music. The performance style did not differ remarkably from earlier staging. The great texts of the Chinese classical theatre were written by Kuan Han-ch'ing (called the father of Chinese drama), Kao Ming, T'ang Hsien-tsu, Shen Ching, Kung Shang-jen, and Li Yu.

The Opera By the mid-nineteenth century, the dominant theatrical form for China was the Beijing Opera. Primarily a theatrical rather than a literary form, its emphasis is upon rigidly controlled conventions of acting, dancing, and singing rather than upon a text.

Many conventions of Beijing Opera, like theatrical conventions the world over, are related to the architectural features of the playhouse. The earliest stages were probably the porches of temples. The traditional

FIGURE 2.15

A representation of a seventeenth-century stage in Beijing, probably in the grounds of a private mansion. The audience would have watched the performances from the courtyard or the halls, separate from the stage itself. Stages such as this still exist in the Summer Palace, Beijing, and elsewhere, but are no longer used.

stage is an open platform, often square and raised a few feet above the ground, covered by a roof supported by lacquered columns. It is equipped with a carpet, two doors in the rear wall (the one on stage right is used for all entrances and that on stage left for all exits), between them hangs a large embroidered curtain. The only permanent properties are a wooden table and several chairs. (See Figure 2.15.)

Many of the early public theatres were temporary. In the seventeenth century actors began to perform in *teahouses* where customers were seated at tables. When permanent theatres were built, this arrangement was retained and the ground floor was fitted out with tables and stools at which spectators were served tea while watching the play. The permanent theatres also included a raised platform around the sides and back of the auditorium where poorer spectators sat on benches. A balcony, divided into sections much like the boxes of the Western theatre, was also added. In some periods the balcony was occupied by the wealthy class; in others, entirely by women. After the Chinese Republic was formed in 1912, the auditoriums were changed to include Western-style seating, but audience behavior changed very little. Spectators still carry on conversations, eat and drink, and come and go freely, usually remaining for their favorite passages while ignoring others.

The performance conditions for the opera are rigid: rapid changes of place are possible through speech, action, or properties. To circle the stage indicates a lengthy journey. The table and chairs are transformed by a prescribed formula into a law court, banqueting hall, or interior scene. For example, an incense tripod on the table indicates a palace; paper and an official seal indicate an office; an embroidered divided curtain hung from a bamboo pole indicates an emperor's chamber, and so on. Throughout the performance, assistants dressed in ordinary street clothes help the actors with their costumes and bring on or remove the properties as needed.

Music is an integral part of every opera performance. It provides atmospheric background, accompanies the many sung passages, controls the timing of movements, and welds the performance into a rhythmical whole. The string, wind, and percussion instruments of the Chinese orchestra have no counterparts in the West. Much of the onstage action is performed to a musical background, and entrances and exits are signaled by deafening percussion passages.

The Actor The heart of the Beijing Opera is the actor. On a bare stage furnished with only a few properties, the colorful and lavishly dressed actors speak, sing, and move according to prescribed conventions. The male roles (*sheng*) include scholars, statesmen, patriots, and similar types. Actors playing these roles wear simple makeup and, except for the young heroes, beards. The female roles (*tan*) are subdivided into six types: the good and virtuous wives and lovers, coquettish types, warrior maidens, young unmarried girls, evil women, and old women. Originally, all *tan* roles were played by women, but in the late eighteenth century actresses were forbidden to appear. After 1911, actresses returned to the stage and have now largely supplanted the male *tan* actors. The *ching* roles include warriors, courtiers, gods, and supernatural beings and are characterized by painted faces in brilliant patterns. The comic actor (*ch'ou*), who combines the skills of a mime and an acrobat, speaks in an everyday dialect and is the most realistic of the characters.

The actors' heavily patterned and colorful costumes likewise signify the wearers' ages, social status, and types. Color is always used symbolically: yellow for royalty, red for loyalty and high position, and dark crimson for barbarians or military advisors. Designs also have symbolic significance: the dragon is the emblem of the emperor; the tiger stands for power and masculine strength; the plum blossom for long life and feminine charm. The actors' visual appearance is completed with makeup and beards for the *sheng* actors. The female roles, with the ex-

MEI LAN-FANG

Mei Lan-fang, the greatest Chinese actor of modern times, as Tu Li-niang in a version of Huan-hun chi (The Return of the Soul), *the masterpiece of T'ang Hsien-tsu (1550–1617).*

Mei Lan-fang (1894–1961), one of the greatest of all Asian actors, was born in Beijing of an old theatrical family and trained at the Fu-lien-ch'eng school there. He made his professional debut at the age of ten and became noted in *tan* (female) roles. He acted chiefly in Beijing until the Japanese occupied Manchuria in 1931, and he moved to Shanghai and then to Hong Kong during the war years. He returned to Beijing in 1949 and remained there until his death in 1961.

Tours to the United States, Europe, and Russia in the 1930s established his fame and popularity as a foremost performer and brought the traditions of Beijing Opera to the West. His appearances in theatres in Moscow, Berlin, London, and Paris made lasting impressions on the leading theatre people of the day, including Bertolt Brecht, Vsevelod Meyerhold, and Sergei Eisenstein.

ception of old women who wear very little makeup, require white painted faces with the eyes surrounded by a deep red, shading into pink. The clown's distinguishing feature is the white patch around the eyes with distinctive black markings.

The actor's delivery of lines is controlled by convention: each role has a required vocal timbre and pitch; spoken passages are governed by strict rhythms and tempos; each word is accompanied by hand and arm gestures that have codified meanings.

Once the communist government assumed control over mainland China in 1949, a number of changes were made in Beijing Opera to make subjects and ideas conform to communist goals. In its traditional form, Beijing Opera is now most fully preserved on Taiwan and to a lesser extent in Hong Kong and Singapore. Although Western influences have brought about changes in Chinese theatre and spoken drama, the Beijing Opera and its symbolic conventions continue to fascinate Westerners and influence modern productions.

EASTERN INFLUENCES ON WESTERN THEATRE

Bertolt Brecht's production of The Caucasian Chalk Circle *at the Theater am Schiffbauerdamm, in (formerly East) Berlin, in 1954 shows the influence of Eastern theatre. In the photo, Grusha journeys with the child to the mountains. On a bare stage she mimes her long journey before a simple white curtain with pine trees in the center.*

Kabuki costumes, like the one worn by this principal actor in Pacific Overtures, *are made of layers of richly embroidered, hand-painted kimonos. This 1975 elaborate Broadway musical was directed by Harold Prince, with lyrics by Stephen Sondheim and dazzling costumes by Florence Klotz.*

Shakespeare's Richard II, *as directed by Ariane Mnouchkine for her celebrated company, the Théâtre du Soleil (Paris), 1981, was visually modeled on the grand theatrical styles of the Kabuki and Noh theatres. Designer Jean-Claude Barriera's costumes are a mix of Japanese and English period dress. Here, actors stand in classical Japanese poses, clad in layered clothing, cutaway kimonos, belted sashes, and heavily lined makeup.*

The King Stag *by Carlo Gozzi in an American Repertory Theatre (Cambridge)*
1991 production designed by Julie Taymor and Michael Yeargan.

FIGURE 2.16
The Noh stage is a square, polished cedar platform open on three sides; it has a temple roof and a back wall with a painted pine tree. In this photo the National Theatre of Japan performs for a modern audience. The musicians and chorus surround the principal actor (shite) on two sides; the audience is seated in front and to the left of the stage.

The Japanese Noh Theatre

The Japanese Noh theatre was established in the fourteenth century and has maintained its present form since the seventeenth century. Unlike Western drama, it is highly stylized and depends heavily on music and mime.

The Noh Stage The stage is situated in a corner of a building at the audience's right hand. A temple roof rises above the stage floor, which is divided into two areas: the stage proper (*butai*) and the bridge (*hashigakari*). All elements on this stage, including the four columns supporting the roof, have names and significance during performances. (See Figure 2.16.)

The stage proper is divided into three areas: The largest is about eighteen feet square and marked off by four pillars and roof; at the rear of the stage are the musicians—a flute player and two or three drummers; and to the left of the main area sits the six-to-ten-member chorus. The stage's two entrances are the bridge, a railed gangway that leads from the dressing room to the stage that is used for all important entrances, and the "hurry door." Only three feet high, the hurry door is used by minor characters, musicians, chorus, and stage assistants. Three small pine trees in front of the bridge symbolize heaven, earth, and humanity. Another pine tree, symbolizing the play's earthly setting, is painted on the center wall behind the musicians. This wall forms the scenic background for all Noh performances.

The Performers Like the stage, all features of a Noh performance are carefully controlled and fixed by tradition. The principal character (*shite*) is usually an aristocrat, lady, or supernatural being. The actor playing this character performs facing the column at the downstage (nearest the audience) right corner. The downstage left column is associated with the secondary character (*waki*).

The conventions of performance are handed down from one generation of actors (all male) to the next. Every movement of the hands and feet and every vocal intonation follow a set rule. The orchestra supplies a musical setting and controls the timing of the action. The chorus sings the actor's lines while he is dancing, and narrates many of the play's events. Song and dialogue outline circumstances.

Some Noh actors wear painted wooden masks (see Figure 2.17) that designate basic types: men, women, aged people, deities, monsters, spirits. The silk costumes and headdresses are rich in color and design.

Japanese Kabuki Theatre

By about 1600 the Noh theatre was replaced in popular taste, first by the Bunraku puppet theatre and then by Kabuki. Whereas Noh largely remained the theatre of the court and nobility, Kabuki—which originated in Edo, Kyoto, and Osaka, and was less formal and restrained—had more popular appeal. The modern Kabuki stage is a rare combination of the old and the new, of thrust- and proscenium-type stages. (See Figure 2.18.)

The Kabuki Stage The Kabuki stage covers the entire front of the theatre and is approached by a ramp, called a *hanamichi*, or "flower way,"

FIGURE 2.17

*The ancient craft of
mask-making for the
Noh theatre has been
handed down from
one generation of
artists to the next.
The masks are made
of wood and painted.
The purity and simpli-
city of the Noh mask
reflect the highly
formal theatrical tra-
dition of which it is
a part.*

FIGURE 2.18

*The theatrical
excitement and
commercialism of
this modern Kabuki
performance are
illustrated by the
painted scenery,
elaborate costumes,
musicians, and the
onnagata in a
climactic pose atop
a giant bell.*

CHIKAMATSU MONZAEMON

Born into a provincial samurai (warrior) family in the seventeenth century, Chikamatsu (1653–1724) became the most important Japanese playwright since the great period of Noh drama 300 years earlier. When he was thirty, Chikamatsu began writing for the Bunraku puppet theatre; he also wrote for the Kabuki theatre, and many of his puppet plays were later adapted for Kabuki.

Chikamatsu wrote both history and domestic plays—loosely constructed stories about the nobility featuring military pageantry, supernatural beings, battles, suicides, beheadings, and many kinds of violent deeds, all rendered through choreographed movements. His domestic plays featured unhappy lovers driven to suicide. Every play was characterized by the beauty of Chikamatsu's poetry.

A prolific writer, Chikamatsu has been compared by Western critics to William Shakespeare and Christopher Marlowe for the power of his verse and the sweep of his social canvas. His best-known plays in the West are *The Battles of Coxinga* (1715) (his most popular work); *The Love Suicides at Sonezaki* (1703); *The Courier for Hell* (1711); and *The Love Suicides at Amijima* (1721).

---

which is a raised narrow platform connecting the rear of the auditorium with the stage proper. The performers (all male) make dramatic entrances and exits on this runway. Occasionally, they perform short scenes on the *hanamichi* as well, literally in the middle of the audience.

The proscenium stage is long (some as long as ninety feet) but has a relatively low opening. Visible musicians (usually seated stage left) generally accompany the stage action. Kabuki plays originally required a full day in performance but today are about five hours long. They deal with vendettas, revenge, adventure, and romance and feature elaborate and beautiful scenic effects, including a revolving stage that was developed in Japan before it was used in the West.

The Performers Like Noh actors, Kabuki actors are trained from childhood in singing, dancing, acting, and feats of physical dexterity. Kabuki roles are divided into such basic types as brave and loyal men, villains, comic roles, children, and women's roles. Male actors who play women's parts are called *onnagata*. They are particularly skillful in their ability to imitate feminine sensibilities through stylized gestures and attitudes.

The Kabuki actor does not use a mask but instead wears boldly patterned makeup—a white base with designs of red, black, brown, or blue. The makeup symbolizes the character and describes the role. The *onnagata* use only white makeup, along with false eyebrows and rouging to shape the mouth and at the corners of the eyes. Each role has its conventional costume, based on historical dress and often weighing as much as fifty pounds.

The Kabuki actor's performance is always highly theatrical, colorful, and larger than life. Since he does not sing, he is often assisted by a narrator and chorus. The narrator may set the scene, speak dialogue, recite passages, and even comment on the action.

In recent years, Western scholars, directors, and actors have become interested in Eastern theatrical practices: minimal staging; revolving stages; fixed conventions of movement, style, and dress; symbolic properties, dress, and masks; musical interludes, visible musicians, and stage assistants. In addition, the main forms of Eastern theatre—the Beijing Opera (China); Noh theatre, Bunraku or puppet theatre, and Kabuki theatre (Japan); shadow puppets (Malaysia); Balinese dance theatre (Bali); and Kathakali dancers (India)—have influenced Western producer-directors such as Edward Gordon Craig, William Butler Yeats, Vsevelod Meyerhold, Antonin Artaud, Bertolt Brecht, Jerzy Grotowski, Ariane Mnouchkine, Harold Prince, and Peter Schumann.

Summary

In Western and Eastern theatre, traditional spaces are divided into stage and auditorium. Beginning with ritual performances in early societies, the theatrical space has always been special—a privileged place, to paraphrase anthropologist Mircea Eliade, where spectators perceive the revelation of a reality separate from that of their daily lives. Those making theatre have traditionally sought out a place—a hillside, a street, a marketplace, a building—to engage audiences in the experience of seeing life imitated by performers. Over the centuries those places have been ritual dancing circles, stone amphitheatres, church naves and choir lofts, fixed platforms and movable wagons in open spaces, and complex thrust and proscenium stages in enclosed buildings. In all cases inflexible conventions eventually developed regarding the relation of spectator to performer. These conventions are played with, violated, even turned upside down, as many contemporary theatre practitioners attempt to engage audiences directly by breaking the established molds of actor–audience relationships. We call this search for new and different spaces *alternative* (and even environmental) theatre. We will examine the use of unusual spaces in our next chapter.

Questions for Study

1. What are the two essential components of theatrical space?

2. In what sense are *enactment, imitation,* and *seasonal rites* forerunners of today's theatre?

3. What are the essential features of the ancient Greek theatre?

4. In what sense is the medieval European theatre a *festival theatre*?

5. How are the medieval theatre's *fixed* and *processional* stages related to our own theatre practices?

6. How did the features of Shakespeare's stage influence his use of space in *Hamlet*?

7. What are the principal features of the proscenium theatre?

8. How are the acting and audience spaces related in proscenium theatres?

9. How does the modern proscenium-thrust stage, or open stage, combine features of the Elizabethan theatre and of the picture-frame stage?

10. What are the fixed traditions of Beijing Opera, Japanese Noh theatre, and Kabuki theatre?

11. Modern directors are interested in Eastern theatre because it does not attempt to create an illusion of life being lived before us. How does Noh or Kabuki staging differ from the Western realistic theatre of Anton Chekhov or Tennessee Williams?

12. How have the physical relationships between actor and audience changed throughout theatrical history?

13. Describe the types of theatres found on your campus.

14. Plays to Read: *The Crucifixion Play* (Wakefield), Shakespeare's *Hamlet*, and *The Story of the Chalk Circle* by Li Ch'ien-fu.

15. Suggested Reading: Joseph Campbell with Bill Moyers, *The Power of Myth* (New York: Doubleday, 1988).

Modern efforts to find new kinds of
theatrical space have created different ways
of seeing theatre. In recent decades Jerzy
Grotowski in Poland, Ariane Mnouchkine
in Paris, Peter Schumann in Vermont, and
Peter Brook in France have rearranged
theatrical space to bring audiences and
actors closer together. As audiences, we are
part of the staged action, seeing both as
spectators and as participants.

3

ALTERNATIVE
THEATRICAL SPACES

Alll theatre people who have performed singly or in groups wherever an audience could be gathered around them are background
to the modern avant-garde creation of alternative performance
spaces. These alternative forms are associated in particular with the
Vietnam War era in the United States, although international in practice
today.

Much of the work of Julian Beck and Judith Malina (the Living Theatre), Jerzy Grotowski (the Polish Laboratory Theatre), Peter Brook (International Centre for Theatre Research), Ariane Mnouchkine (Théâtre
du Soleil), and Peter Schumann (the Bread and Puppet Theatre) within
the last three decades is labeled alternative and/or environmental theatre. This is a type of theatrical performance that rejects conventional
seating and arranges the audience as part of the playing space.

Writing about environmental production as a particular way of
creating and experiencing theatre, American director Richard Schechner says: "The thing about environmental theatre space is not just a
matter of how you end up using space. It is an attitude. *Start with all
the space there is and then decide what to use, what not to use, and
how to use what you use.*"[2] Polish director Jerzy Grotowski describes
the essential concern as "finding the proper spectator–actor relationship for each type of performance and embodying the decision in physical arrangement."[3]

By definition, environmental theatre rejects conventional seating and
includes the audience as part of the performance space. Like the actors,
the spectators become part of what is seen and done; they are both seeing and seen.

Forerunners of Alternative Approaches

In modern Russia and Germany, such leaders as the inventive Vsevelod Meyerhold (1874–c. 1940) and Max Reinhardt (1873–1943) developed unorthodox production methods and uses of theatrical space. They are the chief forerunners of today's many experiments in nontraditional performance styles and alternative spaces. In the 1930s in Moscow, the Russian director Meyerhold, rejecting the proscenium arch as too confining for his actors, removed the front curtain, footlights, *and* proscenium. He had stagehands change properties and scenery in full view of audiences and had actors perform on trapezes, slides, and ramps to arouse exhilarating feelings in both performers and audiences.

Max Reinhardt explored vast acting areas, such as circus arenas to stage *Oedipus the King* (1910) in Berlin's Circus Schumann, which he thought of as a people's theatre—his "theatre of the five thousand." He dreamed of a theatre on the scale of classical Greek and Roman theatres to be used for spectacles and mass audiences. In 1920, he created his most famous spectacle (*Everyman*) in the square before the Salzburg Cathedral.

During the last forty years, especially in the United States, many theatre directors and designers have also looked for new theatrical spaces in warehouses, lofts, and halls. In creating a new performance style, they reshaped *all* of the space available to audience and actor, seeking to bring the audience into direct contact with the actor to make the audience a more obvious part of the theatrical event.

This chapter is a brief discussion of three alternative approaches to the use of theatrical space in the modern theatre: the Polish Laboratory Theatre, the Théâtre du Soleil, and the Bread and Puppet Theatre.

The Polish Laboratory Theatre

Jerzy Grotowski's Poor Theatre

When Jerzy Grotowski founded the Polish Laboratory Theatre in 1959, he set out to answer the question: What is theatre? Grotowski evolved a concept that he called poor theatre. For him, theatre's essentials are the actor and the audience in a bare space. He found that theatre could happen without costumes, scenery, makeup, stage lighting, and sound ef-

JERZY GROTOWSKI

Jerzy Grotowski (b. 1933) was founder and director of the Polish Laboratory Theatre, an experimental company located in Wroclaw. Not a theatre in the usual sense, the company became an institute for research into theatre art in general and the actor's art in particular. In addition, the laboratory also undertook performances for audiences as well as instruction of actors, producers, students (many of them foreigners), and people from other fields. The plays performed were based on Polish and international classics. In the 1960s and 1970s Grotowski's productions of Stanislaw Wyspianski's *Akropolis*, Shakespeare's *Hamlet*, Marlowe's *Dr. Faustus*, and Calderón's *The Constant Prince* attracted worldwide attention. His closest collaborators were actor Ryszard Cieslak and literary adviser Ludwik Flaszen. He wrote about his methods in *Towards a Poor Theatre* (1968).

After 1970, Grotowski disbanded his company to explore human creativity outside the theatre (he called these projects para-theatre). He intended to lead participants back to elemental connections between themselves and the natural world by exposure to basic myths, dancing, playing, bathing, and the elements of fire, earth, air, and water. In 1975 the event called *Holiday* took place in a forest, where participants in a pure ritualized experience were encouraged to rediscover the roots of theatre and themselves.

In 1983 at the University of California–Irvine, Grotowski began a new phase of workshops called Objective Drama to examine the "roots of theatre" common to all cultures. In 1986, he established a Workcenter (*Centro di lavoro*) in Tuscany, Italy, where today he engages in the exploration of "ritual acts."

fects; all it needed was the actor and audience in live communion in a special place. Grotowski wrote:

> I propose poverty in theatre. We have resigned from the stage-and-auditorium plant: for each production, a new space is designed for the actors and spectators. . . . The essential concern is finding the proper spectator–actor relationship for each

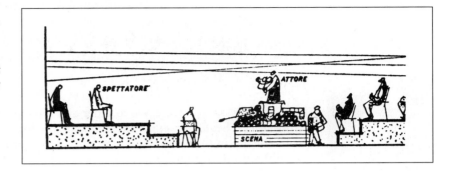

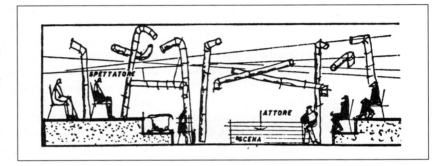

FIGURE 3.1
The theatrical space at the beginning of the performance of Akropolis. *Note that the wire struts above the audience are empty.*

FIGURE 3.2
The theatrical space at the end of Akropolis. *The actors have disappeared, leaving the stovepipes hanging from the wire struts as gruesome reminders of the events in the concentration camps.*

FIGURE 3.3
A view of the scenic action for Grotowski's production of Dr. Faustus, *based on the Elizabethan text by Christopher Marlowe. One hour before his death, Faustus offers a last supper to his friends (the audience) seated at the refectory tables. The theatrical space has been converted into a monastery dining hall.*

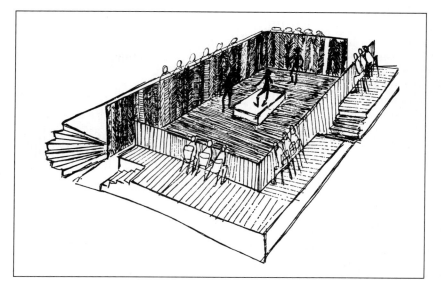

FIGURE 3.4
A view of the scenic action for The Constant Prince, *based on the seventeenth-century Spanish text by Pedro Calderón de la Barca. The audience, seated behind a barrier, looks down on a forbidden act. Their positioning suggests a surgical operating theatre or a bullring.*

type of performance and embodying the decision in physical arrangements.[4]

In his production of *Akropolis* (1962), the actors built structures among the spectators, subjecting them to a sense of congested space (see Figures 3.1 and 3.2). In *Dr. Faustus* (1963), the entire space became a monastery dining hall, and the spectators were guests at a banquet during which Faustus offered them entertaining episodes from his life (see Figure 3.3). In *The Constant Prince* (1965), the audience was separated from the actors by a high fence. They looked down on the actors like medical students watching a surgical operation (see Figure 3.4).

Within the whole space, Grotowski created what he calls holy theatre: The performance is a semireligious act in which the actor, prepared by years of training and discipline, undergoes a psychospiritual experience. Grotowski set about to engage the audience in this act, and thus to engage both actor and audience in a deeper understanding of personal and social truths.

Akropolis

In *Akropolis*, Grotowski adapted a text written by Polish playwright Stanislaw Wyspianski in 1904. In the original, statues and paintings in Cracow Cathedral come to life on the eve of Easter Sunday. The statues

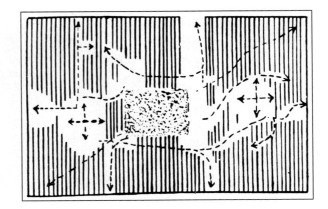

FIGURE 3.5
The diagram shows Grotowski's use of space for Akropolis. *The lines with arrows indicate the actors' movements and areas of action; the straight lines show audience areas. The central playing space is a boxlike "mansion" where pipes are assembled and into which the actors disappear at the end of the performance.*

re-enact scenes from the Old Testament and antiquity. But Grotowski shifted the action to an extermination camp, Auschwitz, in wartime Poland. In the new setting he contrasted the Western ideal of human dignity with the human degradation of a death camp.

Akropolis takes place in a large room. (See Figure 3.5.) Spectators are seated on platforms, and passageways for the actors are created between the platforms. Wire struts are strung across the ceiling. In the middle of the room is a large, boxlike platform for the actors. Rusty pieces of metal are heaped on top of the box: stovepipes, a wheelbarrow, a bathtub, nails, hammers. With these objects the actors build a civilization of gas chambers. They wear a version of a camp uniform—ragged shirts and trousers, heavy wooden shoes, and anonymous berets.

Grotowski juxtaposes Biblical and Homeric scenes and heroes against the grotesque reality of the modern death camp (see Figures 3.6 and 3.7). The love of Paris and Helen, for instance, is played out between two men to the accompaniment of the laughter of the assembled prisoners; Jacob's bride is a stovepipe with a rag for a veil. *Akropolis* ends with a procession around the box in the center of the room led by a Singer carrying the headless corpse of the Savior. As Grotowski describes it:

> The procession evokes the religious crowds of the Middle Ages, the flagellants, the haunting beggars. . . . The procession reaches the end of its peregrination. The Singer lets out a pious yell, opens a hole in the box, and crawls into it, dragging after him the corpse of the Savior. The inmates follow him one by one, singing fanatically. . . . When the last of the condemned men has disappeared, the lid of the box slams shut. The silence is very

This photo depicts a "dialogue between two monuments." The metal stovepipe and human legs with boots make a visual statement about the way human beings can be treated as objects. This is one of many statements in the performance about the effects of inhumanity throughout our history. The actor is Zbigniew Cynkutis.

The character Esau (played by Ryszard Cieslak) sings of the freedom of a hunter's life while enmeshed in the wire struts.

sudden; then after a while a calm, matter-of-fact voice is heard. It says simply, "They are gone, and the smoke rises in spirals." The joyful delirium has found its fulfillment in the crematorium. The end.[5]

Grotowski's poor theatre returns us to the essentials of theatre: actor, audience, space.

Théâtre du Soleil
Ariane Mnouchkine's Environmental Space

Another group having impact on environmental production styles, especially in Europe, is the Théâtre du Soleil ("Theatre of the Sun"), founded in Paris in 1964 by Ariane Mnouchkine and a group of politically committed individuals.

ARIANE MNOUCHKINE

Théâtre du Soleil's 1793, produced in Vincennes in 1972 at the Cartoucherie (a former munitions factory). This view of the performance shows actors on raised platforms and audience seated in a center pit as well as on a balcony (left).

Of the French directors who have come to prominence since 1965, Ariane Mnouchkine (b. 1940) has become one of the most important. She founded the Théâtre du Soleil, a commune composed of about forty members, in 1964. Until 1968 they performed in the Cirque d'Hiver in Paris, creating a considerable stir with productions of Shakespeare's *A Midsummer Night's Dream* and Arnold Wesker's *The Kitchen*.

In 1970 the company moved to an abandoned munitions factory just outside Paris (the Cartoucherie), where they have since produced internationally celebrated environmental productions of *1789* (in 1971) and *1793* (in 1972), treatments of the early years of the French Revolution that argued that the revolution was more concerned with property than with social injustice. *The Age of Gold* (1975) dealt with various aspects of materialism; *The Terrible But Unfinished History of Norodom Sihanouk, King of Cambodia* (1984) and *L'Indiade* (1986), with modern political history. The group traveled with their productions of Shakespeare's *Richard II* and *Henry IV, Part 1* to the 1984 Los Angeles Olympic Arts Festival, and in 1992 the company returned to North America with the ten-hour, four-part cycle of Greek tragedy called *Les Atrides*. Théâtre du Soleil is one of France's finest theatre companies.

In the 1960s the Théâtre du Soleil modeled itself on an egalitarian commune: They arrived at artistic decisions through democratic participation and divided the theatre's profits equally among themselves. The company challenged traditional modes of theatrical presentation in its attempts to create a populist theatre, using improvisation as well as techniques from mime, *commedia*, Chinese opera, Japanese Noh and Kabuki, and circus clowning. Audiences moved from platform to platform to keep up with the play's action or sat around the edge or even in the center of a large pit.

Starting in 1967, with productions of Arnold Wesker's *The Kitchen* and a controversial adaptation of *A Midsummer Night's Dream* that anticipated Peter Brook's legendary 1970 production for the Royal Shakespeare Company, Mnouchkine's company attracted considerable international attention. The company was acclaimed for its radical environmental staging techniques and its explosive politicizing of dramatic materials. Their productions grew out of discussion, group study, improvisations with all members of the group sharing in the research, writing, staging, design, and construction. Their commitment to left-wing political beliefs and to creating vibrant "performance texts" out of the whole cloth of French history resulted in *1789*, then *1793* (see page 68), *The Age of Gold*, and more recently *Sihanouk* and *Les Atrides*. In environmental spaces that directly engaged audiences, these performances dealt with theatre as revolution, historical data, and contemporary social facts; improvised stage action and audience participation; and spectacle and ritual.

Théâtre du Soleil came to symbolize, along with the Living Theatre and the Bread and Puppet Theatre, the best that political theatre had to offer anywhere in the world.

But as political fervor waned worldwide in the late 1970s, along with the winding-down of the Vietnam War, many groups like these either went out of existence or, like Théâtre du Soleil, turned to other artistic experimentations, which overshadowed any "environmental" trendiness or political and sociological messages contained in their works. Théâtre du Soleil's Asian-inspired Shakespearean productions and *Les Atrides*, the four-part cycle of Greek tragedy based on plays by Euripides and Aeschylus, have further challenged contemporary notions of theatrical presentation.

ENVIRONMENTAL THEATRE—A PERSPECTIVE

THE LIVING THEATRE

The oldest of the collective groups creating environmental theatre began in 1948 in a cellar on New York's Wooster Street. Judith Malina and Julian Beck were the foremost gurus of the '60s **Off Off-Broadway** groups. Their zeal and talents were directed toward encouraging a non-violent revolution to overhaul society and creating a performance style to confront that society (the United States).

In 1959, in a converted space on 14th Street in New York, Malina and Beck produced Jack Gelber's *The Connection*, a disturbing play about heroin addicts. The addicts' environment, of which the audience was a part, was naturalistically reproduced, as was the junkies' lifestyle.

After an encounter with the U.S. Internal Revenue Service, which led to prison sentences for tax evasion, the Living Theatre became a nomadic group traveling throughout Europe and South America. They performed outside traditional theatres in streets, prisons, even bars, provoking audience riots and confrontations with civil authorities.

In 1984, after an absence of fourteen years, the Living Theatre returned to New York with four productions, including Brecht's *Antigone*. Although still politically confrontational, these works marked a turning away from street encounters toward performances within identifiable theatres. Julian Beck, who died in 1985, once said that "art opens perception and changes our vision. I think without art we would all remain blind to reality. We go to the theatre to study our-selves. The theatre excites the imagination, and it also enters into the spirit. . . ."[7]

The Living Theatre's 1963 production of Kenneth Brown's The Brig *re-created the repetition and senseless routine of a day in a Marine prison camp, of which the audience was a part.*

The Living Theatre.
Actors form a living totem pole in one of many theatrical rites that composed Paradise Now: The Revolution of Cultures *(1968). The piece was one of the first to incorporate nudity (of the actors and—sometimes—the audience) as an integral part of the performance.*

Théâtre du Soleil production of Shakespeare's Richard II *staged in a munitions factory in Paris in 1981.*

The environmental production of The Age of Gold (L'Age d'Or), *1975, by Théâtre du Soleil. Here, a character declaims while standing in the middle of the audience.*

The Mahabharata, *a nine-hour drama adapted from the Sanskrit (Indian) epic, was initially staged in France by Peter Brook, head of the Paris-based International Centre for Theatre Research. Brook, a celebrated director for more than three decades, brought the production to America on international tour in 1987–88. The initial 1985 staging in a rock quarry near Avignon is shown here.*

PETER SCHUMANN

The Bread and Puppet Theatre performs The Same Boat: The Passion of Chico Mendes *in an open town space as part of the 1990 "Earth Day" celebration. The masked actors, the band, and the larger-than-life-size puppets are traditional features of a Bread and Puppet production.*

Peter Schumann (b. 1934 in Silesia) moved from Germany to the United States in 1961 and two years later founded the Bread and Puppet Theatre in New York City.

Until he was ten, the Schumann family lived in a village near Breslau, renamed Wroclaw at the end of World War II when this part of Germany was incorporated into Poland. In late 1944, the family fled

The Bread and Puppet Theatre

Peter Schumann's Open-Air Performances

Peter Schumann founded the Bread and Puppet Theatre in New York in 1961. Today, the group makes its home in Glover, Vermont, on a farm owned by Goddard College. Unlike many radical theatres that grew out barely ahead of the Soviet army and survived on his mother's baked rye sourdough bread until they reached Schleswig-Holstein. The twin themes of family and survival in Schumann's work stem from this period. In 1956, he met his American wife in Munich, and they emigrated to the United States in 1961 where their artistic collaboration began with the creation and performances of street pageants, anti-Vietnam War parades, productions based on religious themes, and summer workshops with giant puppets.

In 1970, Schumann was invited to take up residency at Goddard College in Plainfield, Vermont, and "practice puppetry." Living now in Glover, Vermont, Schumann has assembled a small troupe of puppeteers and designers. Each August the troupe performs in a grassed-over gravel pit with actors on five- or six-foot stilts, strolling jazz bands, rope walkers, and fire jugglers. Sourdough rye bread that Schumann has baked is passed among audiences.

Schumann's pageants are always about life and death, good and evil. His work with puppets reflects a traditionalism that harks back to Indian effigies, Japanese Bunraku and Noh theatre, and to the masks of African and Alaskan shamans. Mistrusting the power of words, Schumann uses puppets to simplify and caricature the horror of modern living in a time of potential global annihilation. His aim is to bring a spiritual reaction into the lives of ordinary spectators. In a Bread and Puppet performance, the stories are simple, the giant puppets riveting, and the tempo majestically slow. Schumann is best known for his anti-war and nuclear disarmament pieces dating from 1965: *Fire, The Gray Lady Cantata, The Stations of the Cross,* and *A Man Says Goodbye to His Mother.*

of the social and political unrest of the 1960s in America, the Bread and Puppet Theatre flourishes today. Schumann's group does not attempt to create an environment but performs in almost any situation: streets, fields, gyms, churches, and sometimes theatres. Developed from Biblical and legendary sources and using both actors and larger-than-life-size puppets, Bread and Puppet plays advocate the virtues of love, charity, and humility.

The group takes its name from two constant elements of their work: puppets and bread. It was Peter Schumann's idea that "the theatre should be as basic as bread." At the start of a Bread and Puppet performance, loaves of bread are passed among the spectators. Each person breaks off a piece and hands the rest to the next person, who does the same. When everyone has tasted bread, in an act of social and spiritual communion, the performance begins. Thus the audience participates in an instantly recognizable ritual: sharing the staff of life, a symbol of humanity's most basic need.

The Stations of the Cross

Of his unique work with puppets, Peter Schumann has said that "Puppet theatre, the employment of and dance of dolls, effigies, and puppets . . . is an anarchic art, subversive and untameable by nature . . . an art which does not aspire to represent governments or civilizations but prefers its own secret demeaning stature in society, representing, more or less, the demons of that society and definitely not its institutions."[6] *The Stations of the Cross*, first performed at Goddard College (Vermont) in 1972 and then St. Clement's Church (New York City), lasts about seventy minutes. It consists of a prologue followed by the fourteen separate stations of the cross announced by a narrator. Each announcement is followed by a chorus singing a brief hymn and a series of mute "images" created with puppets and performers and punctuated by acoustical effects with such musical instruments as the violin, bass, flute, horn, drum, cymbal, and trombone. Schumann's puppets range from eight to twenty feet in height, and the mechanics of puppetry become an integral part of a Bread and Puppet production. Christ is represented first by an actress dressed in flowing robes with large puppet hands and then in the eighth station by an eighteen-foot puppet.

Schumann's *Stations of the Cross* does not use the playing space environmentally. Although there is no stage or curtain, a proscenium relationship between performer and spectator is maintained. At the rear of the performance space hangs a pink and green backdrop. Exits and entrances are made to and from the area behind the backdrop.

The performance begins with a narrator, a woman dressed in a black and gold showman's suit who comes to the center, does a fast tap dance, and welcomes the audience with "Good evening, ladies and

FIGURE 3.8

From the Bread and Puppet production of The Stations of the Cross *(1972), New York City. This is one of a series of "mute" images combining giant puppet hands and a silent performer. (Photo by Peter Moore)*

gentlemen. . . ." The chorus and musicians sit on stage right throughout the performance. During the prologue, performers representing Earth, Christ, and Death are presented. Then each "station" begins with the narrator ringing a bell and announcing the sequence, "The First Station of the Cross: He is condemned to death." The puppets mime the action, creating images of Christ's travail during the final period of His life. A large blue puppet is Mary, Christ's mother; the Great Warrior puppet who condemns Christ is ten-foot-tall and blue with a gray head topped by a crest of spikes. The eighteen-foot-tall puppet representing Christ has giant hands that move in supplication. At the fourteenth Station when Christ is placed in the grave, all lie down on the floor with the exception of the musicians and narrator (see Figure 3.8). After a long moment of silence, the narrator sings that the Lord is risen and the other performers rise and join in the singing. Finally, horns, cymbals, and drums drown out the singing and the loud clamor ends abruptly. The performance is over and freshly baked bread is given out to the audience in a sharing of sustenance and community.

Schumann's Bread and Puppet Theatre performs in all types of spaces, bringing actors, puppets, and spectators together in celebration of basic human values.

Summary

Many theatrical groups in recent decades have set about to rethink, re-shape, and re-create the theatrical experience for actors *and* audiences. As Grotowski tells us, his experiment to discover the "proper specta-tor–actor relationship" takes place in a bare space where each type of performance requires its own special "physical arrangements." Jerzy Grotowski has worked in large rooms, Ariane Mnouchkine in an aban-doned munitions factory, Peter Brook in rock quarries, and Peter Schu-mann in fields and streets.

Environmental or alternative theatre, as this type of nontraditional performance has been called since the 1960s, rejects conventional seat-ing and arranges the audience as part of the playing space. Like the ac-tors, the spectators become part of what is seen and done; they are both seeing and seen. In contrast, traditional theatre arranges the audience *before* a stage, where they see and hear at a comfortable distance.

Throughout the ages, the theatre's *space* has influenced those who work within it: playwrights, actors, directors, and designers. We are calling these artists "the image makers," for they create the world of the production as theatrical metaphor for us to experience during the per-formance. Let us begin with the playwright who creates the text, thereby most often providing the blueprint for the production.

Questions for Study

1. How does Jerzy Grotowski define "poor theatre"?
2. Why was the work of the Polish Laboratory Theatre important?
3. What were the social and moral objectives of Grotowski's Laboratory Theatre?
4. How did Grotowski's production of *Akropolis* portray these objectives?
5. What is *environmental theatre*?
6. What seating arrangements are used in environmental productions?
7. What was the original environment for Peter Brook's *The Mahabharata*?

8. Describe the performance space used by the Théâtre du Soleil in Paris.

9. Describe the relationship between politics and environmental theatre events. Use as your examples the Théâtre du Soleil and the Living Theatre.

10. What are the distinct elements of a Bread and Puppet performance?

11. What solutions have environmental directors arrived at to discover the proper actor–audience relationship for each production?

12. Are there any created or "found" spaces used for theatrical productions on your campus or in your community? If so, describe them.

13. *Plays to Read:* María Irene Fornés, *Fefu and Her Friends: A Play* (New York: Performing Arts Journal Publication, 1990). Fornés has written an "environmental performance text." Part One situates the audience in the theatre's auditorium to observe Fefu's living room. Part Two takes place in four locations: a lawn, study, bedroom, kitchen. The audience is divided into four groups, and each scene is repeated four times until the audience has seen all four. They return to the auditorium in Part Three to observe the play's ending.

14. *Suggested Reading:* Jerzy Grotowski's *Towards a Poor Theatre* (1968), Richard Schechner's *Environmental Theatre* (1973), and Judith Malina's *Diaries (1947–1957)* (1984).

A play in a book is only the shadow of a play and not even a clear shadow of it. . . . The printed script of a play is hardly more than an architect's blueprint of a house not yet built or built and destroyed. The color, the grace and levitation, the structural pattern in motion, the quick interplay of live beings, these things are the play, not words on paper, not thoughts and ideas of an author, those shabby things snatched off basement counters at Gimbels. . . .

TENNESSEE WILLIAMS
Afterword to Camino Real[1]

The playwright envisions the play's world, its people, environment, objects, relationships, emotions, attitudes, and events. Playwriting is a creative act that enlarges our understanding of human experience and enriches our appreciation of life.

4

THE IMAGE MAKERS:
THE PLAYWRIGHT

Who fills the theatrical space? Who is seen in the space? What methods and materials are used to create the stage environment, what a famous designer called "the machine for acting"? In theatre we continually encounter the idea of building. Actors speak of building a character. Technicians build the set and costumers build costumes. The director often "blocks" the play. The word *playwright* is formed in the same way as *wheelwright* and *shipwright*: It means "playbuilder." Theatre is the creative collaborative effort of all these builders; the whole is greater than the sum of its parts. The American scene designer Robert Edmond Jones (1887–1954) referred to this wholeness when he said, "All art in the theatre should be not descriptive, but evocative."[2] The efforts of many creative talents using various methods and materials evoke an imaginary world, but the initial artist is most often the playwright. In the next five chapters we consider the working methods of *playwrights*: their tools, perspectives, conventions, and styles of writing.

The Playwright
A Personal Vision

The playwright writes a play to express some aspect of reality, some emotions and feelings connected with all of humanity, some measure of experience, some vision or conviction about the world. Like any artist, the playwright shapes a personal vision into an organized, meaningful

SAM SHEPARD

Curse of the Starving Class *deals with a family—father Weston (Will Marchetti), son Wesley with lamb (Paul Richard Connell), and daughter Ella (Kathy Baker)—starved, not for class status, but for selfhood, belonging, and distinctiveness as individuals. Performed by the Magic Theatre, San Francisco, 1982, and directed by its artistic director, John Lion, who called Shepard "the inkblot of the '80s."*[3]

whole. Thus a script is more than words on a page—it is the playwright's *blueprint* of a special kind of experience, created to appeal as much to the eye as to the ear. All in all, playwriting is the search for the truth of human experience as the playwright perceives it.

Playwrights such as Henrik Ibsen write plays to expose truths about the realities of social injustice. Other playwrights, like Bertolt Brecht and Caryl Churchill, make political statements about people, economies,

Question: So, why are you writing plays?
Answer: I have to. I have a mission (*Shepard laughs*). No, I don't
know why I do it. Why not?[4]

Sam Shepard (b. 1943) began his theatrical career as a bit actor. Since
1964 he has explored contemporary American myths among the refuse
of our junk culture. His characters are Americans we all know, but his
situations are often unfamiliar and jarring. Recipient of the Off Off-
Broadway (*Village Voice*) Obie Award for distinguished playwriting on
eight separate occasions, Shepard was awarded the 1979 Pulitzer Prize
for *Buried Child*. Among his other well-known plays are *Cowboys*
(1964); *Chicago* (1965); *Red Cross* and *La Turista* (1967); *Operation
Sidewinder* (1970); *The Tooth of Crime* (1972); *Angel City* and *Curse
of the Starving Class* (1976); *True West* (1980); *Fool for Love* (1982);
A Lie of the Mind (1987); and *States of Shock* (1991).

Shepard also acted in such films as *Days of Heaven, The Right
Stuff, Country, Crimes of the Heart, Steel Magnolias, Thunderheart,*
and *The Pelican Brief,* and wrote the screenplay for *Far North* and for
Paris, Texas, which won the 1984 Cannes Film Festival award for best
film.

In 1984 he shared some of his thoughts on playwriting with a magazine interviewer: "I feel like there are territories within us that are totally unknown. Huge, mysterious, and dangerous territories. We think
we know ourselves, when we really know only this little bitty part. We
have this social person that we present to each other. We have all these
galaxies inside of us. And if we don't enter those in art . . . whether it's
playwriting, or painting, or music, or whatever, then I don't understand the point in doing anything."[5]

and political systems. These writers use the theatre as a vehicle for a
message or ideology. Most writers turn their personal experiences,
wishes, and dreams into drama. For American playwright Adrienne
Kennedy, writing is an outlet for psychological confusion and questions
stemming from childhood. Other writers, like Eugene Ionesco, ridicule
the conventions of theatre and certain kinds of human behavior to persuade us to see the world differently.

The Playwright's Beginnings

The playwright creates on paper an image or sense of life being lived before us. The playwright's script is of major importance because it is the usual starting point for the theatrical production.

Playwrights start with an idea, theme, dream, image, or notes and work out an action; or begin with an unusual character or a real person and develop an action around that character; or start with a situation based on a personal experience, their reading, or an anecdote. Other writers working with groups evolve scenarios with actors and arrange a final script from the group's improvisations, situations, dialogue, and movement. Some write from scenarios or plot summaries; others write from outline, crisis scene, images, dreams, myth, or imagined environment.

Bertolt Brecht usually worked from a story outline, which he called *the draft plan*. Next, he summarized the story's social and political ideas before developing scenes based on the outline. Sam Shepard writes by hand in a notebook first. He wrote literally a dozen different versions of *Fool for Love* (1982), but the first five pages remained the same in each version. Marsha Norman, author of *'Night, Mother* (1983), after spending a long evening in the theatre making script revisions with the director, will return home and type the changes into her computer in the early morning hours. Some playwrights claim their characters talk to them and develop themselves; others claim they hear the play's voices and dialogue in their heads. Some playwrights speak lines out loud before writing them down, or work from mental images of their characters moving and talking.

The Playwright's Role

In the theatre the playwright is an anomaly. Although playwrights win Pulitzer Prizes and Nobel awards, they are both central and peripheral to the production. In the privacy of the home or studio, the playwright turns on the computer and constructs an imaginary world. As the creative imagination takes over, people, events, conflicts, words, and whole speeches resound in the writer's inner eye and ear. The script belongs to the playwright, but once this original creative act—this *blueprint* for performance—is completed and handed over to director, designers, and actors, the playwright in one sense becomes peripheral to the final process. In the harrowing process of transforming the manuscript into a living performance, the writer takes a backseat in the rehearsal hall only to emerge a success or a failure on opening night. One exception is the playwright who also directs his or her own work, such as Bertolt Brecht, Samuel Beckett, María Irene Fornés, or David Mamet. They remain central to the production process. Others, like Shakespeare and Molière, were not only part owners of their companies but were also actors in their plays. To prolong the New York run of *Small Craft Warnings* in 1972, Tennessee Williams, by no means a professional actor, took the role of narrator in his play and his performance was critically acclaimed.

But in the modern rehearsal hall, playwrights usually take a backseat to their collaborators. Huddled in a back row with a legal pad in hand, their job is to note awkward lines and words that don't ring true, to rewrite speeches and even whole scenes when directors find difficulties in making sense of the action or need a few more seconds for an actor to make an entrance.

The playwright's independence also makes him or her an anomaly in the theatre. Like novelists, playwrights usually create alone, though there are exceptions. Their material, even for a political writer like Bertolt Brecht, is personal. For example, Grusha in *The Caucasian Chalk Circle* is a personal creation and a political statement on the human instinct for survival. We look to playwrights to give us insights into the world around us—to provide fresh perspectives and new visions. To do this, they reach inside themselves, in a private act, and pull forth intensely personal feelings, perceptions, and situations to construct the public world of the play.

Where do playwrights come from? What are their origins? Their backgrounds? Though drama departments offer courses in playwriting, no mastery of technique has ever made a writer. Playwrights have come from every conceivable background: acting, literature, gag-writing, teaching, housewifery, politics, medicine, and so on. Lillian Hellman worked as a reader for a literary agent before writing her first play, *The Children's Hour*. Tennessee Williams wandered the United States writing poems, short stories, one-acts, and his first full-length play, *Battle of Angels*. Aeschylus was a soldier, Terence a slave, Shakespeare an actor, Luigi Pirandello a teacher, Anton Chekhov a doctor, and Caryl

PLAYWRIGHT

DAVID MAMET

As David Mamet's Hollywood types, Madonna, Joe Mantegna, and Ron Silver act out movie-biz pathology in Speed-the-Plow, *first presented at Lincoln Center Theater (New York City) in 1988. Directed by Gregory Mosher.*

Churchill a housewife. Among playwrights, there is no common denominator other than the exercise of the creative imagination in dialogue form—the conversion of dreams, fears, thoughts, and inner voices into a concrete, visible world that expands our horizons and our understanding of society and the universe.

The Playwright's Tools

The tools of the playwright's craft are plot, character, and language. These are also familiar to us as the novelist's tools, and, like novels, plays are studied as literature in the classroom and read for pleasure. Although plays are an arrangement of words on a page (as dialogue), the play-as-text is incomplete. It attains its finished form only in perfor-

86   *Chapter Four*

"I think that people are generally more happy with a mystery than with an explanation. So the less that you say about a character the more interesting he becomes."[6]

David Mamet (b. 1947), born in Chicago, attended the Neighborhood Playhouse School of Theatre, New York City, in the '60s and graduated from Goddard College in 1969. He returned to Chicago where he became a founding member of the Nicholas Theatre Company where he began directing plays. His early plays, *Sexual Perversity in Chicago* (1975), *American Buffalo* (1975), and *A Life in the Theatre* (1977), established his style, language, and subjects. Mamet is a playwright of the panic and poetry of the working class in America. He writes of the spiritual failure of entrepreneurial capitalism in the junkyards, real estate offices, and Hollywood agencies of a uniquely American scene. Noted for his distinctive language, Mamet's beleaguered characters demonstrate their frustration, rage, laughter, and incomprehension in undeleted expletives—what one critic has called the "sludge in American language."

More recently, Mamet has written *Glengarry Glen Ross* (1983), which received the Pulitzer Prize for Drama, *Speed the Plow* (1988), and *Oleanna* (1992), and film scripts for *The Postman Always Rings Twice, The Verdict, House of Games,* and *Glengarry Glen Ross.*

mance on the stage. That is why we call the text of the play a blueprint for performance. To look at several lines of dialogue without actors, scenic space, lights, sound, and costumes is to be convinced of the "incompleteness" of a script. The following lines of *Waiting for Godot* strike us as wholly incomplete without the production elements:

Estragon: He should be here.

Vladimir: He didn't say for sure he'd come.

Estragon: And if he doesn't come?

Vladimir: We'll come back to-morrow.

Estragon: And then the day after to-morrow.

Vladimir: Possibly.

Estragon: And so on. (Act I)

AUGUST WILSON

Ma Rainey (Theresa Merritt) performs in the recording studio in Ma Rainey's Black Bottom, *August Wilson's play, produced at The Alley Theatre, Houston, in 1994. (Photo by Jim Caldwell)*

Despite the dialogue's bare bones quality, the playscript is most often the basis for the production that becomes the play's complete realization.

The playwright "builds" that foundation with plot, character, and language. A story is told with characters, physical action, and dialogue. But, the building does not begin until the playwright conceives a whole event with *conflict* (the clashing of personal, moral, and social forces) and then develops a series of related events to resolve that conflict in new and unusual ways. The conflict and events must be compelling. Some are bold and unusual—such as Sophocles' Oedipus unwittingly chasing his own identity through a plague-ridden city, or Shakespeare's Hamlet avenging his father's murder at the invitation of a ghost. Some

August Wilson (b. 1945), born in Pittsburgh, has had five plays produced on Broadway: *Ma Rainey's Black Bottom* (1984), *Fences* (1987), *Joe Turner's Come and Gone* (1988), *The Piano Lesson* (1990), and *Two Trains Running* (1990). He has won two Pulitzer Prizes (for *Fences* and *The Piano Lesson*).

At nineteen Wilson left home to become a writer; he supported himself as a cook and stock clerk; in his spare time he read voraciously in the public library. Writing became his means of responding to changing race relations in America and to the violence erupting within the black community. In 1968, he co-founded Pittsburgh's Black Horizons Theatre and secured a production of his first play, *Black Bart and the Sacred Hills*, in St. Paul, Minnesota, where he has lived since 1977. In St. Paul, Wilson was hired as a scriptwriter for the Science Museum of Minnesota, which had a theatre company attached to the museum. In 1981, after several rejections of other scripts, a draft of *Ma Rainey's Black Bottom* was accepted by the Eugene O'Neill Theatre Center's National Playwrights Conference in Waterford, Connecticut, and Wilson's career was launched.

Wilson's major plays, set in different decades of twentieth-century America, are a series in progress. He is writing a history of black America, probing what he perceives to be the crucial opposition in African-American culture between those who celebrate black Americans' African roots and those who deny that historical reality.

---

are seemingly ordinary, as in domestic situations depicted in modern realistic plays. But, Blanche DuBois' encounter with her brother-in-law in a New Orleans tenement becomes life-threatening in Tennessee Williams' *A Streetcar Named Desire* (1947), and Troy Maxson destroys his domestic tranquility through his need to control his son and assert his manhood in August Wilson's *Fences* (1987).

Playwrights conceptualize events—hear and see them in the mind's eye—for they are to be enacted and must hold the audience's attention. *Performability* is the key to the success of the playwright's story and dialogue. Whether the story is told in a straightforward manner (linear, point-to-point storytelling) or arranged as a series of nonlinear or discontinuous scenes, audiences respond to powerful and sustained dramatic impact. But that impact must be based on the dramatization of events with believable persons that audiences can put together in some sort of meaningful and satisfying fashion.

In the playwright's so-called bag of tools, plot—what Aristotle called "the soul" of drama—requires compression, economy, and intensity. Romeo and Juliet meet, marry, and die within a "two-hour traffic upon the stage." Although plots may encompass many years, the events are compressed so that the story is introduced, told, and resolved within a reasonable amount of time. The intensity of emotions, changed fortunes, and unexpected happenings accounts for our interest in the story and its outcome.

To sustain our interest, the playwright's characters must be believable, rich, and complex. We may never meet a Hamlet, but his dilemma and responses are credible and far more complex and intriguing than events in our daily lives. **Characters**, according to Tennessee Williams, add the mystery and confusion of living to plays.

> My chief aim in playwriting is the creation of character. I have always had a deep feeling for the mystery in life, and essentially my plays have been an effort to explore the beauty and meaning in the confusion of living.[7]

Plot and character are two of the playwright's means of conveying the confusion and mystery of life. Language is the playwright's third essential tool. As dialogue, it must be speakable, actable, and stageable. As justification for the pain he causes his family, Troy Maxson speaks of his plight as an African-American in a predominantly white society:

> . . . you born with two strikes on you before you come to the plate. You got to guard it closely . . . always looking for the curve-ball on the inside corner. You can't afford to let none get past you. You can't afford a call strike. If you going down . . . you going down swinging. (2, i)[8]

Wilson's language is graphic, active, filled with gesture, emotion, and metaphor that convey the essence of Troy's plight and understanding of his situation in life.

In *Fences*, Troy Maxson speaks an ethnic dialect highly charged with feelings, gestures, and baseball images. Wilson's character swings his favorite baseball bat against a rag ball and delivers pronouncements on life in a manner that is at once actable and stageable. No baseball diamond is required to convey Troy's philosophy of life as he stands in his front yard in reduced circumstances and swings the bat against defensive thoughts and lost dreams.

The Playwright and the Industry

Since the Greek festivals in ancient Athens, **producers** have clamored for new and better plays from playwrights. Today, hundreds of producers and literary agents are anxious to discover new authors and new scripts. To do so, they employ a cadre of "readers" to find the exceptional manuscript: the new David Mamet or the undiscovered Marsha Norman. International Creative Management (ICM) is one of the largest literary agencies in New York, representing Arthur Miller and others. For years, Tennessee Williams was represented by Audrey Wood, who guided him through the most successful part of his career. The agent and the producer are two essential connections for the playwright's success. Moreover, some writers develop working relationships with directors; for example, Arthur Miller and Tennessee Williams with Elia Kazan, August Wilson with Lloyd Richards, Neil Simon with Mike Nichols and Jerry Zaks, Wendy Wasserstein with Daniel Sullivan. Others, like David Mamet, direct their own plays.

For the successful Broadway playwright, the rewards are staggering, including television, film, and publishing contracts and interviews in glamorous magazines. Prestigious awards are also forthcoming as indicators of success: the Pulitzer Prize, the Drama Critics' Circle Award, the Antoinette Perry "Tony" Award, and for some, even Nobel Prizes for Literature. Luigi Pirandello and Samuel Beckett both received Nobel awards.

In many respects, playwrights are the most celebrated of the theatre's artists because audiences are aware that they sit in the presence of the writer's world. We listen to and experience a personal vision that makes

TENNESSEE WILLIAMS

Paul Newman as Chance Wayne (left) and Madeleine Sherwood as Miss Lucy confront their personal histories in Tennessee Williams' Sweet Bird of Youth, directed by Elia Kazan and designed by Jo Mielziner for the 1959 Broadway production.

us laugh and cry. The public may revere the actor—a Dustin Hoffman or an Emma Thompson—but the actor's creativity usually begins with the playwright's creation: the characters, situations, environment, and original world of conflicts, feelings, and choices.

In one sense, playwriting is only one facet of the theatre profession and the theatrical machine—the industry. In another sense, it transcends both because when the curtain comes down on a production, there still

Born Thomas Lanier Williams in Columbus, Mississippi, Tennessee Williams (1911–1983) was the son of a traveling salesman and an Episcopalian minister's daughter. The family moved to St. Louis in 1918. He was educated at Missouri University, Washington University in St. Louis, and later the University of Iowa, where he received his B.A. degree.

In 1939, *Story* magazine published his short story "A Field of Blue Children," the first work to appear under his nickname Tennessee, which was given to him because of his Southern accent. That same year he compiled four one-act plays under the title *American Blues*, and won a prize in the Group Theatre's American play contest. This aroused the interest of New York agent Audrey Wood, who asked to represent him.

The Glass Menagerie in 1944–45 marked Williams' first major success and established him as an important American playwright. It was followed by his major plays: *A Streetcar Named Desire* (1947), *The Rose Tattoo* (1951), *Cat on a Hot Tin Roof* (1955), *Sweet Bird of Youth* (1959), and *The Night of the Iguana* (1961). Although his later plays failed to please critics, he continued to write and be produced in New York and London until his death.

remain the playwright's words, ideas, characters, and fictions. As Lillian Hellman, creator of *The Little Foxes*, said: "The manuscript, the words on the page, was what you started with and what you have left" after the production is over. Whereas we might not have an opportunity to see a production of *A Streetcar Named Desire* or *Fences*, we can read the playwright's published script and partake of the playwright's creative act, incomplete though it is.

WOMEN PLAYWRIGHTS: EMERGING VOICES AND PERSPECTIVES

Women playwrights are emerging in growing numbers to provide significant contributions to the contemporary theatre. These are six among many. While Lillian Hellman and Lorraine Hansberry were singular voices for many years, the feminist movement, **Off Broadway**, and regional theatres have provided avenues for women writers both here and abroad.

Lillian Hellman (1905–1984) was produced successfully on Broadway for almost thirty years. Best known for The Children's Hour, The Little Foxes, *and* Toys in the Attic, *Hellman pioneered as a woman in the tough commercialism of the Broadway theatre. She has said of the theatre: "The manuscript, the words on the page, was what you started with and what you have left. The production is of great importance, has given the play the only life it will know, but it is gone, in the end, and the pages are the only wall against which to throw the future or measure the past."[9]*

Lorraine Hansberry (1930–1965) is best known for A Raisin in the Sun *(1959), which ran on Broadway for 530 performances and then was made into a film. She was the youngest American playwright, the first African-American writer, and only the fifth woman to win the New York Drama Critics' Award for the Best Play of the Year. Of playwriting, Hansberry said in 1962: "Plays are better written because one* must, *even if people think that you are being either artsy-craftsy or a plain liar if you say so. One result of this is that I usually don't say it any more, I just write—at my own dismally slow (and, yes, heartbreaking and maddening) commercially disinterested pace and choice of subject matter. . . ."*[10]

María Irene Fornés (b. 1930) emerged in the mid-'60s as a writer, director, and designer. Produced Off Broadway, her plays include Promenade *(1965),* Fefu and Her Friends *(1977), and* Mud *(1984). Of women playwrights she says: ". . . We have to reconcile ourselves to the idea that the protagonist of a play can be a woman and that it is natural for a woman to write a play where the protagonist is a woman. Man is not the center of life. And it is natural when this fact reflects itself in the work of women."[11]*

Caryl Churchill (b. 1938) is a British writer associated with the Joint Stock Theatre Company, the Royal Court Theatre, and the Royal Shakespeare Company. She is best known in this country for Cloud 9 *(1979),* Top Girls *(1980),* Fen *(1983),* Serious Money *(1987), and* Mad Forest *(1991), produced Off Broadway to critical acclaim. Churchill has said: "I believe in the magic of theater, but I think it's important to realize that there is nothing magical about the work process behind it. I spend ages researching my plays and sitting alone writing them."[12]* Mad Forest, *written in collaboration with director Mark Wing-Davey and students from the Central School of Speech and Drama in London, is political theatre that explores the confusion of events and deprivation of the people caught up in the revolution that toppled Romania's Ceauşescu government from power.*

Wendy Wasserstein (b. 1950) was born in Brooklyn, grew up in New York City, and studied playwriting at the Yale School of Drama. She has since been associated with Playwrights Horizons in New York City, which was instrumental in launching her career. Her plays deal with the contemporary woman's hopes, dilemmas, ambitions, and personal conflicts. Uncommon Women and Others, *written in 1977 as a master's thesis, was followed by* Isn't It Romantic *(1981),* The Heidi Chronicles *(1989), and* The Sisters Rosensweig *(1992).* The Heidi Chronicles *won the Pulitzer Prize for Drama and the Tony award for Best New Play of the season. On the difficulties women face as writers and directors in theatre and film, she says, "There are many, many more women playwrights now, and many, many more plays by women being produced. I don't think a play does not get produced because it's by a woman. . . ."*[13]

Marsha Norman (b. 1940), one of many emerging women writers of the past decade, grew up in Louisville, Kentucky, of fundamentalist parents and was encouraged in her writing by Jon Jory, artistic director of Actors Theatre of Louisville. Getting Out, *about a young woman being released from prison, was first produced there and then became an Off Broadway success in 1979. In 1983, she won the Pulitzer Prize for* 'Night, Mother, *about a determined young woman's suicide. In 1991, she wrote the book and lyrics for the musical* The Secret Garden, *winning a Tony Award for Best Book of a Musical, and, in 1993, the book and lyrics for the musical* The Red Shoes. *In trying to explain the increasing numbers of women playwrights in the American theatre, she says, "Plays require active central characters. Until women could see themselves as active, they could not really write for the theater. We are the central characters in our lives. That awareness had to come to a whole group before women could write about it. . . ."[14]*

Summary

Because the whole theatrical process usually begins with the script, the playwright is one of the theatre's most important collaborative artists. The playwright creates the play's world—its events, people, and meaning—on paper. We next consider the playwright's tools, conventions, forms, and styles of writing as he or she creates the world of the play.

Questions for Study

1. What does the word *playwright* mean in its most literal sense?
2. What does designer Robert Edmond Jones mean when he refers to the theatre as "evocative"?
3. What are some of the ways a play takes shape in a playwright's imagination?
4. What is the playwright's function as a collaborator in the theatrical process?
5. What are the playwright's tools for creating a fictional world?
6. What is dialogue?
7. What does Tennessee Williams mean when he refers to the "confusion of living"?
8. How and why have recent women writers placed "women" at the center of their plays?
9. What is the function of a literary agent?
10. *Plays to Read:* Wilson's *Fences*, Shepard's *Buried Child*, Mamet's *American Buffalo*.
11. *Suggested Reading:* David Mamet, *Writing in Restaurants* (New York: Viking Penguin, Inc., 1986); Arthur Miller, *Timebends: A Life* (New York: Grove Press, 1987); *In Their Own Words—Contemporary American Playwrights*, ed. David Savran (New York: Theatre Communications Group, 1988).

Playwrights use different dramatic forms to express their understanding of human experience. Tragedy and comedy are the forms most familiar to us, but there are many other ways to classify plays and to label the playwright's vision—the way he or she *perceives* life in theatrical terms. A study of drama's changing forms is also a study of the playwright's changing perception of the world.

5

DRAMA'S PERSPECTIVES
AND FORMS

Over the centuries, playwrights have developed ways of imitating behavior in different dramatic forms and styles. Drama's forms change as societies and perceptions of the world change. This is what Peter Brook means when he says that every theatrical form, once born, is mortal.[2] Dramatic forms, or as Bertolt Brecht called them, "special mirrors," fall into many categories. The main ones are *tragedy*, *comedy*, *tragicomedy*, *melodrama*, and *farce*. In the twentieth century, two more significant forms have been devised, the *epic* and the *absurd*.

Drama's essential forms are ways of seeing human experience. The words *tragedy*, *comedy*, and *tragicomedy* are not so much ways of classifying plays by their endings as ways of talking about the playwright's vision of experience—of the way he or she perceives life. They furnish clues about how the play is to be taken or understood by audiences. Is the play a serious statement about, say, the relationship between men and women? Does it explore issues of gender and sexual preference? Does it despair at the possibilities of mutual understanding? Or does it hold such attempts up to ridicule? Or does it explore humanity's unchanging existential situation?

Tragedy

It is not altogether simpleminded to say that a tragedy is a play with an unhappy ending. Tragedy, the first of the great dramatic forms in Western drama, makes a special statement about human fallibility.

OEDIPUS THE KING

One of several Greek playwrights whose work survives today, Sophocles wrote three plays about Oedipus. *Oedipus the King* (427 B.C.) is generally considered the greatest of Greek tragedies. (*Antigone*, 441 B.C., and *Oedipus at Colonus*, 406 B.C., are the other two.)

Oedipus the King tells the story of a man who flees from Corinth to avoid fulfilling a prophecy that he will kill his father and marry his mother. On his journey he kills an old man (an apparent stranger but actually his real father, the king of Thebes) at a place where three roads meet. He then proceeds to Thebes and solves the riddle of the Sphinx. As a reward, he is made king and married to the widowed queen, who is actually his mother, Jocasta. He rules well and has four children.

The play opens with Thebes stricken by a plague. Declaring that he will rid the city of infection, Oedipus has sent his brother-in-law Creon to consult the Delphic oracle about the cause of the plague. As he pursues the plague's source, Oedipus comes face to face with himself as his father's killer, as his mother's son and husband, and as his children's father and brother. When the truth is learned, Jocasta kills herself and he puts out his eyes. By his own decree, Oedipus is exiled from Thebes and wanders blind into the countryside.

Oedipus the King explores human guilt and innocence, knowledge and ignorance, power and helplessness. Its fundamental idea is that wisdom comes to us only through suffering.

The Tragic Vision

The writer's tragic vision of experience conceives of people as both vulnerable and invincible, as capable of abject defeat and transcendent greatness. Tragedies like *Oedipus the King, Hamlet, Ghosts,* and *A Streetcar Named Desire* show the world's injustice, evil, and pain. Tragic heroes, in an exercise of free will, pit themselves against forces represented by other characters, by their own inner drives, or by their physical environment. We witness their suffering, their inevitable defeat, and, sometimes, their personal triumph in the face of defeat. The trials of the hero give meaning to the pain and paradox of our humanity.

Some tragedies are concerned with seeking meaning and justice in an ordered world, others with humanity's helpless protest against an irrational one. In both kinds, the hero, alone and willful, asserts his or her intellect and energy against the ultimate mysteries of an imperfect world.

Tragic Realization

The realization (a **recognition** or **anagnorisis**) that follows the hero's efforts usually takes one of two directions: that, despite suffering and calamity, a world order and eternal laws exist and people can learn from suffering; or that human acts and suffering in an indifferent, capricious, or mechanical universe are futile, but at the same time the hero's protests against the nature of existence are to be celebrated. In *Oedipus the King* and *A Streetcar Named Desire* we find examples of these two kinds of tragic realization.

Aristotle on Tragedy

Aristotle spoke of tragedy as "an imitation of an action . . . concerning the fall of a man whose character is good (though not pre-eminently just or virtuous) . . . whose misfortune is brought about not by vice or depravity but by some error or frailty . . . with incidents arousing pity and fear, wherewith to accomplish the catharsis of these emotions."[3]

Aristotle and the Greek playwrights depicted tragedy's action as an imitation of a noble hero experiencing a downfall and tragedy's subjects as suffering and death. The heroes of ancient tragedies were usually aristocrats, to show that even the great among us are subject to the fate of the human condition. In modern plays, the hero's averageness speaks to us of kinship in adversity. Whether the hero is aristocratic or ordinary, his or her actions are influenced by the writer's tragic view of life, which centers on the need to give meaning to our fate despite the fact that we are doomed to failure and defeat.

Comedy

In the eighteenth century, Horace Walpole said: "The world is a comedy to those that think, a tragedy to those that feel." In comedy the playwright examines the social world, social values, and people as social

MOLIÈRE

Tartuffe (Jeffrey Bean) attempts to seduce Elmire (Annalee Jefferies) in the 1994 revival of Moliere's play at the Alley Theatre, Houston. Directed by Gregory Boyd in collaboration with the California-based Dell'Arte Players.

Molière (Jean Baptiste Poquelin, 1622–1673), French playwright-actor-manager, was the son of Louis XIV's upholsterer. Poquelin spent his early years close to the court and received a gentleman's education. He joined a theatrical troupe in 1643 and became a professional actor with the stage name Molière. Molière helped to found the Illustre Théâtre Company in Paris, which soon failed, and spent twelve years touring the French provinces as an itinerant actor and company playwright. He returned to Paris to become the foremost writer and comedian of his time. Within thirteen years (1659–1673), he wrote and acted in *Tartuffe, The Misanthrope, The Doctor in Spite of Himself, The Miser,* and *The Imaginary Invalid*. Written during France's golden age, Molière's comedies balance follies of eccentric and devious humanity against society's reasonable good sense.

Tartuffe (1664) is Molière's comedy about a hypocrite. Tartuffe disguises himself as a cleric, and his apparent piety ingratiates him with the credulous merchant Orgon and his mother, Madame Pernelle. As the play begins, Tartuffe has taken over Orgon's house. Both Orgon and his mother believe that Tartuffe's pious example will be good for the family. But everyone else in the family, including the outspoken servant Dorine, is perceptive enough to see through Tartuffe.

Despite the protests of his brother-in-law Cléante and his son Damis, Orgon determines that his daughter Marianne, who is in love with Valère, will marry Tartuffe. When Orgon's wife Elmire begs Tartuffe to refuse Marianne's hand, he tries to seduce her. Damis, who has overheard, denounces Tartuffe. Orgon banishes his son rather than his guest and signs over his property to Tartuffe.

Elmire then plots to expose the hypocrite. She persuades Orgon to conceal himself under a table while she encourages Tartuffe's advances. Orgon's eyes are opened, but it is too late. The impostor realizes he has been discovered and turns Orgon's family out of the house. Then he reports to the authorities that Orgon has a strongbox containing seditious papers and contrives to have Orgon arrested. But, by the king's order, the arresting officer takes Tartuffe to prison instead.

The play ends with Damis reconciled to his father, Orgon reconciled with his family, and Valère and Marianne engaged.

Differences Between Tragedy and Comedy

Tragedy	Comedy	Tragedy	Comedy
Individual	Society	Terror	Euphoria
Metaphysical	Social	Unhappiness	Happiness
Death	Endurance	Irremediable	Remediable
Error	Folly	Decay	Growth
Suffering	Joy	Destruction	Continuation
Pain	Pleasure	Defeat	Survival
Life-denying	Procreative	Extreme	Moderation
Separation	Union/Reunion	Inflexible	Flexible

beings. Frequently, comic action shows the social disorder created by an eccentric character who deviates from reasonable values like sensibility, good nature, flexibility, moderation, tolerance, and social intelligence. Deviation is sharply ridiculed in comedy because it threatens to destroy revered social structures such as marriage and the family.

The Comic Vision

The writer of comedy calls for sanity, reason, and moderation in human behavior so that society can function for the well-being and happiness of its members. In comedy, society survives the threat posed by inflexible or antisocial behavior. In Molière's *Tartuffe* the title character's greed is revealed and Orgon's family is returned to a normal, domestic existence at the play's end. For the seventeenth-century French playwright, as for some of his contemporary American counterparts, the well-being of the family unit is a measure of the well-being of the society as a whole.

At the end of almost any comedy, the life force is ordinarily celebrated in a wedding, a dance, or a banquet symbolizing the harmony and reconciliation of opposing forces: young and old, flexible and inflexible, reasonable and unreasonable. These social ceremonies allow us to see that good sense wins the day in comedy and that humanity endures in the vital, the flexible, and the reasonable.

Tragicomedy

Tragicomedy, as its name implies, is a mixed dramatic form. Up to the end of the seventeenth century in Europe, it was defined as a mixture of tragedy, which went from good fortune to bad, and comedy, which reversed the order from bad fortune to good. Tragicomedy combined serious and comic incidents as well as the styles, subject matter, and language proper to tragedy and to comedy, and it also mixed characters from all stations of life. The *ending* (up until the nineteenth century) was its principal feature: Tragicomedies were serious and potentially tragic plays with happy endings, or at least with averted catastrophes.

The term *modern tragicomedy* is used to designate plays with mixed moods in which the endings are neither exclusively tragic nor comic, happy nor unhappy. The great Russian playwright Anton Chekhov (1860–1904) wrote plays of mixed moods in which he described the lives of "quiet desperation" of ordinary people in rural Russia around the turn of the century: provincial gentry, writers, professors, doctors, farmers, servants, teachers, government officials, and garrisoned military. What they had in common, finally, was their survival.

Chekhov's most frequently revived play, *The Three Sisters* (1901), tells of the provincial lives of the Prozorov family: three sisters (Olga, Masha, and Irina), their brother (Andrey), his wife (Natasha), their lovers, a brother-in-law, and military friends. The play's only action in the traditional sense is the departure of a military regiment from a small town after an interval of several years. For four acts the sisters dream of returning to Moscow to escape from the dull routine of their lives. But, unlike the regiment, they are unable to move on to new places and experiences.

As we scrutinize the seriocomic quality of Chekhov's play, a theme emerges: *the value of surviving in the face of social change*. The three sisters are emotionally adrift in a society whose institutions supply avenues of change only for the soldier, the upstart, and the entrepreneur. The weak and ineffectual, like the three sisters (and these women are products of their time), are locked into a way of life that is neither emotionally nor intellectually rewarding. The most Chekhov's people can do is endure the stultifying marriage, the routine job, and the tyrannical sister-in-law. But they survive. With no prescription for the future, Masha says only that "We've got to live."

The Three Sisters, with Kim Stanley as Masha, Shirley Knight as Irina, and Geraldine Page as Olga in the 1964 Actors Studio Theatre production, directed by Lee Strasberg, at Broadway's Morosco Theatre.

Chekhov's most critically acclaimed work during his lifetime was first produced at the Moscow Art Theatre in 1901 with Olga Knipper as Masha, Constantin Stanislavski as Colonel Vershinin, and Vsevelod Meyerhold as Baron Tusenbach.

In a garrison town in rural Russia, the cultured Prozorov sisters think longingly of the excitement of Moscow, which they left eleven

Modern Tragicomedy

Samuel Beckett subtitled *Waiting for Godot* a "tragicomedy" though it is also an enduring absurdist play of modern times. In this play, two tramps entertain themselves with comic routines while they wait in a sparse landscape adorned by a single tree for someone named Godot to arrive (see the box on page 110). But Godot never comes. As they react years earlier. Olga, the oldest, is constantly exhausted by her work as a schoolteacher; Masha, married at eighteen to a man she considered an intellectual giant, bitterly realizes that he is merely a pedant; Irina, the youngest, dreams of a romantic future and rejects the sincere love of Lieutenant Tusenbach and the advances of Captain Solyony. Their brother, Andrey, an unambitious man, courts Natasha, the daughter of a local family. Into this circle comes Lieutenant Colonel Vershinin. Like Masha, he is unhappily married. They are immediately attracted to one another.

The Prozorovs and their friends recognize the frustration of their lives, but hope in some vague future keeps their spirits high. For the sisters it is a dream of returning someday to Moscow. The atmosphere changes when Andrey marries Natasha. The sisters' immediate prospects of returning to Moscow are dashed. Irina tries to find relief in her job in the telegraph office. Natasha takes control of the household, and as time goes on the sisters are moved about in the house to make room for her two children. Andrey takes refuge in gambling and mortgages the house that he and his sisters own jointly.

News that the garrison is to be transferred brings depressing prospects for the future. Irina decides to marry Tusenbach, an unattractive but gentle man, who resigns his army commission in the hope of finding more meaningful work. As Masha and Vershinin, who have become open lovers, bid each other goodbye, and the regiment prepares to leave, word comes that Tusenbach has been killed by Solyony in a duel over Irina. The sisters cling to one another for consolation. As the military band strikes up, the gaiety of the music inspires them to hope that there is a new life in store for them in another "millennium."

to this situation, humor and energy are mixed with anguish and despair. In the modern form of tragicomedy, playwrights show people laughing at their anxieties and life's contradictions with little effect on their situations. Beckett's Vladimir summarizes the form when he says, "The essential doesn't change."

Sam Shepard's *Buried Child* and August Wilson's *Fences* are more recent tragicomedies. Although principal characters die in both plays,

SAMUEL BECKETT

Samuel Beckett's tramps, Vladimir and Estragon, entertain themselves by searching for a missing boot. Although Godot has not kept his appointment with them, the tree has grown leaves between the first and second acts. With Godot's absence and the tree's growth, Beckett juxtaposes despair with hope, loss with gain. The photo is from the 1961 Paris revival of Waiting for Godot directed by Jean-Marie Serreau with Lucien Raimbourg as Vladimir and Etienne Berg as Estragon. The tree was designed by sculptor Alberto Giacometti.

the writers affirm humanity's endurance—despite anguish and loss—among little potential for social or personal change.

Melodrama

Another mixed form, melodrama, derives its name from the Greek word for music, *melos*. It is a combination of music and drama in which the spoken word is used against a musical background. Jean Jacques Rousseau, who introduced the term's modern use in 1772, applied it to his *Pygmalion*, a *scène lyrique* in which words and music were linked in the action.

Samuel Beckett (1906–1989) was an expatriate Irishman living in France. Beckett grew up near Dublin and attended Trinity College, where he received two degrees in literature and began a teaching career. In the 1930s Beckett left his teaching position, traveled in Europe, published his first book (*More Pricks Than Kicks*), and wrote poetry in French. During World War II he worked with the French Resistance and barely escaped capture by the Nazis.

Beginning in 1953, Beckett wrote some thirty theatrical pieces, including radio plays, mime sketches, monologues, and four full-length plays (*Waiting for Godot, Endgame, Krapp's Last Tape, Happy Days*), which have become modern classics.

Beckett's last plays were minimal. *Come and Go* (1965) is a 3-minute play, *Breath* (1966) is a 30-second play, *Rockaby* (1980) is a 15-minute play, and *Not I* (1973) consisted of eight pages of text. With these brief pieces Beckett constructed a theatrical image of how we come and go on this earth, briefly filling a void with our bodies and voices, and then disappear into darkness without a trace.

The Mixed Form

Melodrama became widely used in the nineteenth century to describe a play without music but having a serious action usually caused by the villainy of an unsympathetic character. Melodrama's characters are clearly divided—either sympathetic or unsympathetic—and the villain's destruction brings about the happy resolution. Melodrama usually shows a main character in circumstances that threaten death or ruin from which he or she is rescued at the last possible moment. Like a film's musical score, incidental music heightens the mood of impending disaster. The term *melodrama* is most often applied to such nineteenth-century plays as *Uncle Tom's Cabin* (1852), based on Harriet Beecher

Regina Gibbons, played by Tallulah Bankhead (on sofa, center), and her brothers cultivate Mr. Marshall (Lee Baker) to secure the cotton mill and their fortunes while Birdie and Alexandra (right) talk of other matters in the 1939 Broadway production of Lillian Hellman's The Little Foxes.

The Little Foxes, written by Lillian Hellman in 1938–39, is a quintessential melodrama. The play takes place in the American South in 1900 and concerns the wealthy Hubbards, a prosperous family eager to parlay their success as merchants and bankers into vast industrial wealth. "To bring the machines to the cotton, and not the cotton to the machines," as Ben Hubbard says. Regina Hubbard Gibbons is the powerful villainess of the play that demonstrates the corrosive consequences of money and lust.

To compete with her brothers, Oscar and Ben, Regina must persuade her dying husband, Horace Gibbons, to invest one-third interest in their get-rich-quick scheme. Because of a heart condition,

Horace has been in a Baltimore hospital; Regina sends their daughter Alexandra to bring him home so that Regina can invest his Union Pacific bonds in the scheme. Horace arrives but refuses to advance the money. Her brothers tell Regina they will go elsewhere for another business partner, although they would prefer not to bring in an outsider. When the brothers learn from Leo—Ben's son who works in the bank that holds Horace's bonds—that the bonds could be "borrowed" from the bank strongbox without fear of discovery, they take the bonds and tell Regina she's out of the deal. When Horace discovers the bonds are missing and learns of his wife's manipulations, he says he will claim that he lent the bonds to his brothers-in-law. Regina's scathing attack on Horace brings on his fatal heart attack. Because his death will eliminate her problems and make her rich, she stands immobile while he pleads with her for his medicine. She watches his desperate but futile struggle to climb the stairs to reach his medicine. With her husband's death, the bonds now belong to Regina and she is once again victorious. Regina blackmails her brothers into giving her 75 percent interest in the venture for her unauthorized "investment." Their alternative is jail. Alexandra, who suspects Regina's complicity in her father's death, voices her disgust and leaves home, but this is only a minor shadow on the bright horizon of Regina's future.

Hellman's episodes turn on theft, blackmail, sudden and unexpected shifts of fortune, unrelenting greed, and major changes in the balance of power in the Hubbard money game. The play's characters range from the genteel Birdie Hubbard and naive Alexandra to the "little foxes that spoil the vines"—the vicious and manipulative Regina, Ben, and Oscar Hubbard. Hellman does not attempt to deepen our understanding of society or of human values. Rather she shows evil in conflict with evil and the good and decent as merely impotent onlookers. But the fascination with Regina's manipulations and her victory over her pernicious brothers stimulate audiences into applauding her resourcefulness and withholding moral judgment before her wit, glamour, and cunning.

Stowe's novel, and Dion Boucicault's *The Octoroon* (1859). Today, we apply the term to such diverse plays as Lillian Hellman's *The Little Foxes* (1938), Lorraine Hansberry's *A Raisin in the Sun* (1959), and such suspenseful thrillers as Ira Levin's *Death Trap* (1978).

The melodramatic view of life sees human beings as whole, not divided; enduring outer conflicts, not inner ones, in a generally hostile world; and sees these conflicts resulting in victory or defeat as they are pressed to extreme conclusions. Melodrama's characters win or lose in the conflict. The endings are clear-cut and extreme. There are no complex and ambiguous resolutions, as when Hamlet wins in losing. Replying to critics complaining about her melodramatic plots, Lillian Hellman said: "If you believe, as the Greeks did, that man is at the mercy of the gods, then you write tragedy. The end is inevitable from the beginning. But if you believe that man can solve his own problems and is at nobody's mercy, then you will probably write melodrama."[4]

Melodrama oversimplifies, exaggerates, and contrives experience. In short, melodrama is the dramatic form that expresses the truth of the human condition as we perceive it most of the time. We have our victories, and our "accidents" or failures are attributable to external factors.

Farce

Farce is best described as comedy of situation. In farce, pies in the face, beatings, mistaken identities, slips on the banana peel—exaggerated physical activities growing out of situations—are substituted for comedy's traditional concern for social values. The writer of farce presents life as mechanical, aggressive, and coincidental and entertains us with seemingly endless variations on a single situation. A typical farce situation is the bedroom crowded with concealed lovers as the cuckolded husband or deceived wife arrives on the scene.

The "psychology of farce," as Eric Bentley calls it, is that special opportunity for the fulfillment of our unmentionable wishes without taking responsibility for our actions or suffering the guilt[5] Farce as a dramatic form gives us a fantasy world of violence (without harm), adultery (without consequences), brutality (without reprisal), and aggression (without risk). Today we enjoy farce in the films of Charlie Chaplin, W. C. Fields, the Marx Brothers, Woody Allen, Chevy Chase, Steve Martin, and Eddie Murphy; and in the plays of Georges Feydeau, Neil

Michael Frayn's Noises Off, *where the actors are performing "Nothing On." A real-life sex farce backstage parallels the fictional one in which they are appearing. Dorothy Loudon played Dotty Otley in the 1983 Broadway production.*

Noises Off (1982) by British playwright Michael Frayn is a farce about farce. It ridicules the many clichés of the genre within the format of a play-within-a-play. Act I is the final dress rehearsal by a provincial touring company of *Nothing On.* The typical confusions of farce result from actors who can't remember their lines, their entrances, and their stage business. Plates of sardines, doors, and telephones add to the actor's difficulties. Frayn heaps onto his play-within-a-play a melee of stock characters—cheery housekeeper, incompetent burglar, unexpected lovers, outraged wife, harried husband—who stampede in and out of the many doors. The stage clichés of the farce *Nothing On* (*Noises Off*, Act I) are repeated in the backstage confusion of relationships (Act II). Act III takes place at the same time as the second Act, only this time we see Act II from the front of the theatre; there are even further actorly mishaps and temper tantrums.

Frayn's farcical contrivances are further compounded by the onstage versus the backstage view of life. The director of *Nothing On* summarizes the improbable confusions of the genre: ". . . That's what it's all about. Doors and sardines. Getting on—getting off. Getting the sardines on—getting the sardines off. That's farce. That's the theatre. That's life."

Simon, Michael Frayn, and Penn & Teller. Farce has also been an element of some of the world's great comedies, including those of Shakespeare, Molière, and Chekhov.

Adaptations

Nicholas Nickleby, Les Misérables, The Mahabharata, and *The Grapes of Wrath* are enormously successful examples of another play form: *the adaptation.* The current explosion of interest in adaptations in contemporary French, English, Russian, and American theatres is not related to the availability of new plays but to a desire of theatre companies to create their own texts. (See Figure 5.1.)

Dickens' novels, with their wealth of dramatic incident and social detail, have been prime properties for adaptation. Many theatrical adaptations (not counting films and television) have been made of *A Christmas Carol, The Pickwick Papers, A Tale of Two Cities, David Copperfield, Great Expectations, Nicholas Nickleby,* and *Little Dorrit.* In France, novels by Jack London, Voltaire, Honoré de Balzac, Gustave Flaubert, and Marguerite Duras have found their way onto the stages of both established and experimental theatres.

How is a dramatic adaptation created and how does it work theatrically? An adaptation is largely the result of the director's concept and the actors' work. As French director Antoine Vitez says: "The theatre is *someone* who takes his material wherever he finds it—even things not made for the stage—and puts them on stage. Or, rather, stages them."[6] In the process of adaptation, director and actors emerge as primary creators. What matters is not what the author meant the text to say but how the director reads and stages it.

One method of adapting novels to the stage is to retain the novel's narrative voice (with actors as narrators), substituting storytellers for characters. The aim is to blend narrative techniques (descriptions, comments, interior monologues) with dramatic ones (one character speaking directly to another). In some cases, social documents relevant to the action are read aloud. Descriptions are also included in what is spoken. Sometimes actions simply give voice to both descriptions and conversations, including the phrases "he said" or "she said."

FIGURE 5.1

The Life and Adventures of Nicholas Nickleby, *a Dickens novel written in
1838–39, has been one of the most popular stage adaptations of a novel in
modern times. Adapted for the Royal Shakespeare Company by David Edgar
and directed by Trevor Nunn and John Caird,* Nicholas Nickleby *became the
RSC's greatest success since Peter Brook's* A Midsummer Night's Dream. *The
daring concept involved forty-two actors in a production that ran more than
eight and a half hours. Even more so than Dickens' novel, the RSC production
conjured up the seaminess and violence of Victorian England, with its extremes
of cruelty and compassion, wealth and poverty, corruption and innocence. In
this photo, Smike (David Threlfall), center, struggles to communicate to his
friend Nicholas (Roger Rees) against the noises of Victorian London, as
provided by the actors at left.*

THE GRAPES OF WRATH

The Steppenwolf Theatre Company presented the world premiere of *The Grapes of Wrath* in 1988 in Chicago. John Steinbeck's famous novel was adapted and directed by Frank Galati for the ensemble. The 35-member company presented the world premiere of the stage adaptation first in Chicago, then at the La Jolla Playhouse, California, and again at The National Theatre of Great Britain before bringing the production to Broadway where Frank Galati was awarded a "Tony" Award for Best Play of the 1989 season.

Tom and Ma Joad (Gary Sinise and Lois Smith) join in an evening of country dancing to fiddles and guitars.

Gary Sinise as Tom Joad and Terry Kinney as his friend Jim Casy discuss their bleak future at the start of their journey away from the Oklahoma dustbowl and toward the migrant labor camps of California.

The Joad family and friends drive through the night along Route 66 toward the "promised land" of California. Gary Sinise as Tom Joad drives the truck, which moves about the stage; the converted Hudson is the play's most important scenic element made of authentic parts from 1930s vehicles. Sally Murphy (above) is Rose of Sharon.

Lois Smith as Ma Joad holds her son Tom (Gary Sinise) in their farewell scene at the play's end. After the death of his friend Casy and his futile struggle with police and camp guards, Tom must abandon the family for their welfare and to save his life.

The Joad family, having arrived in California, are questioned by a foreman before being admitted inside the wire fence as hired laborers to work the fields. Set designer Kevin Rigdon used old wood planks and corrugated sheet metal to suggest barren earth and cultivated fields with furrows. In this scene, a piece of barbed-wire gate represents the entranceway to the ranch—to work, food, and shelter.

The cast at the curtain call.

The Grapes of Wrath **was first published by John Steinbeck in 1939 and was awarded the Pulitzer Prize in 1940. The novel chronicles the troubled journey of the Joad family, displaced from their Oklahoma**

The Grapes of Wrath

The Grapes of Wrath was commissioned by the Steppenwolf Theatre Company, Chicago, and adapted by the group's writer-director Frank Galati in 1988. Concentrating on the place and time of John Steinbeck's novel, Galati traces a stage action that tells an epic story about dislocation as the Joads move across country (on a bare stage) in the play's most significant stage prop, the heavily laden Hudson Super Six truck (reminiscent of the canteen wagon in Brecht's *Mother Courage and Her Children*), and propelled in time by ballad music played on a guitar.

farm by the dust bowl disaster in the mid-1930s to the migrant labor camps of California. John Ford's classic 1940 film starred Henry Fonda as Tom Joad.

The novel (and the stage adaptation) follows the Joads: their exodus from Oklahoma, their wanderings in the Southwest, and their trials in the "promised" land—California. The spine of the novel follows the growth and discovery of its commonplace though heroic figures (Ma and Pa Joad, Tom Joad, Rose of Sharon, Jim Casy, and to some degree, Uncle John). At the novel's end, Tom's friend Casy has sacrificed his life in a labor dispute with management and the police; Rose of Sharon becomes a mother but loses her child and feeds another from her breast; Ma refuses to be "wiped out" ("We're the people—we go on"); and Tom's rage over Casy's death and the possibility that he has killed a policeman force him to leave the family to join an undefined movement committed to social struggle. He becomes our common hero fighting for human rights. He promises his mother at the novel's end: "Wherever they's a fight so hungry people can eat, I'll be there. Wherever they's a cop beating up a guy, I'll be there."

The Grapes of Wrath is a compelling, realistic treatise on the plight and nobility of ordinary laborers. It is also a bitter commentary on the human costs of industrial "progress" and the radicalization of an individual by social injustice. Centrally concerned with issues of social and economic justice, it is regarded as one of the most important American novels to emerge from the Great Depression.

As the novel's adaptor for a thirty-five member cast, Galati worked with the essential elements of the novel. He concentrated on Steinbeck's language, the journey of the characters, and their strength of spirit in great adversity. Galati also reasoned that Steinbeck's story applies to our own time when so many are homeless and dispossessed and when the hope for the salvation of the world lies with the human heart.

One challenge in adapting the 500-page novel to the stage was how to find an appropriate setting for the Joads' epic saga. After much research into the writings and photographs of the era, an abstract version of the plowed, barren earth was created for the stage out of "corrugated

BERTOLT BRECHT

Bertolt Brecht's The Good Person of Setzuan, *directed by Andrei Serban with music by Elizabeth Swados, was staged by the American Repertory Theatre, Cambridge, in their 1986–87 season. Like Brecht's* The Caucasian Chalk Circle, *this play combines a non-illusionistic performance style with the statement that it is hard for human beings to reconcile our instincts for goodness with the necessity for economic survival.*

sheet metal and old wood." Sections of the stage floor opened up to permit real fire, rain, and water. A piece of barbed wire represents a fence, a gate represents a ranch, a huge wall with doors becomes the solid interior of a barn. The Joads' authentic '30s truck carries twelve people and their belongings in full view of the audience.

Galati paces Steinbeck's story for a two-and-a-half hour dramatic production. He eliminated most of the novel's "general chapters," using songs, music, and some narrative as transitions to trace the family's journey from Oklahoma to California. Galati wrote no dialogue of his own but used Steinbeck's words to create the play's dialogue and to tell

124   *Chapter Five*

Bertolt Brecht (1898–1956) was born in Augsburg, Germany, where he spent his early years. In 1918, while studying medicine at Munich University, he was called up for military service as a medical orderly. He began writing poems about the horrors of war. His first play, *Baal* (1918), dates from this period.

After World War I, Brecht drifted as a student into the bohemian world of theatre and literature, singing his poetry in Munich taverns and coffee-houses. By 1921, Brecht had seriously entered the theatre world as a reviewer and playwright. During the 1920s in Berlin, Brecht became a Marxist, wrote plays, and solidified his theories of epic theatre. *The Threepenny Opera* (1928)—produced in collaboration with the composer Kurt Weill—was an overnight success and made both Brecht and Weill famous.

With the rise of the Nazi movement, many German artists and intellectuals left Germany. Brecht and his family fled in 1933, first to Sweden, and then to the United States, where he lived until 1947. In October of 1947, Brecht was subpoenaed to appear before the House Un-American Activities Committee to testify on the "Communist infiltration" of the motion-picture industry. He left the United States the day following his testimony, eventually settling in East Berlin, where he founded the Berliner Ensemble. This great theatre company continues to perform his works at the Theater am Schiffbauerdamm, where he first produced *The Threepenny Opera*. Brecht's greatest plays date from his years of exile (1933–1948): *The Good Person of Setzuan, Mother Courage and Her Children, Galileo,* and *The Caucasian Chalk Circle.*

the story of an epic adventure in which adversity follows adversity but the human spirit endures.

Epic Theatre

Bertolt Brecht, the director and playwright who has probably had more influence on our postwar theatre than any other theatrical artist, reacted against Western traditions of the **well-made play** and the proscenium theatre of pictorial illusion. Over a lifetime, he adapted methods from Erwin Piscator (who pioneered the docudrama for German working class audiences in the '20s), Chinese opera, Noh drama, chronicle history plays, English music-hall routines, and films to create "epic" theatre.

The Epic Play

When Brecht spoke of *epic* theatre, he was thinking of plays as *episodic* and *narrative*: as a sequence of incidents or events narrated without artificial restrictions as to time, place, or formal plot. Play structure was more like that of a narrative poem than of a well-made play.

Because Brecht wanted to represent historical process in the theatre and have it judged critically by audiences, he departed from many theatrical traditions. First, he thought of the stage as a platform on which political and social issues could be debated. And he rejected the idea that a play should be "well made," reminding us that history does not end but moves on from episode to episode. Why should plays do otherwise? Brecht's plays therefore were a series of loosely knit scenes, each complete in itself. The effect was achieved through the juxtaposition of contrasting *episodes*. The nonliterary elements of production—music, acting style, lighting, and moving scenery—also retained their separate identities. His epic play is, therefore, *historical*, *narrative*, *episodic*, and highly theatrical. It treats humans as social beings in their economic, social, and political milieus.

Dramatic Versus Epic Theatre

Brecht's table, published in *The Modern Theatre Is the Epic Theatre* (1930), shows the difference between dramatic theatre (for example, *Ghosts*) and epic theatre.[7]

Brecht's characters are both individuals and collective beings. This type of characterization dates to the morality plays of the late Middle Ages, where "Everyman" is both a recognizable individual and a representative of all human beings.

In Brecht's plays, character emerges from the individual's social function and changes with that function. In keeping with the idea that the theatre is a platform to discuss political and social issues, theatrical language is discursive and polemical.

DRAMATIC THEATRE	EPIC THEATRE
Plot	Narrative
Implicates the spectator in a stage situation	Turns the spectator into an observer, but
Wears down his capacity for action	Arouses his capacity for action
Provides him with sensations	Forces him to make decisions
Experience	Picture of the world
The spectator is involved in something	He is made to face something
Suggestion	Argument
Instinctive feelings are preserved	Brought to the point of recognition
The spectator is in the thick of it, shares the experience	The spectator stands outside, studies
The human being is taken for granted	The human being is object of inquiry
He is unalterable	He is alterable and able to alter
Eyes on the finish	Eyes on the course
One scene makes another	Each scene for itself
Growth	Montage
Linear development	In curves
Evolutionary determinism	Jumps
Man as a fixed point	Man as a process
Thought determines being	Social being determines thought
Feeling	Reason

Epic Acting as Eyewitness Account

Early in his career Brecht admonished actors not to regard themselves as impersonating or becoming characters so much as narrating the actions of people in a particular time, place, and situation. The model he used to demonstrate this approach was the behavior of an eyewitness to a traffic accident.

In retelling the event, eyewitnesses clearly differentiate between themselves and the victim, although they may reconstruct the victim's reactions and gestures. So, too, Brecht argued, actors clearly differentiate between themselves as actors and the characters in the play. The eyewitness never *becomes* the victim. He further explained:

> It is comparatively easy to set up a basic model for epic theatre. For practical experiments I usually picked as my example of completely simple "natural" epic theatre an incident such as can be seen at any street corner; an eyewitness demonstrating to a collection of people how a traffic accident took place. The bystanders may not have observed what happened, or they may simply not agree with him, may "see things a different way": the point is that the demonstrator acts the behavior of driver or victim or both in such a way that the bystanders are able to form an opinion about the accident.[8]

In Brecht's theatre, the actor did not "become" the character as in the Stanislavski approach to acting; rather, actors "demonstrated" the characters' attitudes while retaining freedom to comment on the actions of the person whose behavior they were displaying. This device of the actor as eyewitness to the play's events was also part of Brecht's efforts to distance or alienate the audience emotionally from what was happening on stage.

The Alienation Effect

Brecht called this jarring of the audience out of its sympathetic feelings for what is happening on stage his **alienation effect** (sometimes called A-effect or *Verfremdungseffekt*). He wanted to prevent the audience's empathetic "willing suspension of disbelief," to force them to look at everything in a fresh light, and, above all, to think. Brecht wanted audiences to absorb his social criticism and to carry new insights out of the theatre into their own lives (see Figure 5.2).

Brecht was certainly aware of the entertainment value of theatre. For Brecht, pleasure in the theatre came from observing accounts of past situations, discovering new truths, and enlarging upon an understanding of the present. What he opposed was a theatre solely of **catharsis**, where the audience lost its critical detachment by identifying emotion-

FIGURE 5.2
The Caucasian Chalk Circle, *1954. The chalk circle test from the Berliner Ensemble production of Brecht's* The Caucasian Chalk Circle, *1954. Judge Azdak gives the child to Grusha because she will not engage in the tug-of-war for Michael for fear of harming him.*

ally with the characters. All of the epic devices—music, scenery, lighting, placards, projections, acting style—reminded audiences that they were in a theatre, that the stage was a stage and not someone's living room.

Absurdist Theatre

In 1961 Martin Esslin, a British critic, wrote a book called *The Theatre of the Absurd* about trends in the post-World War II theatre. He used the label to describe new theatrical ways of looking at existence.

Absurdist writers, like Eugene Ionesco and Samuel Beckett, made their breakthrough in dramatic form by *presenting*, without comment or moral judgment, situations showing life's irrationality. The common factors in the absurdist plays of Ionesco, Beckett, and others are unrecognizable plots, mechanical characters, situations resembling dreams and nightmares, and incoherent dialogue. The absurdist does not tell a story or discuss social problems. Instead, the writer presents in concrete stage images, such as two tramps waiting for a person who never shows up, *a sense of being* in an absurd universe.

The Absurd

Absurdist playwrights begin with the premise that our world is *absurd*, meaning irrational, incongruous, and senseless. Albert Camus (1913–1960)—a French philosopher, novelist, and playwright—diagnosed the human condition as absurd in *The Myth of Sisyphus*.

EUGENE IONESCO

Eugene Ionesco (1912–1994) is a Rumanian-born former schoolteacher and refugee from Nazism who lives in France. Forty years ago he puzzled and outraged audiences with plays about bald sopranos, octogenarian suicides, homicidal professors, and human rhinoceroses as metaphors for the world's absurdity. Today, *The Bald Soprano, The Chairs, The Lesson,* and *Rhinoceros* are modern classics.

Since *The Bald Soprano* was first produced in Paris at the Théâtre de Noctambules in 1950, Ionesco has written over thirty plays in addition to journals, essays, and children's stories. Ionesco said that his theatre expresses the malaise of contemporary life, language's failure to bring people closer together, the strangeness of existence, and a parodic reflection of the world. Breaking with the theatre of psychological realism, Ionesco pioneered a form of theatre closer to our dreams and nightmares.

A world that can be explained even with bad reasons is a familiar world. But, on the other hand, in a universe suddenly divested of illusions and lights, man feels an alien, a stranger. His exile is without remedy since he is deprived of the memory of a lost home or the hope of a promised land. This divorce between man and his life, the actor and his setting, is properly the feeling of absurdity.[9]

Ionesco defined absurd as "anything without a goal . . . when man is cut off from his religious or metaphysical roots, he is lost; all his struggles become senseless, futile and oppressive."[10] The meaning of Ionesco's plays is simply what happens on stage. The old man and old woman in *The Chairs* (1952) gradually fill the stage with an increasing number of empty chairs. They address absent people in the chairs. At the play's end, the two old people leave the message of their life's meaning to be delivered by an orator, and jump out of windows to their deaths. The orator addresses the empty chairs, but he is a deaf-mute and cannot make a coherent statement. The subject of Ionesco's play is conveyed by the empty chairs themselves—the emptiness of the world.

The maid dominates the scene with the Smiths, the Martins, and the fire chief. The photo is from the original Paris production of The Bald Soprano *at Théâtre des Noctambules, 1950, directed by Nicholas Bataille.*

The Bald Soprano (produced at the Théâtre des Noctambules, Paris, 1950) is Ionesco's "antiplay" that dramatizes the absurdity of human existence. In 1948, while taking a course in conversational English, Ionesco conceived the idea of using many of the practice sentences to create a theatre piece.

Mr. and Mrs. Smith talk in clichés about the trivia of everyday life. The meaninglessness of their existence is caricatured in dialogue in which each member of a large family, living and dead, regardless of age or sex, is called Bobby Watson. Mr. and Mrs. Martin enter. They converse as strangers but gradually discover they are both from Manchester, that they arrived in London at the same time, that they live in the same house, sleep in the same bed, and are parents of the same child. The Martins and the Smiths exchange banalities, a clock strikes erratically, and the doorbell rings by itself. A fire chief arrives. Although in a hurry to extinguish all fires in the city. he launches into long-winded, pointless anecdotes. After he leaves, the two couples talk in clichés until language breaks down to basic sounds. The end of the play completes a circle: The Martins replace the Smiths and speak the same lines that opened the play.

Ionesco subtitled his first play, *The Bald Soprano* (1949), "the tragedy of language." In it, he was one of the first to confront the absurdity of the universe with new dramatic techniques. This farce, like many of his early plays, demonstrates the emptiness of middle-class life in a world devoid of significant problems (see excerpt on pages 146–148).

In more recent plays, Ionesco's concerns about middle-class conformity have a more political cutting edge. In *Rhinoceros*, written in 1958, Ionesco's hero, Bérenger, is an individual in a world of conformists. Ionesco's political concern is with people who are brutalized by dogma (in this case, fascism) and changed by it into beasts. The rhinoceros, with its thick hide and small brain, is Ionesco's brilliant analogue for the herd mentality. Bérenger emerges as a lonely but authentic hero, for he resists the physical and moral conformity that overwhelms his world and his loved ones. Like other Ionesco heroes, he represents a genuine assertion of personal value in a world dominated by nationalism, bureaucracy, and "groupthink."

His more recent plays, such as *Exit the King* (1962), *Macbett* (1972), *Man With Bags* (1975), and *Scene* (1982), are parables on human evil, the will to power, and the inevitability of death.

Summary

Drama's forms are the organization of the playwright's vision of and statement about the world. Tragedy, comedy, tragicomedy, melodrama, farce, epic, and absurdist are ways of labeling the playwright's view of the world's substance, shape, and meaning so that we can understand the world's form and substance as the playwright does. Dramatic form is conveyed to us in the theatre through numerous means: endings, situations, reversals, character awareness, social ceremonies, mood, wish fulfillment, episodes, narration, language, and staged images.

However, there is a larger pattern of writing that has the potential for becoming living words and actions. We call this pattern for "doing" or "becoming" *drama*. It all begins with the imitation of human events, speech, and behavior.

Questions for Study

1. Tragedy is the name of one dramatic form. Can you name six others?
2. What terms describe a playwright's vision of his or her world?
3. What was Aristotle's understanding of tragedy?
4. How does the hero of modern tragedy differ from Oedipus or Hamlet?
5. What are comedy's subjects?
6. How does tragicomedy combine elements of comedy and tragedy?
7. What is the origin of the word *melodrama*?
8. What different kinds of melodrama are found today on television?
9. How does farce fulfill our darkest wishes?
10. Can you describe the farce situation in a recent play, film, or television series that you have seen?
11. Why are many theatre companies adapting nondramatic materials for the stage?
12. What methods are used to create a *stage adaptation*?
13. How was *The Grapes of Wrath* adapted for the stage?
14. What is *epic theatre*?
15. What is meant by Brecht's "alienation effect"?
16. In what ways does *The Caucasian Chalk Circle* demonstrate Brecht's concept of epic theatre?
17. How does the playwright Eugene Ionesco define *absurd*?
18. How does Ionesco present life's absurd quality in *The Bald Soprano* without debating or discussing it?
19. *Plays to Read*: *Oedipus the King* by Sophocles, *Tartuffe* by Molière, *The Three Sisters* by Chekhov, and *The Bald Soprano* by Ionesco.
20. *Suggested Reading*: Leon Rubin, *The Nicholas Nickleby Story: The Making of the Historic Royal Shakespeare Company Production* (London: Heinemann, 1981).
21. *Suggested Biography*: Ronald Hayman, *Brecht: A Biography* (New York: Oxford University Press, 1983); William Wright, *Lillian Hellman: The Image, The Woman* (Simon and Schuster, 1986).

The play is a quest for a solution.
DAVID MAMET
Writing in Restaurants[1]

To read drama, the printed page of a script, is to experience much of the playwright's art. Drama has the potential for becoming human speech, action, sound, and movement. Different types of play structures and dramatic conventions help playwrights shape their materials into potential theatrical experiences for us to

6

STRUCTURES OF SEEING

Drama, the playwright's art, takes its name from the Greek verb *dran*, meaning "to do" or "to act." Drama is most often defined as a pattern of words and actions having the potential for "doing" or becoming living words and actions.

On the printed page drama is mainly *dialogue*—words arranged in sequence to be spoken by actors. Stage dialogue can be similar to the dialogue we speak in conversation with friends. In some cases, as with Shakespeare's blank verse or the complex verse forms of the Greek plays, dialogue is more formal. But stage dialogue differs from ordinary conversation in one important way: The playwright creates it and the actor speaks it. *Performability* is the link between the playwright's words and the actor's speech.

Let us begin to think about drama as a way of seeing by discussing *play*, with which it shares similar features.

Drama as Imitation

Children at play are a kind of amateur playwright as they imitate reality through playing such games as "space invaders," "school," and "dinosaurs." Children play to entertain themselves, to imitate adult behavior, and to help fit themselves into an unfamiliar world. In play, children try out and learn roles they will experience in their adult lives. In their imitations they develop what the American psychiatrist Eric Berne called *life-scripts*.

What do we mean by *imitation*, especially imitation at the psychological level? In *Play, Dreams and Imitation in Childhood* (1962), French psychologist Jean Piaget shows that we tend to imitate through play those things that arouse ambivalent emotions within us. We do this to handle the fears those things evoke because of their strangeness. We imitate the unknown as a way of mastering and gaining dominance over it. Children, adults of primitive societies, and artists all use imitation and for many of the same reasons.

So imitation is a process by which we confront and transform our fears of the strange and unknown by becoming one with them. Every drama is an imitation that confronts the mystery of human behavior. It does so concretely through *the living presence* of the actor, who is both a real person and a fictional character. The great British actor Laurence Olivier once remarked, "Acting is an almost childish wish. . . . Pretend to be somebody else. . . . Let's pretend—I suppose that's the original impulse of acting. . . ."[2]

Play and drama have much in common. The child playing firefighter or the actor playing *Hamlet* must start with a scenario or script, or imagined situation, character, dialogue, and locale. Both play and drama entertain. They contribute to a sense of well-being and to an understanding of ourselves and others. They have their own fixed rules. Most important, they *imitate human events*.

In the fourth century B.C. the Greek philosopher Aristotle (384–322) described drama as *mimesis*—the imitation of human beings in action. In his *Poetics* (c. 335–323), he showed that the playwright used certain devices to turn written material into human action: plot, character, language, ideas, music, and visual elements. From our modern perspective, we could add time and space to Aristotle's list of dramatic elements (Figure 6.1).

Drama's Elements

Drama's chief elements are still often modeled on Aristotle's criteria, beginning with plot, character, and language. *Plot* is an arranged sequence of events or incidents usually having a beginning, middle, and end. These incidents spring from an action or motive. *Character* includes the physiological and psychological makeup of the persons in the play.

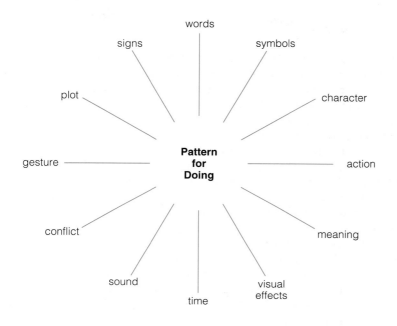

FIGURE 6.1
The elements of drama make up a pattern for doing. Today the list is more extensive than it was in Aristotle's time. Modern elements of drama are words, symbols, signs, plot, action, character, gesture, conflict, time, visual effects, sounds, and meaning.

THE ELEMENTS OF DRAMA

Language is the spoken word, including symbols and signs. The play's *meaning* is its underlying idea—its general and particular truths about experience. Today we frequently use the word *theme* or message when we talk about a play's meaning. A play may have more than one basic theme. *Macbeth*, for example, is a play about crime and punishment, but it is also about the destructive effects of power and ambition on the psyche.

Aristotle used the word *spectacle* to take in all visual and aural elements: costumes, music, and singing. In the modern theatre, we add scenery, properties, stage lighting, and sound technology to this list.

The modern idea of a play's *time* refers not to *actual time*—the length of the performance—but to *symbolic time*, which is integral to the play's structure and may be spread out over hours, days, or years. *Hamlet* takes about four hours to perform, although the story covers

HENRIK IBSEN

Henrik Ibsen (1828–1905), Norwegian playwright, is considered by many to be the most influential playwright since Shakespeare. Finding his early plays (celebrating his country's past glories) poorly received, Ibsen immigrated to Italy. There he wrote *Brand* (1865), a symbolic tragedy in verse, which brought him immediate fame. For twenty-seven years he remained with his family in self-imposed exile in Rome, Dresden, and Munich, writing such plays as *A Doll's House, Ghosts, An Enemy of the People, The Wild Duck,* and *Hedda Gabler.* These plays changed the direction of the nineteenth-century theatre. In 1891 he returned to Norway, and in 1899 completed *When We Dead Awaken,* the play that James Joyce considered his finest. He died there in 1906.

Called the father of modern drama, Ibsen wrote plays dealing with problems of contemporary life, particularly those of the individual caught in a repressive society. Although his social doctrines, radical and shocking in his own day, are no longer revolutionary, his portraits of humanity are timeless.

Ghosts, written in 1881, is the story of the Alving family. Mrs. Alving, widow of the admired and respected Captain Alving, has been living alone on her husband's estate with her maid Regina, carrying on her husband's philanthropic projects. Her son, Oswald, has returned from Paris for the dedication of an orphanage she has built.

many months. In Henrik Ibsen's *Ghosts* we are asked to believe that the incidents take place in a little more than twenty-four hours.

Action is a crucial element of drama. Aristotle did not use *action* to refer to those external deeds, incidents, situations, and events we tend to associate with a play's plot. He likened the relationship of action and drama to that of the soul and the body. He saw action as the source of the play's inner meaning, a spirit that moves through the play, holding all its elements together in a meaningful way.

American scholar Francis Fergusson defines action as "the focus or aim of psychic life from which the events, in that situation, result."[3] The source of the play's outward deeds, action embodies all the physical,

The play opens with a conversation between the carpenter Jacob Engstrand and Regina, his supposed daughter. He tries to convince the girl to do her duty to her father and become the "hostess" of a sailors' hostel, which he plans to open with his savings. Regina refuses; she hopes for a more genteel life. Pastor Manders, a long-time friend of the family, arrives to dedicate the orphanage. He and Oswald heatedly discuss new moral codes. Oswald goes into the dining room, where sounds of his advances to Regina are heard. Mrs. Alving remarks that the "ghosts" of the past have risen to haunt her.

In Act II, Mrs. Alving explains that Regina is actually Captain Alving's daughter by a serving girl, and that his upstanding reputation has been falsely derived from her own good works. At the end of Act II the orphanage burns to the ground as a result of Engstrand's carelessness.

In Act III, it is revealed that Manders' fear of scandal has led him to bribe Engstrand. (Engstrand has convinced Manders that the pastor started the fire himself.) Engstrand goes off with Regina to open the sailors' "home." Oswald confesses that he suffers from syphilis inherited from his father—another ghost. Mrs. Alving promises to give him a deadly drug should he become insane as the disease progresses. As the play ends, Oswald's mind disintegrates under a final seizure, and Mrs. Alving must decide whether to administer the drug as she has promised or to let her son live as a helpless invalid. The curtain falls as she tries to decide.

psychological, and spiritual gestures and motivations that result in the visible behavior of the characters. The action of Oedipus in Sophocles' play occurs on two levels. On one level, Oedipus' action is to find the killer of Laius, the former Theban king, and to purify the city of plague by punishing the guilty person. During his investigation of the plague's cause, Oedipus discovers that he is the guilty man, that he unwittingly killed his father and married his mother. On another, deeper level, the action of *Oedipus the King* is really a man's efforts *to know himself*. In short, action is the play's all-encompassing purpose.

Over the centuries, playwrights have developed different ways of using dramatic forms, structures, and styles to mirror the changing in-

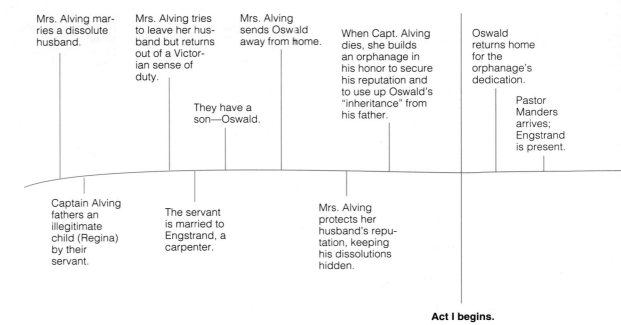

Mrs. Alving marries a dissolute husband.

Mrs. Alving tries to leave her husband but returns out of a Victorian sense of duty.

Mrs. Alving sends Oswald away from home.

When Capt. Alving dies, she builds an orphanage in his honor to secure his reputation and to use up Oswald's "inheritance" from his father.

Oswald returns home for the orphanage's dedication.

They have a son—Oswald.

Pastor Manders arrives; Engstrand is present.

Captain Alving fathers an illegitimate child (Regina) by their servant.

The servant is married to Engstrand, a carpenter.

Mrs. Alving protects her husband's reputation, keeping his dissolutions hidden.

Act I begins.

FIGURE 6.2

Climactic play structure. Ghosts, *like the classical plays* Oedipus the King *and* The Trojan Women, *begins late in the story, near the crisis and climax. All the events of the story's past (to the left of the first vertical line) occur before the play begins and are revealed in exposition. Each act of Ibsen's play ends with a climax, building to the highest point of tension: Oswald's collapse. Since a climactic plot begins late in the story, the period of time covered is usually limited.* Ghosts *begins in the afternoon and ends at sunrise the following day.*

tellectual and emotional life of their cultures. The play's structure is the playwright's way of organizing the dramatic material into a coherent whole.

Play Structures

In Western drama, plot and action are based on a central *conflict* and organized usually in the following progression: confrontation–crisis–climax–resolution. This generalization is true for plays written by William Shakespeare, Henrik Ibsen, or Sam Shepard. The way the playwright varies this pattern determines the play's structure. In general, plays have been organized in three basic ways: *climactic, episodic,* and

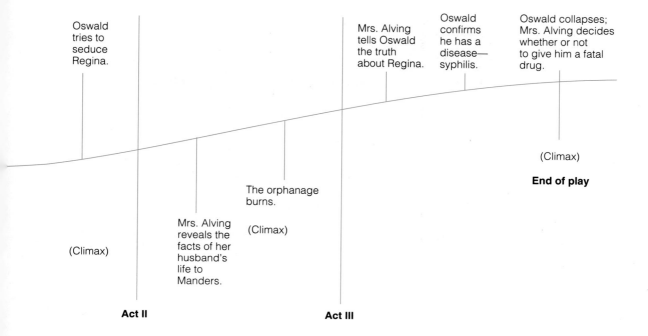

Oswald tries to seduce Regina.

Mrs. Alving tells Oswald the truth about Regina.

Oswald confirms he has a disease— syphilis.

Oswald collapses; Mrs. Alving decides whether or not to give him a fatal drug.

(Climax)

End of play

(Climax)

Mrs. Alving reveals the facts of her husband's life to Manders.

The orphanage burns.

(Climax)

Act II

Act III

situational. Entirely new structures, such as "talking pieces" and "synthetic fragments," have recently been devised.

Climactic Structure

Found in classical and modern plays, climactic structure confines the character's activities and intensifies the pressures on the characters until they are forced into irreversible acts—the **climax**. As the action develops, the characters' range of choices is reduced. In many cases, they are aware that their choices are being limited and that they are being moved toward a crisis and turning point. Climactic structure is a *cause-to-effect* arrangement of incidents ending in a climax and quick resolution.

Ibsen's *Ghosts* Mrs. Alving in Ibsen's *Ghosts* (1881) is progressively shown that the "ghosts" of her past are the cause of the present situation. Her son looks like his father; like his father, he makes advances to the serving girl; he also carries his father's moral corruption within him as a physical disease; and Mrs. Alving is conditioned to do what society dictates is proper and dutiful. Mrs. Alving has two alternatives at the play's end: to kill her terminally ill son or not. (See Figures 6.2 and 6.3.) She must choose *one.*

FIGURE 6.3

In climactic drama the characters are confined within time and space. Ghosts has five characters and takes place in Mrs. Alving's living room. As the pressures of the past go to work in the present, the choices the characters have open to them become limited. An explosive confrontation becomes inevitable. Here Mrs. Alving (Margaret Tyzack) learns the truth from Oswald (Nicholas Pennell) about his terminal disease in the 1977 Stratford Festival Theatre production of Ghosts.

Episodic Structure

Episodic play structure, found in medieval plays and the work of William Shakespeare, Bertolt Brecht, Edward Bond, and Tony Kushner, traces the characters through a *journey* of sorts to a final action and to an understanding of what the journey meant. It can always take a new turn. In Shakespeare's plays, people are not forced immediately into unmaneuverable positions. Possibilities of action are usually open to them until the very end. Events do not accumulate to confine the characters because the play encompasses large amounts of time and distance. *Hamlet* takes place over several years and countries. And the expanding plot takes in a variety of events. In this loose structure, characters are not caught in circumstances but pass through them, as Grusha does in *The Caucasian Chalk Circle*[4] (see Figure 6.4).

Brecht's *The Caucasian Chalk Circle* In *The Caucasian Chalk Circle*, Brecht tells three stories. The setting is a meeting of two Soviet collective farms in 1945 to decide which group should own a certain valley.

THE CAUCASIAN CHALK CIRCLE

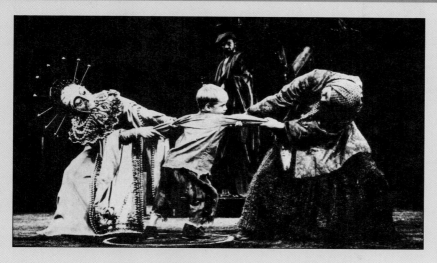

Brecht's gestic language. The circle drawn in white chalk on the stage signifies a test of true motherliness and rightful ownership based on mutual interests and well-being. The governor's wife (left) and Grusha pull at the child as Judge Azdak looks on in the 1965 production of The Caucasian Chalk Circle *at the Guthrie Theater. Grusha (Zoe Caldwell) releases the child before harming him.*

The Caucasian Chalk Circle, written by German playwright Bertolt Brecht in 1944–45, begins in 1945 with two Soviet villages disputing the ownership of a fertile valley.

Before they decide the issue, a singer entertains them with a Chinese parable, the story of the chalk circle. The scene changes to a Georgian city being overthrown by a nobles' revolt. The governor is killed, and his wife abandons their son Michael in order to escape. Grusha, a peasant girl, rescues the child and flees to the mountains. In order to give the child a name and status, she marries a peasant whom she believes is near death. When the revolt ends, the governor's wife sends soldiers to get the child. The scene shifts again, to the story of Azdak, a rogue made village judge by the rebellious soldiers. He is corrupt and prepares to judge the case of Grusha versus the governor's wife for possession of Michael. He uses the test of the chalk circle to identify the child's true mother, but reverses the outcome: The child is given to Grusha because she will *not* engage in the tug-of-war that is supposed to end in the child's being pulled out of the circle by maternal affection. He also decrees Grusha a divorce so that she can return to her soldier fiancé, Simon. Brecht's moral is that things—children, wagons, valleys—should go to those who serve them best.

Grusha's story

Prologue	Narrator tells the story of Grusha, a peasant girl, saving the governor's child in the midst of a revolution.	She flees with the child Michael to the mountains, leaving her fiancé behind.	She bargains to feed the child, escapes pursuing soldiers, and marries to provide food and shelter for Michael.	The soldiers capture Grusha and Michael; they are returned to the city.

1945— People from two valleys dispute the land's ownership.

Azdak's story

The rogue Azdak harbors a fugitive.

He turns himself in for sheltering the grand duke.

FIGURE 6.4

Episodic play structure begins early in the story and involves many characters and events. Place and event do not confine the characters; instead, the plot expands to include a variety of events and activities. Brecht's Caucasian Chalk Circle *is made up chiefly of two stories, Grusha's and Azdak's. The expanding plot moves in a linear fashion, telling the seemingly unrelated stories until Brecht combines them in the chalk-circle test to make his point about decent people caught in the injustices of a corrupt political system.*

Before they vote, they are told the stories of Grusha and the child Michael, which make up the play proper, and of the disreputable career of Azdak, a village rogue whom rebellious soldiers make a judge. The three stories come together as Azdak tries the case of the child's ownership and settles it by reversing the old test of the chalk circle. He awards the child to Grusha rather than to the biological mother (the governor's wife), who had abandoned him in wartime and now, to win custody of the child, pulls him roughly from the circle. The final moral is that both child and valley should go to those who serve them best.

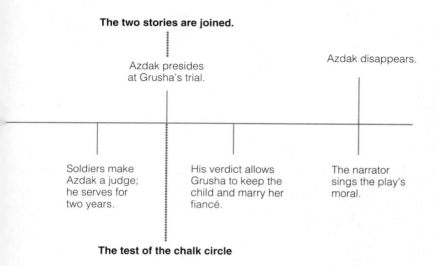

The two stories are joined.

Azdak presides
at Grusha's trial.

Azdak disappears.

Soldiers make
Azdak a judge;
he serves for
two years.

His verdict allows
Grusha to keep the
child and marry her
fiancé.

The narrator
sings the play's
moral.

The test of the chalk circle

Situational Structure

In absurdist plays of the 1950s, *situation* shapes the play, not plot or arrangement of incidents. It takes the place of the journey or the pressurized events. For example, two tramps wait for a person named Godot who never arrives (*Waiting for Godot*); a husband and wife talk in meaningless clichés as they go about their daily routines (*The Bald Soprano*).

The situation has its own inner rhythms, which are like the basic rhythms of life: day, night, day; hunger, thirst, hunger; spring, summer, winter. Although the situation usually remains unchanged, these rhythms move in a cycle.

Ionesco's *The Bald Soprano* In *The Bald Soprano* (1949), Ionesco introduces a fire chief and the Martins into Mr. and Mrs. Smith's typical middle-class English living room. After a series of absurd events, the dialogue crescendos into nonsensical babbling. The words stop abruptly

Ionesco's middle-class English couple, Mr. and Mrs. Smith, discuss dinner, the newspaper, and Bobby Watson in the original 1950 Paris production of The Bald Soprano.

The "Bobby Watson" exchange from Ionesco's *The Bald Soprano* (1950) presents aural and visual images showing the banality of middle-class suburban life. Mr. and Mrs. Smith, seated in their middle-class English living room discussing their middle-class English dinner, engage in conversation about Bobby Watson.

Another moment of silence. The clock strikes seven times. Silence. The clock strikes three times. Silence. The clock doesn't strike.

Mr. Smith *[still reading his paper]*: Tsk, it says here that Bobby Watson died.

Mrs. Smith: My God, the poor man! When did he die?

Mr. Smith: Why do you pretend to be astonished? You know very well that he's been dead these past two years. Surely you remember that we attended his funeral a year and a half ago.

Mrs. Smith: Oh yes, of course I do remember. I remembered it right away, but I don't understand why you yourself were so surprised to see it in the paper.

Mr. Smith: It wasn't in the paper. It's been three years since his death was announced. I remembered it through an association of ideas.

Mrs. Smith: What a pity! He was so well preserved.

Mr. Smith: He was the handsomest corpse in Great Britain. He didn't look his age. Poor Bobby, he'd been dead for four years and he was still warm. A veritable living corpse. And how cheerful he was!

Mrs. Smith: Poor Bobby.

Mr. Smith: Which poor Bobby do you mean?

Mrs. Smith: It is his wife that I mean. She is called Bobby too, Bobby Watson. Since they both had the same name, you could never tell one from the other when you saw them together. It was only after his death that you could really tell which was which. And there are still people today who confuse her with the deceased and offer their condolences to him. Do you know her?

Mr. Smith: I only met her once, by chance, at Bobby's burial.

Mrs. Smith: I've never seen her. Is she pretty?

Mr. Smith: She has regular features and yet one cannot say that she is pretty. She is too big and stout. Her features are not regular but still one can say that she is very pretty. She is a little too small and too thin. She's a voice teacher.

[The clock strikes five times. A long silence.]

Mrs. Smith: And when do they plan to be married, those two?

Mr. Smith: Next spring, at the latest.

Mrs. Smith: We shall have to go to their wedding, I suppose.

Mr. Smith: We shall have to give them a wedding present. I wonder what?

Mrs. Smith: Why don't we give them one of the seven silver salvers that were given us for our wedding and which have never been of any use to us? *[Silence]*

Mrs. Smith: How sad for her to be left a widow so young.

Mr. Smith: Fortunately, they had no children.

Mrs. Smith: That was all they needed! Children! Poor woman, how could she have managed!

Mr. Smith: She's still young. She might very well remarry. She looks so well in mourning.

Mrs. Smith: But who would take care of the children? You know very well that they have a boy and a girl. What are their names?

Mr. Smith: Bobby and Bobby like their parents. Bobby Watson's uncle, old Bobby Watson, is a rich man and very fond of the boy. He might very well pay for Bobby's education.

Mrs. Smith: That would be proper. And Bobby Watson's aunt, old Bobby Watson, might very well, in her turn, pay for the education of Bobby Watson,

continued on next page

continued from page 147

Bobby Watson's daughter. That way Bobby, Bobby Watson's mother, could remarry. Has she anyone in mind?

Mr. Smith: Yes, a cousin of Bobby Watson's.

Mrs. Smith: Who? Bobby Watson?

Mr. Smith: Which Bobby Watson do you mean?

Mrs. Smith: Why, Bobby Watson, the son of old Bobby Watson, the late Bobby Watson's other uncle.

Mr. Smith: No, it's not that one, it's someone else. It's Bobby Watson, the son of old Bobby Watson, the late Bobby Watson's aunt.

Mrs. Smith: Are you referring to Bobby Watson the commercial traveler?

Mr. Smith: All the Bobby Watsons are commercial travelers.

Mrs. Smith: What a difficult trade! However, they do well at it.

Mr. Smith: Yes, when there's no competition.

Mrs. Smith: And when is there no competition?

Mr. Smith: On Tuesdays, Thursdays, and Tuesdays.

Mrs. Smith: Ah! Three days a week? And what does Bobby Watson do on those days?

Mr. Smith: He rests, he sleeps.

Mrs. Smith: But why doesn't he work those three days if there's no competition?

Mr. Smith: I don't know everything. I can't answer all your idiotic questions! . . . [5]

and the play begins again. This time Mr. and Mrs. Martin are seated as the Smiths were at the play's beginning, and they repeat the Smiths' lines from the first scene. With this repetition, Ionesco demonstrates the interchangeability of middle-class lives. (See Figure 6.5. For more on Ionesco, see p. 130.)

Recent Structures

Solo Text

Solo performances have a long stage history, beginning with medieval mimes and jugglers. Most recently in the mainstream of the American commercial theatre, we have seen Julie Harris as Emily Dickinson, Pat Carroll as Gertrude Stein, and Robert Morse as Truman Capote. However, solo performances have also become a vital part of our contempo-

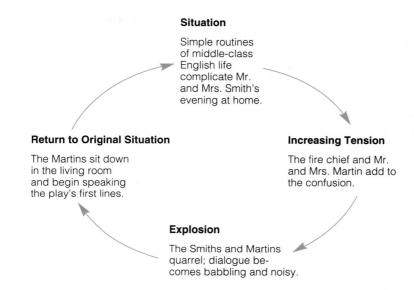

Situation

Simple routines of middle-class English life complicate Mr. and Mrs. Smith's evening at home.

Increasing Tension

The fire chief and Mr. and Mrs. Martin add to the confusion.

Explosion

The Smiths and Martins quarrel; dialogue becomes babbling and noisy.

Return to Original Situation

The Martins sit down in the living room and begin speaking the play's first lines.

FIGURE 6.5

Situational play structure in Ionesco's The Bald Soprano. *The "theatre of the absurd" emerged in Europe following World War II. Absurdist plays convey a sense of alienation, of people having lost their bearings in an illogical or ridiculous world. Situational play structure mirrors this worldview.*

rary avant-garde, as evidenced in the work of Spalding Gray, Anna Deavere Smith, Tim Miller, Karen Finley, and others. In the 1990s, the solo performer has provided a low-budget means of exploring (often with nudity and explicit language) such timely issues as censorship, pornography, AIDS, feminism, dysfunctional families, prostitution, racism, and alternative lifestyles. The solo text is a highly personal response to today's social issues, while at the same time a powerful means of speaking directly to America's collective conscience. Spalding Gray has been working with this minimalist form since the 1960s.

Gray's "Talking Pieces" In the late 1970s, the inflationary economy and the lack of large social and political issues resulted in the disbanding of many of the American theatrical collectives that had gathered momentum in the 1960s over issues like the Vietnam War. Many performers, such as Spalding Gray, who had worked for a time with Richard Schechner's Performance Group in New York, turned to creating a new kind of theatre piece for the solo performer (and also for small casts). Gray's pieces, developed for performance by him, have been called "talking pieces," even "epic monologues." They represent a new and interesting dramatic structure, as well as theatre event.

Gray improvised his memories, free associations, and ideas of childhood, family relationships, and private emotions to create an open narrative of personal actions.[6] Using properties bought at Woolworth's, a tape recorder, old family photograph albums, slide projections, and phonograph records, he worked before small audiences that included director Elizabeth LeCompte of the Wooster Group, giving shape to his autobiographical sketches. The text as it developed was talked through with the director and audiences in what Gray calls "an act of public memory." Once satisfied with the final product, Gray "set" the text. Because of these improvisational methods, Gray refers to the pieces as "poetic journalism" or as "talking pieces"—a series of simple actions using free associations as building blocks to create a series of images like personal, living Rorschachs.

Gray's series of monologues, or talking pieces, include *Sex and Death to the Age 14*; *A Personal History of the American Theatre*; *Booze, Cars and College Girls*; *Terrors of Pleasure*; *Monster in a Box*; and *Gray's Anatomy*. Even in the trilogy *Three Places in Rhode Island*, the monologue remains a foundation stone. *Rumstick Road* opens with a monologue in which Gray discusses his acting career, his mother's psychiatric treatment, her Christian Science faith, her illness from cancer, and her eventual suicide.

Monodrama

Since the original production of *Waiting for Godot* in 1953, Samuel Beckett has been a major influence on experimentalists looking for ways to introduce into the theatre intuitive events, talking pieces, interior monologues, and minimal staging. To do so required new dramatic forms, conventions, and performance techniques. Cause-to-effect plots, soliloquies, and formal exposition were no longer adequate.

Beckett's **monologues** and narrative voices in his novels and plays, together with his minimal staging (an old man, a table, and a tape recorder; a woman buried in a mound of dirt; two lips speaking; a woman in a rocking chair), influenced the work of Lee Breuer, Sam Shepard, Spalding Gray, Harold Pinter, and others. The aim of the convention (let us call it *monodrama*) is the same as that of the stream-of-

SPALDING GRAY

Spalding Gray is a theatre creator, performer, and teacher. A graduate of Emerson College, he came to New York in 1967, where he performed in Off Broadway plays. He worked for brief periods with the Alley Theatre in Houston and with Joseph Chaikin's Open Theatre before joining Richard Schechner's Performance Group in 1969. There he played in Sam Shepard's *The Tooth of Crime* and in Bertolt Brecht's *Mother Courage*. In 1975, he and Elizabeth LeCompte, with other former members of the Performance Group, formed the Wooster Group.

For the Wooster Group, Gray composed and/or performed in *Sakonnet Point, Rumstick Road, Nayatt School, Point Judith*, and *Route 1 & 9*. The first three are known as *The Trilogy: Three Places in Rhode Island*, based on Gray's life. He also created a series of monologues, or talking pieces, with the Wooster Group, including *Swimming to Cambodia* (1983), a monologue about that country, Thailand, Hollywood, and his participation as an actor in the film *The Killing Fields. Terrors of Pleasure* (1990), *Monster in a Box* (1992), *Gray's Anatomy* (1993), and his novel *Impossible Vacation* (1993) are his most recent works.

Gray has taught in the Experimental Theatre Wing of New York University's School of Drama and has led many workshops there and in India and Europe. The emphasis of his workshops for both children and adults is autobiographical; participants are encouraged to develop material and theatrical metaphors from their own lives.

consciousness novel: to present the conscious and unconscious thought processes of the speaker. To take us into the character's or speaker's consciousness in the theatre, playwrights (following Beckett's lead) have introduced electronic amplification, sound tracks, holograms, and voice-overs.

Beckett's *Rockaby* *Rockaby*, written in 1980, was interpreted for New York audiences in 1984 by British actress Billie Whitelaw and directed by Alan Schneider. *Rockaby* is a fifteen-minute monodrama in which a

Billie Whitelaw as the woman in the rocking chair in Samuel Beckett's Rockaby, *directed by Alan Schneider, at the Samuel Beckett Theater, New York, 1984.*

W = *Woman in chair.*
V = *Her recorded voice.*
Fade up on W in rocking chair facing front downstage slightly off centre audience left. Long pause.

W: More.

   Pause. Rock and voice together.

V: till in the end
   the day came
   in the end came
   close of a long day
   when she said

to herself
whom else
time she stopped
time she stopped
going to and fro
all eyes
all sides
high and low

for another
another like herself
another creature like herself
a little like
going to and fro
all eyes
all sides
high and low
for another
till in the end
close of a long day
to herself
whom else
time she stopped
time she stopped
going to and fro
all eyes
all sides
high and low
for another
another living soul
one other living soul
going to and fro
all eyes like herself
all sides
high and low
for another
another like herself
a little like
going to and fro
till in the end
close of a long day
to herself
whom else
time she stopped
going to and fro
time she stopped

time she stopped

Together: echo of "time she stopped,"
coming to rest of rock, faint fade of light.

Long pause.

W: More.

Pause. Rock and voice together.

V: so in the end
close of a long day
went back in
in the end went back in
saying to herself
whom else
time she stopped
time she stopped
going to and fro
time she went and sat
at her window
quiet at her window
facing other windows
so in the end
close of a long day
in the end went and sat
went back in and sat
at her window
let up the blind and sat
quiet at her window
only window
facing other windows
other only windows
all eyes
all sides
high and low
for another

continued on next page

at her window
another like herself
a little like
another living soul
one other living soul
at her window
gone in like herself
gone back in
in the end
close of a long day
saying to herself
whom else
time she stopped
time she stopped
going to and fro
time she went and sat
at her window
quiet at her window
only window
facing other windows
other only windows
all eyes
all sides
high and low
for another
another like herself
a little like
another living soul
one other living soul

Together: echo of "living soul,"
coming to rest of rock, faint fade
of light.

Long pause.

W: More.

Pause. Rock and voice together.

V: till in the end
the day came
in the end came
close of a long day
sitting at her window
quiet at her window
only window
facing other windows
other only windows
all blinds down
never one up
hers alone up
till the day came
in the end came
close of a long day
sitting at her window
quiet at her window
all eyes
all sides
high and low
for a blind up
one blind up
no more
never mind a face
behind the pane
famished eyes
like hers
to see
be seen
no
a blind up
like hers
a little like
one blind up no more
another creature there
somewhere there
behind the pane

another living soul
one other living soul
till the day came
in the end came
close of a long day
when she said
to herself
whom else
time she stopped
time she stopped
sitting at her window
quiet at her window
only window
facing other windows
other only windows
all eyes
all sides
high and low
time she stopped
time she stopped

Together: echo of "time she stopped,"
coming to rest of rock, faint fade
of light.

Long pause.

W: More.

Pause. Rock and voice together.

V: so in the end
close of a long day
went down
in the end went down
down the steep stair
let down the blind and down
right down
into the old rocker

mother rocker
where mother sat
all the years
all in black
best black
sat and rocked
rocked
till her end came
in the end came
off her head they said
gone off her head
but harmless
no harm in her
dead one day
no
night
dead one night
in the rocker
in her best black
head fallen
and the rocker rocking
rocking away
so in the end
close of a long day
went down
in the end went down
down the steep stair
let down the blind and down
right down
into the old rocker
those arms at last
and rocked
rocked
with closed eyes
closing eyes

continued on next page

she so long all eyes
famished eyes
all sides
high and low
to and fro
at her window
to see
be seen
till in the end
close of a long day
to herself
whom else
time she stopped
let down the blind and stopped
time she went down
down the steep stair
time she went right down
was her own other
own other living soul
so in the end
close of a long day
went down

down the steep stair
let down the blind and down
right down
into the old rocker
and rocked
rocked
saying to herself
no
done with that
the rocker
those arms at last
saying to the rocker
rock her off
stop her eyes
fuck life
stop her eyes
rock her off
rock her off

Together: echo of "rock her off," coming to rest of rock, slow fade out.

woman, seated in a rocking chair, rocks herself into the grave (see box, pp. 152–57). The actress speaks only one word ("more") four times. The single word is separated by a litany of other words recorded on tape by the actress. The words on tape represent the final thrashings of the woman's consciousness. As death comes, she ceases rocking. A single stage light picks out the actress' face; her eyes are closed. Then the darkness is total.

With no scenery, one actor, few words, and scant movement, Beckett makes us feel the weight of the solitary, seemingly endless night of living. Death comes as a release—a happy ending.

NOTES

LIGHT

Subdued on chair. Rest of stage dark. Subdued spot on face constant throughout, unaffected by successive fades. Either wide enough to include narrow limits of rock or concentrated on face when still or at mid-rock. Then throughout speech face slightly swaying in and out of light. Opening fade-up: first spot on face alone. Long pause. Then light on chair. Final fade-out: first chair. Long pause with spot on face alone. Head slowly sinks, comes to rest. Fade out spot.

W

Prematurely old. Unkempt grey hair. Huge eyes in white expressionless face. White hands holding ends of armrests.

EYES

Now closed, now open in unblinking gaze. About equal proportions section 1, increasingly closed 2 and 3, closed for good halfway through 4.

COSTUME

Black lacy high-necked evening gown. Long sleeves. Jet sequins to glitter when rocking. Incongruous frivolous headdress set askew with extravagant trimmings to catch light when rocking.

ATTITUDE

Completely still till fade-out of chair. Then in light of spot head slowly inclined.

CHAIR

Pale wood highly polished to gleam when rocking. Footrest. Vertical back. Rounded inward curving arms to suggest embrace.

ROCK

Slight. Slow. Controlled mechanically without assistance from W.

VOICE

Lines in italics spoken by W with V a little softer each time. W's "More" a little softer each time. Towards end of section 4, say from "saying to herself" on, voice gradually softer.[7]

Theatre of Images

In 1976 critic Bonnie Marranca coined the label "The Theatre of Images" to describe the works of American writer-director-designer-composers Robert Wilson, Philip Glass, and Lee Breuer. Revolting against words and "old-fashioned" verbal texts, these innovators independently created theatre events dominated by visual and aural images. Since the early 1970s, their avant-garde experiments have evolved in form and structure to resemble the painter's collage. Absent are climactic drama's cause-to-effect relationships of action, plot, and character.

PLAYWRIGHT-PRODUCER

ROBERT WILSON

The Black Rider: The Casting of the Magic Bullets *premiered in Hamburg, Germany, in 1990 with direction and stage design by Robert Wilson.*

Born in 1941, Robert Wilson created the Byrd Hoffman Foundation to work with autistic children, as well as performers of all ages, on developing a new kind of theatre. The results were unusually long performances—five to seven hours—intended to provoke contemplation rather than to tell a story.

In their place we find actors juxtaposed with holographic shapes, atonal sounds, and sculpted images that develop as large-scale performances requiring more than a few hours to complete. This new mixture of creative sources (sound, music, light, technology, text) ultimately raises the same issues as more traditional theatre: questions of humanity's relationship to society, to environment, and to itself.

Robert Wilson, a student of architecture and painting, creates living pictures on stage with sounds, sculpted forms, music, and visual im-

158   *Chapter Six*

Wilson's productions "assemble" actors, sounds, music, light, and shadow to comment on American society and cultural myths. They are known as much for their length and complexity as for their unique titles:

- *The Life and Times of Joseph Stalin*
- *Einstein on the Beach*
- *The Life and Times of Sigmund Freud*
- *A Letter for Queen Victoria*
- *Death Destruction and Detroit*
- *I was Sitting on My Patio This Guy Appeared I Thought I Was Hallucinating*
- *The Golden Windows*
- *The Knee Plays*
- the *CIVIL warS: a tree is best measured when it is down*
- *The Forest*
- *Danton's Death*
- *The Black Rider: The Casting of the Magic Bullets*

His epic productions stretch the audience's attention in an attempt to alter perceptual awareness of people, places, and things. Wilson has said of his work: "Most theatre that we see today is thought about in terms of the word, the text.... And that's not the case with my work. In my theatre, what we see is as important as what we hear. What we see does not have to relate to what we hear. They can be independent."[8]

ages that require many hours to experience. (One of his productions, *Ka Mountain*, lasted seven days.) *A Letter for Queen Victoria*, which appeared briefly on Broadway in 1974, is composed of bits and pieces of overheard conversations, clichés, newspaper blurbs, colors, spot announcements, television images, and film clips. One theme of the piece was American imperialism, but instead of discussing the topic, Wilson simply projected *images* of it: In Act II, pilots talk about faraway lands against a background of sounds of gunfire and bomb blasts.

THEATRE FOR A
HIGH-TECH WORLD

Robert Wilson, Philip Glass, and Lee Breuer have forged a new kind of theatre for the twenty-first century, manipulating technology to create experiences for audiences that they cannot find in any other medium.

The Forest. *Scene from the 1988 American premiere of Robert Wilson's* The Forest *(with music by David Byrne) based on* The Epic of Gilgamesh *and produced at the Brooklyn Academy of Music. Enkidu (right, actor Howie Seago), the story's hero, confronts images of civilization's history: hunter, whore, slave, priest, scholar, and godhead. Wilson's production takes Enkidu on a journey through the history of civilization from primitive times up through the nineteenth-century industrial revolution and the end of the "modern" world.*

Einstein on the Beach. *Originally produced in 1976 for two sold-out perfor-mances at the Metropolitan Opera House, New York City,* Einstein on the Beach *is a collaboration between Robert Wilson and composer Philip Glass. The five-hour production dealt with contradictions implicit in the genius Albert Einstein and his legacy to our world. Seen here are dancers Sheryl Sutton and Lucinda Childs as sculpted forms. In the background is a projected image of the young Einstein. From the revival staged at the 1984 Next Wave Festival, the Brooklyn Academy of Music, New York. (Photo by Paula Court)*

The Knee Plays. *Originally intended as an interlude between the fifteen scenes of the CIVIL warS (and also used again in The Forest), The Knee Plays, created by Robert Wilson in 1984, consists of thirteen vignettes running about ninety minutes in performance. With music and lyrics by David Byrne (of The Talking Heads), the company of nine dancers creates a cascade of imagery—visual, aural, verbal, and choreographic—focusing on "a tree of life." Using square modules, puppets, and masks, they tell a story dealing with the life cycle through history, beginning with the tree of life and proceeding through the American Civil War.*

1,000 Airplanes on the Roof *(1988).*
Music by Philip Glass and libretto by
David Henry Hwang. The actor is
diminished by the holographic image
of a highrise architectural structure
that dominates the scene.

The Voyage *with music and story created by Philip Glass (with libretto by*
David Henry Hwang) for the Metropolitan Opera Company's Christopher
Columbus Quincentenary celebration in 1992. Production design by Robert
Israel tells the story visually of people who have the courage to follow where
their vision leads.

Wilson's *the CIVIL warS* One of Wilson's boldest ventures is the opera *the CIVIL warS: a tree is best measured when it is down* (1984), a collaborative work involving German playwright Heiner Müller, American composer Philip Glass, and others. Although Wilson first thought of the work as an exploration of the American Civil War and the Industrial Revolution, as he continued to develop his themes he expanded his vision to include all "civil struggles" that have existed throughout history, from mythological Greece to the distant future. With haunting, violent images of the American Civil War at its center, its recurrent theme is destruction and death contrasted with the importance of civilization and the value of life.

Wilson's theatre combines architectural landscapes, striking verbal and musical images, long physical and verbal pauses that exaggerate our sense of time passing, and incongruous characters (including astronauts, Robert E. Lee, and Dorothy and the Tin Man of Oz). Literally towering above them all is Abraham Lincoln, a sixteen-foot-tall figure formed by a singer suspended in a harness and wearing a long black coat—the startling image of the "tree" that is best measured when cut down.

Summary

Drama is a special way of imitating human behavior and events. Just as children imitate adults as a way of mastering the strangeness of the world around them, so playwrights create dramatic blueprints representing physical and psychological experience to give shape and meaning to their world as they see it.

Drama comes from the Greek *dran*, meaning "to do" or "to act." From our modern perspective, it defines an art form having the potential for placing *action* before us in a performance space. That action takes many forms, depending on the playwright's attitudes and interpretations of experience. For 2,500 years, the major Western play structures have been climactic, episodic, and situational, and drama's conventions have been fairly consistent, relying on exposition, crisis, climax, and resolution to convey the play's meaning to audiences.

But in a world of high technology and ambivalent meanings, writers and directors have tried different methods to create verbal and visual texts that speak to audiences familiar with computer graphics, sophisticated electronic sound systems, video equipment, and spectacular holographic effects. Almost in ironic juxtaposition to the elaborate technology being brought into the theatre space is the minimalist art of Samuel Beckett. Imagistic texts, both *elaborate* and *minimal*, by Robert Wilson and Samuel Beckett, have articulated in performance the difficulties of what it means to be a human being in the world of the last quarter of the twentieth century. Like the texts themselves, *language* for the theatre has its own special techniques and ways of communicating to audiences.

Questions for Study

1. What is *dialogue*?
2. What similarities are there between children at play and writers creating plays?
3. What is *mimesis*?
4. What is the difference between a play's *actual time* and its *symbolic time*?
5. What are the basic differences between *climactic*, *episodic*, and *situational* play structure? Give examples of each.
6. Describe the relationship of *solo texts* (and performances) to today's theatre and society.
7. Describe a solo performance that you have seen.
8. What are *talking pieces*? Discuss Spalding Gray's performance work.
9. What is *monodrama*? Describe Beckett's *Rockaby* as monodrama.
10. In what ways does the theatre of Robert Wilson reflect a high-tech world?
11. *Plays to Read*: Henrik Ibsen's *Ghosts*, Bertolt Brecht's *The Caucasian Chalk Circle*, Eugene Ionesco's *The Bald Soprano*.
12. *Suggested Viewing*: Videos of Spalding Gray in *Swimming to Cambodia* or *Monster in a Box*; and Robert Wilson's *Einstein on the Beach*.

All that lives by the fact of living, has a form, and by the same token must die—except the work of art which lives forever in so far as it *is* form.[1]
LUIGI PIRANDELLO

Playwrights have common strategies to develop plot, character, and action; to manipulate time; and to end plays. Taken all together, dramatic conventions are agreed-upon artistic means used to communicate information and experience to audiences.

7

DRAMA'S CONVENTIONS

Over the years, playwrights have worked out various strategies to convey experience and activity to audiences. They have evolved dramatic conventions—their ground rules—to set plot and character in motion. A *convention* is an agreed-upon method of quickly getting something across to an audience. Just as we have social conventions in life to help us meet strangers or answer the telephone, so the playwright has conventions to solve problems, pass along information, develop plot and action, and create interest and suspense. These shortcuts make it possible for the playwright to give information and to present experiences that in life would require weeks or even years, to tell two or three stories at once, and to complicate the stage action without confusing the audience. What follows is a discussion of nine *dramatic conventions*: stage directions, exposition, point of attack, complication, crisis, climax, resolution, double plots, and the play-within-the-play.

Writing Conventions

Stage Directions

Before the printing press made possible a general readership for plays, stage directions (if they existed at all) were used solely by theatre personnel. In modern editions of *Hamlet*, for example, we find such abbreviated directions as "*A flourish,*" "*Exeunt,*" "*Aside,*" "*Dies,*" and "*Exit Ghost.*" We assume that these directions were added later to Shakespeare's original promptbook by playwrights or players. Nevertheless, by modern standards, the directions are sparse.

FIGURE 7.1

Tennessee Williams' A Streetcar Named Desire *(1947) was designed by Jo Mielziner to capture the atmosphere of the cramped apartment where Stanley and Stella live.*

Modern stage directions are included at the beginning of each act and provide information about how the playwright imagined details of the three-dimensional stage space, such as Mrs. Alving's drawing room in *Ghosts* or the Kowalski apartment in *A Streetcar Named Desire*. Often, stage directions are added as a result of the director's and actors' contributions to the script during rehearsals and performance. Stage directions include facts about geography, season of the year, time of day or night, weather conditions, decor, dress, mood, stage properties, music cues, and general impressions of place or environment. The opening stage direction in *A Streetcar Named Desire* is a full page in length. In it, Tennessee Williams evokes atmosphere with graphic details of place, time, light, and sound: New Orleans, Elysian Fields Avenue, a May twilight, blue sky, barroom piano music. The age, dress, and movements of Stanley Kowalski and his friend Mitch are described: They are twenty-eight or thirty years old and wear blue denim work clothes.

SCENE ONE

The exterior of a two-story corner building on a street in New Orleans which is named Elysian Fields and runs between the L & N tracks and the river. The section is poor but, unlike corresponding sections in other American cities, it has a raffish charm. The houses are mostly white frame, weathered grey, with rickety outside stairs and galleries

A tender moment between actors Jessica Tandy as Blanche DuBois and Karl Malden as Mitch in the original New York production of A Streetcar Named Desire *(1947), directed by Elia Kazan.*

Tennessee Williams' *A Streetcar Named Desire* was first produced at the Barrymore Theatre, New York, in 1947. Her family's Mississippi estate sold, Blanche DuBois arrives at the New Orleans tenement home of Stella and Stanley Kowalski, her pregnant sister and her brother-in-law. Blanche's faded gentility clashes with Stanley's brutish masculinity. As she seeks protection from the world, she competes with Stanley for Stella's affections but finds herself no match for his sexual hold over her sister. She tries to charm Mitch, Stanley's poker-playing friend, into marrying her. However, Stanley destroys Blanche's hopes for marriage by telling Mitch about her past drunkenness and promiscuity. As Stella reproaches Stanley for his cruelty, her labor pains begin and Stanley rushes her to the hospital.

Blanche is visited by a drunken Mitch, who accuses her of lying to him and makes an effort to seduce her. Stanley returns to find Blanche dressed for a party, fantasizing about an invitation to go on a cruise with a wealthy friend. Angered by her pretensions, Stanley starts a fight with her that ends in rape. In a final scene some weeks later, Blanche, her tenuous hold on reality shattered, is taken to a mental hospital.

The tragedy of *Streetcar* reveals human duplicity and desperation in Williams' modern South, where fragile people are overcome by violence and vulgarity.

and quaintly ornamented gables. This building contains two flats, up-stairs and down. Faded white stairs ascend to the entrances of both.

It is first dark of an evening early in May. The sky that shows around the dim white building is a peculiarly tender blue, almost a turquoise, which invests the scene with a kind of lyricism and gracefully attenuates the atmosphere of decay. You can almost feel the warm breath of the brown river beyond the river warehouses with their faint redolences of bananas and coffee. A corresponding air is evoked by the music of Negro entertainers at a barroom around the corner. In this part of New Orleans you are practically always just around the corner, or a few doors down the street, from a tinny piano being played with the infatuated fluency of brown fingers. This "Blue Piano" expresses the spirit of the life which goes on here.

Two women, one white and one colored, are taking the air on the steps of the building. The white woman is Eunice, who occupies the upstairs flat; the colored woman a neighbor, for New Orleans is a cosmopolitan city where there is a relatively warm and easy intermingling of races in the old part of town.

Above the music of the "Blue Piano" the voices of people on the street can be heard overlapping.

[Two men come around the corner, Stanley Kowalski and Mitch. They are about twenty-eight or thirty years old, roughly dressed in blue denim work clothes. Stanley carries his bowling jacket and a red-stained package from a butcher's. They stop at the foot of the steps.][2]

Blanche, Stella's sister—dressed for a garden party in white suit, hat, gloves—comes unexpectedly into this setting. Williams describes her appearance:

She is about five years older than Stella. Her delicate beauty must avoid a strong light. There is something about her uncertain manner, as well as her white clothes, that suggest a moth.

In contrast, Shakespeare and his contemporaries did not have the advantage of sophisticated print technology. Nor were they interested in the specifics of environment as a factor that shapes human events. Their writing tradition placed all indications of time, place, weather, and mood in the dialogue of the minor characters in the play's beginning moments. They provided the background information and also captured the audience's attention preparatory to the entrance of the principals. In the jargon of the theatre, these are "weather lines." Within eleven lines at the beginning of *Hamlet*, the two guards give us a sense of place ("castle battlements"), time ("'Tis now struck twelve"), weather ("'Tis bitter cold"), mood ("I am sick at heart"), and what's happening ("not a mouse stirring").

Stage directions are an important part of writing conventions, especially in the modern theatre. They provide crucial information for the reader about how the playwright has imagined the play's environment and the characters' age and appearance.

Exposition

In a play's opening scene we are frequently given certain information about what is going on, what has happened in the past, and who is to be seen. This is one type of *exposition*. In Euripides' *The Trojan Women* (415 B.C.) a prologue, which gives the essential exposition, is spoken by the sea god Poseidon and Athene, the goddess defender of Troy. First, Poseidon describes the treachery of the Greeks' use of the Trojan horse to gain entry into the city of Troy, the city's collapse, and the fate of its defenders. Athene describes how the Greeks defiled her altars in Troy. Second, the exposition then shifts to the human level. Troy's Queen Hecuba describes the physical and mental suffering of the Trojan people. Following this background information, the action begins; we learn one by one the fate of the women and the death sentence assigned to Hector's young son, Astyanax.

Poseidon, the god of the sea, speaks this prologue to Euripides' *The Trojan Women*, describing the destruction of Troy by the Greek armies as well as the action of the play—the assignment by lottery of the captured women to the Greek conquerors. He blames the holocaust on the goddess Athene.

Poseidon:

I come from the salt depths of the Aegean Sea,
Where the white feet of Nereids tread their circling dance:
I am Poseidon. Troy and its people were my city.
That ring of walls and towers I and Apollo built—
Squared every stone in it; and my affection has not faded.

The Greeks *presented by the Royal Shakespeare Company in London, 1979. In the foreground is Billie Whitelaw as Andromache; in the background Eliza Ward as Hecuba holds the child Astyanax, in* Part One: The War *(from* The Trojan Women*). The production was directed by John Barton and designed by John Napier.*

The Trojan Women, written by Euripides and produced in 415 B.C. at the Theatre of Dionysus, Athens, is the third (and only surviving) play in his trilogy about Troy—its destruction, the death of its defenders, and the enslavement of its women.

Now Troy lies dead under the conquering Argive spear,
Stripped, sacked and smouldering.

      Epeius, a Phocian from Parnassus, made
To Athene's plan that horse pregnant with armed men,
Called by all future ages the Wooden Horse, and sent it
To glide, weighty with hidden death, through the Trojan
    walls.
The sacred groves are deserted; the temples run with blood;

In a prologue we witness the sea god Poseidon agree to aid Athene—goddess defender of Troy—in her revenge: To teach them to respect all gods, he will destroy the Greeks on their victorious voyage home.

Amid the ruins of Troy, Queen Hecuba (wife of Troy's dead King Priam and mother of Hector, the chief Trojan warrior slain in battle), describes her physical and mental suffering. She calls on the chorus (the captive women) to lament Troy's fate. Talthybius, the Greek messenger, arrives the first of four times to announce decisions made by the Greek generals about the women. Eventually, Talthybius announces that Cassandra goes to Agamemnon, Andromache to Achilles' son, Helen to Menelaus, and Queen Hecuba to Odysseus. These scenes are further complicated by the trial of Helen of Troy and the execution of Hector's young son, Astyanax. On his third entrance Talthybius brings the child's body carried on Hector's shield. Hecuba pronounces his funeral oration and the body is carried off on the shield for burial.

Talthybius' last entrance ends the waiting period and all suspense. Troy is set afire and the captives are ordered to the ships. Hecuba tries to run into the flames, but Talthybius stops her because she is "Odysseus' property."

In Euripides' universe, gods are as vengeful and irrational as human beings. It is a universe without order; therefore, the spectacle of the human dilemma is pitiable but without moral or ethical meaning. A line in the play sums up his vision: "The man who sacks cities is a fool; he makes temples and tombs, the shrines of the dead, a desert, and then perishes himself."

On Zeus the Protector's altar-steps Priam lies dead.
Measureless gold and all the loot of Troy goes down
To the Greek ships; and now they wait for a following wind
To make glad, after ten long years, with the sight of their
    wives and children
The men who sailed from Greece to attack and destroy this
    town.

  Athene, and Hera of Argos, the gods who joined in league

To achieve this end, have worsted me: now I must leave
Ilion the famous, leave my altars. When desolation
Falls like a blight, the day for the worship of gods is
    past.

    Scamandros echoes with endless cries of captured women
Assigned by lottery as slaves to various Greeks—Arcadians,
Thessalians, or Athenians. Those not yet allotted
Are in this house, reserved for the chiefs of the Greek army;
With them, justly held as a prisoner, is Tyndareus' daughter,
Spartan Helen. But if you would see misery itself,
Here by the door, prostrate, shedding unmeasured tears
For griefs unmeasured, Hecabe lies. She does not know
That her daughter Polyxena died just now most pitiably,
An offering slaughtered at Achilles' grave. Her husband,
    Priam,
Is dead; so are her sons. Her daughter the prophetess,
Cassandra, whom Apollo himself left virgin,—she
Will be taken by force, in contempt of the god and all pious
    feeling
By King Agamemnon as his concubine.
                  Farewell, then, city!
Superb masonry, farewell! You have had your day of glory.
You would stand firm yet, were it not for Athene, daughter
    of Zeus.

    In contrast to the formal exposition of Greek plays, some modern plays begin with a telephone ringing; the person answering—for instance, a maid or butler in drawing-room comedy—gives the background information by talking to an unseen party about the family, its plans, and conflicts.

    In most cases, plays begin with informational exchanges of dialogue. *Macbeth* begins ominously with the three witches in thunder and lightning against a background of battle. They are planning their next meeting "when the battle's lost and won," after which they'll meet Macbeth on the heath. The implication is that no good will come of this meeting.

    Contemporary drama presents less information of this kind. Instead of asking who these people are and what is going to happen next, we usually ask: "What's going on now?"

Point of Attack

The moment early in the play when the story is taken up is the *point of attack*. In *Macbeth*, the point of attack grows out of the victorious battle reports to King Duncan who, learning of the death of the traitorous Thane of Cawdor, rewards Macbeth with that title. In the very next scene Macbeth encounters the witches, who greet him with many prophecies, including the title "Thane of Cawdor." Macbeth begins to consider the witches' prophecy that he might become more than a mere thane and writes to his wife, who initiates the murder of King Duncan.

Complication, Crisis, Climax

The middle of a play is made up of *complications*—new information introduced by new characters, unexpected events, or newly disclosed facts. Macbeth's encounter with the witches is the beginning of many violent complications. In *Ghosts*, Mrs. Alving overhears Oswald seducing Regina, who is the child of her husband and a servant with whom he had an affair and is therefore Oswald's half-sister. Mrs. Alving must deal with this complication.

A play's complications usually develop into a *crisis*, or turning point of the action. In fact, plays like *Ghosts* and *Hamlet* may have several crises. The crisis is an event that makes the resolution of the play's conflict inevitable. In *Macbeth*, the crisis is the murder of King Duncan by the Macbeths. They have killed an anointed king and a universal bloodbath will follow until the murderers are punished and the rightful heir restored to the throne. Even at this point of crisis, Macbeth knows that all great Neptune's ocean will never wash them clean again. (See Figure 7.2.)

A play usually ends when the conflict is resolved in the *climax*, or highest point of intensity, and any loose strands of action are then tied off. When Hector's son, the heir to Troy, is sentenced to die and is carried off to be executed, the highest moment of the play's intensity has been reached. The consignment of the women to the Greek generals is almost anticlimactic because—without a male to procreate the tribe—Troy has no hope of future generations.

Macbeth's climax is the appearance of the murdered Banquo's ghost at the banquet table—further evidence of Macbeth's ongoing bloody

The witches entice Macbeth (Ian McKellen) with voodoo dolls, as they paint symbols on his body in the Royal Shakespeare Company production of Macbeth *(1976), directed by Trevor Nunn:*

MACBETH: Speak, if you can. What are you?

1. WITCH: All hail, Macbeth! Hail to thee, Thane of Glamis!

2. WITCH: All hail, Macbeth! Hail to thee, Thane of Cawdor!

3. WITCH: All hail, Macbeth, that shalt be King hereafter!

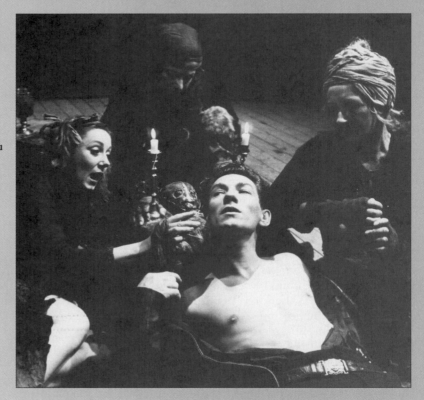

deeds and his unquiet conscience. After the ghost's appearance, forces turn against Macbeth leading him finally to fight his rival Macduff; this secondary climax results in Macbeth's death and the restoration of the rightful heir to Duncan's throne.

Resolution

The resolution usually restores balance and satisfies the audience's expectations. The captive Trojan women are marched away to board the

The last of Shakespeare's four great tragedies (along with *Hamlet*, *Othello*, and *King Lear*), *Macbeth* (1606) was written when his creative powers were at their highest. Macbeth, King Duncan's noble warlord, hears witches prophesy that greatness will be his—that he will be king someday.

When his wife, Lady Macbeth, learns of the witches' prophecy, her imagination—overcharged with ambition—conceives the king's assassination. While he sleeps in their castle, the Macbeths murder Duncan, engendering a seemingly endless series of murders to conceal their original crime and to thwart other pretenders to the throne.

As the play progresses, the disintegrating effects of evil work on a once noble man and his wife. Macbeth's crimes distort his judgment; he is terrified by hallucinations of the ghosts of his victims, symbolizing a warning of retribution to come. He becomes increasingly isolated from his followers and his wife, whose guilty conscience eventually leads her to suicide. Pessimism and despair take hold of Macbeth as he contemplates his inevitable punishment. Only in the end does he revive a part of his former self, as he duels his rival (Macduff) to a certain death.

This story of crime and punishment illustrates the destructive effects of power and ambition on the human psyche. Macbeth's self-awareness endows the action with its tragic dimension: Feeling responsibility for the moral chaos he has created, he explores life's meaning in *soliloquies* that transcend his particular dilemma.

Greek ships; the Macbeths have paid for their crimes with their lives, and Duncan's son is to be crowned king of Scotland. In *A Streetcar Named Desire*, Blanche is taken to an asylum and the Kowalski household settles back into its routines of poker, beer, and Saturday-night bowling. The absurdist play usually completes a cycle in its resolution, suggesting that the events of the play will repeat themselves over and over again. Some plays end with unanswered questions—for example, will Mrs. Alving give Oswald the fatal drug, or won't she?—to stimulate the audience to think about what kind of choice each would make

FIGURE 7.2
Macbeth (Christopher Walken) confronts Banquo's ghost (Christopher Lloyd, at left) in the New York Shakespeare Festival's 1974 production of Macbeth.

in a similar situation. Whatever the case, the resolution brings a sense of completed or suspended action, of conflicts resolved in probable ways, and of promises fulfilled.

In the final scene of *Hamlet*, the succession, in the figure of Hamlet's cousin Fortinbras, is confirmed, and Fortinbras honors Hamlet as a fallen prince.

Hamlet: O, I die, Horatio;
> The potent poison quite o'er-crows my spirit:
> I cannot live to hear the news from England;
> But I do prophesy the election lights
> On Fortinbras: he has my dying voice;
> So tell him, with the occurrents, more and less,
> Which have solicited. The rest is silence.

[Dies.]

Horatio: Now cracks a noble heart. Good night, sweet prince;
> And flights of angels sing thee to thy rest!
> Why does the drum come hither?

[March within.]

[Enter Fortinbras, *the* English ambassadors, *and others.]*

HAMLET

Shakespeare's greatest tragedy, *Hamlet* (c. 1601) tells the story of a man who confronts a task that seems beyond his powers.

Although the Danish court is celebrating King Claudius' wedding to Queen Gertrude, her son Prince Hamlet still mourns the death of his father. The ghost of his father appears and tells Hamlet that he was murdered by Claudius. Hamlet swears to take vengeance, but he must first prove to himself that Claudius is guilty. He has a group of strolling players put on a play in which a similar murder is depicted. Claudius' reaction to the play betrays him and Hamlet plots revenge.

By accident he kills Polonius, the Lord Chamberlain and father to Ophelia, a young woman who loves Hamlet. Hamlet is exiled for killing Polonius, and Ophelia is driven mad.

Laertes, Polonius' son, vows revenge and challenges Hamlet to a duel. To ensure that Hamlet is killed, Claudius poisons Laertes' sword and prepares a cup of poison for Hamlet to drink during the duel. In the closing scene, Gertrude accidentally drinks from the poisoned cup and dies, Hamlet kills Claudius, and Laertes—after mortally wounding Hamlet—is killed by Hamlet with the poisoned sword. Hamlet's cousin Fortinbras is made king of Denmark.

Hamlet is a tragedy about the power of evil to corrupt the innocent, bring chaos to a kingdom, and paralyze the human will. It contains some of the greatest poetry written by Shakespeare.

Fortinbras: Where is this sight?

Horatio: What is it ye would see?
   If aught of woe or wonder, cease your search.

Fortinbras: This quarry cries on havoc. O proud death,
   What feast is toward in thine eternal cell,
   That thou so many princes at a shot
   So bloodily hast struck?

First Ambassador: The sight is dismal;
   And our affairs from England come too late:
   The ears are senseless that should give us hearing,
   To tell him his commandment is fulfill'd,
   That Rosencrantz and Guildenstern are dead:
   Where should we have our thanks?

Horatio: Not from his mouth,
    Had it the ability of life to thank you:
    He never gave commandment for their death.
    But since, so jump upon this bloody question,
    You from the Polack wars, and you from England,
    Are here arrived, give order that these bodies
    High on a stage be placed to the view;
    And let me speak to the yet unknowing world
    How these things came about: so shall you hear
    Of carnal, bloody, and unnatural acts,
    Of accidental judgements, casual slaughters,
    Of deaths put on by cunning and forced cause,
    And, in this upshot, purposes mistook
    Fall'n on the inventors' heads: all this can I
    Truly deliver.

Fortinbras: Let us haste to hear it,
    And call the noblest to the audience.
    For me, with sorrow I embrace my fortune:
    I have some rights of memory in this kingdom,
    Which now to claim my vantage doth invite me.

Horatio: Of that I shall have also cause to speak,
    And from his mouth whose voice will draw on more:
    But let this same be presently perform'd,
    Even while men's minds are wild; lest more mischance,
    On plots and errors, happen.

Fortinbras: Let four captains
    Bear Hamlet, like a soldier, to the stage;
    For he was likely, had he been put on,
    To have proved most royally: and, for his passage,
    The soldiers' music and the rites of war
    Speak loudly for him.
    Take up the bodies: such a sight as this
    Becomes the field, but here shows much amiss.
    Go, bid the soldiers shoot.

[A dead march. Exeunt, bearing off the dead bodies; after which a peal of ordnance is shot off.]

FIGURE 7.3

The secondary plot resolved. Hamlet stands above the wounded Laertes near the end of the duel. Laertes' death concludes the story of his family. Albert Finney as Hamlet watches Simon Ward as Laertes in the 1976 production at London's National Theatre, directed by Peter Hall.

Other dramatic conventions relate past and present events and behavior. Simultaneous plots and the *play-within-the-play* are two important conventions used by Renaissance and modern playwrights.

Simultaneous Plots

The Elizabethans used **simultaneous** or **double plotting** to represent life's variety and complexity. Two stories are told concurrently; the lives of one group of characters affect the lives of the other group. *Hamlet*, for instance, is the story of two families: Hamlet-Claudius-Gertrude, Laertes-Polonius-Ophelia. The secondary plot or subplot is always resolved before the main plot to maintain a sense of priority. For example, Laertes dies before Hamlet in the duel resolving that family's story (see Figure 7.3).

THE PLAY-WITHIN-THE-PLAY: TRADITIONAL AND MODERN

Laurence Olivier as Hamlet (seated at left) watches the king and queen during the play that he has devised to detect Claudius' guilt. From the 1948 film of Shakespeare's play, also directed by Olivier.

Three of Pirandello's fictional "characters" rehearse their play for the play's stage manager in Six Characters in Search of an Author *in the production directed by Liviu Ciulei at the Arena Stage during the 1988–89 season.*

The Caucasian Chalk Circle, *by Bertolt Brecht. The players (center) link the inner play about Grusha, Azdak, and the child to the outer play dealing with the farmer's dispute. Both groups can be seen in this staging. Photo from the 1965 production at The Guthrie Theater, Minneapolis.*

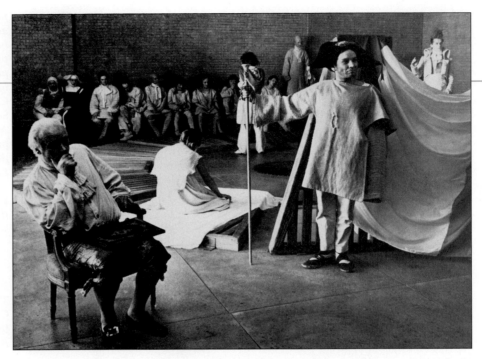

The Marquis de Sade (actor Patrick McGee) rehearses the play-within-the-play with the inmates of Charenton asylum in the 1965 production of Marat/Sade, *directed by Peter Brook for the Royal Shakespeare Company (England).*

Chapter Seven

Conventions of Time
Dramatic versus Actual Time

During a performance, we experience time on several levels. First, there is the amount of actual time that it takes us to see a play. Once begun, the time of a performance is one-directional—from beginning to ending. Dramatic time, however, is a phenomenon of the playwright's text.

Within the fictional world of the play, time can be expanded or compressed. Dramatic time can be accelerated by using gaps of days, months, and even years; or, it can be slowed down by interrupting the forward action with soliloquies. Remembered scenes can take us back into a character's past, like a flashback. Episodes may be shown out of their chronological sequence, or they may be foreshortened so that they occur more swiftly than they would in actuality. Shakespeare's battle scenes, requiring only a few minutes of swordplay on stage, would require days or even months in real time. In Samuel Beckett's plays, characters experience the relentless passage of time as they wait out their uneventful lives. Often in Beckett's plays the experience of dramatic time is cyclical—day becomes night and night becomes day. In his plays, nothing happens in the traditional dramatic sense, but time erodes lives in a relentless journey toward death.

Unlike our own experience of it, time in the fictional universe of drama is highly malleable. Consideration of dramatic time has always played a large part in the different theories and rules of drama. In his *Poetics*, Aristotle briefly suggested that the amount of time it takes the actors to enact the story should ideally be concurrent with the actual time it takes to perform the play. This attention to a *unity of time*, as it was later called, is still found in modern realistic plays in which a situation develops and is resolved within twenty-four hours or less.

Conventions of Metaphor
The Play-Within-the-Play

The play-within-the-play was used by Shakespeare and is still a common plot device, most notably in the work of such modern writers as Bertolt Brecht, Peter Weiss, Tom Stoppard, and Luigi Pirandello. In

PLAYWRIGHT

LUIGI PIRANDELLO

Luigi Pirandello (1867–1936), the son of a rich owner of sulphur mines in Agrigento on the southern coast of Sicily, studied philosophy at the University of Rome and earned a doctorate at the University of Bonn in Germany. In his early years, he wrote poems and short stories for his own enjoyment. He married the daughter of his father's partner in an arranged marriage. Both families lost their fortunes when the mines flooded in 1904. To earn a living for his new family, Pirandello became an instructor at a teacher's college for women in Rome. Shortly thereafter, his wife became mentally ill. Refusing to place her in a public institution and too poor to afford a private one, Pirandello endured life with his wife's mental illness until her death in 1918. Writing to support the family, he had attained international fame as a playwright by the 1920s. In 1925, he founded his own art theatre (Teatro d'Arte) in Rome and was awarded the Nobel prize for literature in 1934.

Pirandello's plays demonstrate a brooding inquiry into the nature of reality. His belief that all experience is illusory and that life itself is a "sad piece of buffoonery" is best illustrated in *It Is So! (If You Think So)* (1917), *Henry IV* (1922), *As You Desire Me* (1930), and in his "theatre trilogy": *Six Characters in Search of an Author* (1921), *Each in His Own Way* (1924), and *Tonight We Improvise* (1930).

Hamlet, the play-within-the-play (called *The Murder of Gonzago*) is used in what is now thought of as a highly traditional way. The strolling players re-create a second play on stage about the murder of Hamlet's father; Claudius' reaction to it gives Hamlet proof of the King's guilt.

Brecht's *Caucasian Chalk Circle*, like Pirandello's *Six Characters in Search of an Author* and Michael Frayn's *Noises Off*, is almost in its entirety a play-within-the-play. The singer-narrator links the outer play (the settling of the farmers' dispute) with the inner one (the stories of Grusha, Azdak, and the chalk-circle test). The long inner play manifests a kind of collective wisdom that has practical applications in an actual dispute over ownership of property (the outer play).

Recent playwrights use the play-within-the-play in a more complex way than even Brecht to demonstrate that *life is like theatre*, and vice

186   *Chapter Seven*

Pirandello's "six characters" make their mysterious appearance in the play-within-the-play. Six Characters in Search of an Author *was directed by Liviu Ciulei for Arena Stage, Washington, D.C.*

Six Characters in Search of an Author, written in 1921 by Italian playwright Luigi Pirandello, begins with a rehearsal of a "Pirandello comedy" by a second-rate acting company. A family of six fictional characters intrudes demanding that their story be performed, for they have been deserted by their author and left in limbo, so to speak. The actors agree to give one rehearsal to the characters' story and chaos ensues in their tale of domestic tragedy that becomes the play-within-the-play. During the rehearsal, the characters insist that the actors cannot portray them in any meaningful way. Characters and actors bicker in a radical questioning of dramatic art. The paradoxes of play and reality, characters and actors, illusion and truth are played out in the rehearsal and in the inner play. Pirandello's influential play anticipated the theatricalism of the modern theatre, along with the mood and questioning of absurdist drama.

ACT 1

At this point, the Door-keeper *has entered from the stage door and advances towards the manager's table, taking off his braided cap. During this manoeuvre, the* Six Characters *enter, and stop by the door at back of stage, so that when the* Door-keeper *is about to announce their coming to the* Manager, *they are already on the stage. A tenuous light surrounds them, almost as if irradiated by them—the faint breath of their fantastic reality.*

This light will disappear when they come forward towards the actors. They preserve, however, something of the dream lightness in which they seem almost suspended; but this does not detract from the essential reality of their forms and expressions.

He who is known as The Father *is a man of about 50: hair, reddish in colour, thin at the temples; he is not bald, however; thick moustaches, falling over his still fresh mouth, which often opens in an empty and uncertain smile. He is fattish, pale; with an especially wide forehead. He has blue, oval-shaped eyes, very clear and piercing. Wears light trousers and a dark jacket. He is alternatively mellifluous and violent in his manner.*

The Mother *seems crushed and terrified as if by an intolerable weight of shame and abasement. She is dressed in modest black and wears a thick widow's veil of crêpe. When she lifts this, she reveals a wax-like face. She always keeps her eyes downcast.*

The Step-Daughter, *is dashing, almost impudent, beautiful. She wears mourning too, but with great elegance. She shows contempt for*

versa. The stage itself becomes a *metaphor* for the world's fictions and self-imposed illusions. The outer play retains the convention that the stage is seen as a real-life living room (or situation), but the real-life living room is seen as a stage. The inner play captures this new look at life's "multiple stages."

In his celebrated masterpiece *Marat/Sade (The Persecution and Assassination of Jean-Paul Marat as Performed by the Inmates of the Asylum of Charenton under the Direction of the Marquis de Sade)*, written in 1964, Peter Weiss (1916–1982) used the play-within-the-play con-

the timid half-frightened manner of the wretched Boy *(14 years old,
and also dressed in black); on the other hand, she displays a lively tenderness for her little sister,* The Child *(about four), who is dressed in
white, with a black silk sash at the waist.*

   The Son *(22) tall, severe in his attitude of contempt for* The Father,
supercilious and indifferent to The Mother. *He looks as if he had
come on the stage against his will.*

Door-keeper *[cap in hand]:* Excuse me, sir . . .

The Manager *[rudely]:* Eh? What is it?

Door-keeper *[timidly]:* These people are asking for you, sir.

The Manager *[furious]:* I am rehearsing, and you know perfectly well
   no one's allowed to come in during rehearsals! *[Turning to the*
   Characters.*]* Who are you, please? What do you want?

The Father *[coming forward a little, followed by the others who seem
   embarrassed]:* As a matter of fact . . . we have come here in search
   of an author . . .

The Manager *[half angry, half amazed]:* An author? What author?

The Father: Any author, sir.

The Manager: But there's no author here. We are not rehearsing a new
   piece.

The Step-Daughter *[vivaciously]:* So much the better, so much the
   better! We can be your new piece. . . .

vention to suggest that our contemporary world is a madhouse. Set in
1808, *Marat/Sade* depicts the production of a play by the inmates of an
insane asylum in Charenton, France. Their text, about the events surrounding the death of political revolutionary Jean-Paul Marat fifteen
years earlier, has been composed by the Marquis de Sade, who is also
director, fellow actor, and fellow inmate.

   Weiss uses two time frames: (1) the events of 1793—the historical
setting of de Sade's play about the French Revolution—that culminate
in the assassination of Marat, and (2) the "present" of 1808, when

de Sade and his mentally deranged cast are staging their play. The madhouse world of Charenton mirrors the violence and irrationality of our modern world. And the play-within-the-play, the story of Marat's murder, forces us to compare the manner in which conflicting political ideologies resolve their differences: then with the guillotine, and now with nuclear weapons.

Summary

Drama's conventions are effective writing strategies to set plot, character, and action in motion. There are conventions for providing background information, manipulating time, plotting suspenseful stories, ending plays, and telling more than one story at a time. The insertion of a minor play within the larger one was a favorite device of Elizabethan writers to enliven the production's theatrics and, as in *Hamlet*, to demonstrate the villain's guilt in the outer play. In the modern theatre, the play-within-the-play has become a means for demonstrating life's theatricality within the medium most accessible to showing artifice, play-acting, and heightened moments. Dramatic conventions are part of the playwright's strategy for communicating with audiences. *Language* written for the stage also has its special techniques and ways of communicating to audiences.

Questions for Study

1. What are the playwright's tools for telling a story? Name nine.
2. Give examples of *exposition.*
3. Why does *complication* often follow the *point of attack*?
4. How are *crisis* and *climax* related?
5. What does an audience expect at a play's *resolution* or ending?
6. What is the function of double plotting?
7. Describe the double plot in *Hamlet* and the point at which the two plots become one.

8. *The Murder of Gonzago* as performed by the strolling players in *Hamlet* is an example of a play-within-the-play. What is the function of this "inner" play?

9. Describe Brecht's variation on the play-within-the-play convention in *The Caucasian Chalk Circle*.

10. How do Luigi Pirandello and Peter Weiss further complicate the play-within-the-play convention in *Six Characters in Search of an Author* and in *Marat/Sade*?

11. *Plays to Read*: Bertolt Brecht's *The Caucasian Chalk Circle*, Luigi Pirandello's *Six Characters in Search of an Author*, Peter Weiss' *Marat/Sade*.

12. *Suggested Reading*: Eric Bentley, *The Life of the Drama* (New York: Atheneum, 1964; reprinted Applause Theatre Books, 1991).

Like other stage elements, theatre's
language is special and complex. It
organizes our perceptions of what is
taking place before us, forcing us into self-
discovery or radical changes of attitude.
Language in the theatre communicates
meaning and activity to us in many ways—
verbal and nonverbal. Theatre's language
is a way of seeing that engages our eyes,
ears, and minds.

8

THEATRE LANGUAGE

I n theatre we see and hear a story being lived before us with the intensity of a traveler experiencing new worlds for the first time. Playwrights, directors, designers, and actors use a special *language* to organize our perceptions, one that is both *visual* and *aural*.

Language in the theatre is both like and unlike the way people talk in real life. First, it is the playwright's means for expressing what characters experience and for developing plot and action. Unlike conversation in real life, actors speak highly selective words supported by highly selective gestures. Hamlet's soliloquies, some of the most beautiful verse written in English for the theatre, express his feelings and thoughts in blank verse. This unusual and eloquent language is acceptable to us because it has its own reality, consonant with a world other than our own.

Theatre language, then, is the language of the characters and of the stage world, and it expresses the life of the play. Language spoken by actors as characters expresses ideas and feelings, revealing the consciousness of the characters; it makes their decisions to act dramatically meaningful.

We are so used to equating language (and communication) with words that we must constantly remind ourselves that in the theatre the *word* is what Peter Brook called "a small visible portion of a gigantic unseen formation."[2] Words in the theatre are enhanced by nonverbal language: for example, gestures, costumes, sounds, and light express moods, intentions, and meanings.

Others have also remarked that one characteristic of theatre language is that words have their source in gesture. To repeat George Steiner's comment about this: "Drama is language under such high pressure

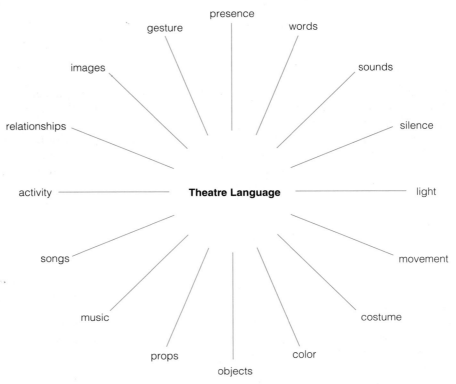

FIGURE 8.1

Theatre language, like our ways of communicating in real life, has both verbal and nonverbal characteristics, and it can be divided into the many different ways that meaning is communicated to an audience. The diagram lists sixteen ways of communicating the characters' experience, the plot and action, and the stage's living reality.

thoughts
attitudes
intentions
presence.

of feeling the words carry a necessary and immediate connotation of gesture. . . ."[3] Theatre language expresses not only the characters' thoughts, attitudes, and intentions, but also the *presence* of human beings in a living world. For this reason, Figure 8.1 includes along with words many other facets of theatre language.

It has been argued that the language we use for communication in real life is also multifaceted and theatrical: Our clothes are costumes, we speak words and make gestures, we carry props (bookbags or sunglasses), we wear makeup, and we are affected by the environment's sounds and silences. Although this is true, there is an important difference between language in the theatre and in life. In the theatre, language (both verbal and nonverbal) is selected and controlled. It shapes the action. Much more must happen through conversation in the theatre than in ordinary life. Our conversations with friends are often random, purposeless, except on formal occasions. But language in the theatre is carefully arranged by playwright, actor, director, and designer in a meaningful pattern that can be repeated night after night.

Let us examine the verbal and nonverbal characteristics of theatre language.

Verbal and Nonverbal Language

On the page of a script, words are signs and symbols with the potential for making something happen in the theatre. When spoken by an actor, they communicate to other actors and to the audience. Besides words, other kinds of signals make up the theatre's language: sound, light, shape, movement, silence, activity, inactivity, gesture, color, music, song, objects, costumes, props, and visual images.

In communication theory, a *sign* has a direct physical relationship to the thing it represents—to its referent. Thunder is a sign of rain: It has a real physical connection with changes in the atmosphere. *Symbols* differ from signs in that they have an arbitrary connection to their referents. The American flag, for example, is a symbol of our country, and many people associate everything good in America with the flag that represents it. But during the Vietnam War, some people associated the flag with everything wrong with America (see Figure 8.2). When they wore motorcycle helmets or clothing painted with the flag, they revised its meaning. This was possible because its meaning was arbitrary—it was a symbol, not a sign. Today, the use and abuse of the American flag have become issues of legal debate, further emphasizing the flag's symbolism.

In the theatre, both verbal and nonverbal symbols and signs are used to enhance our perception of the actors' living presence. In Anton Chekhov's *The Cherry Orchard* (1904), the orchard (usually located offstage) is a verbal symbol variously interpreted as the passing of the old way of life and/or of the coming of a new social order. Characters refer to the orchard as a family treasure, a local tradition, a beautiful object, and the means of saving the estate from auction. The orchard is

Theatre Language **195**

FIGURE 8.2

Actors with the American flag in the rock musical Hair *(1967), directed by Tom O'Horgan, New York, make a visual statement about the attitudes of counter-culture groups in the 1960s toward the establishment.*

symbolic of the ways Chekhov's characters deal with or fail to deal with life's demands. The sound of the ax cutting down the trees at the play's end is a nonverbal sign, communicating the destruction of the family's treasure and their way of life. But it also communicates the arrival of a *new* social order with new values and strengths. Verbal symbol and aural sign reinforce one another in communicating the play's meaning.

Types of Theatre Language

To understand communication in the theatre, we must ask basic questions about theatre language: What do we hear? What do we see? What is taking shape before us? What growing image creates the life of the play? How does the special strength of the language help create the unique presentness of the theatre? When the various elements of theatre

THE CHERRY ORCHARD

The New York Shakespeare Festival production of The Cherry Orchard, *directed by Andrei Serban (1977).*

After some years abroad, the widowed Madame Ranevskaya returns to her Russian estate to find that it has been heavily mortgaged to pay her debts, and that it is to be auctioned. Generous and irresponsible, she seems incapable of recognizing her financial situation. A half-hearted attempt is made to collect money owed her by a neighboring land-owner, but he is also in financial straits. Gaev, Madame Ranevskaya's brother, makes some suggestions, but his chief hope lies in an uncertain legacy from a relative, or a rich marriage for Anya, Madame Ranevskaya's young daughter. The only realistic proposal comes from Lopakhin, a merchant whose father was once a serf of the Ranevskaya family. He suggests cutting down the famous cherry orchard and dividing the land into plots for summer cottages. The family rejects the idea of destroying such beauty and tradition.

With no specific plan in mind for saving the estate, the family drifts aimlessly toward the day set for the auction. On the evening of the sale, Madame Ranevskaya gives a party she cannot afford. In the middle of the festivities, Lopakhin arrives; when questioned, he reveals that he has bought the estate and intends to carry out his plan for cutting down the orchard.

With the estate and orchard now sold, the family prepares to leave. Forgotten in the confusion is the old and dying Firs, the devoted family servant. As the sound of the ax rings from the orchard, he lies down to rest and is soon motionless in the empty house.

FIGURE 8.3

The actor's language. Hamlet's costume in the final two acts is that of a man of action. He is no longer dressed in the "solemn black" of mourning, nor in the disheveled dress of his "antic disposition." In addition, the actor's speech, gestures, and movements convey the character's determination to rid Denmark of the corrupt king. Albert Finney plays Hamlet in the 1976 production at London's National Theatre.

language are really working together, however, we do not ask these questions, for there is no time; we experience sensation, sounds, and presence, without particularly analyzing the experience. Let us consider several examples from familiar plays of theatre language's variety and immediacy.

Shakespeare's Verse

Hamlet The Shakespearean soliloquy is a means of taking the audience into the character's mind to hear its contents. In Hamlet's "How all occasions do inform against me," he begins with concern for his delayed revenge, then meditates on human nature, and on the "thing" to be done. The precision of Hamlet's argument with himself reveals the brilliance of a mind that perceives the cause, proof, and means of revenge. The speech's length betrays the habit of mind that has delayed revenge against Claudius, filling time and space with words rather than actions. Measuring himself against his kinsman, the warrior-soldier Fortinbras, the man of action, Hamlet finds the example by which to act (see Figure 8.3).

SOLILOQUY FROM HAMLET

The Shakespeare soliloquy is a stage convention for expressing a character's inner thoughts and feelings: As the actor speaks, we hear the way the character's mind works and understand those hidden thoughts that result in action. (See Figure 8.3.)

Hamlet: How all occasions do inform against me,
And spur my dull revenge! What is a man,
If his chief good and market of his time
Be but to sleep and feed? A beast, no more.
Sure, He that made us with such large discourse,
Looking before and after, gave us not
That capability and godlike reason
To fust in us unused. Now, whether it be
Bestial oblivion, or some craven scruple
Of thinking too precisely on the event,
A thought which, quartered, hath but one part wisdom
And ever three parts coward—I do not know
Why yet I live to say, "This thing's to do,"
Sith I have cause, and will, and strength, and means
To do't. Examples gross as earth exhort me.
Witness this army, of such mass and charge,
Led by a delicate and tender prince,
Whose spirit, with divine ambition puffed,
Makes mouths at the invisible event,
Exposing what is mortal and unsure
To all that fortune, death, and danger dare,
Even for an eggshell. Rightly to be great
Is not to stir without great argument,
But greatly to find a quarrel in a straw
When honor's at the stake. How stand I then,
That have a father killed, a mother stained,
Excitements of my reason and my blood,
And let all sleep, while to my shame I see
The imminent death of twenty thousand men
That for a fantasy and trick of fame
Go to their graves like beds, fight for a plot
Whereon the numbers cannot try the cause,
Which is not tomb enough and continent
To hide the slain? O, from this time forth,
My thoughts be bloody, or be nothing worth!
(4, iv)

It is important that this speech is delivered as a soliloquy, for Hamlet is indeed alone in the charge from his father's ghost and in the eventual killing of Claudius.

The speech moves in thirty-five lines from inactivity to activity, concluding with: "O, from this time forth,/My thoughts be bloody, or be nothing worth!" Hamlet, the hitherto *invisible* man of action, takes shape before our eyes, ears, and minds in sixty lines of blank verse.

IBSEN'S WORDS AND GESTURES

Ibsen's stage directions relate the characters' words to their physical gestures and to the stage lighting in the final scene from *Ghosts*. His concern is to make visible the symbolic truth of the light (the sunrise illuminating the situation) and the darkness (Oswald's disease and society's repression). Ibsen's symbols are found both in dialogue and stage directions.

Oswald: . . . And now let's live together as long as we can. Thank you, Mother.

(He settles down in the armchair that Mrs. Alving *had moved over to the sofa. The day is breaking; the lamp still burns on the table.)*

Mrs. Alving: Now do you feel all right?

Oswald: Yes.

Mrs. Alving *(bending over him)*: What a fearful nightmare this has been for you, Oswald—but it was all a dream. Too much excitement—it hasn't been good for you. But now you can have your rest, at home with your mother near, my own, my dearest boy. Anything you want you can have, just like when you were a little child. There now, the pain is over. You see how quickly it went. Oh, I knew it would—And look, Oswald, what a lovely day we'll have. Bright sunlight. Now you really can see your home.

(She goes to the table and puts out the lamp. Sunrise. The glaciers and peaks in the back-

Ibsen's Signs and Symbols

Ghosts The language of the nineteenth-century play was influenced by a theatre technology unknown in Shakespeare's day, and it reflects a concern for reproducing speech appropriate to the characters' socioeconomic background and psychological makeup. Ibsen introduces nonverbal signs and symbols in stage directions that are like descriptive passages in realistic novels.

The final scene of *Ghosts* begins with stage directions indicating that Mrs. Alving puts out the table lamp as the sun rises. She is alone with her dying son, Oswald, who is talking about the sun. In Ibsen's play the *sun* (also a play on the word *son*) is a symbol for the *truth* about the secrets of the past.

Oswald is seated in a chair facing the audience, and we see the change that comes over him. As Oswald slumps into the immobile state *ground shine in the brilliant light of morning. With his back toward the distant view, Oswald sits motionless in the armchair.)*

Oswald (abruptly): Mother, give me the sun.

Mrs. Alving (by the table, looks at him, startled): What did you say?

Oswald (repeats in a dull monotone): The sun. The sun.

Mrs. Alving (moves over to him): Oswald, what's the matter?

(Oswald appears to crumple inwardly in the chair; all his muscles loosen; the expression leaves his face; and his eyes stare blankly.)

Mrs. Alving (shaking with fear): What is it? *(in a shriek)* Oswald! What's wrong! *(drops to her knees beside him and shakes him)* Oswald! Oswald! Look at me! Don't you know me?

Oswald (in the same monotone): The sun—the sun.

Mrs. Alving (springs to her feet in anguish, tears at her hair with both hands and screams): I can't bear this! *(whispers as if paralyzed by fright)* I can't bear it! Never! *(suddenly)* Where did he put them? *(Her hand skims across his chest.)* Here! *(She shrinks back several steps and shrieks.)* No, no, no!—Yes!—No, no! *(She stands a few steps away from him, her fingers thrust into her hair, staring at him in speechless horror.)*

Oswald (sitting motionless, as before): The sun—the sun.[4]

of the catatonically ill, Mrs. Alving's truth is made visible. She has not eradicated the ghosts of the past, and she is faced with a terrible choice in the present: to give Oswald drugs that will kill him, or to permit him to live. Ibsen's language reflects Mrs. Alving's horror over the truth and her indecision. Using monosyllables, Ibsen indicates the choice Mrs. Alving will make. Five "no's," indicating that she can't give Oswald the drug, are placed against the one "yes." The repressiveness of nineteenth-century society that has dictated Mrs. Alving's principal life decisions becomes visible in her frantic inability to speak or to act.

Light, gesture, movement, physical relationships—in addition to the spoken word—help convey the play's meaning. The background lighting effect ("the sun rises") reinforces the truth of Mrs. Alving's tragic dilemma: The visual design is repeated in Oswald's words "the sun." Truth and light have come too late for them.

CHEKHOV'S SOUND EFFECTS

In the modern theatre, stage directions have become important means by which playwrights communicate imaginative worlds to directors, actors, and designers. In the final scene of *The Cherry Orchard*, Chekhov describes the stage's appearance; Firs' costume, manner, and words; and the final powerful sounds.

Lyubov: We are coming. (*They go out.*)

(*The stage is empty. There is the sound of the doors being locked up, then of the carriages driving away. There is silence. In the stillness there is the dull stroke of an axe in a tree, clanging with a mournful lonely sound. Footsteps are heard. Firs appears in the doorway on the right. He is dressed as always—in a pea-jacket and white waistcoat with slippers on his feet. He is ill.*)

Firs (*goes up to the doors, and tries the handles*): Locked! They have gone . . . (*sits down on sofa*). They have forgotten me. . . . Never mind . . . I'll sit here a bit. . . . I'll be bound Leonid Andreyevitch hasn't put his fur coat on and has gone off in his thin overcoat (*sighs anxiously*). I didn't see after him. . . . These young people . . . (*mutters something that can't be distinguished*). Life has slipped by as though I hadn't lived. (*Lies down*) I'll lie down a bit. . . . There's no strength in you, nothing left you—all gone! Ech! I'm good for nothing (*lies motionless*).

(*A sound is heard that seems to come from the sky, like a breaking harp-string, dying away mournfully. All is still again, and there is heard nothing but the strokes of the axe far away in the orchard.*)

Curtain.

Chekhov's Sounds and Silences

The Cherry Orchard Chekhov ends *The Cherry Orchard* with language that also combines verbal and nonverbal effects: sounds with silence, words with noise, inactivity with activity.

Firs is the elderly valet left behind by the family in their hurried departure from the estate that has been sold at auction. His last speech is placed between stage directions suggesting offstage sounds of departure, of a breaking string, and of the stroke of an ax. The *pauses* in Firs' speech indicate the ending of a life and also of a way of life. The fact that he is alone, locked in the house, forgotten and dying, tells us more vividly that "life has passed him by" than his saying it.

FIGURE 8.4

At The Cherry Orchard's *end, Firs, the old valet, lies down alone—the final symbol of the passing of a way of life. This visual image of the dying man is reinforced by the sound of a breaking string. Finally, the sounds of ax strokes suggest the arrival of a vital force taking over from the old. This scene was staged by director Andrei Serban in the 1977 New York Shakespeare Festival production at Lincoln Center, New York City.*

In Chekhov's plays, what people do—their gestures—is frequently more important than what they say. Like gesture, the abstract sound of the breaking string in the distance juxtaposed against the immediate sound of the ax is more important than the character's words. Even the order of the sound effects is important. The breaking string's mournful sound, symbolic of the release of tensions and the passing of a way of life, subsides into silence *before* the ax stroke, the sound of the aggressive new order, intrudes on the scene. At the end of *The Cherry Orchard*, the audience hears and sees a world in transition (see Figure 8.4).

Brecht's Gestic Language

The Caucasian Chalk Circle Brecht includes music, songs, placards, film projections, and *gest* in his concept of language in the theatre. Brecht's concept of gest, or gestic language, is a matter of the actors' overall attitude to what is going on around them and what they are

ANTON CHEKHOV

In The Three Sisters, *1983, at the American Repertory Theatre, Cambridge, scenic designer Beni Montresor created a playing space with mirrored floor, massive red velvet curtains in the rear, and banks of footlights on either side of the floor. The Prozorov house becomes a stage within a stage where Chekhov's "poor players" strut and fret away their hours. Director Andrei Serban heightens the actors' energy to show people living to the hilt. Masha (Cheryl Giannini) twirls alone to a Chopin mazurka. All engage frantically in the dance, creating a striking visual image of people trying to forget, to avoid, the inevitability of their lives.*

asked to do on stage. Brecht insisted that words follow the gest of the person speaking.

"Gest" is not supposed to mean gesticulation: it is not a matter of explanatory or emphatic movements of the hands, but of overall attitudes. A language is gestic when it is grounded in a gest and conveys particular attitudes adopted by the speaker towards other men. The sentence "pluck the eye that offends thee

Anton Pavlovich Chekhov (1860–1904) was born in southern Russia and studied medicine at Moscow University. During his student years he wrote short stories to earn money. He began his playwriting career in the 1880s with one-act farces, *The Marriage Proposal* and *The Bear*. *Ivanov* (1887) was his first full-length play to be produced.

Chekhov redefined stage realism during the years of his association with the Moscow Art Theatre (1898–1904). The meaning of his plays is not in direct, purposive action but in the representation of a certain kind of rural Russian life, which he knew firsthand. Director Constantin Stanislavski's style of interpreting the inner truth of Chekhov's characters and the mood of his plays resulted in one of the great theatrical collaborations.

During his last years, Chekhov lived in Yalta, where he had gone for his health, and made occasional trips to Moscow to participate in the productions. He died of tuberculosis in a German spa in 1904, soon after the production of *The Cherry Orchard*, and was buried in Moscow.

During his short life Chekhov wrote four masterpieces of modern stage realism: *The Sea Gull, Uncle Vanya, The Three Sisters,* and *The Cherry Orchard.*

out" is less effective from the gestic point of view than "if thine eye offend thee, pluck it out." The latter starts by presenting the eye, and the first clause has the definite gest of making an assumption; the main clause then comes as a surprise, a piece of advice, and a relief.[5]

The characters' gestic language becomes visible in the test of the chalk circle. To decide who is worthy of rearing the child Michael, the judge orders that a circle be drawn on the floor and that the contestants pull the child from the circle. The materialistic attitudes of the lawyers and the governor's wife toward the child are contrasted with Grusha's humanitarian feelings. Grusha refuses to tug at the child, while the governor's wife pulls the child twice out of the circle. The wife's attitudes, words, and gestures betray the fact that her access to wealth and power depends on the return of the child to her. We see that she is selfish and "grasping."

Brecht used music and song as well as dialogue to express characters' thoughts and feelings. The narrator in *The Caucasian Chalk Circle* (scene vi) sings the girl's thoughts as a means of expressing, without becoming sentimental, Grusha's love for the child.

> **The Singer:** Hear now what the angry woman thought and did not
>   say: (*Sings*)
> If he walked in golden shoes
> Cold his heart would be and stony.
> Humble folk he would abuse
> He wouldn't know me.
> Oh, it's hard to be hard-hearted
> All day long from morn to night.
> To be mean and high and mighty
> Is a hard and cruel plight.
> Let him be afraid of hunger
> Not of the hungry man's spite
> Let him be afraid of darkness
> But not fear the light.[6]

Brecht's working notes call for musicians to be included on stage. A narrator interrupts the play's action to sing songs that pinpoint social attitudes and wrongs. A song is sung to reveal what Grusha *thinks* but does not say. As the narrator sings Grusha's thoughts, Brecht allows us to understand, without sentiment, Grusha's selfless concern for the child.

Contemporary Trends

French playwright and theatre theorist Antonin Artaud (1896–1948), one prophet of the new theatre, militated against traditional dialogue that furthers plot and reveals character. He favored inducing in audiences a shock reaction and a visceral response. He called for a "theatre of cruelty" to purge the audience's feelings of hatred, violence, and cruelty through use of nonverbal effects: sounds, lighting, unusual theatre spaces, violent movements. Artaud wanted to assault the audience's senses, to cleanse us morally and spiritually, for the improvement of humankind. Followers of Artaud, like Peter Brook, have taken theatre language in two directions, toward *violent images* and toward *physicalization*.

Peter Weiss' Visceral Language

Marat/Sade Peter Brook's 1965 production of *Marat/Sade* for the Royal Shakespeare Company played up the grimness of Peter Weiss' play. The opening scenes confront the audience with violent images and sounds of life in a nineteenth-century asylum that communicate more viscerally than intellectually. A quartet of inmates wearing colored sacks sings sardonic songs while the action described by the songs is mimed by other inmates. Some inmates wear shapeless white tunics and straitjackets to contrast with the formal nineteenth-century costumes of de Sade, the asylum director, and his family. The verbal debate between Jean-Paul Marat and the Marquis de Sade is repeatedly interrupted by the lunatics acting out Marat's story and their own passions. In the mass guillotining sequence, inmates make metallic rasping noises and pour buckets of paint—blood—down drains, while other inmates jump into a pit in the center of the stage so that their heads are piled above stage level, next to the guillotine.

Marat/Sade uses shock to make its point. Marat, the political idealist committed to violent social reform (played by a naked asylum inmate seated in a bathtub; see Figure 8.5), and the Marquis de Sade, the skeptic committed to anarchic individualism, debate the value of revolution during one of de Sade's theatrical productions. For de Sade, humanity, not the political or economic system, is the root of all social evil. He argues, therefore, that revolution is futile and merely perpetuates violence. To make his point that the guillotine—the Revolution's tool—made dying wholesale and meaningless, de Sade describes the four-hour execution of Damiens, King Louis XV's would-be assassin. Damiens' death, for de Sade, is an example of significant individual suffering lost in the impersonal mass deaths of the guillotine.

Peter Weiss' images of torture and death express de Sade's attitudes toward human corruption and unreason. The actor playing de Sade can also express, by luxuriating in the vowel sounds, how the witnesses to the execution luxuriated in the spectacle of Damiens' death. By doing so, the actor's word-sounds have a visceral effect on the audience.

De Sade (*to Marat*): Let me remind you of
    the execution of Damiens
after his unsuccessful attempt to assassinate
Louis the Fifteenth (now deceased)
Remember how Damiens died
How gentle the guillotine is
compared with his torture
It lasted four hours while the crowd goggled
and Casanova at an upper window
felt under the skirts of the ladies watching

[*pointing in the direction of the tribunal
where* Coulmier *sits*]

His chest arms thighs and calves were slit
    open
Molten lead was poured into each slit
boiling oil they poured over him burning tar
    wax sulphur
They burnt off his hands
tied ropes to his arms and legs
harnessed four horses to him and geed
    them up
They pulled at him for an hour but they'd
    never done it before
and he wouldn't come apart
until they sawed through his shoulders and
    hips
So he lost the first arm then the second
and he watched what they did to him and
    then turned to us
and shouted so everyone could understand

And when they tore off the first leg and then
    the second leg
he still lived though his voice was getting
    weak
and at the end he hung there a bloody torso
    with a nodding head
just groaning and staring at the crucifix
which the father confessor was holding up
    to him

[*In the background a half-murmured litany
is heard.*]

That
was a festival with which
today's festivals can't compete
Even our inquisition gives us no pleasure
nowadays
Although we've only just started
there's no passion in our post-revolutionary
    murders
Now they are all official
We condemn to death without emotion
and there's no singular personal death to be
    had
only an anonymous cheapened death
which we could dole out to entire nations
on a mathematical basis
until the time comes
for all life
to be extinguished[7]

FIGURE 8.5
Jean-Paul Marat, the social reformer (played by Ian Richardson in the Peter Brook production) debates the importance of violent revolution while an asylum inmate (Susan Williamson) attends to his skin disease.

Words are only one vehicle for the visceral impact of Weiss' language. The verbal images that describe Damiens' violent death are reinforced by the starkness of the white bathhouse where the performance of de Sade's play takes place. The onstage sexual and physical violence of the inmates—Charlotte Corday stabs Marat to death in his bathtub and the inmates revolt against their keepers—blends image and gesture, words and actions, into a total theatrical effect.

Sam Shepard's Magical Realism

By the 1970s with the end of the Vietnam War, American political consciousness was largely dissipated; the new performance techniques of experimental groups in the United States, like The Open Theatre and The Living Theatre, had become stale and predictable; and the games, transformations, and group improvisations of these companies had been appropriated by the commercial theatre as productions of *Hair* (1968)

In Buried Child, *New York, 1978, Bradley (Jay Sanders, right) is threatened with his own artificial leg by Vincent (Christopher McCann). Shelly (Mary McDonnell), Vincent's girlfriend, looks on.*

In Act I of Sam Shepard's *Buried Child*, Halie enters and discovers the corn (and husks) that her son Tilden has brought into the living room. Dodge, the husband and father, is a husk of his former self, emptied of his potency and usefulness by age, sickness, and guilt. He remains indoors, ill, isolated from the soil that holds his crime: child murder.

She stops abruptly and stares at the corn husks. She looks around the space as though just waking up. She turns and looks hard at Tilden *and* Dodge *who continue sitting calmly. She looks at the corn husks.*

Halie: (*pointing to the husks*) What's this in my house! (*kicks husks*) What's all this!

Tilden *stops husking and stares at her.*

Halie: (*to Dodge*) And you encourage him!

Dodge *pulls blanket over him again.*

Dodge: You're going out in the rain?

Halie: It's not raining.

Tilden *starts husking again.*

Dodge: Not in Florida it's not.

Halie: We're not in Florida!

Dodge: It's not raining at the race track.

Halie: Have you been taking those pills? Those pills always make you talk crazy. Tilden, has he been taking those pills?

Tilden: He hasn't took anything.

Halie: (*to* Dodge) What've you been taking?

Dodge: It's not raining in California or Florida or the race track, only in Illinois. This is the only place it's raining. All over the rest of the world it's bright sunshine.

Halie *goes to the night table next to the sofa and checks the bottle of pills.*

Halie: Which one did you take? Tilden, you must've seen him take something.

Tilden: He never took a thing.

Halie: Then why's he talking crazy?

Tilden: I've been here the whole time.

Halie: Then you've both been taking something!

Tilden: I've just been husking the corn.

Halie: Where'd you get that corn anyway? Why is the house suddenly full of corn?

Dodge: Bumper crop!

Halie: (*moving center*) We haven't had corn here for over thirty years.

Tilden: The whole back lot's full of corn. Far as the eye can see.

Dodge: (*to* Halie) Things keep happening while you're upstairs, ya know. The world doesn't stop just because you're upstairs. Corn keeps growing. Rain keeps raining.

Halie: I'm not unaware of the world around me! Thank you very much. It so happens that I have an over-all view from the upstairs. The back yard's in plain view of my window. And there's no corn to speak of. Absolutely none!

Dodge: Tilden wouldn't lie. If he says there's corn, there's corn.

Halie: What's the meaning of this corn Tilden!

Tilden: It's a mystery to me. I was out in back there. And the rain was coming down. And I didn't feel like coming back inside. I didn't feel the cold so much. I didn't mind the wet. So I was just walking. I was muddy but I didn't mind the mud so much. And I looked up. And I saw this stand of corn. In fact I was standing in it. So, I was standing in it.

Halie: There isn't any corn outside Tilden! There's no corn! Now, you must've either stolen this corn or you bought it.

Dodge: He doesn't have any money.

Halie: (*to* Tilden) So you stole it!

Tilden: I didn't steal it. I don't want to get kicked out of Illinois. I was kicked out of New Mexico and I don't want to get kicked out of Illinois.

Halie: You're going to get kicked out of this house, Tilden, if you don't tell me where you got that corn!

Tilden *starts crying softly to himself but keeps husking corn. Pause.*

continued on next page

Dodge: (*to* Halie) Why'd you have to tell him that? Who cares where he got the corn? Why'd you have to go and tell him that?

Halie: (*to* Dodge) It's your fault you know! You're the one that's behind all this! I suppose you thought it'd be funny! Some joke! Cover the house with corn husks. You better get this cleaned up before Bradley sees it.

Dodge: Bradley's not getting in the front door!

Halie: (*kicking husks, striding back and forth*) Bradley's going to be very upset when he sees this. He doesn't like to see the house in disarray. He can't stand it when one thing is out of place. The slightest thing. You know how he gets.

Dodge: Bradley doesn't even live here!

Halie: It's his home as much as ours. He was born in this house!

Dodge: He was born in a hog wallow.

Halie: Don't you say that! Don't you ever say that!

Dodge: He was born in a goddamn hog wallow! That's where he was born and that's where he belongs! He doesn't belong in this house!

Halie: (*she stops*) I don't know what's come over you, Dodge. I don't know what in the world's come over you. You've become an evil man. You used to be a good man.

Dodge: Six of one, a half a dozen of another.

Halie: You sit here day and night, festering away! Decomposing! Smelling up the house with your putrid body! Hacking your head off til all hours of the morning! Thinking up mean, evil, stupid things to say about your own flesh and blood!

Dodge: He's not my flesh and blood! My flesh and blood's buried in the back yard!

They freeze. Long pause. The men stare at her.[8]

and *A Chorus Line* (1975) moved onto Broadway. Powerful new voices emerged in the 1970s and 1980s in the American theatre as a postwar wave of writers, including Terrence McNally, Lanford Wilson, John Guare, Sam Shepard, David Mamet, and many others. All tested the American character, family, and dreams, and found them wanting.

Buried Child Sam Shepard's plays—*Buried Child, True West, Fool for Love,* and *A Lie of the Mind*—take audiences into the inner working of modern American family life, using bizarre and powerful verbal and nonverbal language in a carefully structured, realistic play. Recognizable places and situations are twisted and warped by sexually explicit language, acts of gratuitous violence, and mysterious occurrences like fantastical crops growing in fields not farmed in thirty years. In Shepard's Pulitzer Prize winner *Buried Child* (1978), for example, carrots as phallic symbols are sliced up on stage with malicious energy, an amputee is robbed of his artificial leg, an old man's head is brutally shaved with an electric razor, and a baby's skeleton is brought on stage. But, crops mysteriously grow in abundance and are visible to the innocent and the redeemed.

Shepard's characters are all searching out their personal histories that might explain who they are and how they came to be that way. The central action of *Buried Child* is the grandson Vincent's quest for his roots and identity. Shepard is writing here within the mainstream of Western drama, from Sophocles' *Oedipus the King* to Edward Albee's *Who's Afraid of Virginia Woolf?* The grandson returns to his family, who live in a Midwestern farmhouse, to find out who he is. The past, once so promising, is filled with horror: one son killed in a gangland murder; a baby born of incest drowned; another son maimed in a chainsaw accident. Without the touchstones of normal family life and friendship, Shepard's characters live in a world that is indifferent to their betrayal, guilt, and violence. The family is locked together in mutual dependence, caring for the sick and looking after the physically and psychologically lame. But these are surface, automatic gestures. The characters do not really care about one another. Hostile and ineffectual, they assert themselves in the present with violence, for the past has too many hidden meanings.

David Mamet's Wordsmiths

In language at once fragmented and obscene, Mamet explores the myths of American capitalism—the loss of individual and national enterprise—in the salesmen, confidence men, and tricksters that inhabit *American Buffalo* (1977), *Glengarry Glen Ross* (1983), and *Speed the Plow* (1988).

Mamet's characters are *wordsmiths* who invent lies, sell reassurance, tell stories, and command experience through words alone. His is a

Robert Prosky as Shelly Levene (left) argues for the "leads" in the 1984 Goodman Theatre premiere production (Chicago) of David Mamet's Glengarry Glen Ross. *Directed by Gregory Mosher.*

David Mamet's wordsmiths, like real estate salesman Shelly Levene in Act I of *Glengarry Glen Ross*, articulate in monosyllabic words the panic and sheer poetry of their beleaguered lives. The emphases (the italicized words) in the text underscore the hard-sell core of their lives as they fend off failure in the guise of loss of influence, respect, leads, closings, new deals, and even the job. In Mamet's writing, words bring to the surface the characters' fear, greed, and desperation.

world composed of petty criminals (*American Buffalo*), dubious real estate salesmen (*Glengarry Glen Ross*), and second-rate Hollywood agents (*Speed the Plow*). His urban cowboys, even gangsters, speak a language that is self-serving, caustic, and exploitative. These characters desperately wish to connect with one another, but they have forgotten how to do so except in their "business" relationships. They deploy language

A booth at a Chinese restaurant, Williamson *and* Levene *are seated at the booth.*

Levene: John . . . John . . . John. Okay. John. John. Look: (*Pause.*) The Glengarry Highland's leads, you're sending Roma out. Fine. He's a good man. We know what he is. He's fine. All I'm saying, you look at the *board*, he's throwing . . . wait, wait, wait, he's throwing them *away*, he's throwing the leads away. All that I'm saying, that you're wasting leads. I don't want to tell you your *job*. All that I'm saying, things get *set*, I know they do, you get a certain *mindset.* . . . A guy gets a reputation. We know how this . . . all I'm saying, put a *closer* on the job. There's more than one man for the . . . Put a . . . wait a second, put a *proven man out* . . . and you watch, now *wait* a second—and you watch your *dollar* volumes. . . . You start closing them for *fifty* 'stead of *twenty-five* . . . you put a *closer* on the . . .

Williamson: Shelly, you blew the last . . .

Levene: No. John. No. Let's wait, let's back up here, I did . . . will you please? Wait a second. Please. I didn't "blow" them. No. I didn't "blow" them. No. One kicked *out*, one I closed . . .

Williamson: . . . you didn't close . . .

Levene: . . . I, if you'd *listen* to me. Please. I *closed* the cocksucker. His *ex*, John, his *ex*, I didn't know he was married . . . he, the *judge* invalidated the . . .

Williamson: Shelly . . .

Levene: . . . and what is that, John? What? Bad *luck*. That's all it is. I pray in your *life* you will never find it runs in streaks. That's what it does, that's all it's doing. Streaks. I pray it misses you. That's all I want to say.

Williamson (Pause): What about the other two?

Levene: What two?

Williamson: Four. You had four leads. One kicked out, one the *judge*, you say . . .

Levene: . . . you want to see the court records? John? Eh? You want to go down . . .

Williamson: . . . no . . .

Levene: . . . do you want to go down*town* . . . ?[9]

that is both cynical and exploitative as they hustle in pursuit of the "deal."

Glengarry Glen Ross Written in 1983, *Glengarry Glen Ross* is set in and around a Chicago real estate office and takes its title from a subdivision ripe for the deal. The play concerns a group of none-too-successful real estate salesmen whose company has imposed a ruthless new regimen: The most successful salesman will receive a Cadillac, the runner-up a set of steak knives, the loser will be fired. Mamet contrives a neat paradigm of a competitive capitalist society. The key to success lies in securing the addresses of likely buyers ("the leads"), and the pressure to succeed encourages unscrupulous methods with respect to the clients and even to the company. Increasingly desperate, one of the salesmen, Shelly Levene, breaks into the office and steals the premium address list of potential clients and the police are called to investigate the crime. By contrast, the salesmen's day-to-day fraudulent activities as they deceive their customers is regarded simply as good business, sanctioned by the ethics of a world in which success is the highest value and closing a deal the ultimate achievement.

Mamet's salesmen speak in a code, deploying the jargon of the trade: leads, deals, sales, closings, percentages, marks, streaks, and so on. They speak in incomplete sentences sprinkled with italicized or capitalized words and with obscenities. The characters are consummate story-tellers—wordsmiths. When the need arises, they can improvise a drama or create stories of total plausibility to turn a situation into advantage, a sales, and cash.

It should not be assumed that the ethical failures of Mamet's confidence men lose them the playwright's sympathy nor that of the audience. It is Mamet's concern for the individual's alienation (and isolation) from his own moral nature and fellow human beings that forces us to look at human need and vulnerability among his fellow tricksters and unwary customers.

There is in David Mamet's work a yearning for that very sense of trust denied by every betrayal in the petty wheeling and dealing that he documents. Somewhere at the heart of his characters' being is a sense of need that is the beginning of their *redemption* (and our sympathy). Their words may snap under the pressure of fear or greed; they may try to adjust themselves to the shape of myths and fantasies; they may deny or exploit the desire for companionship. Deep down, however, below the broken rhythms of speech and the four-letter words, beyond the failed gestures at contact, is a surviving need for *connection*. The play enacts the failure of that urge but also suggests its possibility even as the characters pursue the latest advantage and the next deal.

FIGURE 8.6
Director Peter Stein at the Schaubühne am Lehniner Platz, Berlin, 1984, staged the ending of The Three Sisters *so that the empty house, the trunks and valises, the dilapidated fence, the encompassing trees with open space beyond make a visual statement about leave-taking. Vershinin (O. Sander), standing apart, takes his farewell of Olga (Edith Clever), Anfisa (John Hofer), the elderly nurse, and Irina (Corinna Kirchhoff). The total stage picture communicates parting, nostalgia, and change.*

Summary

Language in the theatre is not merely the spoken word, although we tend to equate theatre language with words and words with the playwright's text, meaning, and message. In the theatre we are subjected to sounds, silences, images, and words. All contribute to the overall illusion that life is taking place before us. These images may be familiar, strange, or fantastic. Oedipus' bleeding eyes, Oswald's likeness to his father, Marat's skin disease, and Bradley's artificial leg are *visible* images of certain kinds of experiences.

One critic says: "Theatre is the art of the self-evident, of what everybody knows—the place where *things mean what they sound and look like they mean*."[10] At the end of *The Cherry Orchard*, Chekhov's meaning *is* the sound of the breaking string, for a way of life is dying even as noises from the new order are rapidly encroaching on the scene. In Chekhov's *The Three Sisters*, the fading sounds of the briskly tuneful military band underscore the hopeless isolation of the sisters in their situation (see Figure 8.6).

Chekhov, like most playwrights, shows us that theatre does not communicate images and aliveness through words alone. As Ionesco says, "Words are only one member of theatre's shock troops."[11]

As we have seen, the creators of drama (the playwrights) are some of the most important of the theatre's "image makers." They initially conceive the theatrical metaphor for our world and experiences. That metaphor may be a real estate office, a Russian estate, or a nineteenth-century asylum. Other theatre artists receive the playwright's work and interpret that vision in the theatre's three-dimensional space, giving it shape, sound, rhythm, image, activity, and human presence. Since the time of ancient Greek festivals, the actor's role in the theatre has been revered, although acting styles and training have changed throughout theatrical history, as we will see in the next chapter.

Questions for Study

1. Name the many aspects of theatre language that communicate meaning to audiences.
2. What is a *sign*? Why is a sign important in the theatre?
3. What is the function of a *soliloquy*?
4. Read the section on *Ghosts* (on page 200) and comment on Ibsen's use of lighting, movement, properties, and conversational prose. What are the characteristics of Ibsen's language for the realistic theatre?
5. Describe Chekhov's nonverbal language in the final stage directions of *The Cherry Orchard*.
6. What does Brecht mean by *gest*? Give examples of Brecht's *gestic* language.

7. What is the function of "songs" in the Brechtian text?

8. How does Peter Weiss achieve a visceral impact with language in *Marat/Sade*?

9. How do Sam Shepard's verbal and nonverbal effects reveal the degeneration of American character, values, and family life?

10. Give examples of Shepard's language of "magical realism."

11. How does David Mamet convey exploitation, fraud, and alienation in language of broken sentences and four-letter words?

12. *Plays to Read*: Anton Chekhov's *The Cherry Orchard*, Sam Shepard's *Buried Child*, David Mamet's *Glengarry Glen Ross*.

13. *Suggested Readings*: David Mamet's *Writing in Restaurants* (New York: Viking Penguin, 1986); David Mamet's *Some Freaks* (New York: Viking Penguin, 1989).

1. relationships, images, gesture, presence, words, sounds, silence light, movement, costume, color, objects, props, music, song, activity

2. Sign - has a direct physical relationship to that thing it represents.
   → enhance perception of actors living presence.

3. Soliloquy → taking audience into the characters mind to hear its contents.
   Expressing a characters inner thoughts & feelings.

6. Gest - Actors overall attitude to what's going on around them or what they are asked to do
   eg "if thine eye offend thee, pluck it out."
   instead of "pluck the eye that offends thee out"

7. "Songs" in Brechtian text - used to pinpoint social attitudes and wrongs express character's thoughts & feelings.

8.

For it is not a game of charades, this acting world of ours; it is an everlasting search for truth.

LAURENCE OLIVIER
On Acting[1]

Acting is the belief and technique by which the actor brings human presence and behavior into the theatre. Theatre is, after all, the art human beings make out of themselves. It doesn't require scenery, costumes, or lighting. It does not even require a play text. It requires only people acting and people watching them act.

9

THE IMAGE MAKERS:
THE ACTOR

We discovered in earlier chapters the modern trend to reduce the theatrical experience to essentials. Grotowski's "poor theatre" and Samuel Beckett's minimalist theatre are perhaps the most widely publicized examples of this trend today. However, in the American theatre, the trend has its roots in the 1938 Broadway production of Thornton Wilder's *Our Town*. Director Jed Harris took Wilder's straightforward play about recognizable townspeople in Grover's Corner, U.S.A., and placed the actors on a bare stage framed simply by the theatre's back wall (see Figure 9.1). Virtually no scenery was used, costumes were muted, and hand properties were minimal. Even stage furniture was done away with. The actors told the story using only those properties, such as chairs and umbrellas, that they could move on and off stage for themselves. The *actors* remained the one indispensable element of the theatrical experience.

For over fifty years, actors have re-created *Our Town*, and they have discovered that a new experience occurs for actor and audience when the stage has minimal scenery or properties. When the only object of the audience's focus is the actor, the modern audience *rediscovers* the actor's presence and art. In this chapter we investigate what acting is all about.

Acting—The Astonishing Art

Acting is doing. Acting is portraying a character's wants and needs through artistically truthful personal behavior that *reflects* a character's

FIGURE 9.1

This photo from the 1938 New York production of Our Town *reveals two essential theatrical elements: actors* in the *space.*

psychological and emotional life. As Laurence Olivier said, acting "is an everlasting search for truth."

Let us state at the outset what acting is not. Acting is not showing, narrating, illustrating, or exhibiting. Acting is not dressing up and displaying emotions. Acting is a creative process as old as Thespis entering the ancient Greek theatre. As a creative artist, the actor (1) selects sensory responses (both physiological and emotional) in the search for (2) *selected* behavior pertinent to a character's needs within the (3) *given circumstances* of the play.[2]

Acting does not begin with performing on stage before an audience. It begins with an individual's talent, imagination, discipline, the need to express, and the process of observation through the sensory organs (eyes, ears, skin, tongue, nose). To prepare a role, the actor selects from memory and personal experience what he or she has seen, heard, felt, and experienced over a lifetime. "At its most rewarding," says British actor Ian McKellen, "acting involves an intense combination of intellect, imagination, and hard work, belying the popular distorted image of dressing-up, booming voices, and shrieking exhibitionism."[3]

The Actor's Reality

Reduced to its simplest terms, the actor's goal is to tell the character's circumstances in the play's story as effectively as possible. Those *circumstances* are the essential conditions in the play's world that include time (when), place (where), and surroundings (what). The actor works in rehearsals to behave as a person would in the prescribed circumstances existing among the play's characters. The actor must concentrate on the *truth* of the character's behavior—his or her sensory responses, psychological motives and objectives—in the context of the play, not in the context of the performance or the audience.

Through meticulous "homework," the actor comes to believe in what he or she is doing on stage as truthful to the moment in the play. To understand better the actor's truth or reality, let us compare the situation in a play with that in an event on the sports field. Like baseball, for example, a play has its own rules and regulations, the set dimensions of the playing area, a set number of persons on the field, and a coach. The interactions among the players are real, vital, and intense. For the playing time, the field is the players' whole universe. The game, like a play, has its own reality that is frequently "more real" and vibrant than everyday reality. Likewise, the actor is given a story, an identity, clothing, circumstances, relationships, motives, activities, and environs. The play sets the number of persons; the director and designer set the dimensions of the playing area; and the playwright sets the circumstances under which the actor-as-character appears in the story. The play has its own reality that the actor finds in the exploration of the play's life and in the character's circumstances and needs.

The creative process that brings the actor to the field of play as the character Hamlet or Blanche DuBois, for example, is demanding and complex. Throughout stage history, actors have used both external technique and internal belief to create their reality on stage. Technique and belief are the fundamentals of their craft. Sometimes, however, in the history of the profession one has been favored over the other.

External Technique

External technique is that activity by which one person imitates another. The mimetic actor chooses to imitate or illustrate outwardly the character's behavior. He or she approaches a role through a deep and passionate study of human behavior *in all its outward forms*, with an eye toward reproducing them in a disciplined and sensitive way.

The English actor David Garrick (1717–1779) approached acting as an imitation of life—he called acting *mimical behavior* (see Figure 9.2). To prepare for the role of King Lear, for example, he studied the appearance and behavior of a friend who had been driven mad by his child's death. By his accurate reproduction of such behavior on stage, Garrick introduced what some have called *naturalistic acting* into the English theatre. He believed that the actor could produce emotions by a convincing imitation and skilled projection of those emotions being imitated. He did not believe that the actor should experience anger or sadness or joy to project these emotions to an audience. The following words are ascribed to him: ". . . that a man was incapable of becoming an actor who was not absolutely independent of circumstances calculated to excite emotion, adding that for his own part he could speak to a post with the same feelings and expression as to the loveliest Juliet under the heaven."[4] His contemporaries wrote that on occasion he would delight them in relaxed moments with his face alone, without any outward motivation or any inward feeling of personal emotion. In this external or purely technical approach, actors, like Garrick, aim for a calculated *presentation* of a character's life on stage.

Many actors in England and Europe have followed Garrick's approach, thereby creating one school of thought on the matter of what

FIGURE 9.2

Garrick's Macbeth, which he played in a contemporary military uniform. He was famous for the dagger scene; his contemporaries praised him for his ability to project the fact that he was "seeing" the dagger before him. It has been said that Garrick's "face was a language."

distinguishes great actors. Throughout stage history, actors have been celebrated for their exceptional charisma, their visible and audible theatrical skills, the bravado of their startling choices, and their ability to *illustrate* many different characters in a career. Included among these ranks are not only David Garrick but also Sarah Bernhardt and Laurence Olivier, to name only three among legions. These actors are notable for working from the "outside in." They objectively predetermine the character's actions, as Garrick has told us, and deliberately watch the form as they execute it. Laurence Olivier, celebrated in his lifetime as England's greatest actor, admitted being uncomfortable working in any other way. No one can deny the brilliance of Olivier's career, but he was often criticized for being "too technical"; however, he defended his methods in interviews and autobiographical writings. Once, after playing *The Entertainer*, John Osborne's play, his friends rushed backstage to congratulate him on a spontaneous and deeply moving performance. He admitted the spontaneity but said, "I don't like that kind of acting; I didn't know what I was doing."[5]

English actor John Gielgud—who is counted among the four greatest actors of his generation (Laurence Olivier, Peggy Ashcroft, and Ralph Richardson are the others)—says of his early days in the theatre that he slavishly imitated other actors:

> I imitated all the actors I admired when I was young, particularly Claude Rains, who was my teacher at dramatic school. I admired him very much. I remember seeing him play Dubedat in *The Doctor's Dilemma*, especially his death scene, in which he wore a rich dressing gown and hung his hands—made up very white—over the arms of his wheelchair. And then I understudied him. I also understudied Noel Coward, whom I felt I had to imitate because he was so individual in his style. I followed him in *The Vortex* and, naturally, the only way to say the lines was to say them as near to the way he said them as possible because they suited his style. It was, after all, written by him for him. Of course, it got me into some rather mannered habits. . . . [And Komisarjevsky, the Russian director] was an enormous influence in teaching me not to act from outside, not to seize on obvious, showy effects and histrionics, not so much to exhibit myself as to be within myself trying to impersonate a character

who is not aware of the audience, to try to absorb the atmosphere of the play and the background of the character, to build it outward so that it came to life naturally. . . .[6]

Modern actors, such as Gielgud, strive to simulate the character, to walk, talk, and look like the king or beggar they are playing. But they also reach into the subtleties of the character's psychology and wholly embody the role, filling it with breath, blood, desires, and emotions so that we believe the actor when he says in Hamlet's words: "The time is out of joint. Oh, cursed spite/That ever I was born to set it right!" We forget that we are watching a working actor and become absorbed in the life and trials of Hamlet, the character.

Internal Belief

A second school of thought on acting emerged with those actors who have astonished audiences with a creative process that is intuitive, subconscious, and subjective. As actors, Laurette Taylor, Uta Hagen, and Al Pacino work "from the inside out" to select behavior pertinent to the character's needs within the given circumstances of the play. These "realistic" actors allow personal behavior to develop out of the playwright's prescribed circumstances, knowing that their actions will involve a moment-to-moment subjective experience.

A great deal of the actor's work is a searching within for relevances from one's personal life to give a reality to the new existence (the character). When Uta Hagen played the young, would-be actress Nina in Chekhov's *The Sea Gull* at the age of eighteen, she understood Nina as a naive middle-class girl from the country who has been drawn into the life of her neighbor, a famous actress of whom she is in awe, and the actress' lover, a noted writer whom Nina hero-worshipped. On stage with Lynn Fontanne as Madame Arkadina, Hagen found it easy to use her awe of the famous actress and her husband, Alfred Lunt. She said, "I was in awe of Miss Fontanne and hero-worshipped Mr. Lunt. These particular character relationships were mirrored in my own, and I used their reality directly for my role."[7]

Most modern theories of actor training address methods of working "from the inside out." Constantin Stanislavski's "method" became the most famous and influential in modern times, especially among American actors.

The Actor's Tools

The actor's tools are the body, voice, emotions, imagination, and intellect. They must be flexible, disciplined, and expressive to communicate a wide range of attitudes, traits, emotions, feelings, and behaviors. The range of demands on the actor's abilities during a career will be enormous, for they must be adequate to re-creating classical and modern roles, such as Oedipus, Hamlet, Blanche DuBois, or Shelly Levene. In training and rehearsals, the actor works to understand the body and voice: how to control them; how to release psychological tensions and blocks that inhibit them; how to increase powers of imagination, observation, and concentration; and how to integrate them with the demands of the script and director. In using these tools, the actor combines an inner belief in the role with external performance techniques. Successful acting combines belief and technique to create a sense of truthful behavior—of life taking place on stage as if for the first time.

The Actor's Training

For many years, European and American actors were trained in the theatre itself. A young man or woman who showed ability would be hired to play small parts in a provincial stock company. The older actors would coach the young person, prescribing voice and body exercises that had been handed down for generations. This kind of external training developed a voice capable of being heard in large theatres, exaggerated gestures, and skill in speaking verse and Shakespeare. If actors showed talent, they would be given longer parts and eventually be invited to join the company.

When realism came into fashion late in the nineteenth century, this "large" style of acting began to seem exaggerated and unconvincing. As the stage came to be thought of not as a symbolic world—a place that symbolized the universe the audience lived in (such as Shakespeare's "Globe" theatre)—but as a recognizable place with a reality that corresponded to what ordinary people observed with their own senses, then scenic design, stage decor, and acting styles changed. The play's world—the environment and characters—were to be represented as directly and in as lifelike a way as possible. A middle-class street, house, and living room represented on a stage were to look like middle-class streets, houses, and living rooms outside the theatre. Actors were to be dressed like the businessmen or menial laborers that they were playing and that the audience encountered outside the theatre. So, too, the actor was called upon to set aside declamation and artificial gestures for the speech, walk, and behavior of such a person outside the theatre and to become a living, recognizable human being. To capture on stage and before an audience this sense of life being lived as it actually is, new methods for training actors had to be developed and new approaches arrived at for preparing a role.

Preparing the Role

Stanislavski's "Method" Constantin Stanislavski, the Russian actor-director, set about in the 1900s developing a systematic approach to training actors *to work from the inside outward* (see Figure 9.3). Today, his premises, developed over a lifetime, are accepted as the point of departure for most contemporary thinking about acting. The essence of Stanislavski's achievement (and lasting influence) was that he laid the basis for a psychological understanding of acting and fused it with a deep sense of drama as aesthetic truth. "The fundamental aim of our art," Stanislavski wrote in *An Actor Prepares*, "is the creation of [the] inner life of a human spirit and its expression in an artistic form."[8] To arrive at this truth, which had been lost in the theatre, Stanislavski proposed that actors understand how men and women actually behave physically and psychologically in given circumstances. Stanislavski's approach asked the actor to study and experience subjective emotions and feelings and to manifest them to audiences by physical and vocal means. He also stressed that personal truth in acting had to be balanced by attention to the *text*, to imaginative realities outside the actor's immediate experience. The actor was called upon to enter "the world of the play" as a whole, not just to attend to his or her part. Over the years, Stanislavski developed a means of training actors (his followers in America called it "the Method"; see Lee Strasberg box, p. 230) whereby they would not only create a subjective reality of their own—an inner truth of feeling and experience—but would also represent the "outer" truth of the character's reality in the surrounding world of the play. Speaking of the "external" acting that he had seen and abhorred in his time, Stanislavski said that "the difference between my art and that is the difference between 'seeming and being.'"[9]

FIGURE 9.3
Stanislavski as Gaev, Madame Ranevskaya's brother, in the 1904 Moscow Art Theatre production of Chekhov's The Cherry Orchard.

What distinguished Stanislavski's theory of actor-training was the emphasis on the purpose and objectives of human behavior. For Stanislavski, stage acting rested on the actor's discovery of the purpose and objectives of his or her character and the successful "playing" of those goals.

Stanislavski developed rehearsal methods by which the actor would "live life" onstage. He developed a set of exercises and principles designed to help the actor call on personal feelings and experiences, along with the body and the voice, in the creation of the role. This aspect of his training was called the "psychotechnique." Through the development of self-discipline, observation, relaxation, and total concentration, his actors learned to recall emotions from their own lives that were analogous to those experienced by the characters they played, in much the same manner described by Uta Hagen (see p. 232). What mattered to Stanislavski was the *actor's truth*: What the actor feels and experiences internally expresses itself in what the character says and how the character reacts to given circumstances. Actors learned to experience what their characters experienced *as if* it were actually happening to them.

LEE STRASBERG

Lee Strasberg (1901–1982), one of the best-known acting teachers in America, transformed Stanislavski's system of acting into an American "Method."

In 1947, members of the Group Theatre—an acting ensemble founded in 1931 that included Elia Kazan, Harold Clurman, Cheryl Crawford, and Stella Adler—started the Actors Studio (located today at 432 West 44th Street in New York City) as a workshop for professional actors to concentrate on acting problems away from the pressures of the commercial theatre. Strasberg assumed leadership of the Studio in 1951. As a teacher and acting theorist, he revolutionized American acting, producing such remarkable performers as Marlon Brando, Marilyn Monroe, Julie Harris, Paul Newman, Geraldine Page, Shelley Winters, Ellen Burstyn, and Al Pacino.

The methods of the Studio derived from Stanislavski were tailored by Strasberg for plays of American realism. He demanded great discipline of his actors, as well as great depths of character relationships and inner truthfulness. He once explained his approach in this way:

> The human being who acts is the human being who lives. That is a terrifying circumstance. Essentially the actor acts a fiction, a dream; in life the stimuli to which we respond are always real. The actor must constantly respond to stimuli that are imaginary. And yet this must happen not only just as it happens in life, but actually more fully and more expressively. Although the actor can do things in life quite easily, when he has to do the same thing on the stage under fictitious conditions he has difficulty because he is not equipped as a human being merely to playact at imitating life. He must somehow believe. He must somehow be able to convince himself of the rightness of what he is doing in order to do things fully on the stage.[10]

FIGURE 9.4
*Actor James Earl Jones as Othello in the 1964
New York Shakespeare Festival Theatre pro-
duction, Delacorte Theatre. Jones, who studied
with Lee Strasberg, won Antoinette Perry
("Tony") Awards as the boxer in* The Great
White Hope *(1968) and Troy Maxson in*
Fences *(1987).*

Stanislavski called this "the magic if" by which the actor thinks, "If I
were in Othello's situation, what would I do?" Not "If I were Othello,
what would I do?" By "becoming" a person in the character's *situation*,
the actor could give a performance that became a truthful, living experience, not merely the imitation of a fiction (see Figure 9.4).

Recalling Emotions

How does the actor induce emotion at the moment of performance
night after night? One of the first methods developed by Stanislavski
was "emotional recall" or "affective memory," in which the actor
recalled a situation in his or her own life that corresponded with the
playwright's intention for the character. Julie Harris tells us that she
conjures up something in her own life that produces tears when she is
called upon to cry.

Not only will the actor think of something sad (for example, a relative's death or something connected with the sad event), but the actor

will try to re-create in the mind's eye all of the surrounding circumstances, the sensory and emotional details that were part of the experience. Uta Hagen writes of her work on the role of Tennessee Williams' heroine, Blanche DuBois:

> Suppose I am going to work on the part of Blanche DuBois in *A Streetcar Named Desire*. I have to hunt for an understanding of—and an identification with—the character's main needs: a need for perfection (and always *when* and *how* have I needed these things); a romantic need for beauty; a desire for gentleness, tenderness, delicacy, elegance, decorum; a need to be loved and protected; a strong sensual need; a need for delusion when things go wrong, etc.
>
>   If I return to my cliché image of myself—the earthy, frank, gusty child of nature—I'm in trouble and there will be an enormous distance between Blanche and myself. If, on the other hand, I remember myself preparing for an evening at the opera (bathing and oiling and perfuming my body, soothing my skin, brushing my hair until it shines, artfully applying makeup until the little creases are hidden and my eyes look larger and I feel younger, spending hours over a silky elegant wardrobe, and a day over the meal I will serve before the opera, setting out my freshest linen, my best crystal and polished silver among dainty flowers); if I recall how I weep over a lovely poem by Rilke or Donne or Browning, how my flesh tingles when I hear Schubert chamber music, how tender I feel at a soft twilight, how I respond to someone pulling out a chair for me at the table or opening a car door for me or offering me their arm for a walk in the park—*then* I am beginning to find within myself realities connected with Blanche DuBois' needs.
>
>   I was not raised on an elegant plantation like Belle Reve, nor have I lived in Laurel, Mississippi, *but* I have visited elegant mansions in the East, I have seen many photographs of Faulkner country and estates, I have toured some of the South, and from a conglomerate of these experiences I can now make *my* Belle Reve and start to build a reality for my life there before the play's beginning.
>
>   Unfortunately, I have never been in New Orleans or the French Quarter, but I have read a great deal, seen many films and news-

reels. I have even related the French Quarter of New Orleans, in a way, to a little section of the Left Bank in Paris where I once lived to make it real to myself.

The Kowalski apartment itself, which is dictated for me by the playwright, the designer and the director, must, nevertheless, be made real to me by substitutions from my own life. It is *I* who must make the sense of cramped space, the lack of privacy, the disorder and sleaziness, the empty beer cans and stale cigarette butts, the harsh street noises all move in on me chaotically and frighteningly. Each object or thing that I see or come in contact with must be made particular so that it will serve the new me and bring about the psychological and sensory experiences necessary to animate my actions.[11]

Many actors like Uta Hagen and Julie Harris build an emotion in sympathy with the character's circumstances through the substitution of remembered sensory and emotional details. But the actor does not stop there. In the theatre the emotional impact must be produced night after night with precise timing, on cue, and with a minimum of conscious thought.

Physical and Vocal Training

The Actor's Body Modern movement training provides actors with a wide range of physical choices in the creation of character. It is not simply a matter of physically demonstrating a pompous valet or a nervous debutante. In movement training ("stage movement" is now an old-fashioned term), the emphasis is on developing the actor's body as a more open, responsive, physical instrument by first eliminating unnecessary tensions and mannerisms. Movement training today is not the imposition of arbitrary positions or alignments, as it was when young actors copied the gestures of the leading actor. Rather, it is more a matter of sensitizing actors to the variety of possibilities of human movement *as an expressive signal* of character and intentions.

In recent years movement training in the United States has changed in two fundamental ways. First, the influence of psychology has given insight into the actor's inner world and consequently into how that world may be expressed through the body's motion. Second, numerous approaches to movement or physical training from many different

UTA HAGEN

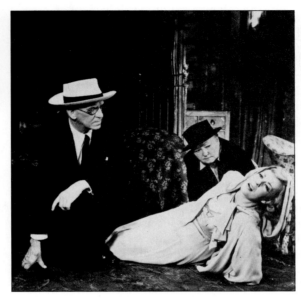

Uta Hagen as Blanche DuBois. She succeeded Jessica Tandy on Broadway in the role in A Streetcar Named Desire *in 1948.*

cultures and traditions have entered our classrooms and rehearsal halls and have had an enormous impact on actor training over the last decade. They range from techniques in martial arts, yoga, juggling and circus arts, stage combat, and mask training to Feldenkrais and the Alexander techniques. Our best movement teachers are familiar with and work through one or more of these approaches.

Today's movement teacher is, above all, an acting teacher who chooses to work through the body. Our best teachers have found ways to train actors to make fresh, often startling, choices—for movement grows from the urge to move as an expression of something that, until one critical moment, is hidden. The violent encounter between Stanley Kowalski and Blanche DuBois in *A Streetcar Named Desire* is an expression of Stanley's pent-up hostility and fear of his sister-in-law. He

Uta Hagen (b. 1919) was born in Gottingen, Germany, and, as a child, moved with her parents to the United States where her father was named head of the Art History Department at the University of Wisconsin, Madison. Inspired by a performance of Elizabeth Bergner as Saint Joan, she determined to be an actress and studied dance, piano, and eventually acting. Her first professional role was as Ophelia in Eva Le Gallienne's 1937 production of *Hamlet*. She played Nina on Broadway in the Alfred Lunt–Lynn Fontanne production of *The Sea Gull* in 1938 and played Desdemona to Paul Robeson's Othello in 1942. She worked with such directors as Guthrie McClintic, Margaret Webster, Marc Connelly, Harold Clurman, and Alan Schneider. She subsequently appeared in *Key Largo, A Streetcar Named Desire, The Country Girl, Saint Joan,* and *Who's Afraid of Virginia Woolf?* She can be seen in the film *Reversal of Fortune.*

Uta Hagen has emerged in recent years as an authority on actor training. Associated for over forty years as a teacher with the HB Studio in New York City, she has written two influential books on acting: *Respect for Acting* (1973) and *A Challenge for the Actor* (1991).

chooses a physical encounter—a fight and sexual assault—to express his fear and rage at this intruder who has so disrupted his household and violated his sense of masculine authority. Blanche, on the other hand, fights for her dignity and life in what is clearly a rape encounter.

Truly expressive stage movement, even combat like the duel in *Hamlet*, begins with the character's inner needs. When those needs are well understood, it is always possible to create physical realities that are compelling—like Laurence Olivier's grotesque, humpbacked Richard III (Shakespeare) or James Earl Jones' Troy Maxson (in *Fences*), whose physical stance is that of an aging athlete.

To be convincing, the actor's movements must *embody* the character's attitudes or needs. In performance, all physical and vocal choices must serve those needs.

The Actor's Voice The voice is our means of communicating to others, presenting ourselves, expressing our personality, thoughts, and feelings. The function of the actor's speech, like our own, is to communicate needs. For example, if we are speaking trivialities, it is not the *triviality* that is important, it is the *need* to speak it that matters. Therefore, however ordinary, stylized, or heightened (as in poetry) stage language is, when the actor speaks lines from the dramatic text, he or she must root those lines in the *need* to speak in a particular fashion and in particular words.[12]

Voice training today happens only in relation to the whole acting process and involves the actor's entire being—the physical and the psychological. Vocal exercises practiced in the classroom are, therefore, aimed at "freeing" the voice. These exercises involve relaxation, breathing, and increased muscularity of lips and tongue. These are followed by particular exercises on texts that stretch the voice, making it more responsive to the demands of the character.

The primary objective in voice training is to open up the possibilities of the voice—its energy, its instinctive responses to what the actor has to say. Correcting one's speech (a regional accent, for example) is not as important in voice training today as it once was, although Standard American Speech is encouraged by the profession. The aim of vocal exercises is to keep the essential *truth* of the actor's own voice, yet make it large and malleable enough for projecting feelings to a large auditorium or modulating to the intimacy of a television studio. To get this balance between the size of the voice and its malleability, vocal work involves both technique and imagination. Unlike the singer whose "sound" is the message, the actor's voice is an extension of the person (and the character). Its possibilities are as complex as the actor's persona. Because actors deal with *words* that come off a printed page, they continually have to find ways to make those words their own. Voice training aims at establishing an ongoing process for the actor to become as sensitive as possible to the physical makeup of the voice in relation to the body (breath, diaphragm, ribs, head, neck). The goal is to merge techniques learned in voice exercises with the actor's imagination to communicate the character's needs through the words of the text. Hamlet's instructions to the Players on the use of the voice and the body, "Suit the action to the word, the word to the action . . . ," are still appropriate to the actor's process.

GREAT MOMENTS OF ACTING

Given 2,500 years of Western theatrical history, the names of great actors illuminating particular roles are legion. The list of great actors of the modern theatre includes such names as Sarah Bernhardt, Eleanora Duse, John Barrymore, Judith Anderson, Ethel Barrymore, John Gielgud, Eva Le Gallienne, Jean-Louis Barrault, Laurette Taylor, Ralph Richardson, and Laurence Olivier. Such legendary performances as Laurette Taylor's Amanda Wingfield, Laurence Olivier's Hamlet, or Jessica Tandy's Blanche DuBois grow out of rigorous training, keen sensitivity, vivid dramatic imagination, and an intelligence equal to the demands of text, director, and stage.

Director Peter Brook describes unforgettable moments in an actor's performance as "a flash of insight that comes from the confrontation of the performer's hidden world and the hidden world of character. . . . For theatre to be seen at its most alive, there has to be a very, very exact balance between the living personality of the performer and the second personality, which is that of the character."[13] Great acting is a seamless integration of the actor's personality and the character in the context of the given circumstances of the play.

This photo essay illustrates unforgettable moments from five plays discussed in this book. They capture a single moment in the work of great actors in the modern theatre whose names have become synonymous with certain roles: Jessica Tandy with Williams' Blanche DuBois, Bert Lahr with Beckett's Estragon, Irene Worth with Chekhov's Madame Ranevskaya, James Earl Jones with Wilson's Troy Maxson, and Ron Leibman with Kushner's Roy Cohn.

JESSICA TANDY (b. 1909) *as Blanche DuBois in the 1947 Broadway production of* A Streetcar Named Desire *with Marlon Brando as Stanley Kowalski and Kim Hunter as Stella in the background.*

Tandy played Blanche, one of the longest and most exacting roles on record, for over two years on Broadway, establishing her as one of America's leading actresses. Critic Brooks Atkinson said of her performance: "She acts a magnificent part magnificently. . . . She plays it with an insight as vibrant and pitiless as Mr. Williams' writing, for she catches on the wing the terror, bogus refinement, and intellectual alertness and the madness that can hardly be distinguished from logic and fastidiousness."

With her husband Hume Cronyn, Tandy formed a distinguished stage partnership. They have appeared together on Broadway, at The Guthrie Theater, and at Stratford Ontario's Shakespeare Festival. Most notable has been their work together in The Fourposter *(1951),* The Gin Game *(1979), and* Foxfire *(1982). Tandy starred on Broadway as Amanda Wingfield in Williams'* The Glass Menagerie *(1984) and re-created the role of Miss Daisy in the film version of Alfred Uhry's play* Driving Miss Daisy *(1989), for which she won an "Oscar" Award for Best Actress. During her distinguished stage career she won three Antoinette Perry ("Tony") Awards as Best Actress for* A Streetcar Named Desire, The Gin Game, *and* Foxfire.

Chapter Nine

IRENE WORTH (b. 1916) as Madame Ranevskaya, one of the great Chekhov roles from The Cherry Orchard, in the 1977 New York Shakespeare Festival production, directed by Andrei Serban at Lincoln Center. Worth has had an extraordinary career on American and British stages in plays by Chekhov, Henrik Ibsen, Edward Albee, Lillian Hellman, Tennessee Williams, and Samuel Beckett, to name only a few. Her work has spanned two continents and included appearances on Broadway, the Edinburgh Festival, London's West End, the Royal Shakespeare Company, the Chichester Festival, Stratford Ontario's Shakespeare Festival, and The Public Theatre. She created the role of Celia Coplestone in T. S. Eliot's The Cocktail Party (1949), starred in Lillian Hellman's Toys in the Attic (1960), played Goneril in Peter Brook's production of King Lear (1962), performed Winnie in Happy Days (1979), directed by Andrei Serban, and Grandma Kurnitz in Neil Simon's Lost in Yonkers (1990) on Broadway, all to vast critical acclaim.

In an interview with the New York Times (February 5, 1976), she talked about the actor's art, which her own work epitomizes: "You know what a salmon does when it goes upstream? It feels about for the point of maximum energy in the water, the point where the water whirls round and round and generates a terrific centrifugal force. It looks for that point, and it finds it, and the water quadruples the salmon's own natural strength, and then it can jump. That's what an actor has to do with the text. The point of maximum energy is always there, but it takes finding."

BERT LAHR *(1895–1967) as Estragon (right) in Beckett's* Waiting for Godot. *Beginning his stage career as a stand-up vaudeville comic, Lahr moved on to Broadway musical comedy, became identified with the role of the Cowardly Lion in the film* The Wizard of Oz *(1939), and closed his career as a distinguished actor best remembered for his performance as Gogo (Estragon) in Beckett's existential masterpiece.*

Lahr created the role in the American premiere of Beckett's play in Miami, 1956, directed by Alan Schneider, continuing on Broadway later that same year (directed by Herbert Berghof) with E. G. Marshall as Vladimir, Kurt Kasznar as Pozzo, and Alvin Epstein as Lucky. These productions are described in Notes on a Cowardly Lion *(1969), a perceptive biography by his son, John Lahr, a notable theatre critic.*

As Estragon, Lahr was unfailing in his instincts to be clear, simple, and to the point. Audiences waited in vain for hints of the famous "cowardly lion," but Lahr refused to retread familiar ground. His warmth and common humanity extended across the footlights and caught up audiences in a shared experience. British critic Kenneth Tynan put it this way: "Mr. Lahr's beleaguered simpleton [Estragon], a draughts-player lost in a universe of chess, is one of the noblest performances I have ever seen."

JAMES EARL JONES *(b. 1931 in Arkabutla, Michigan)* *was educated at The University of Michigan, Ann Arbor, and studied acting in the late 1950s with Lee Strasberg and with the American Theatre Wing in New York City. He made his Broadway debut as an understudy in* The Egghead *(1957) and his London debut in* Paul Robeson *(1978), a one-man show.*

Jones has performed a variety of stage and film roles. He has been seen as Othello, Claudius (in Hamlet*), Macbeth, and King Lear with the New York Shakespeare Festival Theatre; as Jack Jefferson in* The Great White Hope *with Arena Stage in Washington, D.C., and again on Broadway in 1968; and as Troy Maxson (in* Fences*) with the Yale Repertory Theatre in 1985.* Fences *moved to Broadway in 1987. Jones won the Antoinette Perry ("Tony") Award for Best Actor in 1969 for* The Great White Hope *and the American Academy of Arts and Letters Medal for Spoken Language in 1981.*

He has appeared in such major films as Dr. Strangelove *(1964),* The Great White Hope *(1970), and* Hunt for Red October *(1990) and as the voice of Darth Vader in* Star Wars *(1977),* The Empire Strikes Back *(1980), and* Return of the Jedi *(1983).*

The central character, Troy Maxson, in August Wilson's Fences *has been described as the best role of James Earl Jones' career. His performance as Troy was called "mountainous," "magnificent," "towering." One critic called it one of Jones' "most powerful and riveting performances, rising to brilliant outbursts of anguish and irony."*

RON LEIBMAN *as Roy Cohn in* Angels in America: A Gay Fantasia on National Themes. Part 1: Millennium Approaches, *Tony Kushner's 1993 Antoinette Perry ("Tony") Award-winning two-part epic on Broadway. As the maniacal Roy Cohn, the witch-hunting accomplice of Joseph McCarthy, Ron Leibman appears here as the unofficial power broker in the Ed Meese Justice Department during the Reagan administration, who is now New York City's most famous closeted gay AIDS patient. Jack Kroll, writing for* Newsweek, *said ". . . Leibman turns a pit-bull language of chronic rage into a perverse eloquence that is chilling."*

Rehearsals and Performance

This task of creating an emotional impact through the careful reconstruction of one's life experience and then relating those emotions to the character and the situation is carried out in rehearsals, which may last from three to ten weeks. The work of rehearsals is to condition the actor's responses so that during performance emotions flow from the actor's concentration on the material—the character's circumstances and objectives.

In rehearsals the actor works with the director and other actors to find the role and to "set" movement and interpretation. Not until dress rehearsal, as a rule, is an actor able to work with a complete set of properties, settings, costumes, makeup, sound, and stage lighting. However, special rehearsal clothes and properties, like fans, walking sticks, long skirts, and capes are provided if they are significantly different from ordinary dress and handheld objects.

On each night of the play's run, the actor re-creates the character for the audience. Everything the actor has set and made personal in rehearsals—objectives, mannerisms, vocal intonations, movements—stays (or should stay) much the same. But the actor's creativity continues within the boundaries set in rehearsal: This is the actor's art. Each performance requires the actor to give fresh life to the character's feelings, responses, desires, goals—to concentrate anew on the character's speech, behavior, and theatrical effectiveness.

Summary

The actor brings human behavior and a living presence onto the stage. The audience observes and engages in the actor's thinking, planning, working, imagining, and living the life of the character. And the actor must be seen to do all of these things not in the context of the theatre but in the situation shared with other actors onstage—within the world of the play. The actor must be continually redefining relationships with other characters and must be seen as striving to achieve goals and objectives within the play's given circumstances of when, where, and what. This continuous searching for new depths of creative energy and truthful human behavior keeps the actor's performance fresh and alive night after night.

The director, in collaboration with the actor, interprets the playwright's text in the theatre's three-dimensional space, lending shape, sound, rhythm, images, and activity to the creative process. Audiences experience the play through the actor's *and* the director's eyes, ears, emotions, imagination, and intellect, but the director is the final arbiter of choice—the captain and navigator of the theatrical ship. The next chapter deals with the director, who emerged as a creative force in the theatre only in the final days of the previous century.

Questions for Study

1. Study the photo of *Our Town* on page 222. What are the *essentials* that remain onstage after so much has been stripped away?

2. At what point does the actor's artistic process begin?

3. Define a character's *given circumstances* within the play.

4. Describe Blanche DuBois' given circumstances in her first scene in *A Streetcar Named Desire*.

5. What are the goals of movement and voice training for the actor?

6. Who was Constantin Stanislavski? Lee Strasberg?

7. Discuss your understanding of Stanislavski's terms: *the magic if, psychotechnique, objective, emotional recall*.

8. What do we mean when we talk about the American "Method" of acting?

9. According to Peter Brook, what constitutes an "unforgettable moment" in an actor's performance?

10. Select a distinguished actor and study his or her background in the theatre and special accomplishments. Write an essay in which you describe that actor's understanding of the artistic process.

11. *Plays to Read*: Thornton Wilder's *Our Town*; Tennessee Williams' *A Streetcar Named Desire*.

12. *Suggested Readings*: Lee Strasberg's famous entry on "acting" in *Encyclopaedia Britannica* (included in editions printed since 1957); John Gielgud's *Acting Shakespeare* (New York: Charles Scribner's, 1992); Uta Hagen's (with Haskel Frankel) *Respect for Acting*

(New York: Macmillan, 1973) or her *A Challenge for the Actor* (New York: Charles Scribner's, 1991).

13. *Suggested Writings and Biographies*: *Laurette* (about Laurette Taylor) by Marguerite Courtney (New York: Proscenium, 1955); *Confessions of an Actor: An Autobiography* by Laurence Olivier (New York: Simon and Schuster, 1982); *Stanislavski: A Biography* by Jean Benedetti (New York: Routledge, 1990).

The theater of the future, if it is to hold us, will have to shake off a belief it has held only a relatively short time—the belief that it is showing us "a real room with real people." For the theatre's role is to present life not in its literal exactness but rather through some kind of poetic vision, metaphor, image—the mirror held up as 'twere to nature.[1]

ALAN SCHNEIDER

The director, in collaboration with the playwright and with the help of many other artists and assistants, creates the performance in the theatre's space for us to see and hear.

10

THE IMAGE MAKERS: THE DIRECTOR

Forerunners

In the 1860s in Europe, the practice of a single person guiding all aspects of the production process began to take hold. Before that time, leading actors, theatre managers, and sometimes playwrights "staged" the play, thereby setting actors' movements, dictating financial matters, and making decisions on casting, costumes, and scenery. During the first half of the nineteenth century, actor-managers (following the tradition of James Burbage in England and Molière in France) resembled the modern director in some respects. Nevertheless, the actor-manager was first of all an actor and considered the production from the perspective of the role he was playing. David Garrick (1717–1779) was one of England's successful actor-managers. Although the theatre between 1750 and 1850 was immensely popular in Europe, most actor-managers— Garrick was an exception—maintained inferior artistic standards in their pursuit of large box office receipts.

This general condition in the theatre began to worry a growing number of theatre people, who reexamined the production process. With the formation in 1866 of Duke George II of Saxe-Meiningen's company in Germany (known as the Meiningen Players), the director in the modern sense of the term began to emerge. He exercised a central artistic discipline over the company, serving in the modern sense as producer, director, and financial backer. By controlling design, he introduced a unified look in costumes and settings. The Duke's efforts to define the director's role were followed by those of André Antoine in France and Constantin Stanislavski in Russia. Under their influence, the modern stage director's identity took shape in Europe: someone who understood all

[handwritten margin note:] central artistic discipline — producer — director — financial backer.

DUKE OF SAXE-MEININGEN— GEORGE II

Duke of Saxe-Meiningen, George II (1826–1914), transformed the Duchy of Meiningen's court theatre into an example of scenic historical accuracy and lifelike acting. As producer-director, the Duke designed all costumes, scenery, and properties for historically authentic style, and worked for *ensemble acting*. The Duke was assisted by Ludwig Chronegk (1837–1891), an actor responsible for supervising and rehearsing the company. The Meiningen Players were noted throughout Europe for their crowd scenes, in which each member of the crowd had individual traits and specific lines. In rehearsals the actors were divided into small groups, each under the charge of an experienced actor. This practice was in keeping with the company's rule against actors being stars and was the beginning of the new movement in 1874 toward unified production under the director's control. Saxe-Meiningen's example of the *single creative authority* in charge of the total production influenced Antoine and Stanislavski.

theatre arts and devoted full energies to combining them into a unified, artistic whole.

The Director as Artist

The director collaborates with playwright, actors, designers, and technicians to create on stage a carefully selected vision of life—a special mirror. Alan Schneider described the *theatre's* role from a director's viewpoint as presenting life not in its literal exactness but through some kind of poetic vision, metaphor, or image—the mirror held up to nature. The director can have several roles in the theatre, ranging from the mundane, like attending to budgets, publicity, and box office details, to the imaginative discovery and creative interpretation of the playwright's text. In all events, the director is the controlling artist responsible for unifying the production elements, which often includes the use of text, music, sound, and visuals.

Chapter Ten

Director :–
controlling artist
responsible for unifying
the prod'n elements
which often includes the
use of text, music, sound
& visuals. 248

Although each director has his or her own way of working creatively in the theatre, in general three types of directors have evolved over the years. On the first day of rehearsal, one type of director gives a speech to the cast on what the play is about and describes the approach that will be taken to interpreting the text. Actors, directors, and designers are often treated as "servants" to the director's concept and expected to deliver the "look" and "meaning" of the play's world as specified by the director. Another type of director reverses this approach and becomes the servant or coordinator of a group of actors, thereby limiting his or her own vision to the suggestions, criticisms, and encouragements of the group.

The third type of director functions as a guide, or helmsman, who senses at the outset the direction that the production will take but proceeds in rehearsals to provoke and stimulate the actors. This director creates an atmosphere in which actors dig, probe, and investigate the whole fabric of the play. Rehearsals are used to search out ("to harrow" in the original sense of the word *rehearse*), to listen, and to yield to suggestions. The "directional conception" is what Alan Schneider refers to as the director's poetic vision, and it precedes the first day's work. Nevertheless, the "sense of direction" only crystallizes into a consistent stage image at the very end of the process.

The director's question, unlike the critic's, does not deal so much with "What's the event about?" as with questions about the event's *potential.* This is the reason a director chooses one sort of theatrical material over another—because of its potential. It is this realization of a play's or event's potential that motivates directors to find space, actors, and forms of expression. The director, like the hunter or the explorer, intuits that a potential exists within a work (or text) and yet explores the unknown with a sense of expectation and discovery and with a deepening commitment to leading the team. Try to imagine the potential of an untried script called *A Streetcar Named Desire* and the excitement of its first director, Elia Kazan, struggling to find the direction of what he called the spine (or the throughline) of the play's main action. In his notebook, he defined the play's spine as the "last gasp" of a dying civilization: "This little twisted, pathetic, confused bit of light and culture . . . snuffed out by the crude forces of violence, insensibility and vulgarity which exist in our South—and this cry is the play."[2]

Consider a director like Peter Brook who sets out, over a number of years, to explore an ancient Hindu epic (*The Mahabharata*); Brook's

---

Handwritten margin notes:

3 TYPES OF DIRECTORS

(i) gives speech on 1st day to cast on basis of play & describes approach taken in interpreting text.

(ii) Becomes the servant or coordinator of a group of actors, thereby limiting his/her own vision to suggestions, criticisms + encouragement of the group.

(iii) Functions as a guide who senses at the outset the direction that prod'n will take but proceeds in rehearsal to provoke & stimulate actors.

PRODUCER-DIRECTOR

ANDRÉ ANTOINE

André Antoine (1858–1943) was producer-director of the Théâtre Libre, or Free Theatre, in France. Beginning as a part-time actor, Antoine founded in 1887 a theatre and a naturalistic production style that became world-famous. The Théâtre Libre was a subscription theatre, one open only to members and therefore exempt from censorship. It became a showcase for new plays (Ibsen's *Ghosts* was one) and new production techniques. Seeking authentic detail, Antoine tried to reproduce exact environments. In one play he hung real beef carcasses on stage. In an effort to stage "real" life, Antoine developed three important principles: realistic environments, ensemble acting, and the director's authority.

---

nine-hour theatrical realization presents humanity's greatest dilemma: human beings caught up in the conflict of divine versus demonic forces. The story of this 1985 theatre epic is essentially a quest for morality: how to find one's way in an age of destruction regardless of epoch, culture, or society. As director, Brook—with the assistance of collaborators, including writers, designers, and actors—himself created a theatrical epic out of an ancient, sacred poem of Hindu origins. With *A Streetcar Named Desire*, Elia Kazan *interpreted* Tennessee Williams' text. They are both directors creating a "mirror" that is held up to nature in its many forms, varieties, and expressions.

Directors 6 responsibilities
1) agreeing to direct or create a script.
2) deciding on text's interpretation & the "look" & configuration of the stage space
3) casting actors in various parts.
4) working with other artists to plan & execute the prod'n
5) rehearsing the actors
6) coordinating all elements into final stage performance.

Early Responsibilities: Audition, Casting, Assistants

Basically, a director has six responsibilities: (1) agreeing to direct an offered script or selecting or creating a script, especially in college and university productions; (2) deciding on the text's interpretation and the "look" and configuration of the stage space; (3) casting actors in the various parts; (4) working with other theatre artists to plan and execute

CONSTANTIN STANISLAVSKI

A scene from the 1904 Moscow Art Theatre production of The Cherry Orchard, *directed by Constantin Stanislavski.*

Constantin Stanislavski (1863–1938) was producer-director-actor and co-founder of the Moscow Art Theatre (see Figure 9.3). As a director, Stanislavski aimed for ensemble acting and the absence of stars; he established such directional methods as intensive study of the play before rehearsals began, the actor's careful attention to detail, and re-creation of the play's milieu after visiting locales or doing extensive research. The Moscow Art Theatre's reputation was made with Anton Chekhov's plays depicting the monotonous and frustrating life of the rural landowning class.

Stanislavski is remembered most for his efforts to perfect a truthful method of acting. His published writings in English—*My Life in Art* (1924), *An Actor Prepares* (1936), *Building a Character* (1949), and *Creating a Role* (1961)—provide a record of the "Stanislavski System" as it evolved.

ALAN SCHNEIDER

The first American production of Beckett's Waiting for Godot *was directed by Alan Schneider in 1956 at the Cocoanut Grove Playhouse in Miami. Tom Ewell played Vladimir (center) and Bert Lahr was Estragon.*

Casting - matching an actor to a role.

Auditions:- director looks for actors whose physical appearance, personality & acting style flesh out the directors Idea of the characters.

the production; (5) rehearsing the actors; and (6) coordinating all elements into the final stage performance. Nevertheless, none of the director's process is cut and dried. It is as variable as the names, faces, and talents of the team players.

Casting is matching an actor to a role. During *auditions* the director looks for actors whose physical appearance, personality, and acting style flesh out the director's idea of the characters. In college and university theatres, audition or tryout procedures are more or less standardized. Copies of the play are made available and notices of auditions posted. The director holds private interviews or general tryouts, or a combina-

252   *Chapter Ten*

Alan Schneider (1917–1984) was born Abram Leopoldovich Schneider in Kharkov, Russia, the son of medical students. The Schneiders escaped to the United States during the Russian Revolution and settled in Maryland. Educated at Johns Hopkins University and Cornell University, Alan Schneider taught at Catholic University in Washington, D.C. In 1944, he made his acting debut on Broadway in a Maxwell Anderson play. His first work as a director was at Arena Stage in Washington, D.C., where he began the pattern of his distinguished directing career: alternating between professional regional and Broadway theatres.

The turning point in his career was the 1956 American premiere of *Waiting for Godot* (see also box, p. 110). Bringing Samuel Beckett's plays to the public's attention became a lifelong crusade for Schneider. He directed the American premieres of Beckett's *Krapp's Last Tape, Happy Days, Endgame, Not I*, and *Rockaby*. On Broadway he directed the original productions of Edward Albee's *Who's Afraid of Virginia Woolf?, Tiny Alice*, and *A Delicate Balance*. Amid this flurry of activity he became for four years the head of the Juilliard Theatre Center in New York City. At the time of his death he was artistic director of the Acting Company.

Few American directors have been so consistently involved with plays of quality and significance. Few have worked with so many seminal playwrights of our time.

tion of the two. The director usually asks actors to come prepared to illustrate their acting range by performing selections either from plays of their own choosing or from material provided at the audition for them to read aloud.

Beginning with the leads, the director narrows the choices for each part. If circumstances warrant, he or she calls back a final group. This group reads together from the play to be produced so that the director can visualize the actors together. It is important to see how they relate to one another, how they work together, and how they complement one another in physical appearance and in vocal and emotional quality.

Once the director decides on the desired ensemble effect, there is a further elimination process, the casting notice is posted, and rehearsals begin.

To prepare a play within a three- to ten-week rehearsal period, the modern director needs *assistants*. The *assistant director* attends production meetings, coaches actors, and rehearses special or problem scenes. The *stage manager* compiles the promptbook (a copy of the play with directions for performance); records stage business, blocking, lighting, sound, and other cues; makes the rehearsal schedule; takes notes during rehearsals; coordinates rehearsals; and runs the show after it has opened. **Dramaturgs** provide research and write program notes.

Directing Styles

At the most basic level, the director helps the actor find the character's inner life and project this life vocally and visually to the audience. One basic approach still used by some directors is to preplan the actors' movements and, like a photographer composing a group photograph, arrange the actors in the stage space to show their physical and psychological relationships. The director's emphasis here is on where the people are in *space*. Like a photographer, this director composes pictures with actors on stage to show relationships, emotions, and attitudes, to convey truths about human relationships, and to tell the playwright's story.

The first three or four rehearsals are used to *block* the play. In blocking rehearsals, the director goes through each scene line by line, working with the actors on when to come in, where to stand or sit, on what lines to move. As they go through the actions, the actors write down the directions and **stage business** (specific actions, such as answering a telephone or turning on a table lamp) in their scripts.

As we have seen, directors vary a great deal in their approach to beginning rehearsals. Some give full directions immediately; others leave much of the detail to be worked out later as the actors try out their lines and reactions to one another. Almost any director makes adjustments in later rehearsals as director and actors discover better ways of moving and reacting and generally shaping the script into a meaningful performance.

STAGE VOCABULARY

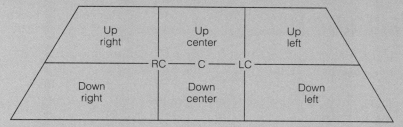

Stage vocabulary is a language that has developed over the years between director and actor to communicate quickly to each other in rehearsals. It is a kind of stage shorthand in which *all directions are to the actor's left or right.*

Upstage means toward the rear of the acting area. *Downstage* means toward the front. *Stage right* and *stage left* refer to the performer's right or left when he or she is facing the audience. The stage floor is frequently spoken of as though it were divided into sections: *up right, up center, up left, down right, down center, down left.*

Body positions are also designated for work largely on the proscenium stage. The director may ask the actor to *turn out*, meaning to turn more toward the audience. Two actors are sometimes told to *share a scene*, or to play in a profile position so that they are equally visible to the audience. An actor may be told to *dress the stage*, meaning to move to balance the stage picture. Experienced actors take directions with ease and frequently make such moves almost automatically.

In the audience we are almost never aware that the actor is taking a rehearsed position. But the actor's movements, along with lighting and sound, often control what we see and hear onstage.

A second basic approach, which most modern directors favor, is the *collaborative approach*. This organic method involves director and actors working together in rehearsals to develop movement, gestures, character relationships, stage images, and line interpretations. Rather than entering the rehearsal period with entirely preset ideas, the director watches, listens, suggests, and selects as the actors rehearse the play.

The methods of German playwright and director Bertolt Brecht (1898–1956) have been described in this way:

> During rehearsals Bertolt Brecht sits in the auditorium. His work as a director is unobtrusive. When he intervenes it is almost unnoticeable and always in the "direction of flow." He never interrupts, not even with suggestions for improvement. You do not get the impression that he wants to get the actors to "present some of his ideas"; they are not his instruments.
>
> Instead he searches, together with the actors, for the story which the play tells, and helps each actor to his strength. His work with the actors may be compared to the efforts of a child to direct straws with a twig from a puddle into the river itself, so that they may float.
>
> Brecht is not one of those directors who knows everything better than the actors. He adopts towards the play an attitude of "know-nothingism"; he waits. You get the impression that Brecht does not know his own play, not a single sentence. And he does not want to know what is written, but rather how the written text is to be shown by the actor on the stage. If an actor asks: "Should I stand up at this point?", the reply is often typically Brecht: "I don't know." Brecht really does not know; he only discovers during the rehearsal.[3]

The importance of the rehearsal process is to discover a unity, rhythm, and meaning for the production. At some point in the rehearsal period, the director sets the performance by selecting from what has evolved in rehearsals. In this second approach, improvisation or game playing is often an important director's tool.

Improvisation (Figure 10.1) can free the actors' imaginations and bodies for spontaneous storytelling. Often the director uses improvisations early in rehearsals to spark the cast's imagination, behavior, reactions, and mood as they begin to work together. In later rehearsals, improvisations can increase concentration, discover dramatic action and character relationships, and develop good working relations among actors.

The modern director uses other tools to stimulate the actors' imaginations so that they will give life to their roles. The director's *ground*

THE DIRECTOR
AS CREATOR

Julie Taymor, as director and designer, created the puppets for the 1988 Off Broadway production of Juan Darien, *based on a Latin American story by Horacio Quiroga.*

The 1984 production of The King Stag, *directed by Andrei Serban, with costumes and masks by Julie Taymor for the American Repertory Theatre, Cambridge, MA. The long arms of the bird-magician figure (front) were inspired by the flowing sleeves of Korean garments.*

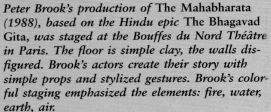

Peter Brook's production of The Mahabharata (1988), based on the Hindu epic The Bhagavad Gita, was staged at the Bouffes du Nord Théâtre in Paris. The floor is simple clay, the walls disfigured. Brook's actors create their story with simple props and stylized gestures. Brook's colorful staging emphasized the elements: fire, water, earth, air.

Peter Brook filled the "empty space" of the stage with circus tricks and techniques borrowed from puppet theatre and the English music halls. Here, trapezes and a feathered bower simulate the magical forest as Titania makes love to Bottom, who wears a clown's red nose, in Peter Brook's acclaimed production of Shakespeare's A Midsummer Night's Dream for the Royal Shakespeare Company (England, 1970).

The Black Rider: The Casting of the Magic Bullets *brought together Robert Wilson, Tom Waits, and William Burroughs in a collaboration based on a German folk tale of a man who, to succeed as a marksman and win his bride, casts magic bullets with the help of the devil. With direction and stage design by Robert Wilson,* The Black Rider *premiered in Hamburg, Germany, in 1990 and was part of the 1993 Next Wave Festival at The Brooklyn Academy of Music, New York City.*

A scene from the CIVIL warS: a tree is best measured when it is down, *conceived and directed by Robert Wilson, juxtaposes actor and puppets in pinpoints of light.*

Ariane Mnouchkine, founding director of the Théâtre du Soleil, removed Shakespeare's plays from traditional Western trappings. Richard II *relies on kabuki traditions of setting, costumes, props, makeup, and movement.*

The chorus of baboon-faced dogs with pointed snouts in masks by Erhard Stiefel from the final part (The Eumenides) *of Ariane Mnouchkine's production of* Les Atrides *(Paris, 1992).*

FIGURE 10.1

Actors improvise movement in Hair *(the 1967 "American tribal love-rock musical" directed by Tom O'Horgan on Broadway). Improvisation is primarily a rehearsal tool and not a performance technique. How much improvisation is used in rehearsal depends on the director's skill with it and on the actors' needs. Viola Spolin's* Improvisation for the Theatre *(1963) is a good book about this approach to freeing the actor from inhibitions.*

Ground Plan

defines the space limitations for the story, such as obstacles furniture, doors, stairs & so on.

plan defines the space limitations for the story, such as obstacles of furniture, doors, stairs, and so on (see Figure 10.2). As the director physically arranges the actors in the ground plan, they discover physical relationships with other characters and come to understand the play's action. As the actors move about the stage, they discover gestures that further illustrate character and emotion. As the director and actors add storytelling details of gesture and speech, the characters' emotional truth is illustrated visually and vocally and the living quality of the play is communicated.

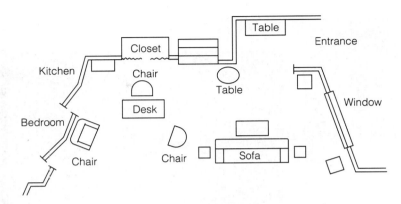

FIGURE 10.2

The ground plan. Director and designer work out the play's environment, noting where the doorways, windows, steps, levels, walls, and furniture are. These are then outlined in tape on the rehearsal-room floor so the actor can visualize the environment in rehearsals.

The Director's Vision

As creative artists, some directors serve the playwright by translating the script as faithfully as possible into theatrical form. Elia Kazan, for example, interpreted Arthur Miller's and Tennessee Williams' plays on Broadway with a faithful concern for the playwright's "intention." Some playwrights, like Edward Albee, Athol Fugard, David Mamet, and María Irene Fornés, direct their own plays. Other directors seek out a controlling idea, image, or sound to define the production's emotional and political meaning. Mike Nichols, in directing Neil Simon's comedies, searches for what he calls the "Event"—the truthful moment or series of moments that will illuminate the author's meaning, that will reveal "real people living their lives." In contrast, JoAnne Akalaitis allows events from the real world, such as songs, pictures, or magazine articles, to trigger the creative process for her. Her work on *Dressed Like an Egg*, which she adapted from French writer Colette's life and works, was inspired by a magazine photograph of Colette leaning against parallel bars in her gym with a poignant, lost, and courageous look.

ELIA KAZAN

Marlon Brando as Stanley (left) prepares to throw his cup and plate on the floor during Blanche's birthday party in A Streetcar Named Desire *(1947). Jessica Tandy as Blanche (center) and Kim Hunter as Stella (right) are seated at the table.*

Elia Kazan (b. 1909 in Istanbul, Turkey) was educated at Williams College and Yale University. He was a member of the Group Theatre and acted in their productions of Clifford Odets' *Waiting for Lefty, Paradise Lost,* and *Golden Boy.*

He is best known today for his direction of plays by Tennessee Williams and Arthur Miller: *A Streetcar Named Desire* (1947), *Death of a Salesman* (1949), *Camino Real* (1953), *Cat on a Hot Tin Roof* (1955), and *Sweet Bird of Youth* (1959). Kazan also directed the films of *A Streetcar Named Desire, On the Waterfront,* and *East of Eden.*

Along with designer Jo Mielziner, Kazan established selected realism as the dominant American theatrical style during the 1950s. The style combined acting of intense psychological truth with simplified but realistic scenery. Marlon Brando as Stanley Kowalski embodied the

continued on next page

style of acting for which Kazan's productions were famous (also see Figure 1.2, page 7).

The following excerpt is from Kazan's director's notebook (dated August 1947), which he kept before and during rehearsals of *A Streetcar Named Desire*:

A thought—directing finally consists of turning Psychology into Behavior.

Theme—this is a message from the dark interior. This little twisted, pathetic, confused bit of light and culture puts out a cry. It is snuffed out by the crude forces of violence, insensibility and vulgarity which exist in our South—and this cry is the play.

Style—one reason a "style," a stylized production is necessary is that a subjective factor—Blanche's memories, inner life, emotions, are a real factor. We cannot really understand her behavior unless we see the effect of her past on her present behavior.

This play is a poetic tragedy. We are shown the final dissolution of a person of worth, who once had great potential, and who, even as she goes down, has worth exceeding that of the "healthy," coarse-grained figures who kill her.

Blanche is a social type, an emblem of a dying civilization, making its last curlicued and romantic exit. All her behavior patterns are those of the dying civilization she represents. In other words her behavior is *social*. Therefore find social modes! This is the source of the play's stylization and the production's style and color. Likewise, Stanley's behavior is *social* too. It is the basic animal cynicism of today. "Get what's coming to you! Don't waste a day! Eat, drink, get yours!" This is the basis of his stylization, of the choice of his props. All props should be stylized: they should have a color, shape and weight that spell: style.

An effort to put poetic names on scenes to edge me into stylizations and physicalizations. Try to keep each scene in terms of Blanche.

1. Blanche comes to the last stop at the end of the line.
2. Blanche tries to make a place for herself.

3. Blanche breaks them apart, but when they come together, Blanche is more alone than ever!

4. Blanche, more desperate because more excluded, tries the direct attack and makes the enemy who will finish her.

5. Blanche finds that she is being tracked down for the kill. She must work fast.

6. Blanche suddenly finds, suddenly makes for herself, the only possible, perfect man for her.

7. Blanche comes out of the happy bathroom to find that her own doom has caught up with her.

8. Blanche fights her last fight. Breaks down. Even Stella deserts her.

9. Blanche's last desperate effort to save herself by telling the whole truth. The *truth dooms her.*

10. Blanche escapes out of this world. She is brought back by Stanley and destroyed.

11. Blanche is disposed of.

The style—the real deep style—consists of one thing only: to find behavior that's truly social, significantly typical, at each moment. It's not so much what Blanche has done—it's how she does it—with such style, grace, manners, old-world trappings and effects, props, tricks, swirls, etc., that they seem anything but vulgar.

And for the other characters, too, you face the same problem. To find the Don Quixote character for them. *This is a poetic tragedy, not a realistic or a naturalistic one. So you must find a Don Quixote scheme of things for each.*

Stylized acting and direction is to realistic acting and direction as poetry is to prose. The acting must be styled, not in the obvious sense. (Say nothing about it to the producer and actors.) But you will fail unless you find this kind of poetic realization for the behavior of these people.[4]

FIGURE 10.3

Director Peter Brook took Shakespeare's
A Midsummer Night's Dream *(1970)*
out of Elizabethan costumes, painted
scenic backdrops, and green forests.
Brook's actors performed while
balancing on trapezes, juggling plates,
hurling streamers, or stumbling about
on stilts.

Many directors today, taking their cues from such great experimental directors as Meyerhold and Brecht, fashion the script into a wholly new and directorially original work of art. In this role, the director alters the play—changes the period represented, cuts the text, rearranges the scenes—and practically takes over the role of author. In his recreation of Shakespeare's *A Midsummer Night's Dream* for the Royal Shakespeare Company in 1970, director Peter Brook worked in this way (see Figure 10.3). Others, like Robert Wilson and Martha Clarke, have their roots in a nonnarrative theatrical tradition. Their work has its inception in images, sounds, and movement, not in a verbal text. For this reason (among many) their work differs from other contemporary directors, such as Elia Kazan, Lloyd Richards, and Lynne Meadow. Their theatre pieces grow out of intense collaboration with different types of theatrical artists, including designers, composers, dancers, and singers.

Martha Clarke, born in 1944 in Baltimore, Maryland, entered the theatre through dance training at the Juilliard School (New York City), and as a member of Anna Sokolow's dance company and later the Pilobolus Dance Theatre. The New York-based Music Theatre Group funded Clarke to develop her own theatrical form. The result was a series of increasingly complex works resulting in *The Garden of Earthly*

FIGURE 10.4
A scene from Endangered Species, *conceived and directed by Martha Clarke, at the 1990 Next Wave Festival at the Brooklyn Academy of Music. The production design, by Robert Israel with lighting by Paul Gallo, had a large cast of humans and circus animals— all endangered species.*

Delights (1984), *Vienna: Lusthaus* (1986), *Endangered Species* (1990), and *Dammerung* (1993). She was awarded a MacArthur "genius" grant in 1990 and has worked as a director with Christopher Hampton on *Alice in Wonderland* for the National Theatre in London.

Working in collaboration with dancers, musicians, designers, actors, and singers, Clarke collects and connects hundreds of imagistic fragments for a theatre piece. First, she asks singers and dancers to move to music, re-creating fragmentary scenes. Later in the collaborative process among the various artists, Clarke superimposes other parts on these early scenes, which may in turn suggest other scenes.

If the pieces connect, she then weaves them into the fabric of the total work that is shaped and reshaped in six months or more of rehearsal, but may last only sixty minutes in performance. Of her process she says: "I'm a very instinctive person and I feel my way around like someone blindfolded in the attic. I stumble the piece into shape and often don't get a vision until late in the process. Then I take out my scissors and my paste and in the very last moments before a first preview it falls together."[5]

The Garden of Earthly Delights, Clarke's 1984 interpretation of painter Hieronymus Bosch's fifteenth-century triptych, gained international attention. This one-hour evocation of the Garden of Eden and the netherworld—inhabited by ten dancers and musicians who at times were earthbound and at others celestially somersaulted through the air

PETER BROOK

The archery contest in Peter Brook's 1986 production of the epic Sanskrit (Indian) work, The Mahabharata, *brought on tour to the United States in 1987–1988.*

on cables—opened in New York City and subsequently toured the United States and Europe.

Clarke's theatre pieces, in which she is the prime creator, are not narrations of a story line but are ultimately expressions of her subconscious. They link the points between inspiration and a volatile inner emotional life. *Vienna: Lusthaus* is made up of forty-four fragments depicting turn-of-the-century Vienna and pairing eroticism and death. Clarke sees lust and death as corrosive powers undermining social order.

Commenting on her collaborative process, she says:

. . . If you watched a rehearsal of mine, you would see that nine-tenths of it is in such disarray. I flounder. . . . I'm foggy a lot of

Chapter Ten

Peter Brook (b. 1925) is a British director and founder of the International Centre for Theatre Research in Paris. He was born in London, educated at Oxford University, and began his directing career in the 1940s. As co-director of England's Royal Shakespeare Company (RSC) from 1962 to 1971, he directed acclaimed productions of *King Lear*, *The Tempest*, *Marat/Sade*, and *A Midsummer Night's Dream*. His activities with the Centre include *Orghast* for the Shiraz Festival at Persepolis (Iran), *The Ik* (based on Colin Turnbull's book *The Mountain People*), and *The Mahabharata*, which toured London and America. He directed the 1963 film *The Lord of the Flies* and wrote influential books on theatre, *The Empty Space* (1968) and *The Open Door* (1993).

Known for his radical adaptations of familiar plays, Brook enjoys an enormous international reputation. His version of *A Midsummer Night's Dream* is not about the romantic fairies and haunted woodlands that Shakespeare imagined. It is an exploration of love performed in a white boxlike set with actors on trapezes and in "mod" clothing and circus costumes (see Figure 10.3).

Since founding the Centre, Brook has experimented with actor training and developed new scripts from ideas taken from myths, anthropology, and fables, producing such international successes as *Conference of the Birds*, *La Tragédie de Carmen*, *The Mahabharata*, and *The Man Who*.

---

the time. And the actors and dancers have to search as much as I do. We're all children dropped on another planet at the beginning of this process and, tentatively, hand-in-hand, we find our way through this mire to whatever. The day-by-day process couldn't be more collaborative.[6]

Robert Wilson is author, designer, and director of nearly 100 theatre, opera, dance, film, and video works. He is best known for such innovative productions as *Einstein on the Beach* (a 1976 opera with composer Philip Glass), *the CIVIL warS: a tree is best measured when it is down* (a 1985 opera with playwright Heiner Müller), *The Forest* (a 1988 production with author Heiner Müller and composer David Byrne), and

JOANNE AKALAITIS

JoAnne Akalaitis (b. 1937) was born in Cicero, Illinois, in a largely Lithuanian community. She studied pre-med at the University of Chicago, switched to philosophy, and graduated in 1960. Attending Stanford University in California to study philosophy, she soon joined Jules Irving's and Herbert Blau's Actors Workshop in San Francisco. There she met Ruth Maleczech, Lee Breuer, and Bill Raymond; in 1969, they founded the Mabou Mines, a theatre collective named after a small town in Nova Scotia. In 1975, she directed her first play, *Cascando* by Samuel Beckett. Since then she has directed *Green Card, Leonce and Lena, The Balcony, Endgame, Through the Leaves, Woyzeck,* and *In the Summer House* for Off Broadway and regional theatres, winning a number of awards along the way. In 1991, she was named Joseph Papp's successor as artistic director for the New York Shakespeare Festival and in 1993 was abruptly dismissed by the theatre's board of directors. Her major directing projects, following her work with the Mabou Mines, have been at the Mark Taper Forum in Los Angeles, the American Repertory Theatre in Cambridge, The Guthrie Theater in Minneapolis, the New York Shakespeare Festival, and Lincoln Center Theater in New York City.

new stagings of *Quartet* (1988), *When We Dead Awaken* (1991), and *Danton's Death* (1992).

Wilson's work is rooted in what he calls the "visual book." He says: "I'm not a writer of words. . . . I usually find a form before I have content. Before I've gathered material, I have a form. Once I have a form, it's a question of how to fill in the form."[7] He then proceeds in workshops and rehearsals to structure time and episodes, to imagine landscapes, and to add themes and references (see Figure 10.5).

Describing his workshop/rehearsal period, Wilson uses the analogy of cooking a meal:

> I've said many times it's like making a dinner. The four of us here at this table are now going to make a dinner. Well, I know I can make a salad, and that's about it. You can make coffee. But

FIGURE 10.5

Actor Richard Thomas as the revolutionary Danton surrounded by his supporters in Danton's Death *by Georg Buchner, conceived and directed by Robert Wilson for the Alley Theatre (Houston, Texas) in 1992.*

maybe he knows how to make pasta, and she knows how to make something else, and then we have this dinner based on what we can do. So Heiner Müller [writer] can do one thing and Darryl Pinckney [writer] can do another, and David Byrne [composer] can do another, and maybe they're all very different, with different aesthetics, different viewpoints. But we make a work together. We have to try to figure out how we can take these different people and make this meal. And then we offer it.[8]

Unlike the stage tradition of the director who carefully interprets the playwright's world for audiences, the "new" collaborators, like Martha Clarke, Robert Wilson, and Philip Glass, develop their own visionary statements with other artists. Referred to as a "theatre of visions," these works *are* the staging with live performers of the maker's vision of a new theatrical reality. In this theatre of visions, there is no concern for verbal analysis, no concern for plausibility, no question of conveying information or of generating meaning. Of ultimate importance is imparting an artistically created vision together with a sense of its significance and visual excitement.

Summary

Emerging in the nineteenth century, the theatre director is one of the most recent additions to the list of principal theatre artists. Before the director became part of theatre, leading actors, theatre managers, and playwrights set the actor's movements, dictated production elements, and took care of financial matters. Nineteenth-century technological advances made stage machinery and lighting more complex; changing social, aesthetic, and political thought so altered the theatre's subjects, characters, and staging that a *coordinating specialist* became necessary.

Whereas the playwright creates the play's world—its events, people, and meaning—on paper, the modern director, with other artists, interprets the playwright's vision in the theatre's three-dimensional space, giving it shape, sound, rhythm, images, activity, and unity. Audiences experience the play largely through the director's imagination—eyes, ears, emotions, and intellect—so the modern director has become as distinct a force in the theatre as the playwright. Other important forces are the designers to whom we turn our attention next.

Questions for Study

1. What is the artistic role of the director in the theatre?
2. What are the director's responsibilities? Name *six* major ones.
3. Why are the Duke of Saxe-Meiningen, André Antoine, and Constantin Stanislavski considered "pioneering" directors?
4. In what ways are auditions important for a director?
5. What does a director look for in casting a play?
6. What is meant by the play's *spine*?
7. How is *improvisation* often a helpful rehearsal tool for director and actor?
8. What are the functions of the *assistant director* and the *stage manager*?
9. What is the director's *ground plan*?
10. What information is given in a Samuel French Publishers' acting edition of a play? Bring several editions to class for illustration.

11. What is a director's *promptbook*?

12. Give examples of the director's wide range of creative possibilities in staging a performance.

13. Describe the work of the contemporary theatre's "new" collaborators.

14. *Plays to Read*: Tennessee Williams' *A Streetcar Named Desire*; Robert Wilson's *A Letter for Queen Victoria*.

15. *Suggested Readings*: Arthur Bartow, *The Director's Voice: Interviews* (New York: Theatre Communications Group, 1989); Elia Kazan, *A Life* (New York: Alfred A. Knopf, 1988); Peter Brook, *The Open Door: Thoughts on Acting and Theatre* (New York: Pantheon Books, 1993).

Theatre artists—actors, directors, and
designers—create the play onstage in
concrete visual terms. Designers of scenery,
costumes, sound, and lighting realize the
playwright's intentions graphically,
aurally, and visually in the theatrical space.

11

THE IMAGE MAKERS: THE DESIGNERS

Designers collaborate with the director to focus the audience's attention on the actor in a special environment: the stage. Designers shape and fill the stage space. They create the actor's environment and make the play's world *visible* and *interesting* to us. Sometimes one person (the **scenographer**) designs scenery, lighting, and costumes. But since scene, costume, light, and sound design are essentially four different arts, we will look at each of them separately.

The Scene Designer

Background

The scene (or stage) designer became part of the American theatre over 100 years ago. The designer's nineteenth-century counterpart was the resident *scenic artist*, who painted the large pieces of scenery for the theatre manager. Scenery's main function in those days was to give the actor a painted background and to indicate time and place. Scenic studios staffed with specialized artists were even set up to turn out scenery on demand. Many of these studios conducted a large mail-order business for standard backdrops and scenic pieces. By the turn of the century, realism had come into the theatre, and the job of making the stage look real became more complex.

Theatre in the late nineteenth century was dominated by a naturalistic philosophy that proclaimed life could be explained by the forces of environment, heredity, economics, society, and the psyche. This being the case, theatre had to present these forces as carefully and effectively as possible. If environment (including economic factors) really did govern people's lives, then it needed to be shown as they actually saw it. The responsibility for creating this stage environment shifted from the playwright and scene painter to the designer. The demands of stage realism called for the stage to look almost photographically like the actual place where the play's action takes place.

Realism has been the dominant convention of the theatre in our time. However, many new and exciting movements in the modern theatre have come about as reactions to this direct representation of reality, which pretends that the stage is not a stage but someone's actual living room and that the audience (seated in a dark auditorium) is really not there beyond the invisible "fourth wall," observing the play. Leaders of many new theatre movements have argued that the stage living room and box set were themselves unnatural; they set about pioneering a special kind of theatrical reality for the stage.

Before World War I in Europe, Adolphe Appia and Edward Gordon Craig became self-proclaimed prophets of a new movement in theatre design and lighting. They were concerned with creating mood and atmosphere, opening up the stage for movement, and unifying visual ideas; they assaulted the illusion of stage realism and led the way to a rethinking of theatrical design (see Figure 11.1). In his *Music and Stage Setting* (1899), Appia called for theatrical art to be expressive. And today, in the same spirit, many modern set designers have extended the traditional media of wood, canvas, and paint to include steel, plastics, projected images, pipes, ramps, light, platforms, and steps to *express* the play's atmosphere and imaginative life instead of attempting to *reproduce* the details of its time and place realistically.

Appia and Craig influenced the young American designers of the 1920s, Robert Edmond Jones, Lee Simonson, and Norman Bel Geddes, who dedicated themselves to bringing the new stagecraft to Broadway. Two generations of American scene designers have followed their lead. Prominent among them are Jo Mielziner, who designed *Death of a Salesman, A Streetcar Named Desire,* and *The King and I*; Boris Aronson, the designer of *Cabaret, Company,* and *Pacific Overtures*; Oliver Smith, designer of *Brigadoon, The Sound of Music,* and *Plaza Suite*; and Ming Cho Lee, designer of *Hair, for colored girls who have considered suicide/when the rainbow is enuf, K2,* and *The Woman Warrior.*

FIGURE 11.1
One model for Edward Gordon Craig's famous setting of Hamlet *for the 1912 Moscow Art Theatre production. Craig designed these huge white screens to be sufficiently mobile so that the appearance of the scene could be changed without closing the front curtain. Unfortunately they did not function with the efficiency he had envisioned.*

The Designer's Training

Sixty years ago the designer, like the actor, was trained in stock and repertory theatres. The scenic artist, with only a rough knowledge of theatrical settings, was concerned almost solely with painting. Design training consisted of an apprenticeship in a scenic studio. With the emergence of the director as artistic coordinator, the concept of the stage designer as a collaborative, interpretive artist with responsibility for all visual and technical elements developed as well. In the 1920s, universities became the training ground for the new theatre artists—the scene, costume, lighting, and later sound designers.

Designing for the Theatre

Scene designers use one of five basic methods to design stage settings:

- Start with a real room or place, select from it, change the dimensions, and reshape it for a particular stage.

APPIA AND CRAIG

Adolphe Appia (1862–1928) and Edward Gordon Craig (1872–1966) built the theoretical foundations of modern expressionistic theatrical practice. For the Swiss-born Appia, *artistic unity* was the basic goal of theatrical production. He disliked the contradiction in the three-dimensional actor performing before painted two-dimensional scenery, and he advocated the replacement of flat settings with steps, ramps, and platforms. He thought the role of lighting was to fuse all visual elements into a unified whole. His *Music and Stage Setting* (1899) and *The Work of Living Art* (1921) are the early source books for modern stage-lighting practices.

Gordon Craig was born into an English theatrical family (he was the son of actress Ellen Terry and architect and scenic designer Edward Godwin) and began his career as an actor in Henry Irving's company. The 1902 exhibit of his work as a stage designer and the publication of his *The Art of the Theatre* in 1905 created controversy throughout Europe; indeed, his entire theatrical life was a storm of controversy. He thought of theatre as an independent art that welded action, words, line, color, and rhythm into an artistic whole created by the single, autonomous artist. Many of his ideas on simplified decor, three-dimensional settings, moving scenery, and directional lighting prevailed in the new stagecraft that emerged after World War I.

- Start with the actors and the play's most important events and then add platforms, shapes, and voids around them.
- Start with the play's mood and find the lines, shapes, and colors that will reflect it.
- Design the scene as an idea or metaphor—in the 1920s, the expressionists in Germany sought to reflect the nightmarish outlook of the disturbed mind in their stage settings (see Figure 11.2).
- Organize the entire space, including actor and audience, as environment.

The environmentalist begins with the notion that the production will both develop from and totally take place in a given space. There is no

FIGURE 11.2
The skeleton scene of the 1922 New York production of German playwright Georg Kaiser's From Morn to Midnight *is a good example of expressionist design and production style, which stressed imaginative lighting (a tree has been transformed into a human skeleton), symbolic decor on an almost empty stage, and the distortion of natural appearances. Notice how the actor is dwarfed by the huge projection. The setting was designed by Lee Simonson.*

effort to create an illusion or imitation; rather, the performer and audience, space and materials, exist as what they are: people, ramps, platforms, ladders, stairs, mazes.

The design process can take months. The designer usually begins by studying the script in much the same way as the director, visualizing details of place, movement, and objects in space. The designer asks certain basic questions about the script's requirements: Where does the play take place? What is the play's historical period? How does the play proceed in time and seasons? What kinds of movements do the characters make? What elements from life are essential parts of the play's world? What is the play's spatial relationship to the audience? Is it close up or far away? Are the play and the audience in the same space? How are character relationships expressed in the space? How much playing space is needed? Is the action to be violent or sedate? What is the play's mood? How many exits, properties, and essential pieces of furniture are needed? What is the director's concept?

As the designer visualizes the space, details are established in *sketches, a ground plan, and a model*. Sketches (or rough pencil drawings) are made in the early period when both the director and the designer are visualizing the stage floor and theatrical space. When their ideas have reached some degree of concreteness, they confer and agree on the ground plan: shape, entrances, exits, and major scenic elements, including color.

The designer also researches the play's historical period, background, and style, including architecture, furniture, and decor. Over the

MING CHO LEE

Ming Cho Lee (born 1930 in Shanghai and educated at Occidental College and UCLA) designed his first Broadway show, O'Neill's *Moon for the Misbegotten*, in 1962. Since then, he has designed settings for Broadway, Off Broadway, regional theatres, opera, and dance.

Speaking of his methods, Lee said: "I generally read the script once just to get an impact from which I will try to form some kind of visual concept. . . . I always design for the total play and let the specifics fit in. The total play demands some kind of expression through materials, and this is something I always first ask a director. . . . And then, I would make the choice as to whether it is a realistic play that requires very literal settings or if it's a play that requires a nonliteral approach and essentially you present it on a platform—you create a framework on which to hang your visual statement."[2]

next several weeks, sketches, color *renderings* (watercolor paintings of the stage with scenery), and a model follow until the director and designer have arrived at the look and details of the setting. The designer, or an assistant, then drafts plans, front elevations (two-dimensional drawings outlining the object as it appears to the eye; see Figure 11.3), and paint elevations (Figure 11.4) to give to the technical director or shop foreman, who converts them into technical drawings, showing how the scenic pieces are to be constructed, their dimensions, and materials. Scenery is basically two- or three-dimensional, framed or unframed. It is built from these drawings and moved onto the stage at the appointed time. (This effort is commonly called "put-in.") The technical drawings detail the profile and outer dimensions of all scenic elements, showing where and how they function and the order in which they will appear onstage.

Scenery must be strong, portable, and dependable. As we look at a set, we are usually not aware of types of scenery, how it fits together, how it is moved about during scene changes—unless the moving is done for theatrical effect.

Chapter Eleven

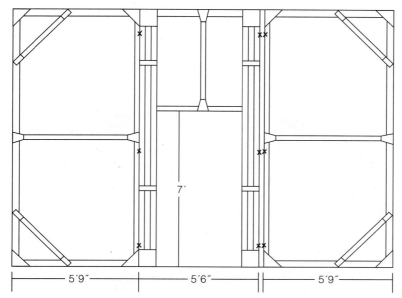

FIGURE 11.3

A designer's elevation is a two-dimensional drawing that shows no perspective. The elevation for the unit of scenery shows overall dimensions, as well as the dimensions of a door.

FIGURE 11.4

The scenic artist, or scene painter—in nonprofessional theatres usually the designer—is a specialized artist who paints the scenery following painter's elevations and a model provided by the designer. Conjoined with lighting, the scene painter's art provides onstage color, perspective, depth, shape, and texture.

The Image Makers: The Designers 277

MODERN
STAGE DESIGNS

Jo Mielziner (1901–1976) pioneered, along with director Elia Kazan, "selective realism" in scenic design. Of his type of design Mielziner said: ". . . If you eliminate nonessentials, you've got to be . . . sure that the things you do put in are awfully good. They've got to be twice as good, because they stand alone to make a comment. . . . I got to feel that even realistic plays didn't need realistic settings necessarily."[3]

In the final scene of A Streetcar Named Desire *(1947) Stanley Kowalski's friends play poker while Blanche DuBois is taken away to an asylum. In the foreground are the selected realistic details of Mielziner's setting: living spaces, beds, tables, and chairs.*

For Arthur Miller's Death of a Salesman *(1949), Mielziner designed the salesman's house on several levels (kitchen, sons' bedroom, porch, and forestage). The actors' movements with area lighting were the only scene-change devices. The large backdrop upstage was painted to show tenement buildings looming over Willy Loman's house in the play's present time. When lighted from the rear, the buildings washed out to be replaced with projections of trees with leaves. The leaves indicated the pleasant atmosphere of Willy's remembered past with its bright sunshine and cheerful ambience.*

Bertolt Brecht's favorite designers—Teo Otto, Caspar Neher, and Karl von Appen—did not create illusions of real places but provided background materials (projections on a rear cyclorama, placards, signs, and set pieces, like Courage's wagon) that commented on the play's historical period and the characters' socioeconomic circumstances. The *setting*

The Berliner Ensemble's 1949 production of Brecht's Mother Courage and Her Children *in (former) East Berlin was originally designed by Teo Otto. In this final scene, Mother Courage's wagon is the main set piece, which actress Helene Weigel as Courage, alone in the harness, pulls toward yet another war.*

Chapter Eleven

itself (the theatrical space) was used to make the dramatic action and individuals appear strange or unfamiliar because it resembled little that was familiar in our daily lives. Brecht did not disguise the fact that all was taking place in a theatre under exposed lighting instruments, creating "white light," and before an audience.

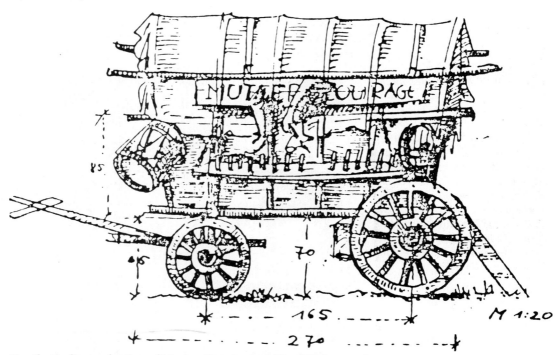

For the Berlin production of Mother Courage and Her Children *at the Deutsches Theater in 1949, Brecht used the set model devised by Teo Otto for the 1941 Zurich production. The wagon and movable screens were the main set pieces of the design.*

Josef Svoboda (b. 1920), chief designer at Prague's National Theatre in Czechoslovakia, is Europe's most celebrated scenographer, making highly imaginative use of an array of contemporary technologies, including computerized s ide and film projections, laser beams, moving platforms, plastics, and netting. His use of surfaces to project images around the actor, creating what he calls "dramatic space" as "psychoplastic," is his trademark. "The goal of the designer," Svoboda has said, "can no longer be a description of a copy of actuality, but the creation of its multidimensional model."[4]

Oedipus the King, *designed and directed by Svoboda at the Smetana Theatre, Prague, 1963. The setting was a vast flight of stairs, starting in the orchestra pit and reaching almost out of sight. The stairs were punctuated by platforms that thrust out from the stairs themselves. The actor playing Oedipus appears on a platform (stage right). "At the end Oedipus was left alone. Virtually all the flat levels disappeared. He climbed an endless staircase, into sharp counterlighting. . . ."*

Designer Ming Cho Lee's spectacular setting for *K2* by Patrick Meyers was a sheer ice wall representing *K2*, the world's second-highest mountain. In the play two climbers are trapped on the icy ledge just below the summit. *K2* opened in 1982 at Arena Stage, Washington, D.C., before going to Broadway.

The elevations for this rock and ice face resembled a government geological survey map. Fifty-thousand board feet of plastic foam were used to build the wall over a wooden frame armature. Finishing touches included an oil fog mist and nightly avalanche of snow from a theatrical-supply house.

The Costume Designer

Costume design has been compared by American designer Patricia Zipprodt to a car trip in which unpredictables of life pop up—unavailable fabric, the inadequate budget, the temperamental actor. The designer, like the car's driver, is in a constant state of problem solving.

The Costume

Costumes include all the character's garments and accessories (purse, cane, jewelry, handkerchief), all items related to hairdressing, and everything associated with face and body makeup, including masks.

Costumes tell us many things about the characters and about the nature, mood, and style of the play. They are visual signals adding color, style, and meaning to the play's environment. Costumes establish period, social class, economic status, occupation, age, geography, weather, and time of day. They help to clarify the relationships and relative importance of various characters. Ornament, line, and color can tie together members of a family, group, faction, or party. Changes in costume can indicate alteration in relationships among characters or in a character's psychological outlook. Similarities or contrasts in costumes can show sympathetic or antagonistic relationships. Hamlet's black costume, for instance, is contrasted with the bright colors worn by the court and speaks eloquently of his altered attitude toward the court. Designer Lucinda Ballard's costumes for *A Streetcar Named Desire* (see Figure 11.5) express Blanche DuBois' self-image of Southern gentility. Jessica Tandy's costume for Blanche's evening with Mitch includes tasteful summer dress, pearls, hat, gloves, handbag, bracelet, and bouquet.

Years ago, the actor, director, or person in charge of stage wardrobe was responsible for costumes. But in the last sixty years, the new stagecraft has required costume designers trained in the visual arts to select and control these visual elements with far more attention to detail. Costume design has become an industry. Professional designers work in film, fashion, theatre, opera, television, dance, commercials, and extravaganzas (ice shows, nightclubs, circuses, and dance revues). Many people are involved in costume research and in sketching, choosing fabric, cutting, fitting, sewing, and making accessories. The large costume houses, such as the Costume Collection (New York City), Western Cos-

FIGURE 11.5

One of designer Lucinda Ballard's costumes created for the 1947 Broadway production of A Streetcar Named Desire. *This is Blanche DuBois' famous party costume. Tennessee Williams described the dress as a "somewhat soiled and crumpled white satin evening gown and a pair of scuffed silver slippers with brilliants set in the heels." Stanley describes the dress himself as a "worn-out Mardi Gras outfit."*

As Blanche, betrayed by Stanley and Mitch, places a rhinestone tiara on her head, she drinks to imaginary "admirers." The costume was completed with bracelet and faded corsage.

tume Company (Hollywood), Eaves-Brooks Costume Company (New York City), and Malabar Ltd. (Toronto) buy stage costumes from closing shows, build costumes on demand, and rent garments to regional, community, and university theatres. A visit to their vast warehouses to select costumes for a play in production is not only an exciting adventure in itself, but also serves as a tour through the history of theatre design.

The Design Conference

Scene and costume designers work with the director to make visible the world in which the play's characters live. They explore verbally and with rough sketches the many different approaches and ideas that might bring the script into dramatic focus onstage. Designers supplement visually the director's concepts and, in so doing, often inspire the director to a new way of thinking about the play. Award-winning designer Theoni V. Aldredge has said: "The costumes are there to serve a producer's vision, a director's viewpoint, and an actor's comfort."

Like the director and the scene designer, the costume designer begins by studying the script and taking note of the story, mood, characterization, visual effects, colors, atmosphere, geography, period, and season. Then the designer asks the practical questions: What is the costume budget? How many costumes (including changes) and accessories are needed? What actors have been cast? What stage actions, such as fighting, will affect the construction or wear of the costumes?

The overall plan of the production is worked out in design conferences. The costume designer brings sketches, color plates, costume charts, accessory lists, and fabric swatches to these meetings to make his or her visual concept clear to the director and scene designer. The designer must be specific to avoid later misunderstandings and costly last-minute changes.

Sometimes a brilliant costume design develops through trial and error. While designing the costumes for the Broadway production of the musical *Pippin* (1972), Patricia Zipprodt and director Bob Fosse had difficulty deciding on the right look for the strolling players. The musical is performed by a group of actors costumed as some kind of theatrical caravan, who relate the story of Charlemagne's eldest son, Pippin, an idealist journeying through courts, battles, and love's intrigues. The script said, "Enter strolling players of an indeterminate period." Zipprodt remembers:

> Now, to me, this meant exactly nothing. I did a lot of sketches, which everybody seemed to like. On the day I was supposed to present finished sketches, time ran short. Instead of fully coloring the costumes of the strolling players as was planned and expected, I just painted beige and off-white washes so that Fosse could read the sketches more easily. I put the whole group of 14 or 15 in front of him and was just about to apologize for not getting the color done when he said, "That's just brilliant, exactly the colors they should be. How clever of you." The minute he said it, I knew he was right.[5]

But more often, the selection is made only after numerous alternatives have been explored.

PATRICIA ZIPPRODT

Patricia Zipprodt's elaborate period costumes for Molière's Don Juan *in the 1981 Guthrie Theatre production, directed by Richard Foreman.*

Patricia Zipprodt studied at Wellesley College and the Fashion Institute of Technology (New York). She has designed costumes for regional theatres, as well as many Broadway musicals and plays, including *Sunday in the Park with George* (with Ann Hould-Ward), *Brighton Beach Memoirs, The Glass Menagerie, Fiddler on the Roof, Cabaret, Zorba, 1776, The Little Foxes, Plaza Suite, Pippin, Chicago,* and *Cat on a Hot Tin Roof.* She has won nine Drama Desk Awards and has been nominated for the Antoinette Perry ("Tony") Award ten times, winning three. She has also designed costumes for opera, dance, and film: the Metropolitan Opera's acclaimed *Tannhäuser* and *The Barber of Seville,* Jerome Robbins' ballets *Les Noces* and *Dybbuk Variations,* and such films as *The Graduate* and *1776.*

THEONI V. ALDREDGE

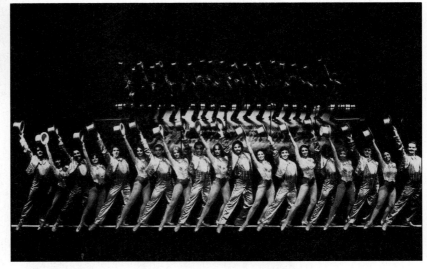

The final musical number of A Chorus Line *(1975), conceived by Michael Bennett and costumed by Theoni V. Aldredge.*

Costume Construction

After approving the sketches and plans, the director turns full attention to rehearsals, and the costume designer arranges for purchase, rental, or construction of costumes and then schedules fitting dates with the actors. If the costumes are being constructed in the theatre's shop (as is most often the case in college and resident theatre productions), actors are measured, patterns cut, garments constructed, dyeing and painting of fabric done, and accessories built or purchased. After several fittings with the actors, the costumes are ready for the *dress parade*, during which designer and director examine the costumes on the actors before the dress rehearsal begins.

BROADWAY DESIGNERS AT WORK

Diana Rigg as Medea in a revival of Euripides' tragedy. The London production originated at the Almeida Theatre and transferred to Broadway in 1994. Peter J. Davison designed the setting of severe, bronze walls enclosing the forecourt of Medea's palace.

The 1994 revival of Richard Rodgers and Oscar Hammerstein's musical Carousel at Lincoln Center Theatre, New York City. Produced by Cameron Mackintosh, this new production was designed by Bob Crowley, who used the theatre's large, open stage with colorful scenic pieces and background cyclorama to recreate Billy Bigelow's world of violence, love, and redemption.

Top, the lavish scenery for the 1994 Andrew Lloyd Webber musical Sunset Boulevard, *starring Glenn Close, was designed by John Napier with costumes by Anthony Powell and lights by Andrew Bridge. Right, the 1991 musical* The Secret Garden *garnered awards for design by Heidi Landesman (scenery), Theoni V. Aldredge (costumes), and Tharon Musser (lighting).*

An Inspector Calls, the 1994 revival of J. B. Priestley's play that opened on London's West End and moved to Broadway with Rosemary Harris and Philip Bosco. The spectacular moving set, designed by Ian MacNeil, unfolds onstage (left) to disclose a realistic interior. Directed by Stephen Daldry, costumes by Ian MacNeil.

Top, Wendy Wasserstein's The Sisters Rosensweig. *The English living room set was designed by John Lee Beatty with costumes by Jane Greenwood and lighting by Pat Collins.* Right, Kiss of the Spider Woman, *designed by Jerome Sirlin (with costumes and lights by Florence Klotz and Howell Binkley), is set in a foul prison transformed in a prisoner's mind into the exotic world of a bygone film goddess (Chita Rivera).*

Theoni V. Aldredge, one of theatre's most gifted and respected designers, has produced over 1,000 costumes and designed costumes for five hit musicals that ran simultaneously on Broadway: *A Chorus Line, 42nd Street, Dreamgirls, La Cage aux Folles,* and *The Rink.* Most recently, she designed the costumes for *The Secret Garden* (1991). She begins her creative process by studying the characters and the cast of any given production: "To me, good design is design you're not aware of. It must exist as part of the whole—as an aspect of characterization. Also, a designer must be flexible and extremely patient. . . . A performance will suffer if an actor doesn't love his costume, and it's your job to make him love it."

For *A Chorus Line* (1975), essentially the story of a Broadway audition, Aldredge closely observed the personalities of the dancers and singers and the outfits they wore to rehearsals. Of this long-running musical, conceived and directed by Michael Bennett, and produced by Joseph Papp for the New York Shakespeare Festival, she has said: "I took millions of snapshots of what the kids came in wearing, and adapted what they had on for my costumes. I didn't depart too much, because it's what made each of them so unique. The only real transformation came with the golden chorus line at the end of the show, which, incidentally, Michael had wanted to be a red chorus line. But I felt red was too definite a color. I thought it should be a fantasy number. I told him it ought to be the color of champagne—of celebration—and that's what we did."[6]

To accomplish this work, the designer may have an assistant designer, shop supervisor, cutters, drapers, seamstresses, crew head, and crew to cut, sew, dye, and make hats, footwear, and wigs. Often in small costume shops this personnel will double up on the responsibilities.

Dress Rehearsal and Wardrobe Personnel

The dress parade and rehearsal (where the costumes, masks, and makeup are worn onstage in front of scenery and under lights) usually take place a week before opening night. It is not unusual to discover that a costume is inappropriate, or that a color doesn't work under the lights or against the scenery. In this event, the designer may redesign the garment, select another fabric or color (or both), and have the costume reconstructed or dyed almost overnight and ready for the next rehearsal or opening performance.

Once costumes and accessories are finished, the costumes leave the shop and usually a new group (the wardrobe crew) takes charge of them during dress rehearsals and performances. Their responsibility is to mend, iron, clean, and generally maintain the costumes for the play's run. Although in the professional theatre there is a clear-cut division between these two groups, in college and university theatres the construction and wardrobe crews may be many of the same people.

The wardrobe supervisor (sometimes called the wardrobe master or mistress) or crew head makes a list of the costumes and accessories worn by each actor before dress rehearsals begin. These lists are used by crew members and actors to check that each costume is complete. The wardrobe "running" crew helps each actor dress and is responsible for the costumes before, during, and after each performance. Wardrobe routines are established during the dress rehearsal period and are followed during the production. The crew is also responsible for "striking" the costumes when the production closes: Costumes are cleaned, laundered, and placed in storage along with accessories, such as hats, wigs, shoes, and jewelry.

Makeup

Makeup enhances the actor and completes the costume. It is essential to the actor's visibility. In a large theatre, distance and lighting can make an actor's features without makeup colorless and indistinct. And makeup, like the costume, helps the actor reveal character by giving physical clues to personality, age, background, race, health, environment.

In the ancient Asian and Greek theatres, actors used a white-lead makeup with heavy accents or they used masks. Today, basic makeup consists of a foundation and color shadings to prevent the actor from looking "washed out" beneath the glare of the stage lights. Pancake makeup has replaced the traditional greasepaint, or oil-base makeup, as the foundation for the actor's basic skin color. Cake makeup—less messy and more flexible than greasepaint—comes in small plastic cases (as does everyday makeup) and is applied with a damp sponge. Color shadings with rouge, lipstick, liners, mascara, and powder are applied with pencils and brushes. A well-equipped makeup kit (which can be purchased inexpensively from theatrical-supply houses) includes the standard foundations and shading colors plus synthetic hair, glue, solvents, wax, and hair whiteners.

Makeup is classified as *straight* and *character*. Straight makeup highlights an actor's normal features and coloring for distinctness and visibility. Character makeup transforms the actor's features to reveal age or attitude. Noses, wrinkles, eyelashes, jawlines, eyepouches, eyebrows, teeth, hair, and beards can be added to change the actor's appearance. Character (sometimes called *illustrative*) makeup can make a young actor look older, can give the actor playing Cyrano his huge, bulbous nose, and can transform Laurence Olivier into Othello the Moor. When misused, makeup can destroy the actor's characterization by giving an external look that conflicts with the character's inner life. The actor must know, then, the basis of makeup as an art and how to work with hair and wigs.

Most frequently, makeup is designed and applied by the actor (especially in the professional theatre), although in fantasy productions, such as the musical *Cats*, makeup and wigs may be designed by someone else.

How does the actor make up? There is no substitute for practice with a basic makeup kit; every actor comes to know his or her face in a new way as soon as practice begins. Each face is different, catching and reflecting light in a different way. Each character presents a new set of challenges in which pancake makeup, rouge, liners, mascara, false eyelashes, wigs, facial hair (usually made from crepe wool), nose putty, and various prosthetic materials for aging, scarring, and disfiguring the skin's appearance are used to accent the character's expressions and attitudes. For this reason, actors should apply their own makeup, since actors know best the expressions, lines, and shadows their characters use.

Masks

In the early theatre, masks had many uses. They enlarged the actor's facial features so that the character's image would be apparent at great distances. The Greek masks expressed basic emotions: grief, anger, horror, sadness, pity. But most important for us today, the masked actor

FIGURE 11.6

The commedia dell'arte *mask. All characters in Italian* commedia, *with the exception of the young lovers, wore masks. Unlike classical masks and those of China and Japan,* commedia *masks did not express any particular emotion like joy or sorrow. Instead, they gave a permanent expression to the character, such as cunning or avarice. The mask's expressiveness varied with the angle from which it was seen. Pantalone, one of the chief* commedia *characters, was a miserly merchant. His mask, brown with a hooked nose, gray, sparse moustache, and a pointed white beard, represented a permanent expression of crafty greed.*

created an altogether different *presence* onstage than the actor without a mask. Although a masked actor may lose something in subtlety of expression, the presence the actor creates can be stately, heroic, awesome, or mysterious; the actor may move the audience simply by standing onstage and reflecting light. Nor is the masked actor totally deprived of the facial subtlety available to the actor whose facial muscles move and change expression. By changing the mask's position (if the mask is made with this effect in mind), by angling the head and catching the light, different emotional responses can be evoked.

Mask-making is an ancient art dating from early cultures where masks were objects of fear; they were thought to have supernatural powers. Masks were used in the Greek and Roman theatres, by the ***commedia dell'arte*** in Renaissance Italy (see Figure 11.6), in Japanese Noh, and in the modern theatre (Figures 11.7 and 11.8). In addition to an artful exterior, a mask must be comfortable, strong, light, and molded to the contours of the actor's face. Today, in college and regional theatres, the costume designer makes the masks as part of the costume, designing for color, durability, and expressiveness.

FIGURE 11.7

These modern stylized versions of classical Greek masks served the chorus in director Andrei Serban's production of Euripides' Medea, *produced at La Mama Experimental Theatre Club (New York City, 1974).*

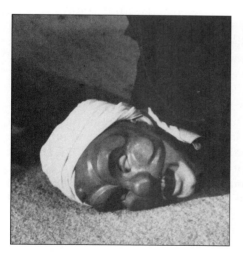

FIGURE 11.8

A modern commedia *mask designed for Théâtre du Soleil's production of* L'Age d'Or *(1975).*

The Image Makers: The Designers   **293**

LIGHTING DESIGNER

JENNIFER TIPTON

Stage lighting controls what we see. Jennifer Tipton's lighting for the 1977 production of Agamemnon *at the Vivian Beaumont Theater, Lincoln Center, New York City, creates a somber atmosphere while calling attention to the bodies of Agamemnon and Cassandra lying before the palace doors.*

The Lighting Designer

Light affects what we see, how we see, how we feel, and even how we hear. It is essential to the modern stage's theatrical effectiveness. It is also one of the most powerful tools the director has to control the audience's focus of attention and to enhance their understanding.

Artificial lighting (first candles and then gas) had been used to illuminate the stage since the seventeenth century, but by 1879 the invention of electric light had transformed overall possibilities for design in the theatre. It made possible complete control of a range of intensities and colors; it could be used flexibly to light or darken different areas of the stage; it provided a source of mood and atmosphere for the actor.

Swiss designer Adolphe Appia (see page 274) understood the artistic possibilities of light in the theatre. In *Music and Stage Setting* he argued that light should be the guiding principle of all design. He believed that light could unify or bring into harmony all production elements, includ-

Jennifer Tipton (b. 1937), born in Columbus, Ohio, graduated from Cornell University in physics, studied dance at the Martha Graham school, and began her career as a lighting designer with the Paul Taylor Dance Company, having studied with Thomas Skelton.

Since the late '60s, she has worked consistently as a lighting designer for regional theatres, dance companies, and on Broadway. In 1974, she began working with Joseph Papp and the New York Shakespeare Festival. She won the Drama Desk Award in 1976 for lighting Ntozake Shange's *for colored girls who have considered suicide/when the rainbow is enuf* and the Antoinette Perry "Tony" Award for *The Cherry Orchard* at Lincoln Center in 1977. She designed Robert Wilson's *CIVIL warS* at the American Repertory Theatre. In 1989, she again received the Drama Desk Award for lighting *Jerome Robbins' Broadway, Long Day's Journey into Night,* and *Waiting for Godot.* Tipton's use of light is characterized by "textured and sculptured space" and by use of a palette based on white. She has summarized the essence of the lighting designer's art: "While 99.9 percent of an audience is not aware of light, 100 percent is affected by it."

ing two- and three-dimensional objects, living and inanimate people, shapes, and things. Appia established light as an artistic medium for the theatre designer.

The Art of Light

Designer Jean Rosenthal defined lighting design as "the imposing of quality on the scarcely visible air through which objects and people are seen." One rule of lighting maintains that *visibility* and *ambience* (the surrounding atmosphere) must be inherent to the total theatrical design, including scenery and costumes. The light designer's tools, other than the instruments themselves, are *form* (the shape of the lighting's pattern), *color* (the lighting's mood achieved by filters—thin, transparent sheets of colored plastic, gelatin, or glass—or by varying degrees of intensity, or by both), and *movement* (the changes of form and color by

FIGURE 11.9

A view of a light booth with computerized control consoles and one of the board operators (seated at right).

means of dimmers, switchboards, and computerized control consoles located in the light booth). (See Figure 11.9.)

Plotting and Cueing

The lighting designer reads the script and confers with the scene designer and director. The basic questions to be answered are: What degree of reality does the director want to suggest? Where are the important scenes placed within the set? What restrictions are there? What forms, moods, color patterns, and movements does the play require? Are special effects needed?

With answers to these questions, the designer sketches out a preliminary *light plot*, starting with a simple sketch of the stage and theatre building as it would be seen from directly above. On this basic plan the designer marks the location of the lighting instruments that will be needed, including type, size, wattage, its wiring and connection to an appropriate dimmer or computer circuit. There are no set rules that any particular instrument may or may not be used in any location. The only limitations in light design are those imposed by the director, by the physical nature of the theatre, by the theatre's available technology, and by safety.

The designer's finished lighting plot (see Figure 11.10) shows: (1) the location of each lighting instrument to be used; (2) the type of

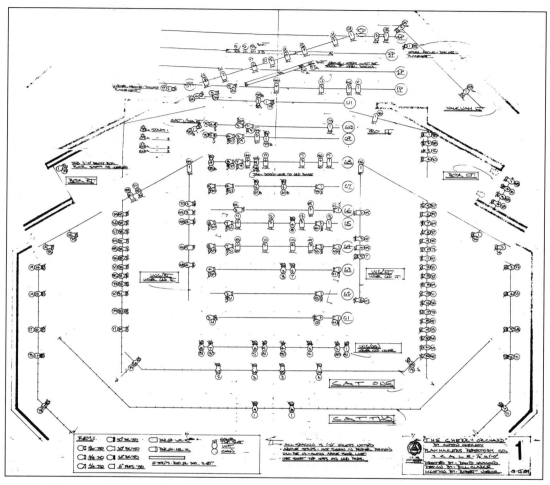

FIGURE 11.10

Design for PlayMakers Repertory Company, Chapel Hill, N.C. (1989); lighting by Robert Wierzel. The light plot by designer Robert Wierzel for The Cherry Orchard *illustrates the positioning of 250 instruments around three sides of the thrust stage, as well as the back-lighting behind the doorways and the overhead chandelier.*

instrument, wattage, and color filter; (3) the general area to be lighted by the instrument; (4) circuitry necessary to operate the instruments; (5) any other details necessary for the electrical operation of the lighting. For example, if a wall fixture is needed onstage so that an actor can turn on a light, the position of this fixture is shown on the light plot.

After the instruments are hung, angled, focused, and circuited, the designer is ready to cue the show. A written cue sheet (or chart of the control board indicating instrument settings and color with each cue numbered and keyed to the script) may be provided in advance to the crew at the control board, or a series of rehearsals may be called during which the designer asks for various intensities of light and makes changes until satisfied. For each change of stage lighting (or light cue), a notation is made that tells how to set the control board and at what point in the stage action to change the lighting's intensity or color. If it is a computerized control console, then it is programmed with cues for the entire show. All of this is done in consultation with the director.

Successful stage lighting complements and unifies the whole without calling attention to itself. It contributes to the play's interpretation with visibility and ambience—controlling what we see and the way we see it (see Figure 11.11).

The Sound Designer

Sound effects have always been a part of the theatre event. In earliest times, music (pipes, drums, lyres), choral chanting, and actors' voices provided the chief sound effects. Until the use of disc recordings in the 1950s, all sound effects in the theatre were produced live offstage; many—such as bells, door slams, and gunfire—still are. In Elizabethan times, "thunder machines" (a series of wooden troughs for cannonballs to rumble down) were invented to simulate tremendous storms, such as the one required in *King Lear*; cannons were fired to convince audiences of fierce battles taking place. Today, advances in sound technology have brought a new artist into the theatre: *the sound designer.*

Theatres today have the capability for both live and recorded sound. Whatever the source or quality of the sound, the sound designer and technicians are responsible for it: mood music, sounds of nature (bird calls, crickets chirping), telephones and doorbells ringing (usually pro-

FIGURE 11.11

For the PlayMakers Repertory Company's 1989 production of Chekhov's The Cherry Orchard, *scenic and costume designer Bill Clarke constructed two set models for the two acts of this production, with lighting by Robert Wierzel.*

The rear and upper levels of the stage were masked with multiple doors and neutral window shades that could be raised and lowered. The thrust stage, designed by Desmond Heeley, is itself a neutral playing space—becoming with different furniture and properties a living room, dining room, riverbank, roadway through woods, and so forth. Here, in Act Two, the house is open, window shades are raised, and the chandelier indicates that it is late.

duced with electrical buzzers), gunshots, abstract sounds, rain and thunder, airplanes and trains passing overhead or in the distance, even military bands marching offstage, as Chekhov requires at the end of *The Three Sisters*.

In consultation with the director, the sound designer plots the effects required by the script (and often added to by the director). The technology available to the sound designer includes tape recorders and playback units, microphones and turntables, mixers and amplifiers, speaker systems of high quality and versatility placed throughout the auditorium, a patch bay (a means of connecting tapes and microphones to any outlet), and a control console. Like the lighting designer, the sound designer develops a cue sheet indicating the placement of each sound in the script, the equipment involved, sound levels, control, and timing of sound modulations.

Just as in our daily lives, sound in the theatre enhances mood, style, atmosphere, and even sense of locale.

Summary

Theatre artists—actors, directors, designers—create the play onstage in *concrete visual and aural terms*. They translate the playwright's words and concepts into a living evocation whose parts are acting, costume, scenery, light, and sound—a visual and aural representation of what occurs in the script. The job of the designer or designers is to convert the stage space into the world of the play. The designer transforms what director Peter Brook refers to as the "empty space" into theatre's special world. Central to the play's world is the actor, and all good stage design enhances the actor's presence in the space. Moreover, all design elements (scenery, costumes, properties, makeup, masks, lighting, and sound) must serve the play's dramatic action—developing, visualizing, and enriching it—without distracting the audience.

Questions for Study

1. What are five methods used by scene designers to design stage settings?
2. How does a designer study a script?
3. How did Appia and Craig pioneer as scenic artists?
4. Why are *ground plans, models,* and *renderings* important in the design process?
5. What is the *technical director's* job?
6. What is a *costume?*
7. How does a costume establish aspects of character, social class, age, weather?

8. What is a design conference? Why is it important?

9. How does the costume designer study a script? What questions do costume designers ask about the script?

10. Why is the dress rehearsal important for designers and directors?

11. What is the function of stage makeup?

12. What is the difference between *straight* and *character* makeup?

13. Why are masks effective onstage?

14. What are the light designer's tools?

15. What is a light plot?

16. What is the function of sound effects in the modern theatre? Give some examples.

17. How do scenery, costume, lighting, and sound enhance the actors' work?

18. *Suggested Reading*: TCI: *The Business of Entertainment Technology and Design*, the leading magazine on American design and technology.

The producer is responsible for financing the production, for hiring and firing the artistic and managerial personnel. The producer is frequently all things to all people: money machine, tyrant, boss, mediator, friend, enemy, gambler, investor, consultant. In a word, the producer's job is to present the play.

12

THE IMAGE MAKERS: THE PRODUCER

T hus far we have been discussing the special contributions of the theatre's *artists*—playwrights, actors, directors, designers—to this highly complex collaborative art form.

The producer is that anomalous person who, in the highly competitive and risky business of theatre, deals with plays, investors, artists, theatre owners, trade unions, agents, contracts, taxes, rentals, deficits, grosses, and the bottom line. The producer is rarely an artist but rather an astute businessperson with creative judgment who knows the demands of the commercial or nonprofit theatre. In answer to the question "What exactly do you do?", producer Cheryl Crawford said: "I find a good play or musical, I find the money required to give it the best physical form on a stage, I find the people to give it life, I find a theatre and try to fill it."[1]

The Broadway Producer

There are thirty-seven Broadway theatres at the present time (see Figure 12.1), sixteen and a half of which are owned by the Shubert Organization of major New York producers. Because of the high cost of producing on Broadway—over $8 million for a musical; $800,000 for a dramatic play—many Broadway producers are seasoned veterans and are collaborating more frequently with one another in their producing efforts. Eight producers joined forces to bring *Angels in America: A Gay Fantasia on National Themes* to Broadway in 1993. As the costs of producing on Broadway continue to skyrocket (*Kiss of the Spider Woman*

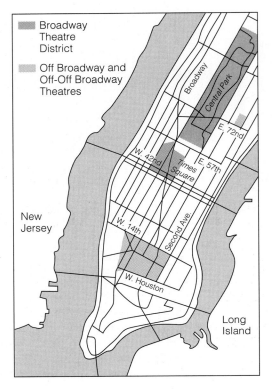

FIGURE 12.1
The New York City theatre districts: Broadway, Off Broadway, Off-Off Broadway.

cost $8 million in 1993), the pattern of producers commingling their know-how and assets has become a trend of the '90s. General managers, accountants, and lawyers assist them with the business of financing a Broadway play from option to opening.

Why is theatre, and especially the commercial Broadway theatre, so costly? Analysts agree that theatre is a service business in which most of the cost of the product is labor. As wages rise with general living standards across the country, most businesses turn to machines or technology rather than to people to blunt the cost of inflation. However, in the theatre, the opportunities for saving labor costs are limited. It takes just as long for actors to bewail the death of Hamlet in 1994 as it did in Shakespeare's day and just as long to design Madame Ranevskaya's living room as it did in Chekhov's. Moreover, unlike the film industry, the multimillion-dollar production cannot be put in a "can" and distributed for tens of thousands of showings in moviehouses to dilute the original costs.

BROADWAY'S "HOTTEST" PROPERTY: THE MUSICAL

Kiss of the Spider Woman, *a musical adapted from Mañuel Puig's novel, opened on Broadway in 1993. It became a star vehicle for Chita Rivera as the bygone film star, Aurora. Here, she—who dwells only in the imagination of the homosexual prisoner, played by Brent Carver—takes center stage.*

The Phantom of the Opera *(above), an Andrew Lloyd Webber production, directed by Harold Prince, opened on Broadway in 1988.*

Sunset Boulevard, *another Andrew Lloyd Webber musical, opened on London's West End with Patti Lupone and in Los Angeles with Glenn Close (above) in 1993. The musical was based on Billy Wilder's film, which starred Gloria Swanson.*

The award-winning musical from the 1993 Broadway season—The Who's Tommy—with music, lyrics, and book by Pete Townshend, a member of the British musical group The Who, from 1963–82. Directed by Des McAnuff, the production was designed by: John Arnone (scenery), David C. Wollard (costumes), and Chris Parry (lights). Above, Tommy's genius as the "pinball wizard" is celebrated in dance and song with Michael Cerveris as Tommy. Left, Cerveris as Tommy and Buddy Smith as the younger boy contemplate mirror images of themselves.

The festive "barn scene" from the 1994 revival of Carousel at Lincoln Center Theater, New York City, with sets and costumes designed by Bob Crowley. Michael Hayden and Sally Murphy (center) are seen here as Billy Bigelow and Julie Jordan.

Jelly's Last Jam *opened on Broadway in 1992 with Gregory Hines as the legendary jazz musician. Book and direction by George C. Wolfe, music by Jelly Roll Morton.*

The Broadway Option

Once a play is written, the playwright usually sends it to an *agent* who contacts the producers and options the play for a commission. The *option*—a payment advanced against royalties to the playwright—is the starting point on that long road to opening night. It is an agreement that grants producers the right to produce a play within a specified period of time and place in exchange for a fee paid to the writer. The amount paid, the length of the option, what the money buys are all negotiable.

Another approach to getting a play produced is to send the script directly to a regional theatre or university theatre department in the hope that the play interests a director. University, regional, and Off Broadway theatres produce new plays, and many Broadway hits are first seen elsewhere, particularly in the professional regional theatres. For example, August Wilson's *Fences* was produced at the Yale Repertory Theatre, a professional regional theatre, before transferring to Broadway. The same has been true in the 1992–93 season of *Angels in America* (the Mark Taper Forum, Los Angeles), *The Sisters Rosensweig* (Lincoln Center Theater, New York City), and *The Who's Tommy* (La Jolla Playhouse, California).

All plays produced on Broadway by an American author are optioned by producers under the Dramatists Guild contract. There are separate contracts for musicals, dramatic productions, stock tryouts, and collaborations; the Dramatists Guild's is a minimum basic contract.

When a commercial producer options, or buys, the exclusive rights to a play for a Broadway production, the playwright then is asked to rewrite parts of the script during rehearsals, out-of-town tryouts, and previews. Tryouts and previews are the testing ground for commercial productions. On the basis of critical notices and audience response during this period, the play is reworked and sometimes completely rewritten before the official New York opening. There is enormous pressure on the playwright to satisfy various interest groups, including director and producer.

The initial option usually lasts for one year from the date of delivery of the completed play. There are permissions for extending the option (if a star is unavailable for six months, for example, or if there is a wait of four to six months to get into a choice Broadway theatre), but that can be expensive.

> "I function in the commercial world, I have to live in the commercial world, I have to finance the productions I do—not by writing a check on what Mr. Ziegfeld left me because he knew I was coming, but by going out and hustling to get the money to produce plays on Broadway. . . ."[2]
>
> **Alexander H. Cohen, producer**

In 1938, producer-director Jed Harris used an unusual strategy to open *Our Town* on Broadway. Convinced that Thornton Wilder's play could not open in just any theatre, but not wanting to extend the option, Harris gambled on a suitable theatre becoming available once the show had opened. He opened the play in a theatre that was available for only one week, reasoning that if the play was a success, another theatre would materialize. And so it did: When the play proved to be a hit, the favored Morosco theatre magically became available.

The producer enters into comparable arrangements with the director, actors, and designers. In addition, the producer will be concerned with potential foreign productions, cast albums, television, video and film rights, and touring companies.

Since producing a Broadway show is an expensive, high-risk investment, the producer usually seeks assistance from co-producers, associate producers, and general managers in raising the money and in handling other business details. Backers, or "angels," are sought to invest in the show, with the full knowledge that they can lose their total investment.

The Associations and Craft Unions

The Broadway producer deals with a variety of organizations. The League of American Theatres and Producers (located at 226 West 47th Street), an association of producers and theatre owners, was founded in 1930 to oversee the common interests and welfare of theatre owners, lessees, operators, and producers. The League's primary function is to act as bargaining representatives for theatre owners and producers with the many unions and associations, ranging from ticket sellers to press agents.

PRODUCER

CAMERON MACKINTOSH

Cameron Mackintosh produced the long-running Andrew Lloyd Webber musical Cats *(1981), directed by Trevor Nunn.*

Born in Enfield, Middlesex, England, in 1946, Cameron Mackintosh has become a leading producer in the commercial theatre on both sides of the Atlantic Ocean—on London's West End and on Broadway. His name is synonymous with such award-winning musicals as *Cats, Les Misérables, Phantom of the Opera*, and *Miss Saigon*.

Casting

General, "open" casting calls (announced in such trade journals as *Variety* and *Backstage*) are conducted by the casting director, and actors are auditioned by the director, author, and producer. The director and producers make the final casting decisions, but the author also has cast approval. The producer does the hiring.

Actors' Equity Association has three basic contracts for actors, singers, dancers, and stage managers: a standard minimum contract for principal actors (at most a Broadway star may make $15,000 a week); a standard minimum contract for chorus; and a standard run-of-play contract. (All of these are spelled out in the *Actors' Equity Rules Handbook*.) Once assembled for rehearsals, the cast elects a deputy to

The Image Makers: The Producer　　　　307

CONTRACTS

Contracts negotiated by the League of American Theatres and Producers include the following:

- Theatre Protective Union, Local No. 1, IATSE: basic theatre house crews, including electricians, carpenters, curtain and property people.

- Treasurers and Ticket Sellers Union, Local No. 751: all box office personnel involved in ticket selling.

- Legitimate Theatre Employees Union, Local No. B-183: all ushers, doormen, ticket takers.

- Theatre, Amusement and Cultural Building Service Employees, Local No. 54: custodians, cleaners, matrons, and the like.

- International Union of Operating Engineers (affiliated with the AFL-CIO), Local No. 30: employees involved in operation and maintenance of heating and air-conditioning systems.

- Mail and Telephone Order Clerks Union Local B-751: all mail clerks and telephone operators employed by theatres.

- Actors' Equity Association: actors, stage managers, singers, dancers.

- Theatrical Wardrobe Attendants Union, Local No. 764: wardrobe supervisors, assistants, and dressers.

- The Society of Stage Directors and Choreographers: directors and choreographers.

- The Dramatists Guild Minimum Basic Production Contract: authors.

- The United Scenic Artists, Local No. 829: set, lighting, costume designers and assistants.

- Associated Musicians of Greater New York, Local No. 802, American Federation of Musicians: musicians.

- Association of Theatrical Press Agents and Managers, Local No. 18032: press agents, house and company managers.

represent Equity members in dealing with the producer over any breach of agreements or other employment terms. Chorus singers and dancers have separate deputies.

The Agent

When asked "What does an agent do?", Audrey Wood, possibly the most famous playwrights' agent of the last forty years, answered as a character in Arthur Kopit's play *End of the World* (1984): "This is a question I am asked all the time. In *theory*, an agent is supposed to find her client *work*! Now, while this has certainly been *known* to happen, fortunately, for all concerned, we do much, much more."

An agent, whether for playwright, director, or actor, acts on behalf of that artist to find theatre, film, television, commercials, and publishing contracts. For a fee, the agent looks after the livelihood of the artist, negotiates contracts and royalties, and writes checks. The agent is as much a part of the artist's professional life and success in the commercial theatre as the director or producer, because it is through the agent that the actor or playwright is seen and heard by directors and producers. As the artist's lifeline into the commercial theatre, the agent is frequently friend, mentor, counselor, parent, psychiatrist, and investment broker.

Preview or Out-of-Town Tryout

Until recently, almost every Broadway show had a trial run in New Haven, Boston, or Philadelphia before its New York opening. The purpose was to get audience response and to fix script and casting problems before subjecting the production to the scrutiny of Broadway critics. Today, out-of-town tryouts as they were conceived in the past are so expensive that producers are trying new options: one is the Broadway preview (of one to three weeks); another is transferring directly onto Broadway a play or musical that has had a successful debut in a regional theatre (*A Chorus Line, Big River, The Who's Tommy*); or transferring directly the successful commercial London production (*Cats, Les Misérables, The Phantom of the Opera*); or opening on campus in a university theatre with commercial producers and moving the

AUDREY WOOD

Playwrights' agent Audrey Wood (1905–1985) helped define the American theatre by representing and guiding the careers of Tennessee Williams, William Inge, Robert Anderson, Clifford Odets, Carson McCullers, Preston Jones, Arthur Kopit, and many others.

Wood discovered Tennessee Williams through his entry in a playwriting contest sponsored by the Group Theatre. It took her eight years to sell the script of *The Glass Menagerie,* but when she did, it launched Williams' international career. When "her" playwrights were young and struggling, she found them jobs and grants and often lent them money herself. She was known for her extraordinary devotion to her clients and was tireless in her calls on their behalf to producers and influential people. Moreover, she was the first agent in the American theatre to be given billing on the bottom of the program: "Mr. Williams' Representative—Audrey Wood." In her autobiography, *Represented by Audrey Wood* (1981), she said: "The theater is a venture (one hesitates to call it a business) built on equal parts faith, energy and hard work—all tied together with massive injections of nerve."[3]

production onto Broadway from there (*Broadway Bound, A Few Good Men, Laughter on the 23rd Floor*).

The pre-Broadway production, like the preview, brings the show into its permanent theatre, thereby avoiding the expenses of the road, and provides a period of time for Broadway audiences to respond to the show and generate word-of-mouth publicity before its official opening.

The Broadway Opening and After

Those late opening-night parties at Sardi's restaurant where everyone connected with the show waits to learn the critics' verdict are legendary. Will the show have a run or won't it? Tension mounts while a group of people wait to learn their fate. Usually the show's press agent or publicity manager reports the television critics' views or brings the newspapers in around midnight.

The morning after the opening, there is a customary meeting among the producer, press agent, and general or company manager (and sometimes an attorney). If the show has received rave reviews, like Andrew Lloyd Webber's *The Phantom of the Opera* (1988) or Harold Prince's *Kiss of the Spider Woman* (1993), the job of planning advertising expenses is an easy one. If the reviews are "pans," the decision to close is equally easy. However, if the reviews are mixed, decisions are difficult. There's always a chance that the show can make it, but figuring out how much money to spend to try to keep it running until expenses can be made is tricky.

Neither is it an easy decision to close a show if the possibility exists of developing business at a later date. So many jobs, from electricians' to actors', depend on this decision. Advance sales to theatre parties have to be weighed against current box office sales. Generally, when a show is panned, it has little chance of making its costs, much less returns on investments.

The National Touring Company

If the show is a hit in New York, a touring company is financed through guarantees from the various theatres where it will appear. A smash hit in New York can gross $350,000 to $800,000 a week in Seattle, Pittsburgh, Detroit, Los Angeles, Philadelphia, and Toronto. During December 1993, the highest-grossing national companies were all musicals with stars.

Producing Off Broadway

Once a haven from the strictures of Broadway commercial contracts and unions, **Off Broadway** is now a smaller, less expensive version of its parent. There is a League of Off Broadway Theatres and Producers; the Dramatists Guild and Actors' Equity have developed Off Broadway contracts, which apply to the smaller theatres (299 seats) and the smaller box office potential.

At one time it was said that producing Off Broadway was unlike anything else in the world, since contractual arrangements were so loosely defined. However, Off Broadway today mirrors the larger enterprise. It all begins when the producer options the play, or *property*. The producer pays for the right to produce it Off Broadway. As soon as the play is presented before paying audiences, the producer makes a weekly payment of an agreed-upon fee to the author. This fee is directly related to gross weekly box office receipts (the author's percentage is anywhere from 8 percent to 12 percent).

Co-producers and associate producers also appear on the Off Broadway scene, since money, regardless of the sum, is always required. A *co-producer* enters into a joint venture (or *limited partnership*, as it is called) to assist the producer in raising money for the production: now a minimum of $350,000 for a musical and $325,000 for a nonmusical. Why use a co-producer? A certain amount of "front money," or risk capital, is needed immediately to pay for the option and printing scripts, for making payments to lawyers and general managers, and to pay for a backers' audition, where potential investors are invited to sample the play. This audition is key to money-raising. The author gives the story line, scenes from the script are presented, musical numbers are sung, and major investors from all areas of the business world are often forthcoming. *Associate producers* also join up for a percentage (1 percent) to get others to invest in the show, and they get billing credits for their efforts.

Once the money is reasonably assured, the producer proceeds to rent a theatre and hire a director, stage manager, actors, designers, press agent, advertising agency, general manager (who oversees the budget and takes care of all financial transactions), accountant, and lawyer. For a musical, additional personnel—musicians, arrangers, choreographers, dancers, and singers—are needed.

Today there is little difference, other than scale and amount of investment, between producing on and off Broadway. The language is the same, contracts similar, key personnel identical, and risks ever-present.

Producing in the Nonprofit Regional Theatre

In **regional theatres**—sometimes referred to as **resident theatres** or companies—a person called an executive producer, producing director, or general manager (the titles vary from theatre to theatre) deals with a board of directors or trustees, corporations, foundations, federal and state agencies, patrons, and subscribers.

Although Broadway remains the mecca for American commercial theatre, both commercial and nonprofit professional theatres have proliferated beyond Broadway and throughout the United States. Just as Off Off-Broadway provides alternative performance spaces for nonprofit groups in New York, so the regional theatre movement, beginning in the '50s, has established a network of nonprofit professional theatres across the country. They have formed a national alliance as the League of Resident Theatres (LORT), which negotiates contracts with all theatre unions, including Actors' Equity, and establishes the general contract under which all nonprofit professional regional theatres operate. It is unusual to find a major city that does not have one or more professional resident theatres, although the majority are clustered in the Northeast (see Figure 12.2).

The terms *resident* and *regional* have been used interchangeably to describe nonprofit professional theatres located outside New York City. Today, there are over sixty theatres in fifty-one cities with operating budgets ranging from $200,000 to more than $9 million. They produce over 600 productions yearly to audiences of 14,000,000. Most perform seasons of from five to ten months, generally to subscription audiences. Many have touring programs. Others have outreach programs for audiences of all ages, which are models for community-wide social organizations. And they all offer opportunities for writers and actors that are unavailable within Manhattan.

Writers have found that the regional theatres have an inherent mandate to develop new works; because New York productions boast prohibitive staging costs, astronomical ticket prices ($45 to $75 for a single Saturday night ticket), and mercurial critics, writers increasingly prefer to have their works initially produced by regional companies. There, during a guaranteed four- to six-week run, writers have time to make changes without the threat of closing notices being posted on opening night. Regional theatres have developed such writers as August Wilson, Wendy Wasserstein, David Henry Hwang, Christopher Durang, David Rabe, Terrence McNally, Marsha Norman, Sam Shepard, Beth Henley, and David Mamet, among others. In 1994, even an established playwright like Arthur Miller eschewed Broadway and unveiled *Broken Glass* at the Long Wharf Theatre in New Haven, Connecticut.

Moreover, New York City has its own resident theatres. Circle Repertory Company, for example, has nurtured writer Lanford Wilson for over a decade. The Manhattan Theatre Club, Playwrights Horizons,

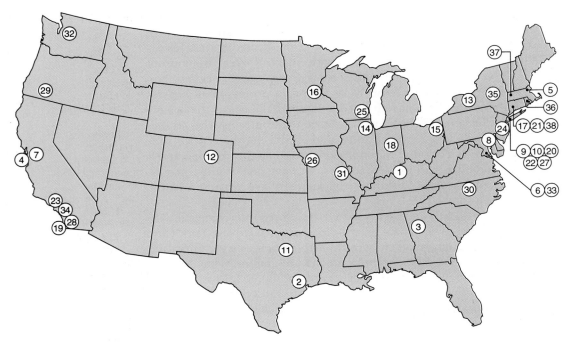

FIGURE 12.2
Some of the 60+ LORT theatres.

the American Place Theater, La Mama ETC (Experimental Theatre Club), the Negro Ensemble Company, the Lincoln Center Theater, and the New York Shakespeare Festival at the Public Theater have all provided stages for the talents of writers Tina Howe, Samm-Art Williams, Wendy Wasserstein, Charles Fuller, A. R. Gurney, Jr., Christopher Durang, David Rabe, George C. Wolfe, Jon Robin Baitz, Terrence McNally, John Ford Noonan, and David Henry Hwang.

The producer's job in the resident theatres is both similar to and different from the Broadway producer's job. He or she deals with Actors' Equity through the special LORT contract; in the New York, Boston, Chicago, and Los Angeles areas, some even deal with craft unions. However, the *regional theatre producer* produces not a single play but a season spanning eight to eleven months. The producer consults with the

Theatre	City	Producing/Artistic Directors
① Actors Theatre of Louisville	Louisville	Jon Jory
② Alley Theatre	Houston	Gregory Boyd
③ Alliance Theatre Company	Atlanta	Kenny Leon
④ American Conservatory Theatre	San Francisco	Carey Perloff
⑤ American Repertory Theatre	Boston	Robert Brustein
⑥ Arena Stage	Washington, D.C.	Douglas C. Wager
⑦ Berkeley Repertory Theatre	Berkeley	Sharon Ott
⑧ Center Stage	Baltimore	Irene Lewis
⑨ Circle Repertory Company	New York City	Tanya Berezin
⑩ CSC Repertory—The Classic Stage Company	New York City	David Esbjornson
⑪ Dallas Theatre Center	Dallas	Richard Hamburger
⑫ Denver Center Theatre	Denver	Donovan Marley
⑬ GeVa Theatre	Rochester	Howard J. Millman
⑭ Goodman Theatre	Chicago	Robert Falls
⑮ Great Lakes Theatre Festival	Cleveland	Gerald Freedman
⑯ Guthrie Theatre	Minneapolis	Garland Wright
⑰ Hartford Stage Company	Hartford	Mark Lamos
⑱ Indiana Repertory Theatre	Indianapolis	Libby Appel
⑲ La Jolla Playhouse	San Diego	Michael Greif
⑳ Lincoln Center Theatre	New York City	Andre Bishop
㉑ Long Wharf Theatre	New Haven	Arvin Brown
㉒ Manhattan Theatre Club	New York City	Lynne Meadow
㉓ Mark Taper Forum	Los Angeles	Gordon Davidson
㉔ McCarter Theatre Company	Princeton	Emily Mann
㉕ Milwaukee Repertory Theatre	Milwaukee	Joseph Hanreddy
㉖ Missouri Repertory Theatre	Kansas City	George Keathley
㉗ New York Shakespeare Festival Theatre	New York City	George C. Wolfe
㉘ Old Globe Theatre	San Diego	Jack O'Brien
㉙ Oregon Shakespeare Festival	Ashland, OR	Henry Woronicz
㉚ PlayMakers Repertory Company	Chapel Hill	Milly S. Barranger
㉛ Repertory Theatre of St. Louis	St. Louis	Steven Woolf
㉜ Seattle Repertory Theatre	Seattle	Daniel Sullivan
㉝ Shakespeare Theatre at the Folger	Washington, D.C.	Michael Kahn
㉞ South Coast Repertory	Costa Mesa, CA	David Emmes
㉟ Syracuse Stage	Syracuse	Tazewell Thompson
㊱ Trinity Repertory Company	Providence	Oskar Eustis
㊲ Williamstown Theatre Festival	Williamstown, MA	Peter Hunt
㊳ Yale Repertory Theatre	New Haven	Stan Wojewodski, Jr.

ZELDA FICHANDLER

Zelda Fichandler, former artistic director of The Acting Company, discusses the distinction between a producer and a manager:
How do you define the difference between a producer and a manager? Well, in my way of thinking (and I'm like the Red Queen, when I use words they mean exactly what I mean them to mean—no more, no less) in my way of thinking, as the Red Queen, they don't belong in the same category, they're two different functions. The producer does what the title says. He or she leads out, leads forth, leads through. The producer is the total organizing human being who generates the impulse from the organization: what direction is it going to take? When is it necessary to move in another direction? The style of the work; are you going to do only new works? Are you going to do only female playwrights between the ages of forty and forty-five? Are you going to do only dead playwrights? Who can come to rehearsals? Are you going to increase your deficit and say "To hell with it, let's see what happens"? Are you going to cut costs? Are you going to have two theatres? Which twin has the Toni?—all of the big questions. The manager, it seems to me, has a very important function. But the manager works within the compass design, works within the full circle to manage whatever area. We're lousy with managers—we've got a box office manager, a house manager, a theatre manager, a production manager. A manager is an executor of the design set by somebody else, in my view. . . .[4]

theatre's *artistic director* (the director in charge of choosing the plays, company, designers) to plan a season of six to ten plays, usually including both classical and modern works (Shakespeare, O'Neill, Miller, and Williams are favorites), musicals, sometimes lesser-known European works, and new American plays. The artistic director usually stages two or more plays within each season, hiring other directors to complete the season, while the producer develops a projected budget to cover all contingencies:

- artistic salaries and fees
- administrative salaries and costs

- travel (for casting and artists)
- marketing and development costs
- production expenses
- equipment, facilities maintenance, and services

In this milieu, producing is precarious. Although there is usually continuity of administrative and artistic leadership within regional theatres, no continuous financial support system exists from season to season, though some theatres have developed endowment funds to offset annual operating costs. The regional theatres and their producers depend on a delicate balance of federal and state dollars (now dwindling), private foundation and corporation money, and subscribers' dollars. The producer must at all times juggle the season's budgeted expenses against real and projected income. Although most theatres hire permanent administrative staff and artistic leadership, they have not yet been able to fund a resident company for the entire season, as do Britain, France, and Germany. At best, a small core of actors remains year after year, playing a broad variety of roles. They are allied with other performers who are hired for a season to play five or six different roles while in residence with the company. The artists themselves often support the theatre by accepting minimal salaries until they grow tired and move on into commercials, film, television, and the commercial theatre. New actors replace them and the cycle begins again. This talent drain is wearing as well as discouraging. But despite the lack of permanent funding and resident companies, the regional theatre movement is strong.

One way a number of producers have chosen to counterbalance the deficit budget that can result in a theatre's closing has been to reestablish connections with the New York commercial theatre. In the last decade, Broadway has been enlivened by shows that established themselves first with regional audiences (a variation on the out-of-town tryout) and then moved with added capital (and co-producers) onto Broadway. A short list includes: *A Chorus Line* and *The Pirates of Penzance* from the New York Shakespeare Festival Theatre (or the Public Theater), *The Gin Game* from Actors Theatre in Louisville, *Fences* and *The Piano Lesson* from the Yale Repertory Theatre, *Glengarry Glen Ross* from the Goodman Theatre in Chicago, *The Sisters Rosensweig* from the Lincoln Center Theater in New York City, and *Redwood Curtain* from the Seattle Repertory Theatre.

Broadway producer Alexander H. Cohen has said that the commercial and nonprofit theatre share something in common: "*What's good succeeds.*" If the material is good—if it addresses the nature of our society—then it will succeed in either the commercial or nonprofit theatre, or in both, as the case may be. There's a great deal of trial and error in choosing material and producing it. But finally the dross sinks beneath its own undistinguished weight and the meaningful, imaginative, and exciting continue on our stages. Out of the commercial and nonprofit theatres, and out of producers' visionary risk taking, have come such American classics as *A Streetcar Named Desire*, *Death of a Salesman*, *Who's Afraid of Virginia Woolf?*, *A Chorus Line*, and *Angels in America: A Gay Fantasia on National Themes*.

Summary

The producer's job, as the name implies, is to produce. However, many businesspeople are attracted to "show biz" and to producing for a variety of reasons, most of them the wrong ones: the glamour of associating with Broadway and "stars"; the get-rich-quick dream of an overnight hit.

But producing means making a lot of difficult, educated decisions about people and money, and carrying them out. It is not for the dilettante or faint of heart. Producing is frequently painful because it can mean firing your favorite actor, director, or designer who turns out not to be right for the show. A producer has to have the personality and experience to influence people, raise money, hire, fire, mediate disputes, encourage and assist people to work together and to get along, option wisely, sell expediently, hold hands and soothe bruised egos, comfort the sick, and be all things to all people. All important is the ability to extract money from investors—in a word, to produce the show.

Questions for Study

1. What is the producer's job in the commercial Broadway theatre?
2. Who works directly with the producer?

3. What is the Dramatists Guild contract? Why is it important?

4. What is an *option*?

5. Name some of the major New York producers.

6. What are the current costs of a Broadway musical? A dramatic play?

7. What is an "angel"?

8. What is the League of American Theatres and Producers?

9. Name some of the unions that operate within the commercial theatre.

10. What is Actors' Equity Association and whom does it represent?

11. What is an "open" casting call?

12. Where are casting calls for the commercial theatre usually posted or announced?

13. What are the three basic contracts used by Actors' Equity Association?

14. What is the job of an Equity "deputy"?

15. What is the function of an agent for an actor or playwright?

16. What is the purpose of an out-of-town tryout?

17. What is a preview performance?

18. What is a national touring company?

19. What is Off Broadway? Off-Off Broadway?

20. How does producing Off Broadway differ from on Broadway?

21. What is a regional theatre?

22. What is a nonprofit or not-for-profit theatre?

23. What regional theatre is located near your campus?

24. *Suggested Readings*: "Profile of Audrey Wood" by Tennessee Williams in *Esquire* magazine (December 1962); Cheryl Crawford, *One Naked Individual: My Fifty Years in the Theatre* (Indianapolis: Bobbs-Merrill, 1977); William Goldman, *The Season: A Candid Look at Broadway* (New York: Harcourt, Brace and World, 1969; Revised Edition—New York: Limelight Editions, 1984).

The reimaging of world cultures by international companies and solo performers has brought cultural diversity onto our stages in a defining way in the last two decades of this century. The fusion of performance styles from different cultures and the return to global moral and social issues have engaged the theatre anew in the fundamental issues of our times—racism, barbarism, hunger, disease, terrorism, discrimination, justice, and the environment.

13

REIMAGING CULTURES: THEATRICAL DIVERSITY

Since its beginnings, the theatre has transgressed the borders of specific cultures through its itinerant audiences, universal subjects, and international touring companies. In the last two decades of the twentieth century, the theatre has assumed a large role in the desire of societies to demonstrate their openness to world cultures. In effect, the theatre's unique ability to blend cultures in the creation of distinctive aesthetic forms has brought theatre to the forefront of the current debate on cultural diversity.

Let us begin this discussion of the theatre's reimaging of cultures with the cultural buzzwords of the '90s—*multiculturalism, transculturalism,* and *interculturalism*—and examine the leading international companies and solo performers who are in the vanguard of artistic efforts to confront the moral, social, and political issues of our time and for all people. This new trend in international theatre requires our attention and understanding because it brings new styles and neglected issues onto our stages.

In the late 1980s, new influences in the ease of world travel, along with the cross-fertilization of aesthetic forms among European and Asian artists and the awakening of America to the riches of a multiracial society, opened doors to new performers, bold texts, and theatrical styles. New multinational productions by Peter Brook, Julie Taymor, and Ariane Mnouchkine transcended borders, languages, and ethnicity. Solo performers, especially in the United States, took up issues of race and class in American culture and thus created a new avant-garde for the '90s.

Webster's Dictionary says that *multiculturalism* means simply "of or pertaining to a society of varied cultural groups." In our newspapers, magazines, and college curriculums, the term has been utilized in two ways: first, to acknowledge the rich diversity of American society—its traditions, learning, and art; and second, to redress the heavy emphasis in our culture on the importance, achievements, and values of Western culture. What is at issue here is the desire to emphasize cultural differences—that is, to allow all cultures self-expression, autonomy, and power. It is fashionable to say that the American effort to emphasize the multicultural is the inversion of the "melting pot" idea; for multiculturalism celebrates the separateness and distinctions of diverse groups existing side by side. Culturally diverse groups set about in today's world to retain their own distinct ethnic qualities: African American, Hispanic, Native American, Asian American, Polish, Korean, Irish, Hasidic, Jamaican, and so on. Nor is the multicultural idea limited to ethnicity. It also includes orientations and ideologies—gay, feminist, environmentalist, creationist, and so on.

Interculturalism is another way of understanding a diverse society, its similarities and differences. Interculturalists directly confront power arrangements and struggles between or among ethnic groups. They explore the confrontations, fears, disturbances, and difficulties at the points where cultures collide, overlap, and pull away—where fissions occur. Interculturalism happens in art, literature, and scholarship when writers and performers examine the causes of conflicts among culturally diverse groups.[2] Performance artist Guillermo Gomez-Peña lives between two cultures—Mexico and the United States—and makes art out of the contradictions. David Henry Hwang's play, *M. Butterfly*, a drama based on the libretto of a nineteenth-century Italian opera, examines Chinese and American culture through the eyes of a Chinese actress who is, in fact, a man.

A third term refers to the "blenders," the *transculturalists*, who borrow forms and styles from various cultures to create new cultural contexts. The three representative companies that we will examine in this chapter are transcultural in the sense that they blend Eastern, European, and Hispanic cultures—texts, styles, nationalities, languages—in the making of new theatre pieces that speak with universal voices on global issues common to all humankind in the late twentieth century.

Transculturalism

Since its beginnings in ancient Greece, theatre has been international and culture specific. Greek writers confronted issues of tribal wars and international imperialism. Aeschylus in *The Persians*, produced in 472 B.C., treated the nation's enemies from the East with deep sympathy and turned their story into a parable on the dangers of pride that goes with power. Euripides in *The Trojan Women* (415 B.C.), written one year following the Athenian armies' destruction of the population of the island of Melos (all male inhabitants were put to death and women and children sold into slavery), condemned Greek barbarity through portraits of war's universal victims—women and children. Twenty-five hundred years later, these ancient theatrical worlds are not far removed from our experiences of modern gang warfare and the tribal and religious conflicts in Eastern Europe, the near East, and Africa. Such large universal issues that transcend specific cultures inform the work of Peter Brook, Julie Taymor, and Ariane Mnouchkine, who base their efforts on Eastern, Latin American, and Greek texts, respectively, to speak to all cultures about good and evil, war and peace, and the common ground of human desires and needs.

Peter Brook and *The Mahabharata* (1985)

In a rock quarry in southern France, Peter Brook first staged the twelve-hour performance of *The Mahabharata*, a cycle of three plays (*The Game of Dice*, *The Exile in the Forest*, and *The War*) adapted by Jean-Claude Carrière in French from the Sanskrit poem dating from 400 B.C. that compiles the myths, legends, wars, folklore, ethics, history, and theology of ancestral India, including the Hindu sacred book *The Bhagavad Gita*. From high in the quarry's rock wall, the piercing fanfare of the *nagaswaram*, an instrument that is half trumpet and half pipe, announces the approach of the first play. Brook's multinational company of twenty-one players, drawn from sixteen nationalities, lends diverse cultural qualities of physical virtuosity, intelligence, humor, and understanding.

In staging this epic struggle between two opposing sets of cousins in an ancient Indian dynasty, Brook begins with the narrative voice of the symbolic poet Vyasa, who is writing a poem about the history of his ancestors (and by inference, the story of humankind) that is taken down by the elephant-man Ganesha, who is also the god Krishna, the supporter of the good and the brave. Throughout, there is the innocence of the young boy who, just as the spectators, listens to the storyteller, watching, questioning, searching. What begins as an austere bargain and a lesson in the right way of life proceeds through adventures that carry an inconsolable sense of loss but that end with a vision of paradise as a gentle place of music, food, cool waters, pleasant conversation, and harmony. At the close, the blind can see, the wounded and slaughtered are restored, and all animosity is forgotten.

The stylization of this global war is achieved almost entirely by ritualistic visual poetry rather than modern stage technology, which is characteristic of Brook's minimal yet spectacular aesthetic. Brook makes dramatic use of the elements (earth, fire, and water) along with brightly patterned carpets, swirling fabrics of red and gold, and masks to transform actors playing half-animal or half-divine characters. Using Asian theatre techniques, billowing cloth represents newborn children, and a single large wooden wheel stands for Krishna's chariot. The battles of multitudes are conveyed by acrobatic displays of Eastern martial arts; dozens of white arrows fly through the air; and, with the flutter of a hand, a god creates a solar eclipse.

For all of the Eastern influences, the common ground shared by *The Mahabharata* and the West are those associations with Oedipus found in the wanderings of the blind prince Dhritarashtra, with the Old Testament in the forest exile of Pandavas, with Shakespeare in the wars of ruling dynasties, and with the *Iliad* and *Odyssey* in the moral struggle of ideal heroes representing divine forces of good arrayed against demonic ones.

Brook's production of the Hindu epic represents a culmination of a lifelong search for theatrical expression of humankind's greatest dramas and deepest dilemmas His efforts to transform Hindu myth into universalized art, accessible to any and all cultures, are triumphant; for embedded in the ancient text are eternal philosophical questions on the paradox of the human condition: Why do people lust for power? What are the causes of humankind's destructiveness? Will humanity survive armageddon? Does the individual have a choice? What is God's game and are we pawns? "Of course, the basic themes are contemporary,"

The dice players toss to determine the fate of the Pandavas in The Mahabharata *at the Bouffes du Nord Théâtre in Paris, 1986. The epic production was directed by Peter Brook.*

The Mahabharata, based on the ancient Hindu poem and first produced at the Avignon Festival in France in 1985, is a cycle of three plays: *The Game of Dice, The Exile in the Forest,* and *The War.*

Part I introduces the main characters, their mythic origins, their characteristics and aims, the role of the gods (especially Krishna), and the growing discord between the Pandavas and the Kauravas, two branches of the Bharata clan. In a game of dice, which the Pandava leader loses to his cousins, the Pandavas forfeit all their property and worldly possessions and are exiled to a forest. In Part II, they live there in a primordial existence while procuring arms for the inevitable battle to come.

In Part III, the devastating war that threatens the entire universe is unleashed—a war foreordained and controlled by the god Krishna. After a gruesome massacre, Pandava regains his rights and is later reconciled with his enemies in heaven. Vyasa, the storyteller, warns that *this*—meaning heaven or earth or the entire play—is "the last illusion." According to Hinduism, life is God's dream and, as rendered by God, is an illusion. At the cycle's end, the characters, dressed in pure white, drop their personae, eat delicacies, and exit, signalling that the game and the performance are over.

Brook says. "One of them is how to find one's way in an age of destruction. What is brought out in *The Mahabharata* is that there is a certain world harmony, a cosmic harmony, that can either be helped or destroyed by individuals. . . . We, too, are living in a time when every value one can think of is in danger."[3]

Julie Taymor and *Juan Darien* (1988)

Julie Taymor and her collaborator, composer Elliot Goldenthal, tell the story of a jaguar cub transformed into a boy in a wordless performance piece about faith and superstition, compassion and revenge, civilization and savagery. *Juan Darien*, produced Off Broadway in 1988, is a compelling narrative, based on the Latin American story by Uruguayan writer Horacio Quiroga, that deals with the bestiality of humans and the humanity of beasts. An accomplished puppeteer and designer, Taymor has banished spoken words from this production, which utilizes puppets, masks, movement, and a musical score sung in Latin and Spanish. Taymor's subjects include maternal love and bereavement, the primitiveness of the natural world, and the malevolence of the human one. Subtitled "A Carnival Mass," the work is described by the creators as a "passion play, a ritualized chronicle of the martyrdom of innocence by bigotry."[4]

The opening images display the play's themes: The deteriorating walls of a mission church are overtaken by giant jungle leaves, while the distant voices of a Latin chorus singing the *Agnus Dei* are drowned out by the buzzing of dragonflies. Unlike the more elaborate staging of Peter Brook's company, Taymor describes *Juan Darien* as "a visual dance of images that have a clear story line, with music—not language—motivating the action."[5]

Created with puppets, actors, and music, *Juan Darien* is a story of transformation brought about by extremes of love and cruelty: of a young jaguar who is transformed by motherly love into a boy, then cruelly executed by superstitious and vengeful villagers, and finally retransformed into the feared jaguar of jungle lore. Understanding the human fear of the jaguar by people living at the edge of civilization, Julie Taymor says, is paramount to understanding this metaphor for human savagery in *Juan Darien*.[6]

Interludes between scenes, called "Tiger Tales," reinforce the culture's obsession with the jaguar as enemy. The "Tales" are a series of shadow puppet plays depicting struggles between humans and beasts presided over by Mr. Bones, the master of ceremonies, a life-size skeleton puppet with a half-jaguar-half-human face, topped with a black bowler hat (See Figure 13.1). These "anti-plays" serve to break the linear flow of the story, interrupt the tension, and introduce crude, scatological jokes. In one instance, a jaguar eats a baby who then drives the animal mad with its loud and ceaseless crying. The jaguar tries to stop the sound within his stomach by covering his various orifices and finally blows his head off, whereupon the baby emerges giggling and gurgling. These interludes further our understanding of the many contrasts in human nature, taking us from the sublime to the ridiculous.

The story begins with images of a tiny church whose windows crumble into lush foliage that descends until the stage becomes a jungle with strange serpentine creatures, night sounds, and flying lizards. A mother jaguar is slain by hunters and her cub stands forlornly in the wilderness. The jungle disappears, and downstage moves an entire hill town in miniature, dotted with houses and with a road that winds to a graveyard at the hill's peak. A funeral procession, also in miniature, proceeds up the hill in this magical landscape that, in the opening moments of the production, has captured Taymor's monumental themes: birth and death, faith and superstition, civilization and savagery.

Juan Darien is a melange of cultural influences that Taymor encountered in the early '70s in Europe, Japan, and Indonesia. The production is a tapestry woven of the Latin American fable, music from the Roman Catholic Mass, life-size Bunraku-type puppets manipulated by three handlers, monumental puppets that recall the Bread and Puppet Theatre, Indonesian shadow puppets, European Punch-and-Judy-style puppets, and Mayan masks. The music—a requiem mass composed for eight musicians—is played on a variety of instruments: Japanese taiko drums, African shakers, Indian temple gongs, Mayan clay flutes, an Australian didgeridoo, Western trumpets, marimbas, a tuba, and an upright piano.

With an ensemble of eleven in which only the actors playing the mother and the boy are identifiable, Taymor captures the story's sense of living at the border between the jungle, with its natural beauty and savagery, and civilization, with its refinement and cruelty. The jaguar is

FIGURE 13.1

A carnival scene with Juan and Mr. Bones, the skeleton puppet who is the play's master of ceremonies, in Juan Darien, a 1988 Off Broadway production directed and designed by Julie Taymor.

feared as a jungle creature that strikes and devours people. As the humans prepare to fight back against an age-old enemy, their innate superstitions and religious beliefs take hold in the most cruel and destructive way. In destroying beauty and innocence, they re-create their worst enemy and perpetuate their worst fears.[7]

Juan Darien is a story of transformation in which Juan is transformed five times. First, he appears as a jaguar cub (a rod and string puppet); second, he becomes an infant (a hand-manipulated doll) cradled by a mother who has lost her own child to the plague; at age ten, he transforms into a four-foot-tall bunraku puppet with realistic features; and upon the death of his mother he becomes a flesh-and-blood child. This is the pivotal moment because, from this point on, Juan is the only human (unmasked) actor in the play. When he is accused by the villagers of being a dangerous jaguar, we realize that everyone around him wears a mask and, unlike Juan, the masked villagers appear as not quite human. The final transformation occurs when the child is burned alive on the Bengal lights (fireworks) and metamorphoses into a jaguar once again. This time, the child's face can be seen through the open mouth of the animal mask, his hands are covered by large paws, and his naked torso has blood-red stripes received during a brutal whipping.[8] The final lesson is that human beings, through abominable acts of torture and murder, unwittingly create beasts of others. Essential

FIGURE 13.2
*Julie Taymor has
directed and designed
Shakespeare's* The
Tempest, The Taming
of the Shrew, *and*
Titus Andronicus
*for the Theatre for
a New Audience
in New York City.
In* The Tempest,
Prospero, *using
his magical powers,
confuses the intruders
to his island while
Ariel (top right),
depicted as a hand-
held mask, looks on.*

questions linger unanswered: Who is really the beast? Are not the defenders of civilization who destroy in the name of piety and order far
more dangerous than creatures of the jungle? And so on.

Taymor's work is a blend of Eastern and Western theatre: puppetry,
masks, and minimalist scenic and performance styles (See Figure 13.2).
The stage is transformed into a poetic realm of myth, dreams, nightmares, and childlike storytelling, where puppets and actors concentrate
meaning on universal issues that extend beyond specific cultures into ar-
chetypes. "A puppet," says Taymor, "is a sort of poetic abbreviation, a
distillation to a character's essence. It is more archetype than individual,
an ideogram for Vulgarity, Brutality, Helplessness, Despair. That these
creatures are inanimate only enhances that concentration of meaning."[9]

Ariane Mnouchkine and *Les Atrides* (1992)

French director Ariane Mnouchkine's ten-hour cycle of Greek tragedy
combined Aeschylus' *Oresteia* (*Agamemnon*, *The Libation Bearers*, *The
Eumenides*) with Euripides' *Iphigenia in Aulis* in the 1992 Théâtre du
Soleil production in Paris. This presentation by a multinational com-
pany of sixty excavates the savage, disaster-cursed story of the House of
Atreus: Agamemnon, Clytemnestra, Menelaus, Orestes, and Electra.

JULIE TAYMOR

The life-size skeleton puppet, Mr. Bones, presides over the interludes (called "Tiger Tales") in Juan Darien, *directed and designed by Julie Taymor in 1988.*

In borrowing from the classical texts and from the arts and crafts of Eastern cultures, Mnouchkine and her collaborators reshaped the form and substance of the Aeschylean story by beginning the cycle with *Iphigenia in Aulis* as a prologue to the causes of genocidelike wars, the death of families, and the role of women in the dissolution and resurgence of civilizations. She draws music, rhythms, costumes, movement, and acting styles from Europe, Africa, China, and India with actors recruited from various ethnic groups and nations: France, Africa, Brazil, Turkey, Mexico, Madras, California. Like Peter Brook, Mnouchkine creates a true theatre of the world informed by the elements of behavior common to all humankind.

Mnouchkine's company, not unlike Brook's, adheres in performance style and visual silhouette to the cultural influences of both East and West. In seeking a "look" for the Greek cycle that was both ancient and modern, Mnouchkine wanted to emphasize Eastern antiquity, such as

Julie Taymor (b. 1953) grew up in a suburb of Boston. She traces her initial interest in puppetry and masks to the École du Mime de Jacques Le Coq in Paris, where she studied before attending Oberlin College in Ohio. On a Watson fellowship earned at Oberlin, she went to Indonesia to study for several months and stayed for four years. There, between 1974 and 1978, she formed her own international company, Teatr Loh (*loh* means "the source"), with performers skilled in traditional dance, t'ai chi, improvisation, mask making, acting, and singing. Her first work, *Tirai* ("Curtain"), was a play in six languages that explored the borders between cultures.

Returning to the United States in 1979, she began creating sets, costumes, puppets, and masks for productions in regional theatres. In 1986, she won her first *Village Voice* ("Obie") award for the stage version of *The Transposed Heads*. Five years later, she received a MacArthur Foundation "genius" award. Her various projects include *The Tempest, Liberty's Taken, The King Stag, Visual Magic* (1985 "Obie" award), *Savages, Black Elk Speaks, Tirai* (1981 Maharan Theatre Design Citation), *The Haggadah, Fool's Fire* (television), and *Oedipus Rex* (opera).

the ancient Indian tradition of Kutiyattam, the only surviving tradition for presenting Sanskrit drama. At least as old as the tenth century, Kutiyattam gave rise to the modern Kathakali dance drama. The result is an amalgam of many cultures and forms of theatre in the colorful costumes and stylized makeup dominated by the Kathakali. The color scheme is deliberately symbolic, using five colors (red, black, white, blue, and saffron yellow) that span the range from the color of wedding ceremonies (yellow), to betrayal and mourning (black), to violence (red), and to innocence and purity (white). The combination of actors surrounded by kinetic choruses, colorful non-Western costumes and painted faces, bloody tableaux, and Eastern sounds of string and percussive instruments signify an artistry unfamiliar to mainstream Western theatre. In *Les Atrides*, the Théâtre du Soleil gives form to passion and deeds by mixing cultural influences of East and West in the theatrical excavation of myth, history, and human drama (see Figure 13.3).

Mnouchkine also brings a modern feminine sensibility to the reading of the classical texts. Her story of the Atridae centers principally on Clytemnestra, who married into the accursed clan and whose doomed passion is central to three of the plays. Prefaced by *Iphigenia in Aulis*, in which Clytemnestra is tricked into bringing her daughter to Aulis—where the Greek fleet is becalmed and where the girl is sacrificed to enable the fleet to sail to Troy—this modern version becomes the story of women betrayed by ambition, power politics, and their own emotions. *The Eumenides*, the final part of *Les Atrides*, is key to Mnouchkine's intentions. Shockingly modern with its nonhuman chorus of leaping, barking dogs, this final episode is presided over by Athene, the goddess of peace and wisdom, who makes peace with the forces of vengeance. She is a fragile, becalmed figure dressed in an East Indian costume of white trousers and tunic who, like a slender reed of peace, positions herself between the audience as democratic populace and the howling forces of barbarism, the perennial "dogs of war." Athene literally stands between the audience and the forces of darkness before which civilizations for 2,400 years have collapsed into savagery and death. However tentative Athene's presence, her pacifying influence is witnessed as the dogs (actors costumed with elaborate baboon-faced masks adorned with swept-back coifs of black hair and pointed snouts) begin to leap about and to stand on two legs as symbolic of the influence of the enlightened way that has led civilizations momentarily out of barbarism and avagery.

The entire production takes place in a forty-foot-wide bullfighting arena of a neutral sand color, textured with smears of "aged blood." It is a ritualized "killing field," a place for confrontation and violence surrounded by three walls with six partitions for the "picadores" and "matadors" to escape to safety from the ensuing violence. There is safety from violence and death only behind or on top of the arena walls, not within the barren and merciless killing field occupied by the doomed **protagonists**. Mnouchkine confessed that she began rehearsals without an "image" of the playing space. Gradually, the arena formed in her imagination with its "wooden enclosure and the spaces where the matador can step away in order to seek protection from the wounded beast sensing its death and seeking the death of its opponent."[10] Boxlike platforms—rectangular second stages—glide into the arena through the rear gates, suggesting alternately a ship, chariot, dais, bed, or monument and carrying its cargo of child, returning warriors, the dead, and the god-

FIGURE 13.3

Achilles (Simon Abkarian) silences Clytemnestra (Juliana Carneiro da Cunha) as she struggles to prevent the sacrifice of her daughter, Iphigenia, in the first of the four plays that make up Les Atrides.

dess. To complete the theatrical landscape (and to provide quick exits and entrances), a raked trolley is pushed by stagehands through the audience to the front of the stage area. As the central characters step onto the trolley, they stand in telling friezelike postures as they exit into an invisible area of unmitigated violence and death. Clytemnestra stands, for example, enfolded in Agamemnon's arms as they are transported to his predetermined death; or she and her lover Aegisthus ride to their violent ends.

The visual and musical effects along with the resonances of Kathakali and other Eastern traditions confirm Mnouchkine's sense that her company members are like archaeologists excavating to uncover in the Greek texts an ancient civilization and to rearticulate their discoveries to a modern world for its understanding of history, myth, and legend. Of the company's choice of the Greek cycle, she said: "It shows that war is fratricidal, that we kill those who are closest to us, members of our own family. . . . Humanity is a cursed family. Why do we make war? Why so many civil wars? That is the theme of the Théâtre du Soleil. . . ."[11]

These themes have also been carried out in the Théâtre du Soleil's earlier productions about the French Revolution (*1789, 1793*), the partition of India (*L'Indiade*), and the catastrophic reign of Norodom Sihanouk (*The Terrible but Unfinished History of Norodom Sihanouk, King of Cambodia*).

REIMAGING CULTURES

Théâtre du Soleil ("Theatre of the Sun"), a Paris-based company under the direction of Ariane Mnouchkine, took four classical texts by Euripides and Aeschylus to bring the ten-hour *Les Atrides* to audiences in the 1992–93 season. Influenced by Eastern dress and makeup, Mnouchkine staged the story of the House of Atreus in a wooden enclosure resembling a bull-fighting arena where violence and death reign in a killing field occupied by the doomed protagonists—Iphigenia, Agamemnon, Clytemnestra, and Orestes. A colorful blue and white canopy arches above the playing space, like a changeable sky bearing witness to human destiny. The disastrous history of the House of Atreus is traced in Mnouchkine's treatment from Euripides' *Iphigenia in Aulis* through Aeschylus' *Agamemnon, The Libation Bearers,* and *The Eumenides.*

One of the many startling images from the nine-hour Sanskrit epic, The Mahabharata, *directed by Peter Brook, that captures the art, culture, and spiritual life of Hindu India.*

In an effort to bring monsters and magical creatures to the American theatre, Julie Taymor designed gigantic flying creatures along with costumes and masks for Andrei Serban's production of The King Stag *at the American Repertory Theatre (Cambridge, MA), in 1984.*

Juan (Lawrence Neals, Jr.) talks with one of Julie Taymor's creature puppets that she designed for the 1988 Off Broadway production of Juan Darien.

The chorus of old men dance around Clytemnestra as she waits for Agamemnon's entrance and his death in the second part of Les Atrides.

The Mahabharata, Les Atrides, The King Stag, and *Juan Darien* are productions that transcend national borders, language, and ethnicity and serve as examples of the "reimaging of cultures" in international theatre. Directed by Peter Brook, Ariane Mnouchkine, Andrei Serban, and Julie Taymor, these productions demonstrate the trend in contemporary theatre toward transculturalism.

Clytemnestra (Juliana Carneiro da Cunha) fights for her life as the chorus of women looks on from a refuge of safety behind the walls of the arena in the third part (The Libation Bearers) of the story about the House of Atreus.

Clytemnestra (Juliana Carneiro da Cunha), Agamemnon's wife, and Achilles (Simon Abkarian), the warrior, in Iphigenia in Aulis, *the first of the four plays in* Les Atrides.

Cultural Diversity and Performance Art

Theatre artists in the United States are also responding to diverse cultural values and political issues that extend far beyond the borders of our current debates over political correctness, affirmative action, equal opportunity, and voting quotas. The cultural pluralism of today's international theatre in the hands of Peter Brook, Julie Taymor, and Ariane Mnouchkine has resulted, first, in a reexamination of our predominantly European tradition in culture and the arts. At home, this pluralism has resulted in our awakening to African American, Hispanic, Native American, and Asian American artists, issues, and cultures. Today, we have the plays of David Henry Hwang, Milcha Sanchez-Scott, August Wilson, Philip Kan Gotanda, Maya Angelou, and Eduardo Machado, and we are developing audiences that mirror a more diverse and complex society.

Performance art and the solo performer are the American theatre's latest means of exploring our cultural diversity and social pluralism. Just as theatre has been forced into the margins of cultural life by film and television, so individual artists have stepped forward to create an artistic means by which the marginalized of our society can express themselves—that is, the poor, nonwhite, gay, old, young, ill, and abused. These artists have come to form the American theatre's avant-garde for the '90s, whose subjects are the excluded, the ostracized, the isolated, and the abandoned.

The solo performer exists on the fringes of the empowered establishment, whether it's the commercial Broadway theatre or the larger political system. In form and substance, the solo performer has antecedents that stretch back to shamanistic practices (see Chapter 2) and modern roots in the great radical "isms" at the beginning of this century in Europe, such as expressionism, cubism, dadaism, futurism. What these performers share in common is their singular *presence*. These contemporary pioneers are positioned not so much on the aesthetic outskirts of the community as on its moral and social extremes. The solo explorations of Holly Hughes, Rachel Rosenthal, Karen Finley, Laurie Anderson, Guillermo Gomez-Peña, Eric Bogosian, and Anna Deavere Smith—as challenging as they might seem artistically—are functions of their overriding concerns with class, ethnicity, gender, sexuality, environment, indeed the entire social and natural environment of American life.

The Solo Performance

Anna Deavere Smith and *Fires in the Mirror: Crown Heights, Brooklyn and Other Identities* (1991)

Created by Anna Deavere Smith, actress and theatre professor at Stanford University in California, *Fires in the Mirror* brought her national attention for its deft biography of people involved in the Crown Heights riots in Brooklyn, New York, in 1991. Her solo work, *Fires in the Mirror* and more recently *Twilight: Los Angeles 1992*, are part of a series begun in 1983 as *On the Road: A Search for American Character* in which she brings onto the stage the "voices of the unheard"—an invisible America. In each of these performance pieces, Smith takes on the roles of the many people she has interviewed about a controversial subject or event. "I try to represent multiple points of view and to capture the personality of a place by showing its individuals," she said in a public-radio interview. In effect, her solo performances are a demonstration of the American character, what she calls "a parade of color," and her theatrical solos create a new framework from which to assess race and class in America.[12] Political, social, and personal, her creations distill over 100 interviews into twenty or more character-narratives that go to the heart of issues of race and class in the United States. Both *Fires in the Mirror* and *Twilight: Los Angeles 1992* take as their impetus historical incidents. The racial conflict between the Lubavitcher and Black communities in Crown Heights, Brooklyn, that resulted in the riots of 1991 became the subject for *Fires in the Mirror*. Racial divisions in Los Angeles between the Rodney King incident of March 3, 1991, and the federal trial that ended in April 1993 with the conviction of two Los Angeles policemen for violating King's civil rights provided the topic for *Twilight*. Of these communities, Anna Deavere Smith said, "They all have a very clear sense of their own difference. I'm interested in capturing the American character through documenting these differences."[13]

Fires in the Mirror This solo piece grew out of interviews with a variety of participants and witnesses from the Black and Lubavitcher communities in Crown Heights. Out of these many voices, Deavere Smith crafted a coherent performance by using the words of the interviewees, thereby developing unique and often contradictory insights into a

FIGURE 13.4
Anna Deavere Smith as the Rabbi Joseph Spielman in her award-winning Fires in the Mirror: Crown Heights, Brooklyn and Other Identities *produced here by the Berkeley Repertory Theatre in 1994.*

complex series of events. As the conflict unfolds in the voices of the Crown Heights community—ranging from the Reverend Al Sharpton, civil rights activist, and Robert Sherman, New York City's Commissioner on Human Rights; to Norman Rosenbaum, Yankel Rosenbaum's brother, and Roz Malamud, a Crown Heights resident—it becomes apparent that there are no simple answers to the questions surrounding the controversy. What Anna Deavere Smith clearly shows, however, is that each person's perspective on the incidents is a reflection of his or her background and experience of race, religion, and gender and is worthy of being heard and understood (see Figures 13.4 and 13.5).

The historical moment occurred on August 9, 1991, in the Crown Heights section of Brooklyn when one of the cars in a three-car procession carrying the Lubavitcher Hasidic rebbe (spiritual leader) ran a red light, hit another car, and swerved onto the sidewalk, killing Gavin Cato, a seven-year-old Black child from Guyana, and seriously injuring his cousin Angela.

As rumors spread throughout the community that a Hasidic-run ambulance service helped the driver and his passengers while the children

Anna Deavere Smith as Sonny Carson, activist, in Fires in the Mirror. *In this series of monologues (using minimal props and costume pieces) she offers a compelling portrait of a society unraveling at the seams of race and class in this part of a series called* On the Road: A Search for American Character.

lay bleeding and dying on the sidewalk, members of the district's Black community reacted with violence against the police and the Lubavitchers. That evening a group of young Black men fatally stabbed Yankel Rosenbaum, a twenty-nine-year-old Hasidic scholar from Australia. For three days, Black people fought the police, attacked Lubavitcher headquarters, and torched businesses while Hasidic patrols responded with equal violence.

This conflict reflected long-standing tensions within Crown Heights between Lubavitchers and Blacks as well as the pain, oppression, and discrimination these groups have historically experienced within and beyond their own communities. Many of the Crown Heights Black community were Caribbean immigrants without U.S. citizenship from Jamaica, Guyana, Trinidad, and Haiti, and they faced discrimination on the basis of both their color and their national origin. The Lubavitchers—members of an Orthodox Jewish sect that fled the Nazi genocide of Jews in Europe during World War II—were particularly vulnerable

ANNA DEAVERE SMITH

Anna Deavere Smith (b. 1950), actress, playwright, and performance artist, grew up in Baltimore, Maryland, as the daughter of Deavere (pronounced "da-veer") Young, a coffee merchant, and Anna Young, an elementary school principal. She trained as an actress at the American Conservatory Theatre in San Francisco, graduating with a Master of Fine Arts degree in 1976. Since then, she has been a teaching artist at Carnegie-Mellon University, New York University, and The University of Southern California–Los Angeles before joining the faculty at Stanford University in California.

In 1983, she began a series of solo performances, entitled *On The Road: A Search for American Character.* She gained national attention with the award-winning *Fires in the Mirror* in 1991 at the New York Shakespeare Festival Public Theatre and on tour, and with *Twilight: Los Angeles 1992* at the Mark Taper Forum in Los Angeles in 1993 and on Broadway in 1994. She has appeared in the film *Dave* and in Jonathan Demme's *Philadelphia.* She collaborated in 1994 on a ballet called *Hymn* for the 35th anniversary season of the Alvin Ailey American Dance Theater. Her solo pieces are sophisticated explorations of race and class in contemporary America.

to anti-Jewish stereotyping because of their religion, style of dress, and insular community. Both communities felt victimized. Black leaders charged that the Lubavitchers enjoyed preferential treatment in the community from police and other city agencies. Hasidic leaders charged Blacks with anti-Semitic street crimes and verbal taunts. Both communities felt victimized by the police, the press, and the legal system. Many viewed the jury acquittal of Yankel Rosenbaum's accused murderer as the most stark example of this mistreatment and injustice.

To prepare this piece, Anna Deavere Smith interviewed over 100 people engaged at all levels of this conflict, and she distilled the interviews into a 90-minute solo performance in which she speaks the words, thoughts, and emotions of eighteen people—male and female, Black and Jewish, activist and resident, parent and teacher.

As a creator and performer, Smith sets out to use the words of the voiceless in society, creating a sophisticated and poetic dialogue about race relations in contemporary America. Onstage among the clutter of chairs and tables, Smith, barefoot with hair pulled back to make the changes of costume and gender easier, neutralizes herself in the task of giving shape to the voices and words of others. She shows culturally diverse people struggling to make coherent their sense of rage, pain, and disbelief. She listens not for the facts but for the inner conflicts of the soul expressed in everyday speech. "I'm interested," she said, "in how language and character intersect."[14]

Fires in the Mirror, like *Twilight*, captures a multicultural America at the edge of consciousness about the death, pain, and guilt generated by racism in the United States.

Summary

Cultural diversity is one of the defining issues in society and the arts—especially in the United States—in the last decade of the twentieth century. What we have called here the "reimaging of cultures" by world theatre artists refers chiefly to the fusion of performance styles from Eastern and Western cultures to engage us anew in a sisterhood of issues on hunger, disease, racism, and justice. The four productions discussed here—*The Mahabharata*, *Juan Darien*, *Les Atrides*, and *Fires in the Mirror* by leading British, French, and American artists—are in the vanguard of blending the arts and styles of many cultures. These productions are examples of the theatre's unique ability to blend cultures in the creation of distinctive aesthetic forms. *Juan Darien*, for example, blends traditions of puppetry and music from many nations in a Latin American story about bigotry and its dreadful results applicable to all peoples. Anna Deavere Smith in her solo performances more directly confronts the voices and words of people caught in historical moments of clashing cultures. What is important to envision here is that the theatre deals with specific and general issues that, in most instances, transcend specific times and places and reach a common ground with all people.

To our understanding of "seeing" theatre our final chapter adds the perspective of the theatre critic. Called "Viewpoints," this last chapter deals with theatre criticism—the critic's role, perspective, and vocabulary—and the ways in which critical perspective often shapes our enjoyment of theatre. Theatre criticism adds a new and final dimension to our discovery of theatre, its people, and forms.

Questions for Study

1. Discuss the uses of the words *multiculturalism*, *interculturalism*, and *transculturalism*.

2. By what combination of means do theatre companies with multicultural interests leap across borders of specific cultures?

3. In what ways is Peter Brook's production of *The Mahabharata* a transcultural theatre piece?

4. Describe the Eastern influences in Peter Brook's production of *The Mahabharata*.

5. How does Julie Taymor blend Hispanic and Eastern cultural traditions in *Juan Darien*?

6. How do Peter Brook's and Julie Taymor's themes transcend specific cultures to embrace all people?

7. Explain Julie Taymor's view of puppets and character.

8. Describe the influence of Kathakali dance drama on Ariane Mnouchkine's production of the Greek cycle of plays.

9. What *feminist* viewpoints are discovered in *Les Atrides*?

10. Describe the visual and thematic effectiveness of Mnouchkine's "bullfighting" arena as setting in *Les Atrides*.

11. What are Anna Deavere Smith's means of creating her character-narratives?

12. In what ways do *Fires in the Mirror* and *Twilight: Los Angeles, 1992* by Anna Deavere Smith capture a "multicultural" America?

13. What questions does *Fires in the Mirror* raise about life in America in the 1990s?

14. *Plays to Read*: *The Mahabharata* by Jean C. Carrière; *Juan Darien: A Carnival Mass* by Julie Taymor and Elliot Goldenthal; *Fires in the Mirror* by Anna Deavere Smith.

15. *Suggested Readings*: Peter Brook, *A Theatrical Casebook* (New York: Methuen, 1988); Adrian Kiernander, *Ariane Mnouchkine and the Théâtre du Soleil* (New York: Cambridge University Press, 1993); *Out from Under: Text by Women Performance Artists*, edited by Lenora Champagne (New York: Theatre Communications Group, 1990).

VLADIMIR: Moron!
ESTRAGON: Vermin!
VLADIMIR: Abortion!
ESTRAGON: Morpion!
VLADIMIR: Sewer-rat!

ESTRAGON: Curate!
VLADIMIR: Cretin!
ESTRAGON: (with finality) Crritic!

SAMUEL BECKETT
Waiting for Godot

Theatre critics add new dimensions to our awareness of the art. Critics acquaint readers and audiences with both good and bad productions; they hope, at best, to connect the good work with audiences and to preserve it for future generations.

14

VIEWPOINTS

Theatre criticism gives us a public view or assessment of what we see in the theatre. There are two distinct kinds of **criticism**: *Drama criticism* comments on the written text from a literary and cultural-historical perspective; *theatre criticism* deals with a play's performance, focusing on all elements of production, including the text in performance.

Present-day theatre criticism reflects the fact that we live in a consumer-oriented society. The business of journalistic theatre reviewers at newspapers and magazines such as the *New York Times, Los Angeles Times, The Washington Post, The New Yorker, New York Magazine*, and *The Village Voice* is to appraise theatrical performances found on Broadway, Off Broadway, and in our regional theatres. But theatre criticism is more than appraisal. It is also an economic force (although many critics often deny this fact). In the commercial theatre, criticism often determines whether a play will continue or close after opening night. Given that critics for the *New York Times* and other metropolitan newspapers and television stations have the power to close a Broadway play or keep it running for months, we would do well to consider how critics' views affect the quality of our theatres and what we are seeing. It is also interesting to reflect on our own roles as critics in which we are cast by simply attending a show.

Seeing Theatre
Audiences as Critics

After the curtain comes down, we often go with friends to our favorite restaurant or hangout to talk about the good and bad points of the production we have just seen. It's hard to put out of our minds a powerful performance of a play, whether we've just experienced Blanche DuBois' dependence on the kindness of strangers or the Orgon family's triumphant return to their house after their ordeal with Tartuffe. As we leave the theatre, we carry with us the emotional residue of the bleak pathos of Blanche's future or pleasure in Orgon's escape. A well-performed and meaningful play remains in our minds and in our emotions.

All audiences are critics by virtue of seeing a play in performance (Figure 14.1). We may like the play and not the performance; or like the performance and not the play; or like neither or both. We may even praise certain strong scenes or single out powerful performances by certain actors. It is generally agreed that audiences bring at least *four viewpoints* to the theatre: We relate to a play's human significance, its social significance, its artistic qualities, and its entertainment value, but not necessarily in any particular order.

Human Significance As we have discussed throughout this book, the playwright and other theatre artists connect us with a common humanity between the stage action and where we are seated in the auditorium, or "the seeing place." Great plays, such as the model plays cited in this book, confront us with life's verities, conveying the hope, courage, despair, compassion, violence, love, hate, exploitation, and generosity experienced by all humankind. They show us ways of fulfilling ourselves in relationships and even with material things; they also show us the possibility of losing our families and property through accidents or catastrophes of war and tyranny. The best plays explore what it means to be human beings in *special* circumstances. These circumstances can be bizarre, like the witches' fortuitous appearance before Macbeth, or recognizable, like an unwanted relative appearing at a New Orleans tenement building. Theatre is an extraordinary medium that links us as audiences with actors as characters. They become reflections of ourselves, or what potentially could be ourselves. Theatre's best achievements lead

FIGURE 14.1
The outdoor stage thrusts toward the surrounding audience at the Delacorte Theatre located in Central Park, New York City. This production by the New York Shake-speare Theatre was titled Wars of the Roses *and included* Henry IV *(2 Pts.),* Henry V, *and* Richard II.

us to discoveries and reflections about our own personalities, circumstances, desires, and anxieties.

Social Significance Of all the arts, theatre has a built-in relation to society because by definition an audience is *an assembled group of spectators*. We become part of a *community* as we watch theatre. Communities vote, express themselves at town council meetings, and respond to local, national, and international events.

Since the days of the classical Greek theatre, the playing space has served as an arena wherein to discuss social and political issues, popular and unpopular. Euripides and the Greek comic playwright Aristophanes were often scorned because of their unpopular pacifist beliefs in a time of great nationalistic fervor. The modern theatre likewise deals with controversial issues. The theatre section of any Sunday edition of the *New York Times* lists plays that deal with almost every imaginable social issue: gay rights, drugs, civil rights, AIDS, abortion, racism, sports scandals, real estate fraud, family strife, sexual discrimination, financial hardship, marriage, show business, incest, feminism, nuclear war, terminal disease, mental illness, capital punishment, political chicanery, and so on. But the best plays and performances present social issues only as fuel for thought, not as propaganda.

Playwrights, along with their artistic associates, focus our attention, compassion, and outrage on social injustices and political corruption. *Tartuffe* celebrates triumph over injustice, and *Macbeth* deplores subversion by evil forces and personal ambition. The playwright stimulates social awareness and puts us, as audiences, in touch with our own thoughts and feelings about issues—both as individuals and as groups. The aim of great playwrights is *to give us new perspectives*, to expand our consciousness, on old and new social issues.

Aesthetic Significance Each of us has aesthetic standards. We know what we like and what we don't like. We have seen a lot of television and many movies. As we attend more and more plays, we quickly come to spot honesty in acting, writing, and directing. We see the gimmicks for what they are. We sense the miscasting and the awkward moments. We have no checklist of what makes one performance more effective, provocative, or moving than another, but there are a number of questions we can ask ourselves about any play or performance. Does the play, as performed, excite or surprise us? Does it barely meet our expectations, or worse? Does it stimulate us to think? Are the actors convincing? Or are they more than just convincing, are they mesmerizing? Does the performance seem wooden or lively? Does what we are seeing seem in any way original, or does it seem a carbon copy of something else? Is it complete and logically sound? Are we caught up in the characters' lives, or are we simply waiting for the play to end?

As we see more theatre, we develop a more sophisticated awareness of sights, words, characters, action, actors, sounds, and colors. We appreciate balance and harmony—beginnings, middles, and ends. We also appreciate stage performances that exceed our expectations—that reveal issues and viewpoints that we did not know existed and in theatrical ways we did not anticipate.

Entertainment Great theatre is always diverting in one or more ways. Even tragedy delights us in an unusual way. Aristotle called the way *catharsis*, or the cleansing of the emotions by pity and fear. In addition, tragedy has its share of just plain thrills. *Hamlet* and *Macbeth* offer ghosts, witches, murders, and duels, but they also please us at a deeper level. By witnessing the trials and insights of the tragic heroes, we are liberated from despair over the senselessness of human deeds.

Comedy and farce openly entertain us with romance, reason, pratfalls, gags, misunderstandings, wit, and nonsense while assuring us that wishes can be fulfilled (and even if *our* wishes cannot, farce assures us that it's safe at least to *wish for* the unheard of or for the socially unacceptable). Comedy and farce persuade us that society is really not so bad after all. In effect, they affirm that society will survive humanity's bungling.

In short, theatre is a dependable source of pleasure, laughter, tears, and companionship in an uncertain world. It is a place where we meet people and join with them in a collective experience: We laugh together and we cry together. Theatre entertains by involving us with others both on the stage and around us in the auditorium.

The Professional Critic
The Critic's Role

Unlike theatre itself, which always takes place in the present, the writing of criticism takes place after the fact. After the curtain comes down on the opening-night performance, critics begin their formal work—writing the review or preparing their sound bites for television journalism. The critic's education, background, experience in the theatre, and critical skills make it possible for him or her to produce instant reviews for radio and television or to write within an hour five paragraphs on the play for the late-night newspaper deadline. Those critics writing for Sunday editions or for weekly or monthly magazines have more leisure and usually write longer reviews. However, in all instances the professional critic has deadlines and a specific number of words allowed for the review. Critic Stanley Kauffmann of the *New Republic* calls the theatre critic "a kind of para-reality to the theater's reality. . . ."

> His [the critic's] criticism is a body of work obviously related to but still distinct from what the theater does; possibly influential, possibly not, but no more closely connected than is political science to the current elections. The critic learns that, on the one hand, there is the theater, with good and bad productions, and, on the other hand, there is criticism, which ought to be good about both good and bad productions. Life is the playwright's

FIGURE 14.2

Artist Jasper Johns demonstrated his sense of irony in "The Critic Sees" in 1961 (sculpmetal on plaster with glass).

subject, and he ought to be good about its good and bad people; the theater is the critic's subject, and he ought to be good about its good and bad plays.[1]

Theatre, according to Kauffmann, is a subject that critics often approach with an attitude of open hostility. And the hostility is frequently requited by artists, producers, and managers. They often resent the critic's power to sit in public judgment on the production. (See Figure 14.2.) The resentment is not so much against the individual critic, or the review, but against the very practice of theatre criticism. Shakespeare has Berowne in *Love's Labour's Lost* speak of "A critic; nay, a night-watch constable." Chekhov, according to one report, referred to critics as "horse-flies . . . buzzing about anything." And Max Beerbohm acknowledged in "The Critic as Pariah" (1903): "We are not liked, we critics."

Critics actually perform many services for the theatregoing public, its artists, and producers. They recognize and preserve the work of good artists for future generations. Plays that receive favorable critical attention are usually published. Critics are also publicists of the good and the bad, helping the public decide what productions to see. Critics mediate between artist and audience. They also serve as historians of sorts. Analyses of the professional theatre by Brooks Atkinson, Robert Brustein, Kenneth Tynan, Claudia Cassidy, David Richards, Richard

Eder, Margaret Croyden, Mel Gussow, and many others provide historical accounts of theatre seasons, special theatre events, and performances. Critics discover new playwrights and call attention to electrifying performances.

The most brutal (and dishonest) argument levied against theatre critics is that they are no more than failed creative artists. This is also said of literary, art, music, and architecture critics. Sometimes first-rate criticism is written by second-rate artists; often the reverse is true. George Bernard Shaw excelled in both. Criticism is a true talent, combining artistic sensibilities, writing ability, performance insights, and knowledge of theatre past and present. It requires a special creative flair. Kauffmann defines *creation* as ". . . the imaginative rendering of experience in such a way that it can be essentially re-experienced by others." This is why the critic writes and why the reader (although he or she may not often go to the theatre) reads. The critic re-creates the experience of theatre in another medium for the reader. And the critic holds a mirror up to theatre's nature, serving in the long run even those who most resent the role of the critic in the theatre.

The Critic's Questions

Theatre criticism evaluates, describes, or analyzes a performance's merits and a production's effectiveness. Since the time of the great German playwright and critic Johann Wolfgang von Goethe (1749–1832), the theatre critic traditionally has asked three basic questions of the work:

- What is the playwright trying to do?
- How well has he or she done it?
- Is it worth doing?

The first question concedes the playwright's creative freedom to express ideas and events within the theatre. The second question assumes that the critic is familiar with the playwright, as well as with the forms and techniques of the playwright's time. The third question demands a sense of production values and a general knowledge of theatre. These questions show up in varying degrees of emphasis in the review.

If critics work with these essential questions (and each one usually generates more questions about the performance), they first consider the imaginative material, the concept, and the themes. Second, they judge how well the performance accomplishes the playwright's intentions. Plot, character, setting, lighting, sound, acting, and directing may be considered, depending on their relative contribution to the effectiveness of the production. Third, the response to the question "Was it worth doing?" is the most sensitive and influential aspect of the review, for critical standards are on the line as well as the fate of the production. Claudia Cassidy and Brooks Atkinson had the innate good judgment to know that Tennessee Williams had said something significant about human vulnerability and anger. Their reviews of *The Glass Menagerie* and *A Streetcar Named Desire* demonstrate the critical standards and evaluations that get at the heart and substance of great plays and performances.

Whatever the order of the critic's essential questions about the performance, theatre criticism *describes*, *evaluates*, and *assesses* to one degree or another depending on the critic's tastes, talents, and preferences. Where the critic places his or her emphasis also depends on the production itself. Is it an old play dressed out in fresh designs and interpretations, as was Peter Brook's *A Midsummer Night's Dream*? Unless the critic *describes* that new look, the reader won't understand the critic's estimation of the production.

Performance Notes

American Theatre, *The Drama Review*, *Theater*, and the *Performing Arts Journal* have in recent years published relatively brief critical descriptions of distinguished productions in the noncommercial theatre both in the United States and in Europe. These performance notes provide, first, a record of a production, stressing its experimental qualities in acting, directing, and design, along with the fresh interpretation that emerged from nontraditional staging. The notes, usually about six paragraphs in length, are accompanied by photographs to give a sense of the performance style.

Performance notes offer an impression of trends in the avant-garde theatre, as well as some familiarity with directors (many of whom we have already mentioned) whose tastes and directorial styles are gradually finding their way into the commercial theatre. A glance at a collec-

GEORGE JEAN NATHAN

George Jean Nathan (1882–1958) was for many years a leading American theatre critic, writing largely for New York City newspapers. He fought for a drama of ideas in America, and championed plays by Henrik Ibsen, George Bernard Shaw, and August Strindberg. He discovered the great American playwright Eugene O'Neill, and published his early work in *The Smart Set*, a magazine he edited with H. L. Mencken. Nathan's more than thirty books on theatre include the volumes on the New York season that he produced annually for many years.

HAROLD CLURMAN

Harold Clurman (1901–1980) was an American director, author, and critic. Founding member and managing director of the Group Theatre (1931–1941), he directed the early plays of Clifford Odets and many distinguished Broadway plays by Eugene O'Neill, Lillian Hellman, Arthur Miller, and Tennessee Williams. Clurman was for over fifteen years theatre critic for *The Nation*. He told the story of the Group Theatre in *The Fervent Years* (1945) and wrote an autobiography, *All People Are Famous* (1974). He published collections of his theatre essays and reviews in *Lies Like Truth* (1958) and *The Naked Image* (1966). The Harold Clurman Theater on 42nd Street in New York is named for him.

tion of performance notes for recent theatrical seasons turns up such directors as Andrei Serban, Lee Breuer, Peter Brook, Ariane Mnouchkine, Martha Clarke, Robert Wilson, Andrei Belgrader, Jonathan Miller, and JoAnne Akalaitis.

It takes years of seeing theatre to develop critical standards. But the best professional critics remain flexible even in their immense knowledge of theatre. George Jean Nathan, writing in the 1920s and '30s, got

CRITICS

CLAUDIA CASSIDY

Claudia Cassidy (b. 1905?) was one of the first women to serve as a long-term theatre critic on a large metropolitan newspaper—the Chicago *Journal of Commerce* and then the Chicago *Tribune*. Her name is part of the legendary success story of Tennessee Williams' *The Glass Menagerie*, which had its premiere in Chicago during 1944. Cassidy praised the new play and its leading actress, Laurette Taylor. When audiences failed to turn out for the play, she mounted a crusade to convince them to attend a theatrical event of first importance. As a result, *The Glass Menagerie* became a Chicago hit, proceeded to Broadway, and became one of the most famous modern American plays.

VINCENT CANBY

Vincent Canby, chief theatre critic of the *New York Times*, succeeded Frank Rich in 1994. Known for many years as a leading film critic, Canby now writes the lead theatre reviews for the Sunday edition of the *New York Times*. His influence determines the fates of multimillion dollar investments in one of the world's major theatre capitals—New York City.

at the heart of the matter: ". . . Criticism, at its best, is the adventure of an intelligence among emotions."[2] After all is said and done, theatre criticism is the encounter of one person's sensibility with the theatrical event. Thus it is important that the critic tells us about the performance, humankind, society, and perhaps even the universe in the course of evaluating the theatre event. Harold Clurman once said that whether the critic is good or bad doesn't depend on his opinions but on the reasons he can offer for those opinions.[3]

". . . to establish some perspective by which 'Streetcar' may be appreciated as a work of art. As a matter of fact, people do appreciate it thoroughly. They come away from it profoundly moved and also in some curious way elated. For they have been sitting all evening in the presence of truth, and that is a rare and wonderful experience. Out of nothing more esoteric than interest in human beings, Mr. Williams has looked steadily and wholly into the private agony of one lost person. He supplies dramatic conflict by introducing Blanche to an alien environment that brutally wears on her nerves. But he takes no sides in the conflict. He knows how right all the characters are—how right she is in trying to protect herself against the disaster that is overtaking her, and how right the other characters are in protecting their independence, for her terrible needs cannot be fulfilled."

Brooks Atkinson,
The *New York Times*,
14 December 1947

"*[Peter Brook] treated* The Mahabharata *with unabashed grandeur and daring theatrics. He evoked every theatrical mode at his command and used all the aspects of his years of travel and research in Asia and Africa—ritual theater, Oriental storytelling, Indian classical theater, magic and clowning, the broad scope of epic staging, the tone and timbre of Shakespearean tragedy and the savagery of the theatre of cruelty. . . .*

At the end of the performance, many in the audience—like the boy—were full of wonderment and awe at what they had seen. For them, Mr. Brook's theatrical magic had worked, evoking the possibilities of live theatre with grand themes in the hands of a master magician."

Margaret Croyden,
The *New York Times*,
25 August 1985

"Angels in America [part one, Millennium Approaches] is, first and foremost, a work about the gay community in the Age of AIDS—an urgent and timely subject fashionable enough off Broadway, now ripe for the mainstream. It is also a 'national' (that is, political) play in the way it links the macho sexual attitudes of redneck homophobes in the '80s with those of red-baiting bullies in the '50s. It is a 'fantasia' not only in its hallucinated, dreamlike style but in the size and scope of its ambitions. . . . And it is a very personal play that distributes blame and responsibility as generously among its sympathetic gay characters as among its villains."

Robert Brustein,
The New Republic,
24 May 1993

Writing the Theatre Review

Although there is no general agreement on criteria for judging a performance, the first step in writing theatre criticism is the ability *to see*. If we can describe what we see in the theatre, then we can begin to arrive at critical judgments. The play or production or both determines the approach—the structure of the review and the critical priorities. If the staging justifies a detailed account of what we observe, then the review incorporates a great deal of description. However, what we see in the theatre must connect with the play's meaning. For this reason, *all theatre criticism involves both description and evaluation.*

Since theatre is something perceived by the audience, writing about performance should be based on sensory impressions. As audiences, we are exposed to many significant details, sounds, and images, and only from them do we derive concepts or abstract meanings. Because we build critical concepts on the foundation of our perceptions, we can begin the process of seeing theatre critically by learning to describe our perceptions. A model for a theatre review written according to this method might take the following form (see Figure 14.3):

Heading or logo

Substance or meaning of play

Setting or environment

Acting (actor and character)

Language   *Select and*

Stage business   *prioritize*

Directing   *these*

Costumes   *elements*

Lighting and sound effects

Other significant human details

In writing any commentary it is necessary, first, to identify the performance to be discussed. Brooks Atkinson identifies both play and playwright in the first paragraph of his review of *A Streetcar Named Desire*. Frank Rich of the *New York Times* identifies actress, play, and playwright in the two short opening paragraphs of his review of *Rockaby*. Margaret Croyden identifies the Hindu poem and the clashing dy-

A STREETCAR NAMED DESIRE, a play in three acts by Tennessee Williams. Staged by Elia Kazan; scenery and lighting by Jo Mielziner; costumes by Lucinda Ballard; produced by Irene M. Selznick. At the Barrymore Theatre.

Negro Woman ... Gee Gee James
Eunice Hubbell .... Peg Hillias
Stanley Kowalski .. Marlon Brando
Harold Mitchell (Mitch) .... Karl Malden
Stella Kowalski ..... Kim Hunter
Steve Hubbell .... Rudy Bond
Blanche DuBois ... Jessica Tandy
Pablo Gonzales ..... Nick Dennis
A Young Collector .. Vito Christi
Mexican Woman ... Edna Thomas
A Strange Woman .... Ann Dere
A Strange Man .. Richard Garrick

FIGURE 14.3
A logo is a standardized format for listing the play's title, author, artists, producer, theatre, and cast list in a box separate from the review. This New York Times *logo for* A Streetcar Named Desire *was published in the December 4, 1947, edition. (Copyright © 1947 by The New York Times Company. Reprinted by permission.)*

nasties in Peter Brook's nine-hour production of *The Mahabharata* for the *New York Times.*

Next, commentary on the play's substance or meaning informs the reader about the playwright's particular perspective on human affairs. Third, the performance involves what J. L. Styan calls "an environment of significant stimuli": sights, sounds, color, light, movement, space.[4] These stimuli can be described by answering questions related to setting, costumes, sound, lighting, acting, and stage business. Is the stage environment open or closed, symbolic or realistic? What are the effects of the stage shape on the actor's speech, gesture, and movement? Is the lighting symbolic or suggestive of realistic light sources? What details of color, period, taste, and socioeconomic status are established by the costumes? What use is made of music and sound or light effects? What details separate the actor-at-work from his or her character-in-situation? What do the characters do in the play's action? What stage properties do the actors use and how are they significant? Finally, what visual and aural *images* of human experience and society develop during the performance? How effective are they?

In his review of *Rockaby* (see Figure 14.4), Frank Rich describes the actress seated in the single piece of furniture (the rocking chair), and the

STAGE: BILLIE WHITELAW IN THREE BECKETT WORKS

BY FRANK RICH

It's possible that you haven't really lived until you've watched Billie Whitelaw die.

The death occurs in "Rockaby," the last of three brief Beckett pieces that have brought the English actress to the newly named Samuel Beckett Theater. In "Rockaby," she plays a woman in a rocking chair, rocking herself to the grave. The assignment looks simple. The only word Miss Whitelaw speaks on-stage is "more," repeated four times. The "more"s are separated by a litany of other words—the tortured final thrashings of a consciousness, as recorded by the actress on tape. Then there is no more.

At that point, Miss Whitelaw stops rocking. The lone light that picks her face out of the blackness starts to dim, and, in the longest of Beckett pauses, we watch the light within the face's hollow eyes and chalky cheeks dim, too. During the long silence, the actress doesn't so much as twitch an eyelash—and yet, by the time the darkness is total, we're left with an image different from the one we'd seen a half minute earlier. Somehow Miss Whitelaw has banished life from her expression: what remains is a death mask, so devoid of blood it could be a faded, crumbling photograph. And somehow, even as the face disintegrates, we realize that it has curled into a faint baby's smile. We're left not only with the horror of death, but with the peace.

And there you have it. With no words, no movement and no scenery, the world's greatest playwright and one of his greatest living interpreters have created a drama as moving as any on a New York stage. Indeed, one might almost say that the entire Beckett canon is compressed into this short coda to a 15-minute play. In the long pause, we feel the weight of the solitary, agonizing, seemingly endless night of living. In Miss Whitelaw's descent to extinction, we see the only escape there can be—and we feel the relief. Death becomes what it must be in a Beckett play: a happy ending.

Like the other works of this evening, "Rockaby" is late Beckett. . . . The author's dramatization of stasis has been distilled to its most austere, pitch-black quintessence; the writing is so minimalist that even the scant, incantatory language has been drained of color, vocabulary and at times even of feeling. Yet if "Rockaby" (1980) and its predecessor on the bill, "Footfalls" (1976), make unusual demands on the audience, they are riveting theater. Or so they are as performed by Miss Whitelaw, for whom Mr. Beckett wrote them, and as impeccably directed by Alan Schneider. . . .

In "Rockaby," the actress continues to create variations within a tiny palette. Each of the four "more"s becomes more fearful; the speaker's "famished eyes" more and more dominate her face. Though the recorded speeches that follow the request for "more" tend to sound alike, subtle differences in both the writing and the performance gradually unfold the desolate tale of a woman's terrifying search for "another creature like herself"—for "one other living soul." An echoed phrase—"time she stopped"—serves as a refrain in each speech until we at last reach the "close of a long day." Then Mr. Beckett and Miss Whitelaw make time stop, and it's a sensation that no theatergoer will soon forget.

FIGURE 14.4

The New York Times *review of Samuel Beckett's* Rockaby, *published February 17, 1984.*[5]

recorded sounds of her voice in contrast to the single word that she speaks ("more"). The stark stage environment, the lighting (or the absence thereof), the rocking movements of the woman in the chair, and the death-masklike makeup Billie Whitelaw wears precede any concern for the "meaning" of it all. The critical properties are clear. The look and minimal speech of the performance project an *image* of the playwright's meaning: ". . . the tortured final thrashings of a consciousness" before her extinction in death, or, as Beckett writes, before "the close of a long day."

Two Critics at Work

Brooks Atkinson (1894–1984) and Kenneth Tynan (1927–1980) wrote significant first-night reviews of two plays that made stage history: *A Streetcar Named Desire* and *Look Back in Anger*. Atkinson reviewed a play enthusiastically embraced by critics and audiences; Tynan, in contrast, found himself a lone voice supporting a play most critics had vilified. Let us examine the choices made by each of these critics as they organized the elements of their reviews. In them, both highly influential critics said to their readers, I have just seen a masterpiece, and so should you.

Brooks Atkinson on *A Streetcar Named Desire*

The opening-night reviewers for three of the New York newspapers—the *Post*, the *Daily News*, and the *Herald Tribune*—were unanimously ecstatic, calling Williams' new play "brilliant," "powerful," and "a smash hit." They compared him to Eugene O'Neill, Clifford Odets, and William Saroyan. But the *New York Times*' Brooks Atkinson, then dean of New York reviewers, best put the play in perspective (see Figure 14.5).

In an unusual approach, Atkinson wrote two reviews of *Streetcar*. The first appeared after opening night. The second, and now very famous, review appeared ten days later, on Sunday, December 14, 1947. In both reviews Atkinson recognized that Williams' play did not address the great social issues of the times, that it solved no problems and arrived at no general moral conclusions. Nor did it deal with "representative" men and women. But, as Atkinson wrote, it was a work of art. Its audiences sat in the "presence of truth."

STREETCAR TRAGEDY: MR. WILLIAMS' REPORT ON LIFE IN NEW ORLEANS

BY BROOKS ATKINSON

By common consent, the finest new play on the boards just now is Tennessee Williams' "A Streetcar Named Desire." As a tribute to the good taste of the community, it is also a smash hit. This combination of fine quality and commercial success is an interesting phenomenon. For if the literal facts of the story could be considered apart from Mr. Williams' imaginative style of writing, "Streetcar" might be clattering through an empty theatre. It is not a popular play, designed to attract and entertain the public. It cannot be dropped into any of the theatre's familiar categories. It has no plot, at least in the familiar usage of that word. It is almost unbearably tragic.

After attending a play of painful character, theatregoers frequently ask in self-defense: "What's the good of harrowing people like that?" No one can answer that sort of question. The usual motives for self-expression do not obtain in this instance. There is no purpose in "Streetcar." It solves no problems; it arrives at no general moral conclusions. It is the rueful character portrait of one person, Blanche DuBois of Mississippi and New Orleans. Since she is created on the stage as a distinct individual, experiences identical with hers can never be repeated.

She and the play that is woven about her are unique. For Mr. Williams is not writing of representative men and women; he is not a social author absorbed in the great issues of his time, and, unlike timely plays, "Streetcar" does not acquire stature or excitement from the world outside the theatre.

Character Portrait
These negative comments are introduced to establish some perspective by which "Streetcar" may be appreciated as a work of art. As a matter of fact, people do appreciate it thoroughly. They come away from it profoundly moved and also in some curious way elated. For they have been sitting all evening in the presence of truth, and that is a rare and wonderful experience. Out of nothing more esoteric than interest in human beings, Mr. Williams has looked steadily and wholly into the private agony of one lost person. He supplies dramatic conflict by introducing Blanche to an alien environment that brutally wears on her nerves. But he takes no sides in the conflict. He knows how right all the characters are—how right she is in trying to protect herself against the disaster that is overtaking her, and how right the other characters are in protecting their inde-

pendence, for her terrible needs cannot be fulfilled. There is no solution except the painful one Mr. Williams provides in his last scene.

For Blanche is not just a withered remnant of Southern gentility. She is in flight from a world she could not control and which has done frightful things to her. She has stood by during the long siege of deaths in the family, each death having robbed her of strength and plunged her further into loneliness. Her marriage to an attractive boy who looked to her for spiritual security was doomed from the start; and even if she had been a super woman she could not have saved it.

By the time we see her in the play she is hysterical from a long and shattering ordeal. In the wildness of her dilemma she clings desperately to illusions of refinement—pretty clothes that soothe her ego, perfumes and ostentatious jewelry, artifices of manners, forms and symbols of respectability. Since she does not believe in herself, she tries to create a false world in which she can hide. But she is living with normal people who find her out and condemn her by normal standards. There is no hope for Blanche. Even if her wildest dreams came true, even if the rich man who has become her

---

FIGURE 14.5

A Streetcar Named Desire *was reviewed for the* New York Times *by Brooks Atkinson as a Sunday edition feature article on December 14, 1947. Williams' play opened at The Barrymore Theatre on December 3, 1947.*[6]

obsession did rescue her, she would still be lost. She will always have to flee reality.

Poetic Awareness
Although Mr. Williams does not write verse nor escape into mysticism or grandeur, he is a poet. There is no fancy writing in "Streetcar." He is a poet because he is aware of people and of life. His perceptions are quick. Out of a few characters he can evoke the sense of life as a wide, endlessly flowing pattern of human needs and aspirations. Although "Streetcar" is specific about its characters and episodes, it is not self-contained. The scenes of present time, set in a New Orleans tenement, have roots in the past, and you know that Mr. Williams' characters are going on for years into some mysterious future that will always be haunted by the wounding things we see on stage. For he is merely recording a few lacerating weeks torn out of time. He is an incomparably beautiful writer, not because the words are lustrous, but because the dialogue is revealing and sets up overtones. Although he has confined truth to one small and fortuitous example, it seems to have the full dimension of life on the stage. It almost seems not to have been written but to be happening.

"Streetcar" deserves the devotion of the theatre's most skillful craftsmen; and, not entirely by accident, it has acquired them. Elia Kazan, who brilliantly directed "All My Sons" last season, is versatile enough to direct "Streetcar" brilliantly also. He has woven the tenderness and the brutality into a single strand of spontaneous motion. Confronted with the task of relating the vivid reality of "Streetcar" to its background in the city and to its awareness of life in general, Jo Mielziner has designed a memorable, poetic setting with a deep range of tones.

Excellent Performances
The acting cannot be praised too highly. Marlon Brando's braggart, sullen, caustic brother-in-law, Karl Malden's dull-witted, commonplace suitor, Kim Hunter's affectionate, level-headed sister are vivid character portraits done with freshness and definition. As Blanche DuBois, Jessica Tandy has one of the longest and most exacting parts on record. She plays it with an insight as vibrant and pitiless as Mr. Williams' writing, for she catches on the wing the terror, the bogus refinement, the intellectual alertness and the madness that can hardly be distinguished from logic and fastidiousness. Miss Tandy acts a magnificent part magnificently.

It is no reflection on the director and the actors to observe that Mr. Williams has put into his script everything vital we see on the stage. A workman as well as an artist, he has not only imagined the whole drama but set it down on paper where it can be read. The script is a remarkably finished job: it describes the characters at full length, it foresees the performance, the impact of the various people on each other, the contrasts in tone and their temperaments and motives.

In comparison with "The Glass Menagerie," "Streetcar" is a more coherent and lucid drama without loose ends, and the mood is more firmly established. "Summer and Smoke," which has not yet been produced in New York, has wider range and divides the main interest between two principal characters. If it is staged and acted as brilliantly as the performance of "Streetcar," it ought to supply the third item in a notable trilogy. For there is considerable uniformity in the choice of characters and in the attitude toward life. That uniformity may limit the range of Mr. Williams' career as a playwright; so far, he has succeeded best with people who are much alike in spirit. In the meantime he has brought into the theatre the gifts of a poetic writer and a play that is conspicuously less mortal than most.

LOOK BACK IN ANGER AT THE ROYAL COURT

BY KENNETH TYNAN

"They are scum" was Mr. Maugham's famous verdict on the class of State-aided university students to which Kingsley Amis' *Lucky Jim* belongs; and since Mr. Maugham seldom says anything controversial or uncertain of wide acceptance, his opinion must clearly be that of many. Those who share it had better stay away from John Osborne's *Look Back in Anger*, which is all scum and a mile wide.

Its hero, a provincial graduate who runs a sweet-stall, has already been summed up in print as "a young pup," and it is not hard to see why. What with his flair for introspection, his gift for ribald parody, his excoriating candour, his contempt for "phoneyness," his weakness for soliloquy, and his desperate conviction that the time is out of joint, Jimmy Porter is the completest young pup in our literature since Hamlet, Prince of Denmark. His wife, whose Anglo-Indian parents resent him, is persuaded by an actress friend to leave him; Jimmy's prompt response is to go to bed with the actress. Mr. Osborne's picture of a certain kind of modern marriage is hilariously accurate: he shows us two attractive young animals engaged in competitive martyrdom, each with its teeth sunk deep in the other's neck, and each reluctant to break the clinch for fear of bleeding to death.

The fact that he writes with charity has led many critics into the trap of supposing that Mr. Osborne's sympathies are wholly with Jimmy. Nothing could be more false. Jimmy is simply and abundantly alive; that rarest of dramatic phenomena, the act of original creation, has taken place; and those who carp were better silent. Is Jimmy's anger justified? Why doesn't he *do* something? These questions might be relevant if the character had failed to come to life; in the presence of such evident and blazing vitality, I marvel at the pedantry that could ask him. Why don't Chekhov's people *do* something? Is the sun justified in scorching us? There will be time enough to debate Mr. Osborne's moral position when he has written a few more plays. In the present one he certainly goes off

FIGURE 14.6

Kenneth Tynan reviewed Look Back in Anger *for the* Observer, London. *Osborne's play opened at the Royal Court Theatre on May 8, 1956, and was produced by the English Stage Company.*[7]

Atkinson's review is organized so that he deals first with the play's truthfulness about the human beings portrayed. He then deals with Williams' "poetic language," directing and scenic details, the fine performances of the actors, and, finally, with Williams' career as the author of two Broadway successes in two years: *The Glass Menagerie* and *A Streetcar Named Desire*.

Kenneth Tynan on *Look Back in Anger*

After John Osborne's *Look Back in Anger* by the English Stage Company opened in London on May 8, 1956, critic Kenneth Tynan found himself in the minority, defending a play that many considered offensive and dismissed as self-indulgent drivel (see Figures 14.6 and 14.7).

the deep end, but I cannot regard this as a vice in a theatre that seldom ventures more than a toe into the water.

Look Back in Anger presents post-war youth as it really is, with special emphasis on the non-U intelligentsia who live in bed-sitters and divide the Sunday papers into two groups, "posh" and "wet." To have done this at all would be a signal achievement; to have done it in a first play is a minor miracle. All the qualities are there, qualities one had despaired of ever seeing on the stage—the drift towards anarchy, the instinctive leftishness, the automatic rejection of "official" attitudes, the surrealist sense of humour (Jimmy describes a pansy friend as "a female Emily Brontë"), the casual promiscuity, the sense of lacking a crusade worth fighting for, and, underlying all these,

the determination that no one who dies shall go unmourned.

One cannot imagine Jimmy Porter listening with a straight face to speeches about our inalienable right to flog Cypriot schoolboys. You could never mobilise him and his kind into a lynching mob, since the art he lives for, jazz, was invented by Negroes; and if you gave him a razor, he would do nothing with it but shave. The Porters of our time deplore the tyranny of "good taste" and refuse to accept "emotional" as a term of abuse; they are classless, and they are also leaderless. Mr. Osborne is their first spokesman in the London theatre. He has been lucky in his sponsors (the English Stage Company), his director (Tony Richardson), and his interpreters: Mary Ure, Helena Hughes, and Alan Bates give fresh and unforced perfor-

mances, and in the taxing central role Kenneth Haigh never puts a foot wrong.

That the play needs changes I do not deny: it is twenty minutes too long, and not even Mr. Haigh's bravura could blind me to the painful whimsey of the final reconciliation scene. I agree that *Look Back in Anger* is likely to remain a minority taste. What matters, however, is the size of the minority. I estimate it at roughly 6,733,000, which is the number of people in this country between the ages of twenty and thirty. And this figure will doubtless be swelled by refugees from other age-groups who are curious to know precisely what the contemporary young pup is thinking and feeling. I doubt if I could love anyone who did not wish to see *Look Back in Anger*. It is the best young play of its decade.

FIGURE 14.7
Look Back in Anger *by John Osborne opened at the Royal Court Theatre (London) on May 8, 1956 with Alan Bates, Mary Ure, Helena Hughes, and Kenneth Haigh.*

Again, Tynan focused on the play's central character and Jimmy Porter's "desperate conviction that the time is out of joint. . . ." Praising the character as an act of original creation on Osborne's part—a truthful portrait of postwar youth—he wrote, "Mr. Osborne is their first spokesman in the London theatre. . . ." Tynan emphasized the human, social, and political significance of Osborne's young people as characters never before seen on the British stage.

Summary

As we gain experience seeing theatre and describing our perceptions from a critical viewpoint, we learn that in some performances, elements such as costumes or lighting may be more important than in others. We become able to arrange priorities, to describe those details that enhance the performance, and omit those that contribute little to it. We develop criteria based on sensory stimuli for judging the performance's effectiveness.

Meaning does not *precede* the performance. A performance's meaning is the sum total of the audience's perceptions. Our experience of the relationship among visual and aural stimuli during a performance leads us to conclusions about the meaning of *Hamlet* or *Rockaby*, for example. To become skilled theatre critics is to hone our perceptions of the when, where, and how of the event taking place before us.

The professional theatre critic confronts the work in performance as the end product of the theatre's creative process. At best, the theatre critic enhances our understanding of the play as performance by enabling us to perceive the theatrical experience from a perspective other than our own or that of our friends.

Theatre criticism—carefully weighed by the reader—adds a new dimension to our discovery of theatre.

Questions for Study

1. What are the essential differences between *drama criticism* and *theatre criticism*?
2. In what way can theatre criticism be an *economic* force?

3. In what ways do general audiences become critics of the performances they see?

4. Name four main viewpoints that audiences bring to the theatre. Can you think of others?

5. Discuss these four viewpoints in relation to one or more of the model plays we have talked about.

6. Comment on the strengths and weaknesses of the most recent production you have seen.

7. How does theatre entertain us?

8. What is the job of the professional theatre critic?

9. What were Brooks Atkinson's special insights into *A Streetcar Named Desire*?

10. What were Kenneth Tynan's arguments in favor of an unusual and potentially unpopular play like *Look Back in Anger*?

11. What information is contained in the *logo* for theatre reviews printed in the *New York Times*?

12. Bring the theatre section of the Sunday edition of the *New York Times* to class and discuss the different issues that playwrights are presenting to audiences today.

13. Select a production that you have seen recently and discuss the basic questions dating from Goethe's time: *What is the playwright trying to do? How well has he or she done it? Is it worth doing?* How well do these questions help you get at the merits of a play in performance?

14. Around what priorities did Frank Rich organize his review of *Rockaby*? See page 362.

15. Attend one or more plays on your campus or in your community during the semester. Write one or more *reviews* of these performances keeping in mind the model on page 360.

16. *Suggested Reading*: Bring reviews to class from various local and national newspapers and magazines. Comment on the content and structure of the review, as well as the critic's viewpoint. Read Diana Rigg's collection of the world's most unfavorable theatre reviews, *No Turn Unstoned: The Worst Ever Theatrical Reviews* (New York: Silman James Press, 1991).

GLOSSARY

Actors' Equity Association   The professional union for actors, stage managers, dancers, and singers. The union controls contracts on Broadway and in the professional regional theatres. It classifies theatres, sets a minimum wage scale, and prescribes the percentage of actors and stage managers who must be members of Equity for any show within a given professional theatre. The union also prescribes conditions for auditions, working conditions, and sets down rules for becoming an "Equity" actor.

Aesthetic distance   A theatre term implying a detachment between the work of art and the receptor. In order to experience a play as a work of art and not as life, there must be some sort of "psychical distance" between the viewer and the theatre event itself. If we become too involved in a play for personal reasons (perhaps its subject matter is too painful for us based on a recent experience, like rape), then we may not be able to view the play as art but only as a real life experience.

Aesthetic distance does not mean that we are totally detached or unmoved by a play or a production; rather, it means we are aware of ourselves as receptors and can experience with a new interest the work of art as something that is like life, but is not life. Our thoughts and feelings evoked by a play are not the same as those evoked by a roughly similar situation in real life. There exists emotional and intellectual distance between us and the art work.

Agon   A Greek word meaning contest or debate between opposing characters and viewpoints in Greek tragedy and comedy. The fierce debate between Oedipus and Teiresias in *Oedipus the King* is called an *agon*.

Alienation effect (Verfremdungseffekt) Bertolt Brecht called his theory and technique of distancing or alienating audiences from emotional involvement with characters and situations an "alienation effect." Brecht wanted a thinking audience rather than an emotionally involved audience. To break down emotional involvement Brecht used white light, placards, loudspeakers, projections, loosely connected scenes, songs, and music to make things on stage appear unfamiliar, even strange, so audiences would observe and think about what they were seeing. Brecht's staging devices were employed to break with traditional stage illusion; that is, we are peering into others' lives and feeling what they feel.

Allegory   A narrative in which abstractions, such as virtue, charity, hope, are made concrete for the purpose of communicating a moral. In a drama, like *Everyman* (written around 1500), characters are personified abstractions, a device typical of a morality play for teaching lessons to audiences. In *Everyman*, the most famous dramatic allegory of its time, we find Good Deeds, Beauty, Five Wits, Death, and more, represented on stage by actors.

Amphitheatre   Today, the term refers to a building with tiers of seats around a central area, such as a stadium, arena, or auditorium. The term originates to describe a Roman building of elliptical shape, with tiers of seats enclosing a central arena, whose purpose was for gladiatorial contests, wild beast shows, and staged sea battles. The first amphitheatre was probably built by Julius Caesar in 46 B.C. The most famous was the Colosseum in Rome, completed in A.D 80, and which is still extant.

Anagnorisis, Recognition Aristotle introduced *recognition* in the *Poetics* as a simple recognition of persons by such tokens as footprints, clothes, birthmarks, and so on. The term has since taken on a larger meaning to include the tragic hero's self-understanding. All of Shakespeare's heroes have great moments of recognition wherein they realize who they are, what they have done, and what their deeds mean for others as well.

Antagonist The character in a play who commonly opposes the chief figure or *protagonist*. The *agon* in Greek tragedy is usually centered on the debate between protagonist and antagonist; for example, in *Oedipus the King* the great antagonists to Oedipus in various debates are Teiresias, Creon, Jocasta, and the Shepherd.

Arena stage See **Stages**

Aside A short statement made by a character directly to the audience to express aloud a personal attitude or to comment upon another character or event. The convention of the aside is that it cannot be overheard by another character. The aside is one of drama's many unrealistic devices, such as the soliloquy, that audiences readily accept.

Black box See **Stages**

Box set An interior setting, such as a living room or a dining room, using flats to form the back and side walls and often the ceiling of the room. The Moscow Art Theatre settings for Chekhov's *The Three Sisters* and *The Cherry Orchard* have box settings.

Broadway Broadway is one of the longest streets in Manhattan, extending diagonally the length of the island. However, for theatregoers, "Broadway" is the thirty to forty theatres clustered between 44th Street and 52nd Street two or more blocks to the west and east of the thoroughfare. Most Broadway playhouses were built at the turn of the century, tending to have small foyers, proscenium stages, outmoded equipment, and drafty dressing rooms. Called the "Great White Way" for its glitter, Broadway remains the area where the most important commercial theatre in the world is produced. When it has a dud of a season, it is then referred to as "the fabulous invalid."

Catharsis Aristotle considered *catharsis* the release of twin emotions of pity and fear in the audience as it experienced tragedy. Catharsis is thought of as psychologically purgative, for it produces in an audience a purgation (or purification) of the emotions of pity and fear. Thus, an audience comes away from tragedy having felt and even modified these emotions. Catharsis, it has been argued, produces a psychologically useful role for tragedy in society.

Character Drama's characters are sometimes divided into two types: *flat* and *round*. Flat characters represent a single trait (for example, a lecherous villain or faithful wife) and are highly predictable. Round characters are more complex, seen as it were from many sides. Like Hamlet, Mrs. Alving, and Troy Maxson, their motives, insights, and behavior, though sometimes unexpected, are credible and provocative. See **Stock character**.

Climax A decisive turning point in the plot where tension is highest. The burning of the orphanage in *Ghosts* is a good example of climax.

Comic relief Humorous episodes in tragedy that briefly lighten the tension and tragic effect. Scenes of comic relief often deepen rather than alleviate the tragic effect. One such scene of comic relief is the gravedigger's scene in *Hamlet*, which, despite its jocularity, calls attention to the common end of all humanity—death and the grave.

Commedia dell' Arte Professional, improvisational companies of actors, including women, that flourished in Italy in the sixteenth century. The average size *commedia* company was ten to twelve members, divided usually into stock characters of two sets of lovers, two old men, and several *zanni* (the array of comic servants, braggarts, buffoons, tricksters, and dupes). Each character had an unvarying name, like Pantalone, costume, mask, and personality. The actors worked from a basic story outline (posted backstage), improvising dialogue, action, and stage business (called *lazzi*) from that outline. They performed on improvised platform stages; the best companies performed in the halls and palace theatres of dukes and kings. Since the *Commedia dell' Arte* was improvised theatre, even though we have some 700 or more *scenarios*, or plot outlines performed by the companies, we are left with only the bare bones of a theatre tradition: its characters, events, disguises, *lazzi*, and illustrations of costumes and masks.

Convention An understanding established through custom or usage in the theatre that certain devices will be accepted or assigned specific meaning or significance on an arbitrary basis, that is, without requiring that they be natural or real. In a soliloquy the actor stands alone on the stage speaking to himself or herself so that the audience can "overhear" private thoughts. Since this behavior is accepted as a convention we do not think it odd or unnatural when it occurs.

Criticism Criticism is the understanding and assessing of the play either as a literary text or as a play in performance. These types of criticism are called respectively drama and theatre criticism. Drama (or interpretive) criticism is usually associated with scholarly articles, books on theatre, and classroom teaching. The critic is concerned with the what and how of the play—with historical background, themes, genre, character, plot, and action. Theatre criticism is found in newspapers, magazines, and journals; it deals with the productions of new and revived plays as performances, not literary texts. Such specialized theatre journals as *The Drama Review, Theater, American Theatre,* and *The Performing Arts Journal* publish articles mainly on contemporary theatre performance and avant-garde movements both in the United States, Europe, and Latin America.

Deus ex machina ("a god out of the machine") In Greek plays, a cranelike device (the *mechane*) was used to raise or lower "gods" into the playing space. It came to be used by playwrights, like Euripides, to solve a problem in a story, usually the ending. Hence, the term has come to mean in drama and literature any unexpected or improbable device used to unknot a plot and thus conclude the work. The king's officer who arrests Tartuffe and rewards Orgon in Molière's comedy is one such example.

Dionysus Greek god of wine, fertility, the phallus, and irrational impulses. It is commonly held that Greek tragedy evolved from choral celebrations (dithyrambic odes) in Dionysus' honor. The Greater Dionysia (or City Dionysia) in Athens was a festival held each year in the god's honor; popular dramatic contests—with Aeschylus, Sophocles, and Euripides competing—were held in the Theatre of Dionysus.

Double plot, subplot, simultaneous plots

Drama's *plot* is the arrangement of incidents or sequences in the story, that is, the order of events. Aristotle not only called plot the "soul of tragedy" but "the whole structure of the incidents." He considered it more important than character or the personalities of the story's individuals. We discussed the elements of plot (exposition, point of attack, complication, crisis, climax, reversal, resolution) in Chapter 7 and the appeal of double plots to Renaissance writers.

The double or simultaneous plot (sometimes called a subplot or underplot) develops two plots, usually with some sort of connection between them. In the order of things, one will be more important than the other. The secondary plot (the story of Polonius' family in *Hamlet* or the Gloucester plot in *King Lear*) is a variation on the main plot. In *Hamlet*, the main plot and the subplot deal with two families whose children suffer parental loss, grief, and untimely deaths. In repeating themes, problems, and events, the double plot demonstrates the world's complexity by engaging a large number of people, events, and locales.

Dramaturg

The dramaturg's profession, which was created in eighteenth-century Germany, has only recently been instituted in American regional theatres. Most often called a *literary manager* in this country, the dramaturg is a critic in residence who performs a variety of tasks before a play opens. He or she selects and prepares playtexts for performance; advises directors and actors on questions of the play's history and interpretation; and educates audiences by preparing lectures, program notes, and essays. To accomplish all of this, the dramaturg serves as script reader for new scripts, theatre historian, translator, play adaptor, editor, director's assistant, and critic of the work in progress. The commitment to producing new plays by our regional theatres has given rise to the dramaturg's employment by a number of not-for-profit regional theatres.

Ensemble acting or performance

Acting that stresses the total artistic unity of the performance rather than the individual performance of a specific (or "star") actor. The photos of Stanislavski's productions of *The Three Sisters* and *The Cherry Orchard* show the unity of acting style for which the Moscow Art Theatre became renown.

Epilogue

Usually a concluding address following the play's ending. Many epilogues were written to encourage applause or to feature one final time a popular actor.

Hamartia (hybris; hubris)

A Greek word variously translated as "tragic flaw," or "tragic error." Though Aristotle used *hamartia* to refer to those personality traits that lead heroes to make fatal mistakes, the idea of tragic flaw became simplified over the centuries to mean a single vice, frailty, or even a virtue (for example, pride, ambition, arrogance, overconfidence) that brings about the tragic hero's downfall. When applied to Sophocles' and to Shakespeare's great heroes, *hamartia* becomes a very complex concept related to human choice and action.

Hand properties   See **Properties**

Irony

Dramatic irony (Sophoclean irony or tragic irony) refers to a condition of affairs that is the tragic reverse of what the participants think will happen but what the audience knows at the outset. Thus, it is ironic that Oedipus accuses the blind prophet Teiresias of corruption and lack of understanding. By the play's end, Oedipus learns (as the audience has known from the beginning) that he himself is corrupt, that he has been mentally blind (ignorant), and the prophet has had superior sight (knowledge).

Dramatic irony also occurs when a speech or action is more fully understood by the audience than by the characters. Found in both tragedy and comedy, this sort of irony is usually based on misunderstanding or partial knowledge. It is ironic, for example, that Tartuffe thinks the king's officer has come to arrest Orgon when, in fact, he has come to arrest Tartuffe.

Mise-en-scène   The arrangement of all the elements in the stage picture either at a given moment or dynamically throughout the performance. Modern directors give careful attention to the mise-en-scène, or total stage picture, integrating all elements of design, lighting, acting, and so forth. The mise-en-scène established by director Andrei Serban and designer Santo Loquasto for the 1977 New York production of *The Cherry Orchard* reflects the director's emphasis on the cherry trees and the dying civilization (see Photo Essay, Chapter 8).

Monologue   Usually a long speech delivered by one character that may be heard but not interrupted by others. Or, it may refer to a performance by a single actor, which is called today a "solo performance." The term *monologue* has been applied to the soliloquy, the aside, and to "direct address" where a character steps out of the world of the play and speaks directly to the audience, like the narrator in Bertolt Brecht's *The Caucasian Chalk Circle*.

Off Broadway   A term that came into theatrical usage in the 1950s; defined by the Actors' Equity Association minimum basic contract as theatres located in the Borough of Manhattan outside the area bounded by Fifth and Ninth avenues, from 34th to 56th street, and by Fifth Avenue to the Hudson River from 56th to 72nd street. In addition to being outside that area, an Off Broadway theatre has no more than 299 seats.

Off Broadway playhouses developed in the '50s as alternatives to Broadway's commercial-ism. Today, the term refers to professional (Equity) theatres operating on significantly reduced budgets in comparison to Broadway, but under a financial structure prescribed by the Actors' Equity Association. Sam Shepard's plays are performed Off Broadway, and some Broadway plays, like Marsha Norman's *'Night, Mother*, are reopened Off Broadway once they have closed on Broadway. This latter practice, of course, depends on the popularity of the play.

Off Off-Broadway   A term that came into theatrical usage in the 1960s, referring to experimental theatres (and spaces) located between West Houston Street ("Soho"), Greenwich Village, and the Bowery. These theatres are lofts, garages, warehouses, studios, churches, and coffee houses where noncommercial and experimental workshops and performances take place. As Broadway's commercialism and Actors' Equity encroached on the Off Broadway theatres, adventuresome producers and artists moved elsewhere, looking for solutions to high production costs and union demands. The work of the Open Theatre, the Living Theatre, the Performance Group, the Wooster Group, and La Mama Experimental Theatre Club is in this category.

Open stage   See **Stages**

Performance   A word used, especially in modern theatre criticism, to describe the whole theatrical event. In environmental theatre the performance begins as the *first* spectator enters the performing space and ends when the *last* spectator leaves.

Producer   In the American theatre the person who puts together the financing and management, publicity and artistic teams to "produce" a show, usually commercial. The producer is ordinarily not involved directly in the artistic direction of the production. The producer hires (and even fires) the artistic personnel and in this way may put a kind of stamp on the overall artistic effect. Producers who have significantly affected the Broadway theatre for some years are: Roger L. Stevens, David Merrick, Bernard Jacobs and Gerald Schoenfeld (the Shuberts), Alexander H. Cohen, James M. Nederlander, Emanuel Azenberg, Andrew Lloyd Webber, Cameron Mackintosh, Hal Prince, and Rocco Landesman.

Properties   These fall into two categories: *set* and *hand* properties.

Set properties are those items of furniture or set pieces that the actor uses; they are placed on stage for design reasons, to accommodate the actor's movement, and to place the actors in the right degree of emphasis with relationship to them. The size and structure of properties, especially furniture, determine the sort of movement the actor can make around them and the use of costume.

Hand properties, such as fans, pistols, swords, or telephones, are required for personal use by the actor. Sometimes the distinction between the set and hand prop is unclear, but design is the main function of the set prop; the hand prop first satisfies the needs of the actor using it even though its "look" is important to the designer. The table lamp that Mrs. Alving turns out in the final act of *Ghosts* is a hand prop, one with symbolic significance. As a set prop, the tree in *Waiting for Godot* is part of the scenic design. Properties are the initial responsibility of the designer. There is a property head and crew responsible for acquiring or making props, supplying rehearsal props, handing out and storing props during the production, and repairing and returning props to storage at the production's close.

Proscenium theatre   See **Stages**

Protagonist   The major character in a play. The Greek word literally means "first" (*protos*), that is, the first contender or chief actor in the perfor-

mance. For example, Oedipus, Hecuba, Hamlet, Macbeth, and Othello are all protagonists. The Greeks labeled the second role the *deuteragonist*, and the third the *tritagonist*. The character in conflict with the protagonist is the *antagonist*.

Regional or resident theatres   The terms *regional* and *resident* have been used interchangeably for the past twenty years to describe professional (Equity) not-for-profit theatres. Today, there are over sixty theatres (members of the League of Resident Theatres) in fifty-one cities with operating budgets ranging from $200,000 to more than $9 million. They produce over 600 productions yearly to audiences of more than 12,000,000. Most perform seasons from five to eleven months, generally to subscription audiences. Established in the '50s and '60s, these theatres from Seattle to Boston have been heralded as alternatives to the commercialism of Broadway and to the theatre's centralization in New York. In a society as diverse and as farflung as that of the United States, these theatres make up a matrix that many call our *national theatre*. Among the most prestigious of the regional theatres are: the Guthrie Theater (Minneapolis), American Repertory Theatre (Cambridge), the Arena Stage (Washington, D.C.), the Yale Repertory Theatre (New Haven), the Mark Taper Forum (Los Angeles), the New York Shakespeare Festival Theatre (New York), the Milwaukee Repertory Theatre (Wisconsin), the Goodman Theatre (Chicago), and Actors Theatre of Louisville.

Revenge play   The development of revenge plays was influenced in the Renaissance by the work of the Roman author Seneca (4 B.C.–65 A.D.). Seneca's ten extant Roman tragedies, probably written not for the stage but for private readings, were filled with deranged heroes, ghosts, deeds of vengeance and horror, stoical speeches, messengers reporting offstage horrors, and pithy moralisms (called *sententiae*).

The Elizabethans read the Roman writers in their classrooms and transposed revenge conventions to the public stage. *Hamlet* has its ghost; its variety of deaths by sword, poison, trickery; and its revengers (Hamlet, Laertes, Fortinbras). In *King Lear*, Gloucester is blinded on stage and *Titus Andronicus* is a virtual feast of atrocities. The revenge play had its own excitement in its many variations on patterns and conventions (like today's horror films) but some, like *Hamlet*, achieved greatness in the writing, characters, originality, and universal insights.

Reversal (peripeteia; peripety)   A plot reversal occurs when an action produces the opposite effect of what was intended or expected. Reversals occur in tragedy, comedy, and tragicomedy. A complex play may have several reversals before its ending. The reversal that occurs when Tartuffe's true nature is revealed to Orgon in the seduction scene is not at all what the characters anticipate. In fact, this reversal "reverses" their situation in the sense that it only makes it worse. The king's officer brings about the final reversal by restoring Orgon's family to good fortune and by punishing Tartuffe.

Satyr play   The fourth play in the series of fifth-century classical Greek tragedies functioned as an afterpiece to the tragic trilogy. The satyr play burlesqued the serious themes or the major characters of the three earlier plays (the trilogy) by showing persons in ludicrous situations. The piece had a chorus of lewd satyrs (creatures half-man, the other half either horse or goat). Euripides' *The Cyclops* is the only complete satyr play in existence. It travesties the legend of Odysseus' encounter with Polyphemus.

Scenographer   A designer with artistic control over all design elements, including set, lighting, and costume. The recent development of theatre technology, particularly the use of film projections and moving scenery, has called for unified production with one person integrating the various design elements. Although the scenographer works closely with the director, he or she is responsible for the totality of theatrical expression in time and space. Artistic unity is the goal. The idea that one person must have total control over design is derived from the theatrical concepts of the early twentieth-century theorists Adolphe Appia and Edward Gordon Craig.

One of the world's most famous scenographers today is Josef Svoboda (b. 1920), the leading designer of the Prague National Theatre in Czechoslovakia. He became known in America through the Czech Pavilion at the 1967 Montreal Exposition, where he orchestrated films and stills, cascading images over surfaces and spectators. The result was a visually kinetic assault on the spectators. Svoboda's stage designs feature moving blocks, projections, and mirrors. The basis of his theory is that all scenic elements must appear and disappear, shift and flow, to complement the play's development.

Set properties   See **Properties**

Simultaneous plots   See **Double plot**

Soliloquy   A speech delivered by an actor alone on stage, which, by stage convention, is understood by the audience to be the character's internal thoughts, not part of an exchange with another character or even with the audience.

Spine   In the Stanislavski method, a character's dominant desire or motivation, which underlies his or her action in the play. For a director, the spine is the throughline of a character's action that propels the play forward toward its conclusion. Director Elia Kazan conceived of the spine of Tennessee Williams' character Blanche DuBois in *A Streetcar Named Desire* as the search for refuge from a brutal and hostile world.

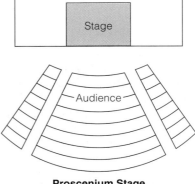

Proscenium Stage

Stage business   An actor's "business" in a role can be anything from the reading of a newspaper to smoking a cigarette to drinking a cup of coffee while he or she performs the text. Stage business is the actor's "busyness," activities devised by the actor (sometimes at the director's suggestion) to create a sense of character apart from the dialogue.

Stages—proscenium, arena, thrust or open, and black box   Throughout theatre history, there have been five types of theatre buildings and basic arrangements of audience seating: (1) the proscenium or picture-frame stage, (2) the arena stage, or theatre in the round, (3) the thrust or open stage, (4) the black box, and (5) created or found space of the kind discussed as environmental theater in Chapter 3.

The proscenium or picture-frame stage is most familiar to us. Almost all college campuses have proscenium theatres, and our Broadway theatres have proscenium stages. The word *proscenium* comes from the wall with a large center opening that separates the audience from the raised stage. In the past the opening was called an "arch" (the proscenium arch), but it is actually a rectangle. The audience faces in one direction before this opening, appearing to look through a picture frame into the locale on the other side. The auditorium floor slants downward from the back of the building to provide greater visibility for the audience; usually there is a balcony above the auditorium floor protruding about halfway over the main floor. Frequently there is a curtain just behind the proscenium opening that discloses or hides the event on the other side. The idea that a stage is a room with its fourth wall removed comes from this type of stage; the proscenium opening is thought of as an "invisible wall."

The *arena* stage (also called a theatre in the round) breaks away from the formality of the proscenium theatre. It places the stage at the center of a square or circle with seats for the spectators around the circle or on the four sides. This stage offers more intimacy between actor and audience since the playing space usually has no barriers separating them. In addition, productions can usually be produced on low budgets since they require only minimal set pieces and furniture to indicate scene and place. Margo Jones (1913–1955) pioneered arena theatre design and performance in America, establishing Theatre 47 in Dallas, Texas, in 1947. Today, the Arena Stage in Washington, D.C., founded by Zelda Fichandler and Edward Mangum, is one of the most famous.

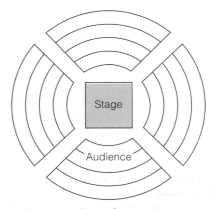

Arena Stage

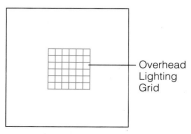

Black Box

The *thrust* or *open* stage, which combines features of the proscenium theatre and the arena stage, usually has three-quarter seating for the audience. The basic arrangement has the audience sitting on three sides or in a semicircle around a low platform stage. At the back of the stage is some form of proscenium opening providing for entrances and exits as well as scene changes. The thrust stage combines the best features of the other two stages discussed here: the sense of intimacy for the audience, and a stage setting against a single background that allows for scenic design and visual elements. After World War II a number of important thrust stages were built in the United States and Canada, including the Guthrie Theater in Minneapolis and the Shakespeare Festival Theatre at Stratford, Ontario.

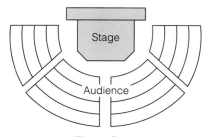

Thrust Stage

The *black box* is a type of minimal performance space developed in the '60s for experimental work and/or new plays. Essentially a large rectangular room (painted a flat black to avoid glare from the overhead lighting instruments), the black-box theatre is usually equipped with a complex overhead lighting grid with instruments and movable seating (approximately 90 to 200 seats). The movable seating permits experimentation with the shape and size of the performance space. The Cottesloe Theatre at the National Theatre, London, is a black-box theatre with two galleries surrounding three sides

of the rectangular space. Designed along the lines of an Elizabethan innyard, the galleries are permanent but the risers of seats positioned along the floor are movable. (See page 9.)

Stock character   The stock character is not only a "flat" character but a generic type found throughout drama: jealous husband, clever servant, braggart soldier, hypocrite, pedant, cuckold, miser. Though most common to comedy (Molière has a number of stock characters in *Tartuffe* ranging from hypocrite to clever servant), stock characters are also found in serious plays. In tragedy we find the avenger, the usurper, the tyrant, and so on.

Thrust stage   See **Stages**

Tiring-house   The backstage space in the Elizabethan public theatre. We know little about this area behind the stage wall used for preparing and maintaining productions. Some reconstructions suggest the space was used for dressing rooms, and for storing costumes, furniture, properties, and other equipment.

United Scenic Artists   The union composed of scenic designers, art directors for television and movies, scenic artists, costume designers, lighting designers, mural artists, as well as members in diorama and display. In order to accept jobs with some theatre organizations, designers must join the United Scenic Artists Union. There are two U.S.A. locals, No. 829 in New York City and No. 350 in Chicago. Both are affiliated with the International Brotherhood of Painters and Allied Trades of the AFL-CIO. There is a parallel union on the West Coast, local 816, the Scenic and Title Artists union, affiliated with the International Alliance of Theatrical Stage Employees (I.A.T.S.E.), the "stagehands" union.

To qualify for membership in the United Scenic Artists Union, an interview and samples of the designer's work are required. Those who become applicants are given rigid examinations in one or more categories chosen by the candidate (scenic designer, costume designer, lighting designer, and scenic artist). Sooner or later, membership in the union becomes an important professional step for the designer.

Unity   A critical term implying a coherence in which the parts of a piece work together to contribute to the whole. *Unity* suggests completeness or a recognizable pattern that ties together beginning, middle, and ending. Aristotle thought a tragedy should have a unified action, meaning a completeness without loose ends or the *deus ex machina* abruptly resolving the play.

Italian critics of the late sixteenth century codified Aristotle's comments in *The Poetics* on unity of action and themselves established "three unities" of time, place, and action. These unities have often mistakenly been passed down to generations as Aristotle's prescription. The unities so revered by sixteenth-century Italian critics and by seventeenth-century French neoclassical writers were: (1) the action of a play must not cover more than twenty-four hours; (2) it must occur in a single place or room; and (3) it must be entirely tragic or entirely comic with no mixture of plots or characters from either kind of writing. What is interesting is that most Greek tragedies in some way violate these unities.

Well-made play (pièce bien faite)   A commercially successful pattern of play construction. Its techniques were perfected by the nineteenth-century French playwright Eugène Scribe (1791–1861) and his followers. The well-made play uses eight technical playwriting elements:

(1) a plot based on a secret known to the audience but withheld from certain characters until it is revealed at the climax to unmask a fraudulent character and restore the suffering hero, with whom the audience sympathizes, to good fortune; (2) a pattern of increasingly intense action and suspense prepared by exposition, contrived entrances and exits, and devices like unexpected letters; (3) a series of gains and losses in the hero's fortunes, caused by a conflict with a hostile opponent or force; (4) a major crisis in the hero's bad fortune; (5) a revelation scene brought about by the disclosure of a secret that brings a turnabout in the hero's bad fortune and defeats the opponent; (6) a central misunderstanding made obvious to the audience but withheld from the characters; (7) a logical, credible resolution or tying-up of events with appropriate dispensations to good and bad characters; and (8) an overall pattern of action repeated in each act, and act climaxes that increase tension over the play's three or four acts.

The features were not new in Scribe's day, but represented the technical methods of most great writers of comedy and even serious drama. Scribe and his followers turned the techniques into a formula for commercially entertaining plays as well as serious plays dealing with social and psychological subjects. In plays by Henrik Ibsen, George Bernard Shaw, and Oscar Wilde we can see the well-made play machinery underpinning the action.

West End, London   The theatre district in central London equivalent to our Broadway where commercial plays are produced. *Cats* and *The Phantom of the Opera* were first produced in the West End rather than in one of the government-subsidized theatres.

APPENDIX A

SUGGESTED READINGS

CHAPTER 1

Blau, Herbert. *The Audience*. Baltimore, Md.: Johns Hopkins University Press, 1990.

Brook, Peter. *The Empty Space*. New York: Macmillan, 1978.

Cole, David. *The Theatrical Event: A Mythos, A Vocabulary, A Perspective*. Middletown, Conn.: Wesleyan University Press, 1975.

Kott, Jan. *The Theatre of Essence*. Evanston, Ill.: Northwestern University Press, 1984.

Schechner, Richard. *The End of Humanism: Writings on Performance*. New York: Performing Arts Journal Publications, 1982.

CHAPTER 2

Bowers, Faubion. *Japanese Theatre*. New York: Hill and Wang, 1952.

Brockett, Oscar G. *History of the Theatre*. 4th ed. Boston: Allyn & Bacon, 1982.

Hodges, C. Walter. *The Globe Restored*. 2nd ed. London: Oxford University Press, 1968.

Kirby, E. T. *Ur-Drama: The Origins of Theatre*. New York: New York University Press, 1975.

Lommel, Andreas. *Shamanism: The Beginnings of Art*. New York: McGraw-Hill Book Company, 1967.

Mackerras, Colin. *The Chinese Theatre in Modern Times: From 1840 to the Present Day*. Amherst: University of Massachusetts Press, 1975.

Mullin, Donald C. *The Development of the Playhouse: A Survey of Theatre Architecture from the Renaissance to the Present*. Berkeley: University of California Press, 1970.

Schechner, Richard and Willa Appel. *By Means of Performance: Intercultural Studies of Theatre and Ritual*. New York: Cambridge University Press, 1990.

Southern, Richard. *The Seven Ages of the Theatre*. New York: Hill and Wang, 1961.

Turner, Victor. *From Ritual to Theatre: The Human Seriousness of Play*. New York: Performing Arts Journal Publications, 1982.

CHAPTER 3

Brecht, Stefan. *Peter Schumann's Bread and Puppet Theatre*. 2 vols. New York: Routledge, 1988.

Carriere, Jean-Claude. *The Mahabharata*. Trans. Peter Brook. New York: Harper & Row, 1987.

Grotowski, Jerzy. *Towards a Poor Theatre*. New York: Clarion Books, 1968.

Kiernander, Adrian. *Ariane Mnouchkine and the Théâtre du Soleil*. New York: Cambridge University Press, 1993.

Malina, Judith. *The Diaries of Judith Malina 1947–1957*. New York: Grove Press, 1984.

McNamara, Brooks, Jerry Rojo, and Richard Schechner. *Theatres, Spaces, Environments: Eighteen Projects*. New York: Drama Book Specialists, 1975.

Roose-Evans, James. *Experimental Theatre from Stanislavsky to Peter Brook*. London: Routledge & Kegan Paul, 1984.

Schechner, Richard. *Environmental Theatre*. Revised Ed. New York: Applause Theatre Books, 1993.

Schevill, James. *Breakout! In Search of New Theatrical Environments*. Chicago: University of Chicago Press, 1972.

CHAPTER 4

Brater, Enoch, ed. *Feminine Focus: The New Women Playwrights*. New York: Oxford University Press, 1989.

Conversations with Lillian Hellman. Ed. Jackson R. Bryer. Jackson: University Press of Mississippi, 1986.

Conversations with Tennessee Williams. Ed. Albert J. Devlin. Jackson: University Press of Mississippi, 1986.

DiGaetani, John L. *A Search for a Postmodern Theatre: Interviews with Contemporary Playwrights*. Westport, Conn.: Greenwood Press, 1991.

Harriott, Esther. *American Voices: Five Contemporary Playwrights in Essays and Interviews*. Jefferson, NC: McFarland, 1988.

Interviews with Contemporary Playwrights. Eds. Kathleen Betsko and Rachel Koenig. New York: Beech Tree Books, 1987.

Macgowan, Kenneth. *Primer of Playwriting*. New York: Random House, 1962. Reprinted Greenwood Press, Westport, Conn., 1981.

Mamet, David. *Writing in Restaurants*. New York: Viking Penguin, Inc., 1987.

Miller, Arthur. *Timebends: A Life*. New York: Grove Press, 1987.

Murphy, Brenda. *Tennessee Williams and Elia Kazan: A Collaboration in the Theatre*. New York: Cambridge University Press, 1992.

"Playwrights and Playwriting Issue." *The Drama Review*, 21, No. 4 (December 1977).

Playwrights on Playwriting: The Meaning and Making of Modern Drama from Ibsen to Ionesco. Ed. Toby Cole. New York: Hill and Wang, 1961.

Savran, David, ed. *In Their Own Words. Contemporary American Playwrights: Interviews*. New York: Theatre Communications Group, 1988.

Wager, Walter H. *The Playwrights Speak*. New York: Delacorte Press, 1967.

"The 'Woman' Playwright Issue." *Performing Arts Journal 21*, 7, No. 3 (1983): 87–102.

Women in American Theatre. 2nd Edition. Eds. Helen Krich Chinoy and Linda Walsh Jenkins. New York: Theatre Communications Group, 1987.

CHAPTERS 5, 6, AND 7

Beckerman, Bernard. *Dynamics of Drama: Theory and Method of Analysis*. New York: Alfred A. Knopf, 1970.

Bentley, Eric. *The Life of the Drama*. New York: Applause Theatre Books, 1990.

Bermel, Albert. *Farce: A History from Aristophanes to Woody Allen*. New York: Simon & Schuster, 1982.

Brecht, Stefan. *Theatre of Visions: Robert Wilson*. New York, Routledge, Chapman, & Hall, 1984.

Brownstein, Oscar. *Strategies of Drama: The Experience of Form*. Westport, Conn.: Greenwood Press, 1991.

Corrigan, Robert W., ed. *Comedy: Meaning and Form*. Rev. ed. New York: Harper & Row, 1980.

———, ed. *Tragedy: Vision and Form*. Rev. ed. New York: Harper & Row, 1980.

Davis, Jessica Milner. *Farce*. London: Methuen, 1978.

Esslin, Martin. *An Anatomy of Drama*. New York: Hill and Wang, 1977.

———. *The Theatre of the Absurd*. 3rd ed. New York: Penguin, 1983.

Fergusson, Francis. *The Idea of a Theater: A Study of Ten Plays. The Art of Drama in Changing Perspective*. New Jersey: Princeton University Press, 1987.

Goldman, Michael. *The Actor's Freedom: Toward a Theory of Drama*. New York: Viking, 1975.

Heilman, Robert B. *Tragedy and Melodrama: Versions of Experience*. Seattle: University of Washington Press, 1968.

Hinchliffe, Arnold P. *The Absurd*. London: Methuen, 1961.

Hirst, David L. *Tragicomedy*. London: Methuen, 1984.

Hoy, Cyrus. *The Hyacinth Room: An Investigation into the Nature of Comedy, Tragedy, and Tragicomedy*. New York: Alfred A. Knopf, 1964.

Langer, Susanne K. *Feeling and Form: A Theory of Art*. New York: Charles Scribner's Sons, 1953.

Marrance, Bonnie. *Theatre of Images*. New York: Drama Book Specialists, 1977.

Schechner, Richard. *Public Domain: Essays on the Theatre*. Indianapolis: Bobbs-Merrill, 1969.

Smith, James L. *Melodrama*. London: Methuen, 1973.

Szondi, Peter. *Theory of the Modern Drama*. Ed. Michael Hays. Minneapolis: University of Minnesota Press, 1987.

Willett, John. *The Theatre of Bertolt Brecht: A Study of Eight Aspects*. New York: New Directions, 1959.

Wilson, Robert. *The Theatre of Images*. 2nd ed. New York: Harper, 1984.

CHAPTER 8

Bigsby, C. W. E. *A Critical Introduction to Twentieth-Century American Drama: Beyond Broadway*. Vol. 3. New York: Cambridge University Press, 1985.

———. *Modern American Drama, 1945–1990*. New York: Cambridge University Press, 1992.

Blau, Herbert. *Blooded Thought: Occasions of Theatre*. New York: Performing Arts Journal Publications, 1982.

Cole, David, *The Theatrical Event: A Mythos, A Vocabulary, A Perspective*. Middletown, CT: Wesleyan University Press, 1975.

Ionesco, Eugene. *Notes and Counter Notes: Writings on the Theatre*. Trans. Donald Watson. New York: Grove Press, 1964.

Mamet, David. *Writing in Restaurants*. New York: Viking Penguin, 1986.

Pavis, Patrice. *Languages of the Stage: Essays in the Semiology of Theatre*. New York: Performing Arts Journal Publications, 1982.

Styan, J. L. *Drama, Stage and Audience*. New York: Cambridge University Press, 1975.

CHAPTER 9

Adler, Stella. *The Technique of Acting*. New York: Bantam, 1990.

Berry, Cicely. *The Actor and The Text*. Revised Ed. New York: Applause Theatre Books, 1992.

———. *Voice and the Actor*. New York: Macmillan, 1974.

Boal, Augusto. *Games for Actors and Non-Actors*. Trans. Adrian Jackson. New York: Routledge, 1992.

Boleslavsky, Richard. *Acting: The First Six Lessons*. New York: Theatre Arts Books, 1933.

Brown, Jared. *The Fabulous Lunts: A Biography of Alfred Lunt and Lynn Fontanne*. New York: Atheneum, 1986.

Carnovsky, Morris, with Peter Sander. *The Actor's Eye*. New York: Performing Arts Journal Publications, 1984.

Chaikin, Joseph. *The Presence of the Actor: Notes on the Open Theatre, Disguises, Acting and Repression*. New York: Atheneum, 1972.

Cohen, Robert. *Acting Professionally: Raw Facts About Careers in Acting*. 4th ed. New York: Harper & Row, 1990.

Cole, Toby, and Helen Krich Chinoy, eds. *Actors on Acting: The Theories, Techniques, and Practices of Great Actors of All Times as Told in Their Own Words*. Rev. ed. New York: Crown Publishers, 1980.

Diderot, Denis. "The Paradox of Acting," in William Archer, *Masks or Faces?* New York: Hill and Wang, 1957.

Gielgud, John. *Acting Shakespeare*. New York: Charles Scribner's Sons, 1992.

Hagen, Uta. *A Challenge for the Actor*. New York: Charles Scribner's Sons, 1991.

———. *Sources: A Memoir*. New York: Performing Arts Journal Publications, 1984.

——— with Haskel Frankel. *Respect for Acting*. New York: Macmillan, 1973.

Hill, Holly. *Actors' Lives On and Off The American Stage: Interviews*. New York: Theatre Communications Group, 1993.

Hirsch, Foster. *A Method to Their Madness: The History of the Actors Studio*. New York: W. W. Norton, 1984.

King, Nancy. *Theatre Movement: The Actor and His Space*. New York: Drama Book Specialists Publications, 1971.

Lewis, Robert. *Advice to the Players*. New York: Theatre Communications Group, 1989.

———. *Slings and Arrows: Theater in My Life*. New York: Scarborough House, 1986.

Linklater, Kristin. *Freeing the Natural Voice*. New York: Drama Book Specialists Publications, 1976.

Marowitz, Charles. *The Act of Being: Toward a New Theory of Acting*. New York: Taplinger, 1978.

Mekler, Eva. *Masters of the Stage: Twenty-Seven British Acting Teachers Talk about Their Craft*. New York: Grove Press, 1989.

Olivier, Laurence. *Confessions of an Actor: An Autobiography*. New York: Simon & Schuster, 1982.

———. *On Acting*. New York: Simon & Schuster, 1986.

Peters, Margot. *The House of Barrymore*. New York: Alfred A. Knopf, 1990.

Redfield, William. *Letters from an Actor*. New York: Limelight Editions, 1984.

Rubin, Lucile S., ed. *Movement for the Actor*. New York: Drama Book Specialists Publications, 1980.

Saint-Denis, Michel. *Training for the Theatre: Premises and Promises*. Ed. Suria Saint-Denis. New York: Theatre Arts Books, 1982.

Skinner, Edith. *Speak with Distinction*. 2nd ed. Eds. Timothy Monich and Lilene Mansell. New York: Applause Theatre Book Publishers, 1989.

Stanislavsky, Constantin. *An Actor Prepares*. Trans. Elizabeth Reynolds Hapgood. New York: Theatre Arts Books, 1948.

———. *Building a Character*. Trans. Elizabeth Reynolds Hapgood. New York: Theatre Arts Books, 1977.

————. *Creating a Role.* Trans. Elizabeth Reynolds Hapgood. New York: Theatre Arts Books, 1961.

————. *My Life in Art.* Trans. J. J. Robbins. New York: Theatre Arts Books, 1952.

Strasberg, Lee. *A Dream of Passion: The Development of the Method.* Ed. Evangelina Morphos. Boston: Little, Brown, 1987.

Suzuki, Tadashi. *The Way of Acting: The Theatre Writings of Tadashi Suzuki.* Trans. J. Thomas Rimer. New York: Theatre Communications Group, 1986.

CHAPTER 10

Bartow, Arthur. *The Director's Voice: Twenty-one Interviews.* New York: Theatre Communications Group, 1989.

Berry, Ralph. *On Directing.* New York: Hamish Hamilton/Viking, 1991.

Brecht, Stefan. *The Theatre of Visions: Robert Wilson.* New York: Routledge, 1988.

Brook, Peter. *The Shifting Point: Theatre, Film, Opera 1946–1987.* New York: Harper & Row, 1987.

Chekhov, Michael. *To the Director and Playwright.* Comp. Charles Leonard. New York: Limelight Editions, 1984.

Clurman, Harold. *On Directing.* New York: Macmillan, 1972.

Cole, Toby and Helen Krich Chinoy, eds. *Directors on Directing.* Rev. ed. New York: Macmillan, 1976.

Guthrie, Tyrone. *A Life in the Theatre.* London: Harrap Ltd., 1987.

Hall, Peter. *Peter Hall's Diaries: The Story of a Dramatic Battle.* Ed. John Goodwin. London: Hamish Hamilton, 1983.

Kazan, Elia. *A Life.* New York: Alfred A. Knopf, 1988.

Miller, Jonathan. *Subsequent Performances.* New York: Viking Penguin, Inc., 1986.

Murphy, Brenda. *Tennessee Williams and Elia Kazan: A Collaboration in the Theatre.* New York: Routledge, 1992.

Schneider, Alan. *Entrances: An American Director's Journey.* New York: Viking Penguin, Inc., 1986.

Shyer, Laurence. *Robert Wilson and His Collaborators.* New York: Theatre Communications Group, 1989.

The Theatre of Images. Ed. Bonnie Marranca. New York: Drama Book Specialists, 1977.

Willett, John, ed. and trans. *Brecht on Theatre: The Development of an Aesthetic.* New York: New Directions, 1964.

CHAPTER 11

Anderson, Barbara, and Cletus Anderson. *Costume Design.* New York: Holt, Rinehart and Winston, 1984.

Aronson, Arnold. *American Set Design.* New York: Theatre Communications Group, 1985.

Bay, Howard. *Stage Design.* New York: DBS Publications, 1974.

Bellman, Willard F. *Scenography and Stage Technology: An Introduction.* New York: Thomas Y. Crowell, 1977.

Burdick, Elizabeth B., and others, eds. *Contemporary Stage Design U.S.A.* Middletown, Conn.: Wesleyan University Press, 1975.

Burris-Meyer, Harold. *Sound in the Theatre.* Rev. ed. New York: Theatre Arts Books, 1979.

Burris-Meyer, Harold, and Edward C. Cole. *Scenery for the Theatre.* 2nd ed. Boston: Little, Brown, 1972.

Collison, David. *Stage Sound.* 2nd rev. ed. New York: DBS Publications, 1982.

Corey, Irene. *The Mask of Reality: An Approach to Design for Theatre.* New Orleans: Anchorage Press, 1968.

Corson, Richard. *Stage Makeup*. 7th ed. Englewood Cliffs, N.J.: Prentice-Hall, 1986.

Ingham, Rosemary, and Liz Covey. *The Costume Designer's Handbook: A Complete Guide for Amateur and Professional Costume Designers*. Englewood Cliffs, N.J.: Prentice-Hall, 1983.

Izenour, George C. *Theatre Design*. New York: McGraw-Hill, 1977.

James, Thurston. *The Theater Props Handbook: A Comprehensive Guide to Theater Properties, Materials and Construction*. Crozet, Va.: Betterway Publications, 1989.

Jones, Robert Edmond. *The Dramatic Imagination: Reflections and Speculations on the Art of the Theatre*. New York: Methuen, 1987.

Leacroft, Richard, and Helen Leacroft. *Theatre and Playhouse: An Illustrated Development of Theatre Building from Ancient Greece to the Present Day*. New York: Methuen, 1984.

Palmer, Richard H. *The Lighting Art: The Aesthetics of Stage Lighting Design*. Englewood Cliffs, N.J.: Prentice-Hall, 1985.

Parker, Oren, and Harvey K. Smith. *Scene Design and Stage Lighting*. 5th ed. New York: Holt, Rinehart & Winston, 1985.

Pecktal, Lynn. *Designing and Painting for the Theatre*. New York: Holt, Rinehart & Winston, 1975.

Rich, Frank, with Lisa Aronson. *The Theatre Art of Boris Aronson*. New York: Alfred A. Knopf, 1987.

Rosenthal, Jean, and Lael Wertenbaker. *The Magic of Light*. New York: Theatre Arts Books, 1972.

Russell, Douglas A. *Costume History and Style*. Englewood Cliffs, N.J.: Prentice-Hall, 1983.

———. *Stage Costume Design: Theory, Technique and Style*. 2nd ed. Englewood Cliffs, N.J.: Prentice-Hall, 1985.

Simonson, Lee. *The Stage Is Set*. New York: Theatre Arts Books, 1962.

CHAPTER 12

Botto, Louis. *At This Theatre: Playbill Magazine's Informal History of Broadway Theatres*. New York: Dodd, Mead, 1984.

Crawford, Cheryl. *One Naked Individual: My Fifty Years in the Theatre*. Indianapolis: Bobbs-Merrill, 1977.

David, Christopher. *The Producers*. New York: Harper & Row, 1972.

Farber, Donald C. *From Option to Opening: A Guide to Producing Plays Off-Broadway*. Rev. ed. New York: Limelight Editions, 1989.

———. *Producing Theatre: A Comprehensive Legal and Business Guide*. New York: Drama Book Specialists, 1981.

Frohnmayer, John. *Leaving Town Alive: Confessions of an Arts Warrior*. Houghton Mifflin Company, 1993.

Goldman, William. *The Season: A Candid Look at Broadway*. Rev. ed. New York: Limelight Editions, 1984.

Hay, Peter. *Broadway Anecdotes*. New York: Oxford University Press, 1989.

Hirsh, Foster. *Harold Prince and the American Musical Theatre*. New York: Cambridge University Press, 1990.

Jacobs, Susan. *On Stage: The Making of a Broadway Play*. New York: Alfred A. Knopf, 1972.

Kessel, Howard. *David Merrick: The Abominable Showman*. New York: Applause Theatre Books, 1993.

Langley, Stephen, ed. *Producers on Producing*. New York: Drama Book Specialists, 1976.

———. *Theatre Management in America, Principles and Practices: Producing for*

Commercial, Stock, Resident, College and Community Theatre. New York: Drama Book Publishers, 1980.

Marsolais, Ken. Broadway Day and Night. Ed. Bill Grose. New York: Pocket Books, 1992.

Newman, Danny. Subscribe Now! New York: Theatre Communications Group, 1977.

Reiss, Alvin. The Arts Management Handbook. Rev. ed. New York: Law-Arts Publishers, 1973.

Shagan, Rena. The Road Show: A Handbook for Successful Booking and Touring in the Performing Arts. New York: ACA Books, 1984.

Theatre Profiles 11: The Illustrated Guide to America's Nonprofit Professional Theatre. New York: Theatre Communications Group, 1994.

CHAPTER 13

Brook, Peter. Peter Brook: A Theatrical Casebook. Comp. David Williams. New York: Methuen, 1988.

———. The Shifting Point: Theatre, Film, Opera 1946–1987. New York: Harper & Row, 1987.

"Brook's Mahabharata." The Drama Review, 30, 1 (Spring 1986).

Carrière, Jean C. The Mahabharata. Trans. Peter Brook. New York: Harper & Row, 1987.

Feral, Josette. "Building Up the Muscle: An Interview with Ariane Mnouchkine." The Drama Review, 33, No. 4 (Winter 1989): 88–97.

Interculturalism and Performance. Eds. Bonnie Marranca and Gautam Dasgupta. Baltimore, Md.: Johns Hopkins University Press, 1991.

Juan Darien: A Carnival Mass. Scenario by Julie Taymor and Elliot Goldenthal with Notes from the Authors, in Theater, 20, No. 2 (Spring/Summer 1989): 43–53.

Kiernander, Adrian. Ariane Mnouchkine and the Théâtre du Soleil. New York: Cambridge University Press, 1993.

"Multiculturalism" Issue. American Theatre, 8, No. 7 (October 1991).

Out From Under: Texts by Women Performance Artists. Ed. Lenora Champagne. New York: Theatre Communications Group, 1990.

Pavis, Patrice. Theatre at the Crossroads of Culture. Trans. Loren Kruger. New York: Routledge, 1991.

Schechner, Richard and Willa Appel, eds. By Means of Performance: Intercultural Studies of Theatre and Ritual. New York: Cambridge University Press, 1990.

Smith, Anna Deavere. Fires in the Mirror: Crown Heights, Brooklyn and Other Identities. New York: Doubleday Anchor Books, 1993.

CHAPTER 14

Atkinson, Brooks. Broadway. New York: Macmillan, 1970.

Brustein, Robert. Reimagining American Theatre. New York: Hill and Wang, 1991.

———. Who Needs Theatre: Dramatic Opinions. New York: Atlantic Monthly, 1990.

"Criticism Issue." Drama Review, 18, No. 3 (September 1974).

Clurman, Harold. Lies Like Truth: Theatre Reviews and Essays. New York: Macmillan, 1958.

———. The Naked Image: Observations on the Modern Theatre. New York: Macmillan, 1966.

The Collected Works of Harold Clurman: Six Decades of Commentary on Theatre, Dance, Music, Film, Arts, Letters and Politics. Eds. Marjorie Loggia and Glenn Young. New York: Applause Theatre Books, 1993.

Kauffmann, Stanley. *Persons of the Drama: Theater Criticism and Comment*. New York: Harper & Row, 1976.

———. *Theatre Criticisms*. New York: Performing Arts Journal Publications, 1984.

Nathan, George Jean. *The Critic and the Drama*. New York: Alfred A. Knopf, 1922.

Rigg, Diana. *No Turn Unstoned: The Worst Ever Theatrical Reviews*. New York: Silman James Press, 1991.

Rogoff, Gordon. *Theatre Is Not Safe*. Evanston, Ill.: Northwestern University Press, 1987.

Sontag, Susan. *Against Interpretation and Other Essays*. New York: Doubleday, 1966.

Tynan, Kenneth. *Curtains: Selections from the Drama Criticism and Related Writings*. New York: Atheneum, 1971.

APPENDIX B

RELATED FILMS AND VIDEOCASSETTES

CHAPTER 1

Hamlet, by William Shakespeare. With Laurence Olivier. (153 min., black & white, video, 1948; also 16mm.) Rank Productions, Learning Corporation of America, and Paramount Home Video, distributors.

Henry V, by William Shakespeare. Directed by Kenneth Branagh, with Emma Thompson, Derek Jacobi, Paul Scofield, and Kenneth Branagh as King Henry. (138 min., color, video, 1989) Fox Video, distributors.

Much Ado About Nothing, by William Shakespeare. Directed by Kenneth Branagh, with Emma Thompson, Denzel Washington, and Kenneth Branagh as Benedick. (110 min., color, 16 mm, 1993) Samuel Goldwyn, distributors.

Oedipus Rex, by Sophocles. Directed by Tyrone Guthrie with Douglas Campbell and the Stratford (Ontario, Canada) Festival Theatre company. (87 min., color, video, 1957) Insight Media, distributors.

CHAPTER 2

Aspects of Peking Opera. (15 min., color) Insight Media, distributors.

Bunraku Puppet Theater. (35 min., black & white, 1968) NBCEE, producers; Films, Inc., distributors.

Kabuki: Classic Theater of Japan. (30 min., color) MTP, producers; Modern Talking Picture Services, distributors.

The Noh Drama: Hagoromo. (43 min., color, 1968) Kajima, producers; UNIJAP, distributors.

CHAPTER 3

Akropolis, by Jerzy Grotowski with the Polish Laboratory Theatre. (60 min., black & white video, VHS) Arthur Cantor Film Collection, distributors.

The Brig, by Kenneth Brown, performed by The Living Theatre. Directed by Jonas Mekas. (65 min., color, video, 1964) Facets Multimedia, distributor.

The Connection, by Jack Gelber, performed by The Living Theatre. Directed by Shirley Clarke. (105 min., color, video, 1961) Facets Multimedia, distributor.

Dionysus in 69, performed by The Performance Group. Directed by Richard Schechner. (90 min., black & white, 1970) Sigma III, distributors.

1789, performed by Théâtre du Soleil. Directed by Ariane Mnouchkine. (35 mm., color, 1974) M. Mnouchkine Films Ariane, 44 Champs-Elysée, 75008 Paris, distributor.

CHAPTER 4

NPR Beckett Festival of Radio Plays (1989). A series of 5 cassettes, including Samuel Beckett's plays: *All That Fall* (2 cassettes), *Embers* (1 cassette), *Words and Music* (1 cassette), *Cascando* (1 cassette), *Rough for Radio 2* (1 cassette). NPR Cassette Department N, Washington, D.C., distributors.

David Mamet, An Interview with the Playwright. (55 min., video) Facets Multimedia, distributor.

Death of a Salesman, by Arthur Miller, with Dustin Hoffman, Kate Reid, and John Malkovich. (135 min., video, 1986). Facets Multimedia, distributor.

'Night, Mother, by Marsha Norman, with Sissy Spacek and Anne Bancroft. Directed by Tom Moore. (96 min., video, 1986). MCA/Universal Home Video, distributor.

A Raisin in the Sun, by Lorraine Hansberry, with Sidney Poitier, Claudia McNeil, and Ruby Dee. (128 min., video, 1961) RCA/Columbia Pictures Home Video.

True West, by Sam Shepard, with Gary Sinise and John Malkovich. (110 min., color, video, 1983) Academy Entertainment, distributors.

CHAPTER 5

Beckett Directs Beckett (Waiting for Godot, Krapp's Last Tape, Endgame), performed by the San Quentin Drama Workshop with mise-en-scène derived from Beckett's production scripts. (Visual Press, video, 1990). Smithsonian Institution, distributor.

The Cherry Orchard, by Anton Chekhov. Performed by Jessica Tandy and Hume Cronyn. (3 audiocassettes, 1966) Caedmon/HarperAudio, distributor.

The Grapes of Wrath, adapted from John Steinbeck's novel by director John Ford, with Henry Fonda and John Carradine. (129 min., video, 1946) Facets Multimedia, distributor.

Hamlet, by William Shakespeare. Directed by Franco Zeffirelli with Mel Gibson, Glenn Close, Alan Bates, Paul Scofield, and Helena Bonham-Carter. (135 min., color, video, 1990; also 16mm.) Warner Home Video, distributor.

The Life and Adventures of Nicholas Nickleby, by Charles Dickens with Roger Rees and the Royal Shakespeare Company. Directed by Trevor Nunn. (7 hours, 59 min., color, video), Films for the Humanities, distributor.

The Little Foxes, by Lillian Hellman. Directed by William Wyler, with Bette Davis and Herbert Marshall. (116 min., black & white, video, 1941; also 16mm.) Orion Home Video, distributors.

Molière. The Royal Shakespeare Company (England) presents a version of Mikhail Bulgakov's comedy based on the life of the French playwright. With Anthony Sher as Molière and directed by Bill Alexander. (112 min., color, 1990) Turner Home Entertainment, distributor.

Tartuffe, by Molière. Directed by Jean Gascon with the Stratford National Theatre of Canada. (Sound recording, 1968) Caedmon Records, distributor.

The Three Sisters, Anton Chekhov. Directed by Laurence Olivier with Alan Bates, Joan Plowright, Derek Jacobi, Laurence Olivier, and the National Theatre Company of London. (165 min., color, 16 mm., AFT 1973) The American Film Institute, distributor.

CHAPTER 6

A Doll's House, by Henrik Ibsen. Directed by Joseph Losey with Jane Fonda, Edward Fox, Trevor Howard, and David Warner. (99 min., color, video, 1973; also, 16mm.) RCA Video, distributors.

Monster in a Box, by Spalding Gray. Directed by Nick Broomfield with Spalding Gray in a solo performance doing battle with a 1800-page "monster"—a novel. (96 min., color, video, 1992) Columbia Tristar Video, distributor.

Rockaby, by Samuel Beckett, directed by Alan Schneider with Billie Whitelaw. The film documents the preparation and rehearsals of the director with the star, through the complete recording of the play at the Beckett Festival in Buffalo, New York. (60 min., color; also 16mm.) Pennebaker Associates, Inc., distributor.

Stations: Robert Wilson. An original work for video by Robert Wilson. (60 min., video, 1985) Facets Multimedia, distributors.

Spalding Gray—Terrors of Pleasure, by Spalding Gray. Directed by Thomas Schlamme with Spalding Gray in a solo performance about dreams and nightmares. (60 min., color, video, 1988). Columbia Tristar Video, distributors.

Swimming to Cambodia, by Spalding Gray. A solo performance by Spalding Gray. (85 min., video, 1986) Facets Multimedia, distributors.

CHAPTERS 7 AND 8

Glengarry Glen Ross, by David Mamet. Directed by James Foley with Al Pacino, Jack Lemmon, Alec Baldwin, Ed Harris, and Alan Arkin. (100 min., color, video, 1992; also 16mm.) Hi Fi Stereo Video, distributor.

Macbeth, by William Shakespeare. Directed by Roman Polanski with Jon Finch and Francesca Annis. (139 min., color, video, 1971; also 16mm.) Swank Motion Pictures and Columbia/Tristar Video, distributors.

Marat/Sade, by Peter Weiss, directed by Peter Brook with the Royal Shakespeare Company. (116 min., color, 1966; also 16mm.) United Artists, distributors.

Six Characters in Search of an Author, by Luigi Pirandello. (52 min., color, video) Films for the Humanities, distributor.

A Streetcar Named Desire, by Tennessee Williams. Film directed by Elia Kazan, starring Vivien Leigh, Marlon Brando, Karl Malden, and Kim Hunter. (122 min., black & white, video, 1951) CBS/Fox Video, distributors.

The Trojan Women, by Euripides. Filmed in Greece by director Michael Cacoyannis with Katherine Hepburn, Genevieve Bujold, Vanessa Redgrave. (105 min., video, 1971) Facets Multimedia, distributors.

CHAPTER 9

Acting in Film with Michael Caine. (60 min., video, 1987) Insight Media/Applause Theatre Books, distributors.

Approaches to Hamlet. With John Barrymore, Laurence Olivier, John Gielgud, and Nicol Williamson. (45 min., color, video; also 16mm.) Films for the Humanities, distributor.

Preparing to Perform Shakespeare. With members of the Royal Shakespeare Company, including actors Ian McKellen and Alan Howard; and directors John Barton and Trevor Nunn. (50 min., color, video) Films for the Humanities, distributor.

Speaking Shakespearean Verse. With members of the Royal Shakespeare Company, including actors Ian McKellen and Alan Howard; and directors Trevor Nunn, John Barton, and Terry Hands. (50 min., color, video) Films for the Humanities, distributor.

Speak with Distinction, by Edith Skinner. Revised by Timothy Monich and Lilene Mansell. (90 min., audiocassette) Applause Theatre Books, distributor.

The Stage Fight Director, with David Boushey. (33 min., color, video) Theatre Arts Video Library, distributor.

"What's the Score?": Text Analysis for the Actor. With Arthur Wagner. (85 min., color, video) Theatre Arts Video Library, distributor.

CHAPTER 10

Master Class in Directing with Joanne Akalaitis (40 min., 1991) Insight Media, distributor.

CHAPTER 11

Fundamentals of Scenic Painting. With Ron Ranson, Jr. (81 min., color, video, 1989) Theatre Arts Video Library, distributor.

The Three Sisters, by Anton Chekhov. Directed by Laurence Olivier, with settings by Josef Svoboda and costumes by Beatrice Dawson, from the National Theatre production (London) with Alan Bates, Joan Plowright, Derek Jacobi, and Laurence Olivier. (165 min., color, 16mm., AFT 1973) The American Film Institute, distributor.

CHAPTER 12

Presenting Performance. A slide–tape presentation by Thomas Wolf on all aspects of performance administration, finances, promotion, hiring, fundraising. (Carousel; 30 min., slide-and-sound) ACA Books, distributor.

The Producers. Directed by Mel Brooks, with Zero Mostel and Gene Wilder. (88 min., color, video, 1968; also 16mm.) Hi Fi Video, distributors.

CHAPTERS 13 AND 14

Anna Deavere Smith: In Her Own Words. Program features the actress performing excerpts from *Fires in the Mirror* and talking about her observations on racism and her creative process. (60 min., audiotape, 1993) WGBH Radio, Boston, distributor.

Fires in the Mirror, by Anna Deavere Smith. A film of Anna Deavere Smith's solo performance on the Crown Heights (Brooklyn) riots, directed for television by George C. Wolfe. (60 min., color, video, 1993) PBS Video, distributors.

The Glass Menagerie, by Tennessee Williams. Directed by Paul Newman with Joanne Woodward, Karen Allen, John Malkovich, and James Naughton. (134 min., color, video, 1987; also 16mm.) HBO Video, distributors.

Look Back in Anger, by John Osborne. Directed by David Jones, with Kenneth Branagh and Emma Thompson. (114 min., color, video, 1989) HBO Video, distributors.

The Mahabharata, written and directed by Peter Brook, with the International Centre for Theatre Research. (360 min., color, video, 1989) Parade Video, distributors.

A Streetcar Named Desire, by Tennessee Williams. Film directed by Elia Kazan with Vivien Leigh, Marlon Brando, Karl Malden, and Kim Hunter. (122 min., black & white, video, 1951) CBS/Fox, distributors.

APPENDIX C

NOTES

CHAPTER 1

1. Peter Brook, *The Empty Space* (New York: Atheneum, 1968): 3. Copyright © 1968 by Peter Brook. Reprinted with permission of Atheneum Publishers, New York, and Granada Publishing Ltd., England.
2. Martin Esslin, *The Theatre of the Absurd*, 3rd ed. (New York: Pelican Books, 1980): 19–21.

CHAPTER 2

1. Mircea Eliade, *The Sacred and the Profane: The Nature of Religion*, trans. Willard R. Trask (New York: Harcourt, 1959): 24. Copyright © 1957 by Rowohlt Taschenbuch Verlag GmbH, trans. © 1959 and renewed 1987 by Harcourt Brace Jovanovich. Reprinted by permission of Harcourt Brace Jovanovich, Inc.

CHAPTER 3

1. Jerzy Grotowski, *Towards a Poor Theatre* (New York: Clarion Press, 1968): 19–20. Reprinted by permission of H. M. Berg, Odin Teatret, Denmark.

2. Richard Schechner, *Environmental Theater* (New York: Hawthorn, 1973): 25. Copyright © 1973 by Richard Schechner. All rights reserved. Reprinted by permission of Hawthorn Books, Inc.
3. Grotowski: 19–20. Reprinted by permission.
4. Grotowski: 19–20. Reprinted by permission.
5. Grotowski: 75. Reprinted by permission.
6. Peter Schumann, "The Radicality of the Puppet Theatre," *The Drama Review*, 35, 4 (Winter 1991): 75. See also Peter Schumann, "The Bread and Puppet Theatre (Interview)," *The Drama Review*, 12, 2 (Winter 1968): 62–73.
7. Mel Gussow, "The Living Theater Returns to Its Birthplace," *New York Times* (15 January 1984): II, 6.

CHAPTER 4

1. Tennessee Williams, Afterword to *Camino Real* (New York: New Directions, 1953): xii. Copyright © 1948, 1953 by Tennessee Williams. Reprinted by permission of New Directions Publishing Corporation.
2. Robert Edmond Jones, *The Dramatic Imagination: Reflections and Speculations*

on *The Art of the Theatre* (London: Methuen Theatre Arts Books, 1969): 81.

3. John Lion, "Rock 'n' Roll Jesus with Cowboy Mouth," *American Theatre*, 1, No. 1 (April 1984): 8. Reprinted by permission of the Theatre Communications Group Inc.

4. Amy Lippman, "Rhythm & Truths: An Interview with Sam Shepard," *American Theatre*, 1, No. 1 (April 1984): 12. Reprinted by permission of the Theatre Communications Group Inc.

5. Lippman: 9. Reprinted by permission of the Theatre Communications Group Inc.

6. "David Mamet," *Contemporary Authors*, Vol. 15, New Revision Series (Chicago: Gale Research Company, 1985): 300.

7. R. C. Lewis, "A Playwright Named Tennessee," *New York Times Magazine* (7 December 1947): 19. Copyright © 1947 by The New York Company. Reprinted by permission.

8. August Wilson, *Fences* (New York: NAL Penguin, 1986): 69.

9. Lillian Hellman, *Pentimento: A Book of Portraits* (Boston: Little, Brown & Company, 1973): 151–152.

10. Lorraine Hansberry. *To Be Young, Gifted and Black*, adapted by Robert Nemiroff (Englewood Cliffs, N.J.: Prentice-Hall, 1969): 133–134. Copyright © 1969 by Prentice-Hall, Inc. Reprinted by permission.

11. María Irene Fornés, "The 'Woman' Playwright Issue," *Performing Arts Journal*, 7, No. 3 (1983): 91. Reprinted by permission.

12. Carol Lawson, "Caryl Churchill Wins Blackburn Drama Prize," *New York Times* (25 February 1984), I, 16:5. Copyright © 1984 by The New York Times Company. Reprinted by permission.

13. "Wendy Wasserstein," *Contemporary Authors*, Vol. 129 (Detroit, Mich.: Gale Research Inc., 1990): 452–457.

14. Mel Gussow, "Women Playwrights: New Voices in the Theater," *New York Times Magazine* (1 May 1983): 6, 26. Copyright © 1983 by The New York Times Company. Reprinted by permission.

CHAPTER 5

1. Bertolt Brecht, "A Short Organon for the Theatre," *Brecht on Theatre: The Development of an Aesthetic*, trans. and ed. John Willett (New York: Hill and Wang, 1964): 204.

2. Peter Brook, *The Empty Space* (New York: Atheneum, 1968): 15.

3. Lane Cooper, *Aristotle on the Art of Poetry* (Ithaca, N.Y.: Cornell University Press, 1947): 17.

4. "Lillian Hellman, Playwright, Author and Rebel, Dies at 79," *New York Times* (1 July 1984): 20.

5. Eric Bentley, "The Psychology of Farce," in *Let's Get A Divorce! and Other Plays* (New York: Hill and Wang, 1958): vii–xx.

6. Danielle Sallenave, "Entretien avec Antoine Vitez: Faire théâtre de tout," *Digraphe* (April 1976): 117.

7. John Willett, trans. *Brecht on Theatre: The Development of an Aesthetic* (New York: Hill and Wang, 1964): 37. Copyright © 1957, 1963, and 1964 by Suhrkamp Verlag, Frankfurt Am Main. This translation and notes © 1964 by John Willett. Reprinted with permission of Hill and Wang, a division of Farrar, Straus & Giroux, Inc. and A.B. P. Ltd.

8. Willett: 121. Reprinted by permission.

9. Albert Camus, *The Myth of Sisyphus and Other Essays* (New York: Alfred A. Knopf, 1955): 5. Reprinted by permission.

10. Eugene Ionesco, *Notes and Counter Notes: Writings on the Theatre*, translated by Donald Watson (New York: Grove Press,

1964): 257. Copyright © 1964 by Grove Press, Inc. Reprinted with permission.

CHAPTER 6

1. David Mamet, *Writing in Restaurants* (New York: Viking Penguin, 1986): 8.
2. Laurence Olivier, *On Acting* (London: George Weidenfeld & Nicolson Limited, 1986): 192. Reprinted by permission of the publisher.
3. Francis Fergusson, *The Idea of a Theatre* (Princeton: University Press, 1949): 36.
4. For my understanding of climactic and episodic drama I am indebted to material from Bernard Beckerman, *Dynamics of Drama: Theory and Method of Analysis* (New York: Alfred A. Knopf, 1970).
5. Eugene Ionesco, *The Bald Soprano*, translated by Donald Watson (New York: Grove Press, 1958): 11–13. Copyright © 1958 by Grove Press, Inc. Reprinted with permission.
6. Spalding Gray, "About *Three Places in Rhode Island*," *Drama Review*, 23, No. 1 (March 1979): 31–42.
7. Samuel Beckett, *Rockaby* (New York: Grove Press, 1980). Reprinted by permission of Grove Press.
8. Robert Wilson, *The CIVIL warS*, edited by Jan Graham Geidt (Cambridge, Mass.: American Repertory Theatre, 1985): 16. Reprinted by permission.

CHAPTER 7

1. From *Naked Masks: Five Plays* by Luigi Pirandello, ed. Eric Bentley, p. 372. Trnsl. copyright 1922 by E. P. Dutton. Renewed 1950 in the names of Stefano, Fausto, and Lietta Pirandello. Used by permission of Dutton Signet, a division of Penguin Books USA, Inc.
2. Tennessee Williams, *A Streetcar Named Desire*.

CHAPTER 8

1. Eugene Ionesco, *Notes and Counter Notes: Writings on the Theatre*, translated by Donald Watson (New York: Grove Press, 1964): 27.
2. Peter Brook, *The Empty Space* (New York: Atheneum, 1968): 12.
3. George Steiner, *The Death of Tragedy*. Copyright © 1963, renewed 1989 by George Steiner. Reprinted by permission of the author's agent, George Borchardt, Inc.
4. *Henrik Ibsen: The Complete Major Prose Plays*, translated by Rolf Fjelde. Copyright © 1965, 1970, 1978 by Rolf Fjelde. Reprinted with permission of The New American Library, Inc.
5. Bertolt Brecht, "On Gestic Music" in *Brecht on Theatre: The Development of an Aesthetic*, translated by John Willett (New York: Hill and Wang, 1964): 104. Reprinted by permission.
6. Bertolt Brecht, *The Caucasian Chalk Circle*, translated by Ralph Manheim, in *Collected Plays*, Volume 7, edited by Ralph Manheim and John Willett (New York: Random House, Inc., 1975). Reprinted with permission of Random House, Inc.
7. Peter Weiss, *The Persecution and Assassination of Jean-Paul Marat as Performed by the Inmates of the Asylum of Charenton Under the Direction of the Marquis de Sade*; English translation copyright © 1965 by John Calder Ltd.; originally published in German under the title *Die Verfolgung und Ermordung Jean Paul Marats Dargestellt Durch die Schauspielgruppe des Hospizes zu Charenton unter Anleitung des Herrn de Sade*; copyright © 1964 by Suhrkamp Verlag, Frankfurt Am Main. Reprinted with permission of Atheneum Publishers and Calder and Boyars Ltd.

8. Sam Shepard, *Buried Child* (Urizen Books, 1979). Included in *Seven Plays* by Sam Shepard. Copyright © 1979 by Sam Shepard. Reprinted by permission of Bantam Books. All rights reserved.

9. David Mamet, *Glengarry Glen Ross* (New York: Grove Press, 1984).

10. David Cole, *The Theatrical Event: A Mythos, A Vocabulary, A Perspective* (Middletown, Conn.: Wesleyan University Press, 1975): 141. Reprinted with permission.

11. Eugene Ionesco, *Notes and Counter Notes: Writings on the Theatre*, translated by Donald Watson (New York: Grove Press, 1964): 23.

CHAPTER 9

1. Laurence Olivier, *On Acting* (New York: Simon & Schuster, 1986): 192.

2. Uta Hagen, *A Challenge for the Actor* (New York: Charles Scribner's Sons, 1991): 50.

3. Lionel Gracey-Whitman, "Return by Popular Demand," *Plays and Players*, No. 367 (April 1984): 21–25. Reprinted by permission.

4. Toby Cole and Helen Krich Chinoy, eds. *Actors on Acting: The Theories, Techniques, and Practices of the Great Actors of All Times as Told in Their Own Words* (New York: Crown, 1959): 132. Reprinted by permission.

5. Hagen 47. See also Laurence Olivier, *On Acting* (New York: Simon & Schuster, 1986).

6. Lewis Funke and John E. Booth, eds. *Actors Talk About Acting* (New York: Random House, 1961): 14. Reprinted by permission.

7. Hagen 70. See also Jared Brown, *The Fabulous Lunts: A Biography of Alfred Lunt and Lynn Fontanne* (New York: Atheneum, 1986).

8. Konstantin Stanislavsky, *An Actor Prepares*, trans. Elizabeth Reynolds Hapgood (New York: Routledge, 1989): 14.

9. Robert Hethmon, *Strasberg at the Actors Studio* (New York: Viking Press, 1965): 78.

10. Konstantin Stanislavsky, *An Actor's Handbook*, ed. and trans. Elizabeth Reynolds Hapgood (New York: Theatre Arts, 1963): 100

11. Uta Hagen with Haskel Frankel, *Respect for Acting* (New York: Macmillan, 1973): 37–38. Reprinted by permission.

12. Cicely Berry, *The Actor and The Voice* (New York: Macmillan, 1973): 121.

13. Richard Eder, "The World According to Brook," *American Theatre*, 1, No. 2 (May 1984): 38. Reprinted by permission of the Theatre Communications Group, Inc.

CHAPTER 10

1. Alan Schneider, "Things to Come: Crystal-Gazing at the Near and Distant Future of a Durable Art," *American Theatre*, 1, No. 1 (April 1984): 17. Reprinted by permission of the Theatre Communications Group Inc.

2. Elia Kazan, "Notebook for *A Streetcar Named Desire*" in *Directing The Play: A Source Book of Stagecraft*, eds. Toby Cole and Helen Krich Chinoy (Indianapolis: The Bobbs-Merrill Company, 1953): 296.

3. Hubert Witt, ed., *Brecht: As They Knew Him* (New York: International Publishers, 1974): 126. Reprinted by permission.

4. Toby Dole and Helen Krich Chinoy, eds. *Directors on Directing*, second revised edition (Indianapolis, IN: The Bobbs-Merrill Company, 1977): 364–366.

5. Arthur Bartow, " 'Images from the Id': An Interview," *American Theatre*, 5, No. 3 (June 1988): 56-57. Courtesy of the Theatre Communications Group Inc.

6. Bartow: 17.
7. Robert Wilson and David Byrne, *The Forest* (West Berlin: Theater der Freien Volksbühne, 1988): 29-32.
8. Wilson and Byrne: 36.

CHAPTER 11

1. Robert Edmond Jones, *The Dramatic Imagination: Reflections and Speculations on The Art of The Theatre* (New York: Methuen Theatre Arts Books, 1987): 26.
2. Lynn Pecktal, "A Conversation with Ming Cho Lee," in *Designing and Painting for the Theatre* (New York: Holt, Rinehart, & Winston, 1975): 242. Reprinted by permission.
3. Pecktal: 51. Reprinted by permission.
4. Jarka Burian, *The Scenography of Josef Svoboda* (Middletown, Conn.: Wesleyan University Press, 1971): 31. Copyright © 1971 by Jarka Burian. From a speech by Josef Svoboda, the text of which was printed in *Zprávy Divadelního Ústavu*, no. 8 (1967): 28-29. Reprinted by permission of Wesleyan University Press.
5. Patricia Zipprodt, "Designing Costumes," in *Contemporary Stage Design U.S.A.* (Middletown, Conn.: Wesleyan University Press, 1974): 29.
6. John Gruen, "She Is One of Broadway's Most Designing Women," *New York Times* (8 April 1984): II, 5, 14. Copyright © 1984 by The New York Times Company. Reprinted by permission.

CHAPTER 12

1. Cheryl Crawford, *One Naked Individual: My Fifty Years in the Theatre.* (Indianapolis: Bobbs-Merrill, 1977): 4.
2. Alexander H. Cohen, "Broadway Theatre," in *Producers on Producing*, ed. Stephen

Langley (New York: Drama Book Specialists, 1976): 15.
3. Audrey Wood with Max Wilk, *Represented by Audrey Wood* (Garden City, N.Y.: Doubleday and Company, 1981): 7.
4. *Producers on Producing*: 78.

CHAPTER 13

1. Bree Burns, "Breaking the Mold: Julie Taymor," *Theatre Crafts*, 22, No. 3 (March 1988): 51.
2. Richard Schechner, "An Intercultural Primer," *American Theatre*, 8, No. 7 (October 1991): 28–31, 135.
3. Margaret Croyden, "*The Mahabharata*: A Review," *New York Times* 25 August 1985: II, 20.
4. Miriam Horn, "A Director Who Can Conjure Up Magic Onstage," *Smithsonian* (February 1993): 72.
5. Burns 49.
6. Julie Taymor, "*Juan Darien*: Notes," *Theater*, 20, No. 2 (Spring/Summer 1989): 51.
7. Eileen Blumenthal, "An Eerie Tale of Civilization and the Jungle," *New York Times* 6 March 1988: II, 5.
8. Taymor 52.
9. Horn 66.
10. Rosette C. Lamont, "Ariane Mnouchkine's Theater of History," *TheaterWeek* (October 5–11, 1992): 19.
11. Lamont 18.
12. John Lahr, "Under the Skin," *The New Yorker* (June 28, 1993): 90.
13. Simi Horwitz, "About Face," *TheaterWeek* (June 22, 1992): 25.
14. Cathy Madison, "Hearing Voices: Portraits of America at the Public," *The Village Voice* (December 10, 1991): 106.

CHAPTER 14

1. Stanley Kauffmann, *Persons of the Drama: Theater Criticism and Comment* (New York: Harper & Row, 1976): 369–380.

2. George Jean Nathan. *The Critic and the Drama* (New York: Alfred A. Knopf, 1922): 133.

3. Eric Bentley and Julius Novick, "On Criticism," *Yale/Theatre*, 4, No. 2 (Spring 1973): 23–36.

4. J. L. Styan, *Drama, Stage and Audience* (London: Cambridge University Press, 1975): 33.

5. Frank Rich, "Stage: Billie Whitelaw In Three Beckett Works," *New York Times* (17 February 1984): III, 3. Copyright © 1984 by The New York Times Company. Reprinted by permission.

6. Brooks Atkinson, "'Streetcar' Tragedy, Mr. Williams' Report on Life in New Orleans," *New York Times* (14 December 1947): II, 3. Copyright © 1947 by The New York Times Company. Reprinted by permission.

7. Kenneth Tynan, "*Look Back in Anger*, by John Osborne, at the Royal Court," in *Curtains: Selections from the Drama Criticism and Related Writings* (New York: Atheneum, 1971): 130–132.

ACKNOWLEDGMENTS

Frontispiece: Joan Marcus; opposite Contents: Richard Feldman; opposite Preface: Richard Feldman; p. 2 Joan Marcus; p. 6 The Museum of Modern Art/Film Stills Archive; p. 7 Eileen Darby; pp. 8–9 Courtesy Royal National Theatre; p. 10 (top) Courtesy The Guthrie Theatre; p. 10 (bottom) Courtesy Oregon Shakespeare Theatre; p. 11 Courtesy Arena Stage; p. 12 Carol Pratt; C1.1 (top left) Jerry Ohlinger (top right) Photofest (bottom) The Museum of Modern Art/Film Stills Archive; C1.2 (top left) Jerry Ohlinger (top right) Photofest (bottom) Jerry Ohlinger; C1.3 (top) Jerry Ohlinger (bottom) The Museum of Modern Art/Film Stills Archive; C1.4 (top) Jerry Ohlinger (bottom) Photofest; p. 19 Courtesy Shakespeare Centre Library, Stratford-Upon-Avon; p. 20 Courtesy George Karger/PIX; p. 24 Johan Elbers; p. 27 Courtesy Staatliches Museum fur Volkerkunde; p. 29 Courtesy Greek National Tourist Organization; p. 31 Courtesy Greek National Tourist Organization; p. 33 Bibliotheque Nationale, Paris; p. 34 Courtesy Columbia University Press; p. 35 from Glynne Wickham, *Early English Stages, Vol. 1* (1959), reprinted by permission of Routlege & Kegan Paul and Columbia University Press; p. 36 Courtesy Folger Shakespeare Library; p. 37 Courtesy Shakespeare Centre Library, Stratford-Upon-Avon; pp. 38–39 Reprinted by permission of Oxford University Press; p. 40 Courtesy Oregon Shakespeare Theatre; p. 43 The New York Public Library at Lincoln Center; p. 44 Courtesy John F. Kennedy Center for the Performing Arts; p. 45 Robert C. Ragsdale/Courtesy Stratford Festival Theatre; pp. 46, 47, 49 From *The Chinese Theatre in Modern Times* (1975), Colin Mackerras; p. 51 (top) Martha Swope; p. 51 bottom Martine Franck/Magnum; p. 52 Courtesy Richard Feldman/American Repertory Theatre; p. 53 Courtesy Japan National Tourist Organization; p. 55 (all) Courtesy Japan National Tourist Organization; p. 56 from *Naniwa Miyage* (souvenir from Naniwa, 1738.) Courtesy Torigoe Bunzo and C. D. Gerstle, *Circles of Fantasy* (Harvard University Press); p. 60 Richard Feldman; p. 63 Zbigniew Raplewski/KaiDib Films International, Glendale, CA; pp. 64–67 Photographs and drawings courtesy H. M. Berg, Odin Teatret, Denmark; p. 68 (both) Martine Franck/Magnum; p. 71 (top) AP/Wide World Photos; p. 71 (bottom) Gianfranco Mantegna/Courtesy Mark Hall Amitin and The Living Theatre; p. 72 (both) Martine Franck/Magnum; p. 73 Gilles Abegg; p. 74 Dan Charlson/ Durham *Herald-Sun*; p. 80 Martha Swope; p. 82 (left) Courtesy Buena Vista Distribution Co.; p. 82 (right) Allen Nomura; p. 86 (right) Courtesy Brigitte Lacombe/The New York Public Library at Lincoln Center; p. 88 (right) Courtesy Jim Caldwell/The Alley Theatre; p. 92 (right) New York Public Library at Lincoln Center; p. 92 (left) Martha Swope; p. 94 National Archives; p. 95 Robert Nemiroff; p. 96 (top) Fred W. McDarrah; p. 96 (bottom) Paul Harter/Courtesy Methuen, Inc.; p. 98 Courtesy Stokely Towles, *The Patriot Ledger*; p. 100 Richard Feldman; p. 104 (left) Courtesy French Press and Information Office; p. 104 (right) Courtesy Alley Theatre; p. 108 Martha Holmes; p. 110 (left) Jerry Bauer/Courtesy Grove-Weidenfeld; p. 110 (right) Courtesy French Press and Information Office; p. 112 New York Public Library at Lincoln Center; p. 115 Martha Swope; p. 117 Martha Swope; pp. 118–122 All photos courtesy Peter Cunningham/Fred Nathan Co. except top photo p. 121 Michelle V. Agins NYT pictures; p. 124 (left) Courtesy German Information Center; p. 124 (right) Richard Feldman/Courtesy American Repertory Theatre; p. 129 Courtesy Berliner Ensemble; p. 130

Courtesy French Press and Information Office; p. 131 Courtesy French Press and Information Office; p. 134 Michal Daniel/Courtesy Guthrie Theater; p. 138 Culver Pictures; p. 142 Robert C. Ragsdale/Courtesy Stratford Festival Theatre, Ontario, Canada; p. 143 Courtesy Guthrie Theater; p. 146 Courtesy French Press and Information Office; p. 151 Paula Court; p. 152 Irene Haupt; p. 158 (left) Ralf Brinkoff/Courtesy Byrd Hoffman Foundation; p. 160 Gerhard Kassner; p. 161 Paula Court; p. 162 Courtesy American Repertory Theatre; p. 163 (top) Tom Caravaglia; p. 163 (bottom) Courtesy Metropolitan Opera, Lincoln Center, New York; p. 166 Michal Daniel/Courtesy The Guthrie Theater; p. 168 Eileen Darby; p. 169 Vandamm Collection/New York Public Library at Lincoln Center; p. 172 Donald Cooper/Photostage; p. 176 Donald Cooper/Photostage; p. 178 George E. Joseph; p. 181 Anthony Crickmay; p. 182 Culver Pictures; p. 183 (both) New York Public Library at Lincoln Center; p. 184 Jerry Ohlinger; p. 186 UPI/Bettmann Newsphotos; p. 187 Joan Marcus; p. 192 Courtesy Alley Theatre; p. 196 Martha Swope; p. 197 George E. Joseph; p. 198 Anthony Crickmay; p. 203 George E. Joseph; p. 204 (left) The Bettmann Archive; p. 204 Richard Feldman; p. 209 Courtesy Royal Shakespeare Theatre; p. 210 Gerry Goodstein; p. 214 Brigitte Lacombe; p. 217 Ruth Walz; p. 220 Joan Marcus; p. 222 New York Public Library at Lincoln Center; p. 224 Courtesy Theatre Museum/Victoria and Albert Museum; p. 229 New York Public Library at Lincoln Center; p. 230 The Lee Strasberg Theatre Institute; p. 231 George E. Joseph; p. 234 (left) Springer/Bettmann Film Archive; p. 234 (right) New York Public Library at Lincoln Center; p. 238 New York Public Library at Lincoln Center; p. 239 George E. Joseph; p. 240 New York Public Library at Lincoln Center; p. 241 Bill Carter; p. 242 Joan Marcus; p. 246 Martha Swope; p. 248 New York Public Library at Lincoln Center; p. 250 New York Public Library at Lincoln Center; p. 251 (left) Culver Pictures; p. 251 (right) New York Public Library at Lincoln Center; p. 252 (left) Frederic Ohringer/Courtesy The Acting Company; p. 252 (right) New York Public Library at Lincoln Center; C2.1 (both) Richard Feldman; C2.2 (top left and right) Martha Swope (bottom) Max Waldman/Max Waldman Archives; C2.3 (top left and right) Courtesy Byrd Hoffman Foundation (bottom) Richard Feldman; C2.4 (top) Martine Franck/Magnum (bottom) Michele Laurent/Gamma-Liaison; p. 259 (both) New York Public Library at Lincoln Center; p. 262 Max Waldman Archives; p. 263 Martha Swope; p. 264 (left) Courtesy Centre International de Recherche Theatrale; p. 264 (right) Martha Swope; p. 266 Martha Swope; p. 267 Courtesy Alley Theatre; p. 270 Richard Feldman; p. 273 Courtesy The Victoria and Albert Museum; p. 274 (both) New York Public Library at Lincoln Center; p. 275 New York Public Library at Lincoln Center; p. 276 Courtesy Mark Taper Forum Press; p. 277 (bottom) From Harold Burris-Meyer and Edward C. Cole, *Scenery for the Theatre*, ©1938, renewed ©1966, 1971 by Harold Burris-Meyer and Edward C. Cole. Reprinted by permission of Little, Brown and Company; pp. 278–279 New York Public Library at Lincoln Center; p. 280 Courtesy KaiDib Films International, Glendale, CA; p. 282 Courtesy KaiDib Films International, Glendale, CA; p. 283 George de Vincent/Courtesy Arena Stage; p. 285 New York Public Library at Lincoln Center; p. 287 (left) Courtesy Patricia Zipprodt; p. 287 (right) Bruce Goldstein/Courtesy Guthrie Theatre; p. 288 (left) Courtesy William Morris Agency; p. 288 (right) Martha Swope; C3.1 (both) Joan Marcus; C3.2 (top) Joan Marcus (bottom) Martha Swope; C3.3 (both) Joan Marcus; C3.4 (both) Martha Swope; p. 292 Illustration of Pantalone from Jacques Callot's etchings, c. 1622, of commedia actors in costume; p. 293 (top) Kenn Duncan; p. 293 (bottom) Martine Franck/Magnum; p. 294 (left) T. Charles Erikson/Courtesy Yale University Office of Public Information; p. 294 (right) George E. Joseph; p. 296 From the Collection of the Metropolitan Opera Archives; p. 299 Courtesy Bill Clarke Designs; p. 302 Courtesy Ken Friedman/American Conservatory Theatre; C4.1 Martha Swope; C4.2 (left) Peter Cunningham (right) Joan Marcus; C4.3 (both) Marcus/Marc Bryan Brown; C4.4 (top) Joan Marcus (bottom) Martha Swope; p. 307 (left) Courtesy Michael Le Poer Trench; p. 307 (right) Martha Swope; p. 310 NYT Pictures; p. 316 Annalisa Kraft/Courtesy Arena Stage; p. 320 *San Francisco Chronicle*; p. 325 Martha Swope; p. 328 Carol Rosegg/Martha Swope Associates; p. 329 Richard Feldman; p. 330 (left) Carol Rosegg/Martha Swope Associates; p. 330 (right) Courtesy Kenlan Sickle; p. 333 Martine Franck/Magnum; p. 334 Martha Swope; p. 335 (both) Richard Feldman; pp. 336–337 (all) Martine Franck/Magnum; pp. 340–342 *San Francisco Chronicle*; p. 346 New York Public Library at Lincoln Center; p. 349 George E. Joseph; p. 352 Courtesy Jasper Johns and Leo Castelli Gallery; p. 355 (top) UPI/Bettmann Newsphotos; p. 355 (bottom) Courtesy New York Public Library at Lincoln Center; p. 358 Gilles Abegg; p. 359 Joan Marcus; p. 367 Wide World Photos; p. 356 (top) Courtesy *The Chicago Tribune*; p. 356 (bottom) Courtesy *The New York Times*.

INDEX

Saroyan, William, 363
Satyr play, 30
Savages (Taymor), 331
Saxe-Meiningen, Duke George II, 247, 248
  biography of, 248
Scenery, 276–277
Scenic artist, 271, 277
Scenographer, 271
Schaubühne, The (Berlin, Germany), 217
Schechner, Richard, 61, 79, 151
Schneider, Alan, 151, 152, 235, 240, 246, 248,
    252, 253
  biography of, 253
Schumann, Peter, 57, 60, 61, 74–77, 78
  biography of, 74–75
Sea Gull, The (Chekhov), 205, 226, 235
Season: A Candid Look at Broadway, The (Goldman),
    319
Seattle Repertory Theatre (Washington), 315, 317
Secret Garden, The (musical), 98, 289, C3.2
Seinfeld, Jerry, 18
Selective realism, 278
Serban, Andrei, 124, 197, 203, 204, 239, 293,
    355, C2.1
Serious Money (Churchill), 96
Serlio, Sebastiano, 42
1776 (musical), 287
1789 (Théâtre du Soleil), 69, 333
1793 (Théâtre du Soleil), 69, 333
Sex and Death to the Age 14 (Gray), 150
Sexual Perversity in Chicago (Mamet), 87
Shakespeare, William, 4, 5, 7, 13, 14, 23, 37, 40, 51,
    63, 68, 72, 85, 88, 116, 135, 138, 140, 142, 167,
    170, 185, 227, 262, 316
  biography of, 37
Shakespeare Theatre at the Folger (Washington, D.C.),
    315
Shaman, 27, 75
Shange, Ntozake, 295
Shaw, George Bernard, 353, 355
Shepard, Sam, 82–83, 109, 140, 151, 209, 210, 212,
    213, 313
  biography of, 83
Short Organum for the Theatre, A (Brecht), 100
Simon, Neil, 91, 116, 239, 258

Simonson, Lee, 272
Sinise, Gary, 118, 119, 120, 121
Sirlin, Jerome, C3.4
Sisters Rosensweig, The (Wasserstein), 97, 305,
    317, C3.4
Six Characters in Search of an Author (Pirandello),
    183, 186, 187, 188–189.
  plot of, 187
  text of, 188–189
Skelton, Thomas, 295
Skene, 28
Small Craft Warnings (Williams), 85
Smetana Theatre (Prague, Czechoslovakia), 282
Smith, Anna Deavere, 149, 320, 338, 339–343
  biography of, 342
Smith, Lois, 118, 121
Smith, Oliver, 272
Society of Stage Directors and Choreographers, The
    (SSDC), 308
Soliloquy, 198–199
Solo performance, 148–150, 338, 339–343
Solo text, 148–149
Some Freaks (Mamet), 219
Sondheim, Stephen, 51
Sophocles, 15, 23, 28, 30, 31, 88, 102, 139, 213
Sound design, 298–300
Sound effects, 202–203
Sound of Music, The (musical), 272
South Coast Repertory (Costa Mesa, CA), 315
Spectacle, 137
Speed the Plow (Mamet), 87, 213, 214
Spine, 249
Spolin, Viola, 257
Stage business, 254
Stage directions, 167–171, 200–201, 260
Stage manager, 254
Stanislavski: A Biography (Benedetti), 245
Stanislavski, Constantin, 108, 128, 205, 226,
    228–229, 230, 247, 248, 251
States of Shock (Shepard), 83
Stations of the Cross, The (Bread and Puppet Theatre),
    75, 76–77
Stein, Peter, 217
Steinbeck, John, 118, 122, 123
Steiner, George, 193

Steppenwolf Theatre Company, The (Chicago, IL), 118, 122
Stoppard, Tom, 185
Stowe, Harriet Beecher, 111
Strasberg, Lee, 108, 228, 229, 230, 231, 241, 244
  biography of, 230
Stratford Festival Theatre (Ontario, Canada), 45, 142, 238, 239,
Streetcar Named Desire, A (Williams), 6, 7, 12, 23, 89, 93, 102, 103, 168–170, 177, 232–233, 234, 235, 238, 249, 250, 259, 260–261, 272, 278, 284, 285, 318, 354, 357, 360, 361, 363, 364–365, 366
  film of, 259
  plot of, 169
Strindberg, August, 355
Sullivan, Daniel, 91, 315
Summer and Smoke (Williams), 365
Sunday in the Park with George (musical), 287
Sunset Boulevard (musical), C3.2, C4.2
Svoboda, Josef, 282
Swados, Elizabeth, 124
Swan Theatre (London, England), 38
Sweet Bird of Youth (Williams), 92, 93, 259
Swimming to Cambodia (Gray), 151, 165
Sydney, Basil, C1.1
Syracuse Stage (New York), 315

T

Tale of Two Cities, A (Dickens), 116
Talking pieces, 149–151
Tandy, Jessica, 6, 7, 169, 237, 238, 259, 357, 361, 364–365
Tartuffe (Molière), 5, 104, 105, 106, 350
  plot of, 105
Taylor, Laurette, 6, 226, 237
Taymor, Julie, 52, 320, 321, 326–329, 330–331, 338, C2.1
  biography of, 331
TCI: The Business of Entertainment Technology and Design (magazine), 301
Teatr Loh (Indonesia), 331
Teatro d'Arte (Rome, Italy), 186
Television, 4–5
Tempest, The (Shakespeare), 37, 329, 331
Terence (Publius Terentius Afer), 85

Terrible But Unfinished History of Norodom Sihanouk, King of Cambodia, The (Théâtre du Soleil), 68, 333
Terrors of Pleasure (Gray), 150, 151
Terry, Ellen, 274
Theater am Schiffbauerdamm (Berlin, Germany), 50, 125
Theatre, The (London, England), 36
Theatre at Delphi (Greece), 29
Theatre criticism, 347
Théâtre de Babylone (Paris, France), 20
Théâtre des Noctambules (Paris, France), 130, 131
Théâtre du Soleil (Paris, France), 51, 61, 62, 67–69, 72, 293, 329, 331
Theatre language, 192–219
  diagram of, 194
  nonverbal, 193, 195
  verbal, 191, 193
Théâtre Libre (Paris, France), 250
Theatre of Dionysus (Greece), 30, 172
Theatre of Images, 157–164
Theatre of the Absurd, The (Esslin), 129
Theatre of visions, 267
Theatrical Casebook, A (Brook), 345
Theatrical diversity, 320–369
Theatrical space, 16–17, 24–59, 60–79
Theatron, 16, 22
Thespis, 17, 222
Thomas, Richard, 267
Thompson, Emma, 92, C1.3, C1.4
Thompson, Tazewell, 315
Threepenny Opera, The (Brecht), 125
Three Places in Rhode Island (Gray), 150, 151
Three Sisters, The (Chekhov), 107, 108–109, 204, 205, 217, 299
  plot of, 108–109
Threlfall, David, 117
Through the Leaves (Kroetz), 266
Thrust stage, 10, 44, 45, 299
Time, 185
Timebends: A Life (Miller), 99
Tiny Alice (Albee), 253
Tipton, Jennifer, 294, 295
  biography of, 295
Tirai (Taymor), 331